NATIONAL GEOGRAPHIC

ALMANAC

2020

Climbing the Athabasca Glacier in Alberta's Jasper National Park

NATIONAL GEOGRAPHIC

ALMANAC
2020

NATIONAL GEOGRAPHIC
WASHINGTON, D.C.

CONTENTS

FOREWORD 8
by Cara Santa Maria

TRENDING 2020 10

QUIZMASTER
Planet in Balance
Future Food
Connected World
Pioneering Women
Into Outer Space

EXPLORATION & ADVENTURE 34

QUIZMASTER
EXPLORATION
Exploration Time Line
Nat Geo Explorers
Robert Ballard, Marine Geologist
Exploring Deep Oceans
Get Out Into Your Country
Best of @NatGeo: Adventure
EXTREMES
A History of Climbing Everest
Earth's Extremes
Underwater Museum
The Speed of Innovation
Mirna Valerio, Ultra Runner
Redefining What Is Possible

CLASSIC TRAVEL
Transportation Time Line
Iconic Destinations
Savor the World's Best Cities
A Taste of Italy
Greatest Expeditions
U.S. National Parks
Australia's Barrier Reef
Best of @NatGeo: Travel
TRAVEL TRENDS
Tokyo
Sustainable Travel
Marvels of the Maya
Off the Beaten Path
America's Best Eats
Iceland's Hot Springs
FURTHER

Yellowstone's Grand Prismatic Spring

Honeybee emerging from brood cell

Hubble image of the Bubble Nebula

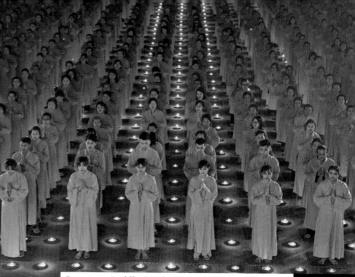

Prayers on Buddha Day in Bac Ninh Province, Vietnam

THIS PLANET & BEYOND 92

QUIZMASTER
PLANET EARTH
Earth Science Time Line
Clarifying Climate
Drought
Reading the Clouds
Combating a Blaze
Hurricanes
Volcanoes
Tim Samaras, Storm Chaser
Best of @NatGeo: Extreme Weather
EARTH, SEA & SKY
Minerals Revealed
Saving Pristine Seas
Volcanic Islands
Winter Sky
Summer Sky
Shapes in the Stars
Space Science Time Line
THE SOLAR SYSTEM
Our Neighborhood
Dwarf Planets
Earth's Moon
On to Mars
Martian Probes
Jupiter & Its Moons
Best of @NatGeo: Night Sky

THE UNIVERSE & BEYOND
Birth of the Universe
Ann Druyan, Science Communicator
When a Star Explodes
Space Radiation
Exoplanets: Is There Life?
Dark Matter
FURTHER

LIFE ON EARTH 156

QUIZMASTER
ALL LIVING THINGS
Life Science Time Line
Domains of Life
Plants Up Close
Talking Trees
Fossils: Past Lives
Nodosaur
OF THE EARTH
Best of @NatGeo: Life on Land
Telltale Tracks
Domestication Transformation
Meet the Quoll
Primate Family Tree
Koko the Signing Gorilla

A pensive pause in the Sahara

THE SCIENCE OF US 220

QUIZMASTER
ORIGINS
  Human Evolution Time Line
  Meet Our Human Ancestors
  Paul Salopek, Immersive Journalist
  Our Deep Ancestry
  Neanderthals Join the Family
THE HUMAN JOURNEY
  Intangible Culture
  Seeking Refuge
  Best of @Nat Geo: World Traditions
  Disappearing Languages
  Kate Orff, Landscape Architect
  Urbanization
  Urban Nature
  Religion Around the World
  Religious Holidays
  Best of @NatGeo: People
BODY & BRAIN
  The Science of Sleep
  Eating Insects
  How the World Gives Birth
  Understanding Gender
  Chinese Traditions
  Jennifer Doudna, Biochemist
HEALTH & MEDICINE
  Medicine Time Line
  Eyes on the Prize
  Antibiotic Resistance
  Future Prosthetics
  Psychobiome
  Herbs & Spices for Health
  Mindfulness
FURTHER

OF THE SEA
  Best of @Nat Geo: Sea Life
  Save the Reefs
  Whales
  Sea Shells
  The Amazing Octopus
OF THE SKY
  Best of @NatGeo: Life on the Wing
  Backyard Birds
  Hummingbirds: Winged Wonders
  Parrots
  Whose Caterpillar?
  Plight of the Honeybee
CARE FOR ALL LIFE
  Conservation Time Line
  Photo Ark
  Biodiversity
  Plastic in Our World
  Heather Koldewey, Marine Biologist
  Earth Day: 50 Years Later
FURTHER

Pineapple fields bump up against native cloud forest in Maui, Hawaii.

YESTERDAY TO TOMORROW 282

QUIZMASTER
WORLD HISTORY
   Prehistory to 1600 Time Line
   Tales Older Than the Hills
   1600 to Recent Past Time Line
   Semiramis, Queen of Babylon
   A History of Democracy
   Ada Lovelace, Early Programmer
   Best of @NatGeo: Historic Places
   Terra-Cotta Warriors
   Genome Clues in Egypt
   Innovations Time Line
   War in Our Times
U.S. HISTORY
   United States Time Line
   America's Other Lost Colonies
   Woman Suffrage
   The Politics of Cherry Blossoms
   Stars and Stripes Through the Centuries
   Flags of the United States
   Territories of the United States
FURTHER

OUR WORLD 326

QUIZMASTER
WORLD VIEWS
   Our Physical World
   Our Political World
   Best of @NatGeo: Landscapes
CONTINENTS & OCEANS
   The Continents
   North America
   South America
   Europe
   Asia
   Africa
   Australia & Oceania
   Antarctica
   Oceans of the World
   Atlantic Ocean
   Pacific Ocean
   Indian Ocean
   Arctic Ocean
   Ocean Around Antarctica
   Best of @NatGeo: Oceanscapes
COUNTRIES OF THE WORLD
   Flags of the World
   United Nations
THE FUTURE
   Future of the Planet
   Future of the Wild on Earth
   Future of Humans on Earth
FURTHER

CREDITS 382
INDEX 386

Katydids at New Orleans' Insectarium

ALWAYS
MORE TO LEARN

A climber glories in the panorama of Norway's Husfjellet.

Nacional Geographic has always had a special place in my heart. It's been a source of inspiration, excitement, and wonder ever since I was a young girl. As an adult, I've been lucky enough to join the NatGeo family, traveling the world in search of knowledge and adventure. I've investigated the global meteorite trade in Morocco, observed brain surgery in Boston, discovered the future of food in the Netherlands, and marveled at a total solar eclipse in the northwestern United States. During my travels for National Geographic's *Explorer* series and other projects, I've had the incredible opportunity to experience the stunning majesty of our planet's wildlife, people, and landscapes firsthand.

That's why I'm pleased to share the *National Geographic Almanac 2020* with you. From the comfort of your home (or wherever else you may find yourself), this book will transport you around the globe to places you could conjure only in your wildest imagination. Wherever you may be on your lifelong journey, this book was written for *you*. And it couldn't have happened without the tireless effort of an incredible team of writers, photographers, editors, and explorers who will stop at nothing to bring the awe and wonder of the natural world within reach for all of us.

The National Geographic Society's central mission is to promote "the power of exploration, science, and storytelling to change the world." With this in mind, the *Almanac 2020* is packed full of stunning scenery, cutting-edge experiments, and deeply personal tales of adventure. From hydrothermal vents at the bottom of the ocean to craters on the far side of the moon, we travel together to the ends of the Earth and beyond, unlocking their brilliant secrets. But as we learn about the awesome beauty of our

Cara Santa Maria sizes up a tiger shark jaw at London's Natural History Museum.

home, we are also confronted with an unfortunate reality. Humankind's actions have taken a toll on Earth's interconnected systems currently hanging in the balance. Its landscape is forever changed due to our shortsightedness. Species are going extinct at an alarming rate, and once biodiversity is lost, it's gone forever. Ocean warming, acidification, and sea level rise affect us all, and the coming years will see climate refugees around the globe.

Yet I remain optimistic about the innovative technologies and problem-solving strategies humanity has to offer. With global connectivity at an all-time high, we have the capability to work together to heal the planet and restore balance to its varied inhabitants. Together, we can make a difference. But we have to act now.

Thank you for joining me on this colorful journey of exploration and adventure. In the following pages, we venture to the ends of the cosmos and dig deep into the mysteries of our own backyards. As your guide through the *Almanac 2020,* I open each section with Quizmaster pages full of fascinating trivia to whet your appetite for what lies ahead. Whether we are celebrating our primate family tree or the deep ripples in spacetime caused by gravitational waves, our eyes will be opened to nature's amazing power.

TRENDING
2020

PLANET IN BALANCE | FUTURE FOOD | CONNECTED WORLD

Massive photovoltaic arrays have been operational in southwestern Spain, a world leader in solar energy, for more than a decade.

QUIZ MASTER

The Journey Starts Here What are the most exciting things happening in science and discovery today? As we put this almanac together, we asked ourselves that question—and here are our answers: the perfect place to begin!

—CARA SANTA MARIA, *Our Favorite Nerd*

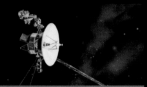

IN WHAT YEAR WAS NASA'S VOYAGER SPACE PROGRAM LAUNCHED?

p32

p33

BY 2018, HOW MANY **BLACK HOLE** MERGERS HAD BEEN DETECTED?

ABOUT HOW MUCH **MEAT** DOES THE AVERAGE AMERICAN CONSUME IN A YEAR?

p32

p20

IN WHAT YEAR IS NASA'S NEW **JAMES WEBB SPACE TELESCOPE** DUE TO LAUNCH?

ON WHICH ISLANDS DO MORE THAN 99% OF RESIDENTS USE THE INTERNET, HIGHEST PERCENTAGE **IN THE WORLD?**

p18

ABOUT HOW MUCH OF THE FOOD WE GROW GOES TO WASTE?

p24

WAX WORMS HAVE THE ABILITY TO BREAK **DOWN** WHICH NOTORIOUSLY RESILIENT SUBSTANCE?

p16

ON WHICH ISLANDS IN THE ATLANTIC OCEAN CAN YOU FIND THE GRAN TELESCOPIO CANARIAS?

p33

WOMEN MADE UP WHAT FRACTION OF THE U.S. CONGRESS IN 2019?

p26

p16

NAME THE COLLINS DICTIONARY 2018 WORD OF THE YEAR.

ABOUT HOW MUCH OF THE EARTH'S SURFACE IS DEDICATED TO AGRICULTURE?

p18

WHAT FRUIT IS THE PREDOMINANT CROP OF UGANDA?

p21

p16

HOW MANY TONS OF PLASTIC ARE CREATED EVERY YEAR?

WHAT COUNTRY FIRST GRANTED FULL VOTING RIGHTS TO WOMEN?

p29

PLANET IN BALANCE

CONFRONTING CLIMATE CHANGE

In October 2018, one of the strongest hurricanes ever in the Pacific scraped an entire Hawaiian island off the map. The island, uninhabited by humans but home to monk seals, sea turtles, and shorebirds, disappeared beneath wind and wave. The next month, the town of Paradise, California, burned to the ground in the deadliest fire in the state's fiery history. Species are going extinct and biodiversity levels are crashing so severely that some call it a new mass extinction. The clock is ticking, but scientists are finding new ways to undo the harm and protect untouched places. The race for a sustainable planet is on.

Morning mist floats over the Danum Valley Conservation Area rainforest in Borneo.

OVER THE PAST CENTURY, THE GLOBAL AVERAGE SURFACE TEMPERATURE INCREASED BY MORE THAN 1.6°F (0.9°C)— AND SOME PREDICT IT WILL RISE ANOTHER 1.5°F BY 2032.

CREATIVE SOLUTIONS

FINDING WAYS TO REGAIN A PLANET IN BALANCE

Mounds of plastic accumulate worldwide.

PLASTIC-EATERS

ANIMALS THAT CAN DIGEST PLASTIC

Our world is awash in plastic. Every year humans create more than 400 million tons of it, of which some eight million flow into our oceans. Even the most remote ocean trenches contain plastic debris, and each bit of plastic may take centuries to break down. One way to reverse this disaster might be found inside beehives.

Insect larvae known as wax worms, which naturally feed on wax and honey, have digestive systems that seem able to break down the long molecular chains known as polymers, whether those polymers are beeswax or plastic. Isolating the chemicals at work inside these natural recyclers could be one way to address our plastic problems.

JUST SAY NO

THE DISAPPEARING PLASTIC STRAW

When the *Collins English Dictionary* chose "single-use" as the 2018 word of the year, it presaged a massive international move away from plastic objects and containers designed to be used once and thrown away. Change has come swiftly. By 2019 many businesses, cities, and even countries had set regulations banning various single-use plastic items.

No longer will you be served a drink with a plastic straw at the Hilton Waikoloa Village Hotel on Hawaii's Big Island, at Disneyland or Disney World, anywhere in the cities of Seattle and Washington, D.C., on United Airlines flights, soon at Red Lobster restaurants—and the list keeps growing. The alternative? Paper or compostable straws, personally owned reusable straws, or no straw at all.

Paper straws are making a comeback.

A Sami herder leads his reindeer in Finland.

Planting tree seedlings is a step anyone can take.

INDIGENOUS PRACTICES

MASTERS OF SUSTAINABILITY

Indigenous peoples are masters of sustainable living—not only sources of wisdom but also activists fighting to protect natural habitats, preserve cultural traditions, and keep their parts of the planet in balance. The Sápara of Ecuador are organizing to resist oil extraction in their rainforest territory. The Karen of northern Thailand clear patches of forest for short-term cultivation and then allow wild greenery to return, a practice that supports pollinators better than continuous monoculture does. In Finland, efforts to develop wind and hydroelectric energy for populated regions interfere with the herding practices of the Sami, who depend on reindeer for survival. There, government and indigenous representatives are working to find common ground.

Many countries are establishing indigenous protected areas, where ancient tradition and modern conservation efforts can work side by side—a powerful team-up to protect both culture and nature.

GREEN WAYS OUT

REDUCING CARBON EMISSIONS BY PLANTING MORE TREES

When we burn fossil fuels—to drive cars, stoke factories, fly jumbo jets—we release massive amounts of carbon dioxide into the atmosphere—a key cause of climate change and global warming. A recent study suggests that one way to reduce carbon emissions is by using nature better.

Plants absorb carbon dioxide, so the more green things we can establish, the better: for example, by reforesting after timber harvesting, planting and plowing in field crops between growing seasons, and greening up cities with more tree-filled parks. Solutions can start in your own backyard, but changes must happen on a national and even global scale to make a real difference.

FUTURE FOOD

FARMING 2.0

More than a third of the planet's surface is dedicated to agriculture, but roughly a third of the food we grow goes to waste. If the world is going to feed an increasing population reliably, we need to do more, and with a smaller footprint. In the Netherlands, farmers have been able to more than double yields by working in massive greenhouses and controlling every part of the process, a technique known as precision farming. Each plant is individually monitored, and regular soil analysis gives information on temperature and water levels. Livestock too are getting an upgrade with humane housing for over 150,000 chickens in a single climate-controlled facility. These methods have helped the Netherlands, a small country with a cold climate, lead the world in tomato, potato, and onion exports.

Greenhouses light up at night in Westland, Netherlands, world renowned as an innovative hub of horticulture.

ONE DUTCH PLANT BREEDER HAS DEVELOPED A TYPE OF TOMATO THAT CAN PRODUCE 150 POUNDS OF FRUIT FROM A SINGLE SEED.

REVOLUTIONIZING THE WAY WE EAT

The Atlantic bluefin tuna, a sushi mainstay, is an endangered species.

SANE SEAFOOD

PROTECTING WILD FISH

Every year, we remove 170 billion pounds of fish from the ocean. Eating wild-caught fish depletes the marine food web, which can take generations to restore. Our preference for large, slow-growing fish like tuna and swordfish is like eating lions and gazelles rather than farmed cattle.

Thankfully, there are more sustainable approaches to fishing. This can mean eating only fish that grow rapidly and reproduce easily, or favoring farm-raised fish over wild-caught. In this way, the fishing industry can keep working and humanity can keep eating. Oceana, the Monterey Bay Aquarium, and other groups offer guides to environmentally friendly seafood choices.

LAB-GROWN MEAT

NOT YOUR ORDINARY VEGGIE BURGER

We're getting more carnivorous: Global consumption of meat has doubled in the past 50 years, and the average American now consumes over 220 pounds of red meat and poultry every year. Livestock accounts for some 15 percent of climate emissions and an increase in animal husbandry has been driving deforestation as trees are cleared to make room for pastureland.

To counter these effects, scientists and conservationists have been working to develop plant-based substitutes that can sizzle like steak, bleed like a burger, and look like ground beef. The Impossible Foods company creates proprietary recipes with protein-based plants and fats, while at Mosa Meat laboratory, chemists are growing beef from stem cells.

Meat lab-grown from stem cells may be on menus soon.

GMO techniques may rescue economies depending on banana exports.

GMOS

GENETIC MODIFICATION FOR GOOD

In Uganda, 75 percent of farmers grow bananas, a staple in a country where some eat two pounds of bananas a day. In recent years, a bacterial plague has devastated the crop. Scientists, however, have found a modification to a banana's base DNA that would prevent the disease and boost nutritional value. Uganda's bananas would become genetically modified organisms (GMOs).

For thousands of years, humans have deliberately bred plants and animals to shape them for our use. The discovery of DNA and the development of gene editing tools have led to new methods that can radically alter organisms in a single generation. As genetic modification becomes increasingly common, debates have arisen about how best to monitor and regulate these new organisms.

A WORD FROM

Do Your Part Food waste can be seen as a massive and daunting problem but within it lie great opportunities. Everyone can get up today and make a difference—volunteer your local gleaning effort, investigate recipes that use up that odd onion in the fridge, or donate to food waste fighting charities like Feedback [feedbackglobal.org]. The solutions are simple and positive, from farm to the fork.

—TRISTRAM STUART, *food waste activist*

IN AUSTIN, TEXAS, RESTAURANTS ARE REQUIRED BY CITY ORDINANCE TO DONATE OR COMPOST UNUSED FOOD. THEY MAY NO LONGER DISPOSE OF IT IN LANDFILLS.

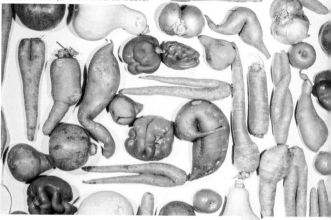
Misshapen vegetables, even if they are delicious, are considered waste.

FOOD WASTE

SAVING THE SCRAPS

Every year, more than 2.9 trillion pounds of food is thrown away, enough to feed the 800 million people suffering from hunger around the world. While some spoilage is inevitable, much of the food being tossed is edible. Markets and restaurants pride themselves on selecting the best produce—perfect peppers, the freshest fruit. So-called ugly food often never hits the market.

To fight this, new start-ups are promoting ugly produce, creating pathways to purchase it, donate it to food banks, or recycle leftovers into animal feed. Food waste will always be with us, but making even a small dent in the problem could lead to more food for the masses.

CONNECTED
WORLD

AN EXPANDING NETWORK

Our world has never been more connected, both literally and figuratively. A vast web of communication satellites allows us to make phone calls from the top of Mount Everest to the Australian outback. Business supply chains flow around the world almost effortlessly, leading to a global rise in countries exporting their goods—and where goods connect, so do people. More than 250 million people relocate their lives each year internationally, and even more travel for work or play. Industry data shows 4.1 billion passenger trips in 2017, up 7.3 percent from 2016. Global connectivity shapes the ways we work and live.

Nighttime satellite views, here of the Gulf coastline from Texas to Alabama, show how interconnected our world is today.

THE PATHWAYS THAT CONNECT US IN THE DIGITAL AGE ARE UNDERWATER. ALMOST 450 SUBMARINE FIBER-OPTIC CABLES CARRY MESSAGES AROUND THE WORLD AT A SPEED OF ABOUT A MILLION MEGABITS A SECOND.

GLOBAL CONNECTIVITY

AS ACCESS INCREASES, SO DO CONTROLS

UNITED STATES
Passage of the USA Patriot Act after September 11, 2001, expanded government surveillance of individuals. Civil liberties groups argued that privacy safeguards in the 2015 Freedom Act did not go far enough.

NORTH AMERICA

SOUTH AMERICA

Access to the Internet, 2016
Percent of population

- 80-100%
- 60-79%
- 40-59%
- 20-39%
- 1-19%
- 0 or no data

Government Restrictions to the Internet, 2016–17

- ☐ Government restricted internet access through blocking websites and internet blackouts.
- ☐ Government restricted internet access through monitoring email and social media and/or regulating published content.
- ☐ Government did a combination of both.

BOLIVIA AND PARAGUAY
Landlocked countries without easy access to undersea fiber optic cables have found themselves trying to catch up, often by launching expensive communications satellites.

FALKLAND ISLANDS
More than 99% of the 3,000 people living in the Falkland Islands use the internet, the highest percentage in the world. Luxembourg comes in second.

AS OF 2018, 3.9 BILLION PEOPLE—MORE THAN HALF THE PEOPLE ON EARTH—WERE USING THE INTERNET.

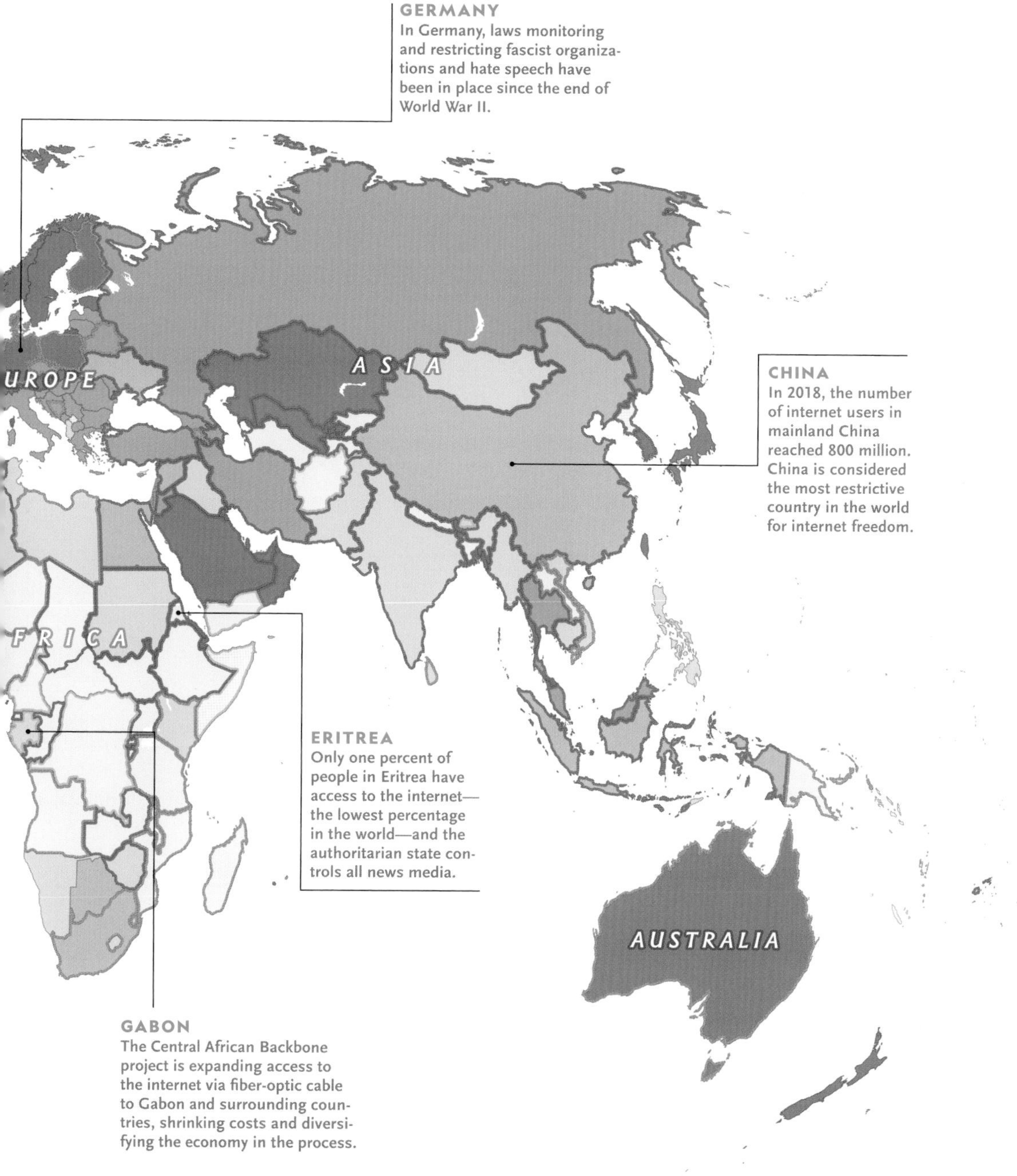

GERMANY
In Germany, laws monitoring and restricting fascist organizations and hate speech have been in place since the end of World War II.

CHINA
In 2018, the number of internet users in mainland China reached 800 million. China is considered the most restrictive country in the world for internet freedom.

ERITREA
Only one percent of people in Eritrea have access to the internet—the lowest percentage in the world—and the authoritarian state controls all news media.

GABON
The Central African Backbone project is expanding access to the internet via fiber-optic cable to Gabon and surrounding countries, shrinking costs and diversifying the economy in the process.

EUROPE

ASIA

AFRICA

AUSTRALIA

PIONEERING
WOMEN

THE FUTURE IS FEMALE

For eons, men have been the decision-makers in society, holding most of the leadership positions in politics, arts, and science. But things are changing. Events like the Women's March of 2017 have put a spotlight on women's interests, and a wave of female legislators have run for office. Today, more women than ever before are in positions of leadership. As of 2019, nearly a quarter of the U.S. Congress is made up of women—the highest portion in history. Around the world, women are challenging traditional expectations around gender and building a more inclusive future.

Millions around the world participated in January 2017 Women's Marches, here shown in Washington, D.C.

ACCORDING TO A UNESCO ESTIMATE, 28.8% OF THE WORLD'S SCIENTIFIC RESEARCHERS WERE WOMEN IN 2018. CENTRAL ASIA HAD THE MOST FEMALE REPRESENTATION IN THE SCIENCES, AT 48.1%.

WOMEN OF POWER

EXTRAORDINARY FEMALES PAST & PRESENT

Scidmore's photograph of Japanese girls and cherry blossoms

EXPLORATION

ELIZA SCIDMORE

As the first female writer and photographer at National Geographic, Eliza Scidmore exemplified the brand in its first decades. Invited onto the governing board in 1892, she championed color photography. Her legacy persists around the tidal basin of Washington, D.C., where she helped bring much beloved cherry trees to the nation's capital.

BETH WALD

Beth Wald journeys around the world documenting how indigenous groups adapt to a changing world. She often treks far off the grid, where survival skills matter. Her work with National Geographic, the Wildlife Conservation Society, and other organizations has taken her from Nepal to Patagonia, Cuba to Alaska.

ARTS & CULTURE

JUANA INÉS DE LA CRUZ

In 1670, an immense library crowded the quarters of a Mexican nun, Sor Juana Inés de la Cruz. Sor Juana was a self-taught poet, a playwright, a scholar, and an advocate for women's education. Today, her former cloister is a college bearing her name.

MARGARET ATWOOD

Canadian writer Margaret Atwood's work includes 17 books of poetry, 16 novels, 10 nonfiction books, eight children's books, and a graphic novel. She's a powerful voice for environmentalism, and her dystopian work, *The Handmaid's Tale,* has reached millions.

Margaret Atwood, whose fiction portrays women's issues

Donna Strickland, physicist and 2018 Nobel Prize winner

THE COUNTRY WITH THE HIGHEST PROPORTION OF FEMALE REPRESENTATIVES IS RWANDA, WHERE 61.3% OF SEATS IN THE LOWER HOUSE OF PARLIAMENT AND 38.5% IN THE UPPER ARE HELD BY WOMEN.

POLITICS

KATE SHEPPARD

New Zealander Kate Sheppard led the first successful effort to extend full voting rights to women. When the government granted women the vote in 1893, Sheppard became a titanic figure, traveling the world, inspiring women to follow her example and claim their natural rights.

ALEXANDRIA OCASIO-CORTEZ

When Alexandria Ocasio-Cortez decided to run for Congress, she was a bartender with no political experience challenging an incumbent nearly twice her age. With her surprise victory in 2018, 28-year-old Ocasio-Cortez became the youngest congresswoman in American history.

SCIENCE

WANG ZHENYI

In the feudal Qing dynasty of 18th-century China, women were not scholars. But Wang Zhenyi broke the mold. A scientist, poet, and author, she wrote at least 12 books, some to simplify mathematical ideas for the public and others to explain her own research on the astronomical movements of a solar eclipse. While much of her work has been lost, books of her poetry survive.

DONNA STRICKLAND

In 2018, Canadian scientist Donna Strickland became the third woman to win the Nobel Prize in Physics, joining the ranks of Maria Goeppert Mayer, a 20th-century expert in atomic structure, and Marie Curie. A self-described "laser jock," Strickland and her team found a new way to stretch and shape light into ultrafast, superstrong pulses. This work unlocked new fields of science in optics and has led to important advances in laser surgeries and laser-cut manufacturing.

AYCHECK FAIRNESS ACT
& Women: Same Job, Same Pay.

Alexandria Ocasio-Cortez, elected to Congress in 2018

INTO
OUTER SPACE

THE VOYAGE CONTINUES

Voyager 1 and Voyager 2 keep sailing on, out into deep space, past the edge of our solar system. Launched in 1977, their power systems will slowly decline over the next decade, but some data may flow back to Earth as late as 2036. The Voyager mission may be our first small step beyond our own star, but thanks in part to its success, we are one giant leap closer to understanding the universe beyond.

The two Voyager spacecraft led the way and have departed our solar system, while NASA's Juno stopped at Jupiter, returning this color-processed image of storms on the planet's surface.

VOYAGERS 1 AND 2 COMBINED HAVE EXPLORED JUPITER, SATURN, URANUS, AND NEPTUNE ALONG WITH 48 MOONS SURROUNDING THOSE PLANETS.

DEEP SPACE
OUTSIDE THE EDGES

WE EXPLORE DISTANT STARS AND GALAXIES IN AN ARRAY OF WAYS

Artist's concept of Voyager passing by the outer planets

SPACECRAFT TRAVEL THE DISTANCE

INTERSTELLAR TRAVELERS

A rare alignment of the outer planets of our solar system in the late 1970s and early 1980s inspired the Voyager mission. Twin craft launched in 1977, originally built to last five years and visit Uranus and Neptune, Voyager 1 and 2 have exceeded all expectations and lasted now more than 40 years, sending back information not only about the outer planets and their moons in our solar system but also about the space beyond.

Both Voyagers are now exploring what is termed interstellar space—the region beyond the reach of our sun's particles and magnetic force—with Voyager 1 nearly 13.5 billion miles and Voyager 2 more than 11 billion miles away from the sun.

SPACE TELESCOPES

OBSERVING DISTANT STARS

Earth's atmosphere can shimmer and distort the view from distant light sources—that's why stars seem to twinkle. Satellite telescopes orbit above the atmosphere, where they operate free from that distortion to create clearer images of distant stars, stellar nurseries, colliding galaxies, and the deepest reaches of space.

Orbiting cameras can be hard to maintain, and the Hubble, which launched in 1990, needs an upgrade. NASA's new James Webb Space Telescope, set to launch in 2021, will be able to see even farther and across a wider spectrum of light. It's expected to be able to photograph the first galaxies formed in our infant universe.

NASA's logo reflected in the James Webb's giant mirror

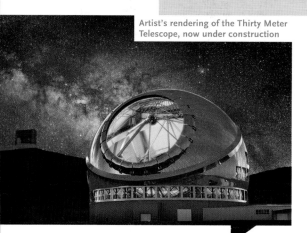
Artist's rendering of the Thirty Meter Telescope, now under construction

NASA IS PERFECTING A DEEP SPACE ATOMIC CLOCK—A MERCURY-ION TIME-KEEPER 50 TIMES MORE PRECISE THAN CURRENT NAVIGATIONAL DEVICES—THAT WILL GUIDE CRAFT AND CREW INTO DEEP SPACE IN THE COMING CENTURY.

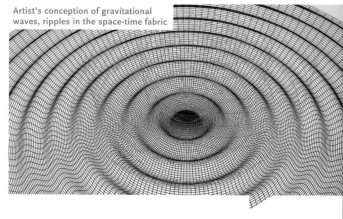
Artist's conception of gravitational waves, ripples in the space-time fabric

EARTHBOUND TELESCOPES

THE BIGGER THE BETTER

Land-based telescopes can be much larger and heavier than satellites, and for telescopes, a larger mirror means a better view. Spain's Gran Telescopio Canarias, located in the Canary Islands, has a single mirror, 34 feet across, made up of multiple segments that can be adjusted individually to eliminate atmospheric distortions. The new 39-meter telescope currently under construction in Hawaii will have 492 linked mirrors stretching almost 100 feet across, able to capture images 12 times as sharp as those from Hubble. The new telescope will join the Keck 1 and Keck 2 scopes atop Hawaii's Mauna Kea.

A WORD FROM

Listening for Others We are now, on an unprecedented scale, listening for radio signals from possible other civilizations in the depths of space. Alive today is the first generation of scientists to interrogate the darkness. Conceivably it might also be the last generation before contact is made—and this the last moment before we discover that someone in the darkness is calling out to us.

—**CARL SAGAN,** *astronomer*

GRAVITATIONAL WAVE OBSERVATORIES

REMNANTS OF THE ANCIENT UNIVERSE

The fabric of space-time is stiff. But according to Einstein's model of general relativity, that fabric ripples when certain events happen—titanic forces, such as black holes absorbing other black holes, ultra-dense neutron stars slamming into each other, or a massive supernova. The ripples are infinitesimal, though, by the time they reach Earth.

But thanks to gravitational wave observatories positioned on Earth, astronomers can now witness these waves. By 2018, 10 black hole mergers and one neutron star merger had been detected by coordinating signals received by laser interferometer observatories in Washington State, Louisiana, and Italy. Tracing the ripples in the fabric may give scientists new ways of obtaining information about deep space and the forces of galactic creation far, far away.

EXPLORATION
& ADVENTURE

EXPLORATION | EXTREMES

Two bikers pedal across a natural sandstone arch in the desert near Moab, Utah.

Intrepid Explorer? Does your spirit carry you to all corners of the globe? Which are you—sophisticated traveler or courageous adventurer? Either way, you'll journey to even more destinations in this chapter.

—CARA SANTA MARIA, *Our Favorite Nerd*

HOW LONG CAN A DUGONG STAY UNDER-WATER?

p75

WHICH TWO EXPLORERS WERE THE FIRST TO SUMMIT MOUNT EVEREST?

p51

p87

IN WHAT YEAR DID CAPTAIN JAMES COOK BEGIN EXPLORING THE PACIFIC OCEAN?

p39

ACCORDING TO LEGEND, IN WHAT YEAR WAS THE FIRST PEACH TREE PLANTED IN GEORGIA?

CHICHÉN ITZÁ WAS THE URBAN CENTER OF WHICH ANCIENT MESOAMERICAN CULTURE?

p83

HOW LONG WAS THE ROAD SYSTEM BUILT BY THE INCA EMPIRE IN THE 15TH CENTURY?

p62

WHAT ICONIC WORLD LANDMARK WAS BUILT TO SERVE AS THE CENTERPIECE FOR THE 1889 WORLD'S FAIR?

p67

IN WHICH COUNTRY WILL YOU FIND THE MAMMOTH-FLINT RIDGE CAVE SYSTEM, THE LONGEST IN THE WORLD?

p53

IN WHICH REGION OF ITALY IS COOKING CHICKEN UNDER A BRICK A COMMON CULINARY TECHNIQUE?

p69

IN WHICH U.S. STATE WILL YOU FIND TABLE ROCK MOUNTAIN?

p47

IN WHICH U.S. NATIONAL PARK CAN YOU SEE THE CONTINENTAL DIVIDE?

p73

IN WHAT YEAR WAS THE FIRST HELICOPTER BUILT?

p63

WHICH SPORT DOES MIRNA VALERIO COMPETE IN?

p58

IN WHAT YEAR DID BOB BALLARD DISCOVER THE WRECK OF THE TITANIC?

p43

EXPLORATION
TIME LINE

| PREHISTORY | 2000 to 1 BC | AD 1 to 1000 | 1000 to 1500 |

PREHISTORY

■ **80,000 ya***
Homo sapiens moves out of Africa.

■ **ca 75,000 ya**
Modern humans reach Southeast Asia.

■ **ca 65,000 ya**
Humans reach Australia.

■ **ca 15,000 BC**
First settlements appear in North America.

■ **ca 8000 BC**
Dogs help pull sleds over snow.

■ **ca 6300 BC**
Earliest known boat is made.

■ **ca 2300 BC**
The earliest known maps are produced in Mesopotamia.

* years ago

2000 to 1 BC

■ **ca 2000 BC**
Austronesians settle on various islands in the South Pacific.

■ **ca 700 BC**
Celts are introducing Iron Age technology to Europe.

■ **240 BC**
Greek mathematician Eratosthenes calculates the circumference of the Earth.

■ **ca 115 BC**
Early trade agreements form between Chinese and European powers.

AD 1 to 1000

■ **150**
Ptolemy maps the world in his *Geography*.

■ **271**
A compass is first used in China.

■ **ca 400**
Polynesian seafarers settle the Hawaiian Islands.

■ **ca 600**
Silk Road is in full use, with China absorbing influences from the West.

■ **1000**
Viking longships under the command of Leif Eriksson cross the Atlantic and reach North America.

1000 to 1500

■ **1050**
Arab astronomers and navigators introduce the astrolabe to Europe.

■ **1271**
Marco Polo sets off on a four-year, 7,500-mile journey from Venice, Italy, to Shangdu, China.

■ **1331**
Arab traveler Ibn Battuta visits East Africa as part of a long voyage through the Islamic world.

■ **1492**
Christopher Columbus lands on a Caribbean island that he names Hispaniola.

■ **1499**
Italian navigator Amerigo Vespucci explores the northeast coastline of South America.

| 1500 to 1750 | 1750 to 1900 | 1900 to 1950 | 1950 to PRESENT |

■ 1513
Ponce de León arrives
in today's Florida,
first of the Spanish
conquistadors in
the Americas.

■ 1519
Ferdinand Magellan
begins his circum-
navigation of the globe.

■ 1535
Jacques Cartier travels
up St. Lawrence River to
site of today's Montreal.

■ 1595
Gerardus Mercator's
first atlas is published.

■ 1607
The English establish
Jamestown on the James
River in North America.

■ 1722
The Dutch land
on Easter Island.

■ 1768
Britain's Capt. James Cook
begins exploring
the Pacific Ocean.

■ 1799
The Rosetta Stone is
discovered in Egypt.

■ 1804–1806
Lewis and Clark run
an expedition across
the western territory
of what is now the
United States.

■ 1841
The first wagon trains
to cross the Rocky Moun-
tains arrive in California.

■ 1891
Construction begins
on the Trans-Siberian
Railroad.

■ 1901
The city of Fairbanks
is settled on the
Alaskan frontier.

■ 1904
Much of Chichén Itzá
is discovered, in Mexico.

■ 1909
Cmdr. Robert E.
Peary and Matthew
Henson lead the first
expedition to the
North Pole.

■ 1937
Amelia Earhart disappears
during an attempt at a
flight around the world.

■ 1946
Richard E. Byrd leads
an expedition to
the South Pole.

■ 1953
Edmund Hillary and
Tenzing Norgay reach
Mount Everest's summit.

■ 1957
The U.S.S.R. launches
Sputnik 1, setting off a
space race with America.

■ 1960
Jacques Piccard becomes
the first human to visit
the Challenger Deep, the
deepest point in the ocean.

■ 1969
Apollo 11 lands men
on the moon.

■ 1990
The Hubble Space
Telescope is put
into operation.

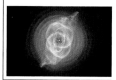

■ 2004
NASA's Spirit and
Opportunity rovers
land on Mars.

NAT GEO
EXPLORERS

THE NEXT GENERATION

These explorers are using conservation, photography, science, and innovation to better understand our world and work toward improving it.

ANNE PRINGLE
UNITED STATES
Pringle, a fungal biologist, works with urban arborists and mycologists in the U.S. and Colombia to assess the health of city trees, including which mycorrhizal fungi are present, and plans to generate a globally applicable approach.

NORTH AMERICA

ELLA AL-SHAMAHI
UNITED KINGDOM
Al-Shamahi is a paleoanthropologist who searches for fossils in Paleolithic caves in the world's most hostile areas—including Syria, Iraq, and Yemen. Scientists avoid many of these spots, which increases Al-Shamahi's chances of making an important discovery.

ATLANTIC

OCEAN

THER WINT AUNG
UNITED STATES
An environmental health researcher working with young citizen scientists on issues of energy poverty in Myanmar, Ther Aung studies the effects of household air pollution associated with cooking and ambient air pollution from sources including industrial emissions.

PACIFIC

OCEAN

JAMAL ALLEN GALVES
BELIZE
Passionate about manatee conservation since he was 11 years old, Galves joined the nonprofit Sea to Shore Alliance to advance the health and safety of these marine mammals, earning a Meritorious Service Award from the governor-general of Belize.

SOUTH AMERICA

NORA SHAWKI
EGYPT
Shawki works in the field of settlement archaeology, which focuses on remnants of community members' daily lives. She investigates the relationships between cities and satellite settlements, as well as the domestic and religious habits of people in those settlements.

EMILIANO DONADIO
ARGENTINA
As mining expands in the Andes, Donadio, a conservation biologist, is studying the effects of this development on canyons and meadows used by migrating guanacos (close relatives of the llama) and proposing strategies to protect these animals.

MARTIN C. WIKELSKI
GERMANY
By tracking intercontinental migrant songbirds via satellite, physiological biologist Wikelski seeks to identify the factors behind their shrinking populations—for these same factors may give insight into challenges facing other life-forms and lead to conservation strategies.

" BELIEVE IN YOURSELF, AND STRIVE TO MAKE A DIFFERENCE. PUSH BOUNDARIES, MEET PEOPLE, TRAVEL, AND UNDERSTAND THE WORLD AROUND YOU. " —TASHI DHENDUP, CONSERVATION BIOLOGIST

RCTIC OCEAN

EUROPE

ASIA

AFRICA

TASHI DHENDUP
BHUTAN
A conservation biologist and forestry officer, Dhendup uses noninvasive camera traps and genetic sampling in Bhutan to educate local communities, reduce human-wildlife conflict, and strategize local conservation initiatives, with a particular focus on tigers.

PACIFIC

OCEAN

ERINA PAULINE MOLINA
PHILIPPINES
Focusing on conservation and community, Molina uses knowledge gleaned from local fishermen to identify vulnerable or locally extinct reef fish species. She partners with communities to research ways to protect dugongs, a marine mammal.

INDIAN

OCEAN

FRIDAH KATUSHEMERERWE
UGANDA
To help preserve, respect, and nurture the resources in African communities, Katushemererwe, a linguist, is using modern language technology to document and share indigenous beliefs, taboos, and proverbs that promoted sustainable practices in previous generations.

AUSTRALIA

HOLLY JONES
AUSTRALIA AND NEW ZEALAND
Islands are home to 20 percent of species but account for 60 percent of contemporary extinctions. Jones, a restoration ecologist, is a pioneer in the area of invasive-pest eradication and how island size affects outcomes.

HANS COSMAS NGOTEYA
TANZANIA
Ngoteya cofounded an organization that promotes, supports, and improves community livelihoods through sustainable environmental practices. He also created a youth-focused project that provides conservation education and alternative livelihood options to reduce pressure on natural resources.

ROBERT BALLARD
MARINE GEOLOGIST

A BOY'S DREAM COME TO LIFE

Twenty Thousand Leagues Under the Sea and a childhood in San Diego, California, awakened in Bob Ballard a love of the ocean and its mysteries. That love eventually led to his discoveries of hydrothermal vents in the Galápagos Rift and numerous shipwrecks, including the *Titanic*. In all, he has conducted more than 150 expeditions coaxing secrets from the world's oceans.

Bob Ballard stands next to the *Hercules* vehicle, which can descend to underwater depths of 2.5 miles.

Before setting the gold standard for ocean exploration, Ballard studied marine geology and served in the U.S. Navy as an oceanographer. In 1985, he returned to temporary active duty for a top-secret Navy-funded mission to assess two sunken nuclear submarines. When he finished that task with 12 days to spare, Ballard was granted permission and resources to spend the remaining days attempting to locate the *Titanic*—which he did.

REWRITING TEXTBOOKS

Between those Navy assignments, Ballard's discoveries changed the way scientists understood not just the ocean but Earth and the universe as well. First, in 1975, Ballard and his colleagues explored the Mid-Atlantic Ridge, the largest mountain range beneath the sea. Their discoveries helped confirm the newly emerging theory of plate tectonics that explains how planet Earth works.

Two years later, Ballard was co-chief scientist on a team that made one of the greatest deep-sea discoveries ever when they found thermal vents off the Galápagos Islands and first reported on the exotic life-forms that live at these vents, using methane—the energy of Earth—instead of light—the energy of the sun—to survive. This discovery changed our definition of life, and that is now helping to guide our search for life elsewhere in the solar system and beyond.

All along, Ballard has been designing remote-controlled, camera-equipped submersibles such as *Jason* and *Hercules,* which can remain on the ocean floor for days on end, beaming their high-definition images to the surface in real time and then via satellite to anyone in the world. Online, 24/7, observers can now watch with Ballard's team on the research vessel *Nautilus* as their deep-sea subs explore the ocean floor.

> **❝ I THINK THE MOST FASCINATING THING I EVER SAW WERE THE CREATURES LIVING IN AND AROUND DEEP-SEA VENTS.❞**

The aged bow of the R.M.S. *Titanic*, first discovered by Bob Ballard

KEY DATES

Some of Ballard's ACHIEVEMENTS

- **1973**
  Explores Mid-Atlantic Rift

- **1977**
  Discovers deep-sea vents and new life-forms

- **1985**
  Finds the *Titanic*

- **1989**
  Finds German battleship *Bismarck*

- **1998**
  Finds aircraft carrier *Yorktown*

- **1999–2000**
  Finds ancient shipwrecks in Black Sea and off Sinai

- **2002**
  Finds JFK's *PT 109*

- **2009**
  Launches exploration vessel E/V *Nautilus*

EXPLORING DEEP OCEANS

95 PERCENT OF EARTH'S LARGEST HABITAT IS UNEXPLORED

Deepsea Challenger sub carries James Cameron to Challenger Deep.

NEW TECHNOLOGY

A DIFFERENT KIND OF SPACECRAFT

The ocean, many say, is the next frontier for humans to explore, map, and exploit. This sentiment takes on urgency when one considers how the negative effects of our presence—pollution, climate change, mining, and fishing—are changing the seas and the creatures in them. Though we are eager to mount expeditions into space as quickly as possible, the cosmos will remain largely unchanged in the meantime. We may, however, have only centuries or even decades to explore our oceans before they are irreversibly altered—as widespread coral reef die-offs make evident. Demand is growing for submersible remotely operated vehicles, cameras, and other instruments that are resilient enough to withstand the pressures, temperatures, and trip durations that make some destinations inhospitable to humans.

DEEP-SEA CREATURES

LUMINOUS LIFE

As scientists explore the deeper reaches of the sea, they discover previously unknown luminous species, such as "green bombers"—deep-sea swimming worms that release sacs of bright green light when attacked—which were identified and described by marine biologists at the Monterey Bay Aquarium Research Institute. They estimate that three-quarters of the animals dwelling in depths up to two and half miles have bioluminescence. Near the surface are jellyfish, followed deeper down by worms and then larvaceans, a zooplankton resembling tadpoles. Some upcoming challenges in this growing field of research include measuring bioluminescence and understanding how these creatures will be affected by changing oxygen levels due to climate change.

A pink helmet jellyfish glows in the Arctic Ocean.

Giant tube worms cluster near a vent in the Galápagos Rift.

THERMAL VENTS

UNEXPECTED COLONIES

The study of hydrothermal vent ecosystems has redefined our understanding of the requirements for life. It was thought that all life on Earth depended on the sun's energy, through photosynthesis. But in 1977, while exploring the Galápagos Rift, scientists came across hydrothermal vents and, shockingly, a robust local community of creatures. Despite extreme temperatures and pressures, toxic minerals, and lack of sunlight, life was thriving because it generated food via chemosynthesis: the absorption of chemicals found in vent water to make organic carbon. Since then, 550 active hydrothermal vent sites have been identified.

Continued exploration of these ecosystems is also challenging models of how life began on Earth. Some scientists say that Charles Darwin's pond-and-lightning model should be replaced by the high-pressure environment found near a vent. In fact, the oldest fossils of living organisms ever found, which could be over four billion years old, come from rock in northern Quebec, Canada, that was once on the ocean floor and likely near a hydrothermal vent.

KEY DATES

Modern Exploration of DEEP SEAS

■ **1872–1876**
H.M.S. *Challenger* circles the globe conducting research for the Royal Society of London, laying the groundwork for modern oceanography.

■ **1943**
Jacques Cousteau and Émile Gagnan engineer the Aqua-Lung, forever changing the course of human-sea interaction.

■ **1961**
The Scripps Institution of Oceanography develops the Deep Tow System, the forerunner of all remotely operated unmanned oceanographic systems.

■ **1977**
Hydrothermal vents are discovered, along with an ecosystem that survives without the energy of the sun, by a team led by Robert Ballard.

■ **2010**
The first ever Census of Marine Life catalogs the diversity, abundance, and distribution of marine species in an online database.

GET OUT INTO
YOUR COUNTRY

WONDERS & THRILLS BOTH NEAR & FAR

Adventure enthusiasts from all over the world travel to the United States to explore stunning national parks, trek iconic trails, and immerse themselves in America's vast wilderness. Each state has its own unique landscape, packed with outdoor activities for every skill level. Don't overlook some obvious choices, for the changing seasons can bring new displays of beauty even to well-known locales.

POP!

ROAD TRIP PLAYLIST

- "Big Sky Country," Chris Whitley
- "The Distance," Cake
- "Edge of Town," Middle Kids
- "Horizon," Tycho
- "Light Enough to Travel," The Be Good Tanyas
- "Lovely Day," Bill Withers
- "Ocean to City," High Highs
- "On the Road Again," Willie Nelson
- "Plan the Escape," Bat for Lashes
- "Wish You Were Here," Pink Floyd

Redwoods tower in Stout Grove at Jedediah Smith Redwoods State Park. Ancient trees there reach up to 300 feet.

CALIFORNIA

Jedediah Smith Redwoods State Park in Northern California is home to trees that date back thousands of years and are only able to thrive in the state's North Coast. Take a scenic drive, snorkel in the Smith River, or camp among the majestic trees.

COLORADO

Adventurers can bike, hike, or four-wheel-drive to Bridal Veil Falls, a 365-foot free-falling waterfall, before continuing on to the Colorado Basin for expansive mountain vistas or ascending cliffs along Telluride's Via Ferrata, a route with metal ladder rungs.

FLORIDA

Large schools of fish flurry throughout the Snapper Ledge dive site in the Florida Keys National Marine Sanctuary. One of 15 marine protected areas of the National Marine Sanctuary System, this sanctuary protects 2,900 square nautical miles of water—including shipwrecks.

KANSAS

The native habitats and ecosystems of Konza Prairie in the Flint Hills of Kansas remain largely untouched for research and conservation, though bison are present. Close to 80 percent of the world's remaining unplowed tallgrass prairie is within this four-million-acre terrain.

MARYLAND

Maryland's Blackwater National Wildlife Refuge is home to three major habitats—forest, marsh, and shallow water—visible from walking trails, water trails, and an auto tour route. Originally a waterfowl sanctuary, it now hosts more than 85 species of birds, including bald eagles.

NEW HAMPSHIRE

Frankenstein Cliff (not as scary as it sounds) in New Hampshire's Crawford Notch State Park is a popular destination for ice climbers. Stunning icefalls, with routes to

A sea kayaker paddles around the Apostle Islands National Lakeshore in Wisconsin.

match every visitor's skill level, are usually found here from December to March.

PENNSYLVANIA

Hyner View State Park has one of the most scenic overlooks in Pennsylvania, with a glorious view of the Susquehanna River. The six-acre park is also popular with hang gliders, who sail over the river's west branch.

RHODE ISLAND

Junior sailors train on Narragansett Bay, which covers 150 square miles and sits at the geographic center of Rhode Island. Sunset sails and fishing cruises promise exciting wildlife viewing, including harbor seals in winter, and uninterrupted sea views.

SOUTH CAROLINA

Table Rock Mountain stands tall above South Carolina's Pinnacle Lake, a popular draw for kayakers. Serious hikers will find access to the 77-mile Foothills Trail that connects Table Rock State Park and Oconee State Park.

TENNESSEE

Churning white-water rapids draw professional and recreational kayakers to the Caney Fork River

Gorge in Tennessee's Rock Island State Park. Highlights are the ruins of an old mill and an unusual waterfall—created by the nearby dam—that comes through the walls of a gorge.

TEXAS

The dynamic desert dunes of Monahans Sandhills State Park in Texas grow and change each season, making each trip different from the previous one. Visitors rent sand disks on-site to surf the dunes or bring horses for a different encounter.

WASHINGTON

Climbers are drawn to the steep slopes found in Washington's Icicle Creek Canyon, a beloved spot in the Okanogan-Wenatchee National Forest. Hikers, families, birders, and runners can take in views of Icicle River and Tumwater Canyon along trails to the mountain summit.

WISCONSIN

The Apostle Islands National Lakeshore—a 21-island archipelago in Wisconsin known as the Jewels of Lake Superior—is home to thousands-year-old ice caves open to visitors for winter exploration.

BEST OF @NATGEO

TOP PHOTOS OF ADVENTURE

@jimmychin | JIMMY CHIN
After his free-solo ascent of Yosemite's El Capitan, Alex Honnold examines the state of his hands.

@renan_ozturk | RENAN OZTURK
Pilots steer an ultralight trike—a type of powered hang glider—over the sandstone formations of Monument Valley in Utah.

@carltonward | CARLTON WARD
The Florida Wildlife Corridor Expedition team paddled, hiked, and biked more than a thousand miles from the northern Everglades to southern Georgia.

@pedromcbride | PETE MCBRIDE
A hockey player skates across fresh black ice in the stark cold of an early morning.

@jimmychin | JIMMY CHIN
Mountaineer Conrad Anker looks over the landscape on a
bright end of day in Antarctica when there is no sunset.

@salvarezphoto | STEPHEN ALVAREZ
An adventurer makes the 600-foot drop into one of the
world's largest caves, Majlis al Jinn in Oman.

@renan_ozturk | RENAN OZTURK
Ice climber Anna Pfaff makes her way up the side of Iceland's
Vatnajökull glacier, the largest in Europe.

@paulnicklen | PAUL NICKLEN
Sunlight illuminates water from above as a diver explores a
deep sinkhole in Mexico.

A HISTORY OF
CLIMBING EVEREST

PROPELLED BY AMBITION AND AWE

For generations, the mountain we know as Everest was a presence to be honored, not conquered. But once British mountaineers attempted to reach its summit in 1922, Everest became an irresistible challenge to climbers from all over the world, forever altering the lives of people living around it. Adventurers have brought wealth and high-tech gear to the region, but they've also introduced pollution and a demand for guides willing to endure dangerous treks. Many hope that, in light of recent tragedies, ambition will be tempered by care and caution.

A WORD FROM

Working Together To be successful, you have to trust the other people you're climbing with, and be inherently playing on the same team, pardon the cliché. From a climbing standpoint, gravity is the adversary. You and your fellow humans are striving together to get to the same place at the same time. And I think that's a really good way for humans to interact.

—CONRAD ANKER, *mountaineer*

"The mountain remains unvanquished," wrote Barry Bishop after the 1963 American Everest expedition, shown here.

Setting Records on
EVEREST

■ **MAY 1953 (SOUTH FACE)**
Edmund Hillary (New Zealand) and
Tenzing Norgay (Nepal) accomplish
the first recorded summit of Everest.

■ **MAY 1963 (WEST RIDGE AND
NORTH FACE)**
First successful American expedition:
Team members Thomas Hornbein
and Willi Unsoeld traverse Everest
via West Ridge.

■ **MAY 1975 (SOUTH FACE)**
Junko Tabei (Japan) becomes first
woman to reach summit—just 12 days
after being injured in an avalanche.

■ **AUG. 1980 (NORTH FACE)**
Reinhold Messner (Italy) makes
first solo ascent—notably without
supplementary oxygen, as on his
previous summit in May 1978.

■ **SEPT. 1988 (SOUTH RIDGE)**
Jean-Marc Boivin (France) accomplishes
the first paraglider descent from the
summit, thus also clocking the fastest
descent ever.

■ **MAY 2010 (NORTH FACE)**
Jordan Romero (U.S.) becomes the
youngest person to summit, at 13 years
and 10 months old.

■ **MAY 2012 (NORTH FACE)**
Tamae Watanabe (Japan) becomes the
oldest female to summit, at age 73 years
and 180 days—breaking her own record.

■ **MAY 2013**
Yuichiro Miura (Japan) reclaims title
of oldest man to summit, at age 80.

■ **MAY 2013**
Dave Hahn (U.S.) sets a new
record, 15, for number of ascents
by a non-Sherpa.

■ **MAY 2018**
Kami Rita Sherpa, age 48, sets record for
number of summits by accomplishing
his 22nd.

EARTH'S EXTREMES

PUTTING THE AWE BACK IN AWESOME

Sunrise over Lake Superior

WATER RECORDS

LARGEST FRESHWATER LAKE

Lake Superior stretches across 31,700 square miles of the United States and Canada, making it the largest lake by surface area. It was formed about 10,000 years ago.

LOWEST POINT

The Challenger Deep in the Pacific is the lowest point on Earth: 36,037 feet below sea level. Mount Everest could be sunk into its depths and still be covered by more than one mile of water.

DEEPEST LAKE

Russia's Lake Baikal is both the deepest lake, at 5,387 feet, and the oldest, at 25–30 million years old. It is part of a rift valley, where tectonic plates are breaking apart.

LARGEST RIVER

There is no competition here: The Amazon River and its tributaries flow through Peru, Bolivia, Venezuela, Colombia, Ecuador, and Brazil before emptying into the Atlantic Ocean. The next largest, India's "Mother Ganges," discharges a significantly lower volume of water than the Amazon does.

LONGEST RIVER

Calculating the length of rivers is a complicated and controversial process. Freshwater scientists often cannot agree on a river's precise source or on how far to extend its watershed boundaries. But most agree that the Nile, stretching through northeast Africa, is the longest in the world at 4,160 miles. The Amazon is a close second at 4,150 miles and the Yangtze clocks in at 3,880 miles long.

The Nile in Sudan

The Valle de la Luna in Chile's Atacama Desert

SCIENTISTS THINK THE DRY VALLEYS OF ANTARCTICA MAY BE THE CLOSEST OF ANY ENVIRONMENT ON EARTH TO THE PLANET MARS.

Bore hole inside Mammoth Cave

LAND RECORDS

DRIEST PLACE
Parts of the high plateau of the Atacama Desert in Chile and the Dry Valleys of Antarctica have never recorded a drop of rain. They are ringed by high mountains that prevent moisture from reaching the dry basins.

HIGHEST POINT
Mount Everest is the world's highest elevation, 29,035 feet above sea level—a figure that increases as the Indian subcontinent crashes into Asia. Hawaii's Mauna Kea is the world's tallest mountain, 33,000 feet from seafloor to summit.

WETTEST PLACE
Asian monsoons make the Indian state of Meghalaya the rainiest place in the world. The town of Mawsynram received about 83 feet of rain in 1985. In 1861, nearby Cherrapunji received 86.6 feet.

FARTHEST FROM THE OCEAN
About 200 miles north of Urumqi, a city in Xinjiang, China, is a "pole of inaccessibility"—a location that is "challenging to reach owing to its remoteness from geographical features that could provide access." The most remote pole of inaccessibility—the place farthest from the ocean—is also in Xinjiang, about 1,644 miles from the coast.

LONGEST CAVE SYSTEM
The Mammoth-Flint Ridge cave system in Kentucky stretches about 400 miles, nearly twice the length of the next longest cave system, Mexico's Sac Actun underwater cave.

HOTTEST PLACE
The temperature at Furnace Creek Station in Death Valley National Park, which straddles California and Nevada, reached 134°F (56.7°C) on July 10, 1913. However, the Danakil Depression—which reaches into Eritrea, Djibouti, and Ethiopia—has the highest average year-round temperature—93.92°F (34.4°C).

COLDEST PLACE
A region near Vostok Station, a Russian research station in Antarctica atop ice almost two and a half miles thick, set the world record on August 10, 2010, when the temperature dipped to minus 135.8°F (−93.2°C).

UNDERWATER MUSEUM

SWIMMING WITH SCULPTURE

A barren sand flat does not typically inspire creativity, but it happens to be a perfect setting for the first Underwater Museum of Art (UMA) in the United States. Located just off the Florida Panhandle, near Walton County's Grayton Beach State Park, the UMA installed its first seven sculptures in 2018. Over time, the collection will become a marine habitat. As at similar projects near Cancún and the Canary Islands, the experience is best suited for scuba divers. On clear days, snorkelers will also be able to enjoy the submerged journey, which sits at a depth of around 60 feet.

POP!

MOVIES WITH UNDERWATER WORLDS

- *The Little Mermaid* (1989)
- *Sphere* (1998)
- *Atlantis: The Lost Empire* (2001)
- *Finding Nemo* (2003)
- *Deepsea Challenge* (2014)
- *Aquaman* (2018)
- *Avatar 2 and 3* (in production)

A school of gray snappers swims among the sculptures at the Underwater Museum of Art in Cancún, Mexico, precursor to the new one in Florida.

Inaugural Class of
SUBMERGED ART

■ **ANAMORPHOUS OCTOPUS**
This perforated steel sculpture was created
by artist Allison Wickey, who first proposed the museum. Her painter's eye is
evident in the textured, shaded surface
of her piece.

■ **CONCRETE ROPE REEF SPHERES**
With a goal of supporting oyster colonies,
architecture professor and artist Evelyn
Tickle developed a concrete formula that
matches the constitution of oyster shells
and used it to make the nooks and crannies
of her creature-friendly tangled sculpture.

■ **THE GRAYT PINEAPPLE**
In the American colonies, rare and expensive
pineapples symbolized hospitality. Artist
Rachel Herring's steel sculpture is welcoming to small fish in particular. Its name refers
to Grayton Beach.

■ **JYC'S DREAM**
In a nod to explorer Jacques Cousteau's
Aqua-Lung, designer Kevin Reilly created
this oversize stainless-steel depiction of a
diver's head gear with rising bubbles—some
containing children's art.

■ **PROPELLER IN MOTION**
Furniture designer Marek Anthony based his
stainless-steel sculpture on a ship's propeller to elicit thoughts of motion and of nature
reclaiming what humans have discarded.
Swimming creatures can easily move
through the hollow blades.

■ **SELF PORTRAIT**
Justin Gaffrey's eight-foot-tall stag evokes
the stillness of an encounter on land. Its
steely presence invites parallels between the
underwater setting and a forest scene—with
dashing fish instead of scurrying forest
animals.

■ **SWARA SKULL**
The steel, cement, and limestone hollow
skull created by film designer (and divemas-
ter) Vince Tatum aims to attract corals and
reclusive marine life. (SWARA stands for
South Walton Artificial Reef Association.)

The Speed of Innovation

Progression of 100-meter dash world record,
1910-2018

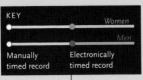

KEY

Women
Men

Manually timed record   Electronically timed record

Male and female runners have bested world records in the 100-meter dash over the past century. But the gear and the track infrastructure are what have changed most dramatically since the first competitions were run with the help of nails driven into the soles of dress shoes.

Stronger starts
Early racers dug holes into the tracks, which were usually laid with cinders. The introduction of solid starting blocks in the late 1920s led to new world records.

Lighter shoes
The first running shoes were simply leather dress shoes, with nails to provide grip. Today's shoes boast nylon, fiberglass, and single-use spikes.

10.6 seconds
Donald Lippincott, U.S.
July 6, 1912

10.2
Jesse Owens, U.S.
June 20, 1936

13.0
12.5
12.0
11.5
11.0
10.5
10.0

1910   1920   1930   1940   1950

ATHLETIC ACHIEVEMENTS IMPROVED FOR DECADES,
IN PART BECAUSE OF NEW TECHNOLOGY AND THE USE
OF PERFORMANCE-ENHANCING STEROIDS.
WITH ATHLETES UNDER INCREASED SCRUTINY,
WORLD RECORDS ARE STILL GETTING BROKEN—BUT
NOT INCREMENTALLY, SUGGESTING THAT WE ARE
PUSHING THE LIMITS OF OUR ATHLETIC POTENTIAL.

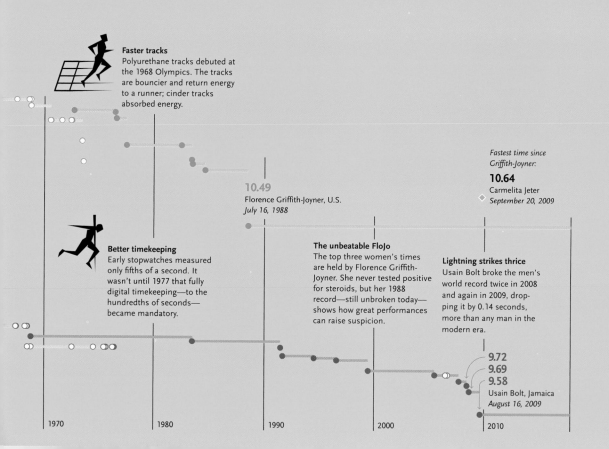

Faster tracks
Polyurethane tracks debuted at
the 1968 Olympics. The tracks
are bouncier and return energy
to a runner; cinder tracks
absorbed energy.

Fastest time since
Griffith-Joyner:
10.64
Carmelita Jeter
September 20, 2009

10.49
Florence Griffith-Joyner, U.S.
July 16, 1988

Better timekeeping
Early stopwatches measured
only fifths of a second. It
wasn't until 1977 that fully
digital timekeeping—to the
hundredths of seconds—
became mandatory.

The unbeatable FloJo
The top three women's times
are held by Florence Griffith-
Joyner. She never tested positive
for steroids, but her 1988
record—still unbroken today—
shows how great performances
can raise suspicion.

Lightning strikes thrice
Usain Bolt broke the men's
world record twice in 2008
and again in 2009, drop-
ping it by 0.14 seconds,
more than any man in the
modern era.

9.72
9.69
9.58
Usain Bolt, Jamaica
August 16, 2009

1970   1980   1990   2000   2010

MIRNA VALERIO
ULTRA RUNNER

CHARTING A COURSE FOR EVERY BODY

"I'm good in my big body." That's what Mirna Valerio—ultramarathon runner, author, and educator—wants her naysayers to know. A few years after starting her blog, Fat Girl Running, Valerio's story went viral, subjecting her to both praise and public scrutiny. Despite racism and body-shaming, she continues challenging stereotypes and inspiring others to do the same.

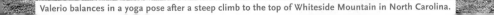

Valerio balances in a yoga pose after a steep climb to the top of Whiteside Mountain in North Carolina.

With an unwavering spirit that solidified her place as a 2018 National Geographic Adventurer of the Year, Mirna Valerio is challenging stereotypes in the running world and bringing a community of body-positive athletes along with her.

Valerio discovered her own athleticism and love of the outdoors at overnight camp in the Catskill Mountains when she was eight years old. She played high school sports and kept running through her college years. But over time, Valerio's exercise routines fell away—until a health scare in 2008. When she came back to running, she weighed more than 300 pounds. Even with running 25 to 35 miles a week and frequently participating in marathons and ultramarathons, Valerio's weight has plateaued at about 240 pounds.

WHAT DOES FIT LOOK LIKE?

This raises the question: Is a BMI score the best indicator of health? "I think that people are really having trouble grappling with the idea that fit comes in many forms," Valerio says, "and that people can still participate in athletics no matter what kind of body they have."

Her blog gained national attention, giving voice to her determination, positivity, and insistence that people of all sizes can be fit. Her message is so inspiring that she has been given a platform and held up as a role model by corporations and media alike.

"We are much more than our bodies. Whether it's body image, our choices to be moms or not, our career choices—we are more than our bodies," Valerio says. "We're so powerful beyond our wildest dreams."

> **" I KNOW THERE'S GOING TO BE UPS AND DOWNS. THAT'S THE BEAUTIFUL CHALLENGE OF RUNNING LONG RACES. I THINK THEY REALLY PREPARE YOU FOR DIFFICULT THINGS IN LIFE."**

Valerio started training for her first marathon in 2011.

KEY DATES

Mirna Valerio's
JOURNEY

■ **DEC. 2011**
Completes first marathon, Marine Corps Marathon, Washington, D.C.

■ **OCT. 2015**
Completes Javelina Jundred, her first 100k run, Fountain Hills, AZ

■ **2016**
Named ambassador for Merrell

■ **OCT. 2017**
Publishes memoir, *A Beautiful Work in Progress*

■ **2017**
REI releases documentary short, *The Mirnavator*

■ **MARCH 2018**
Named a National Geographic Adventurer of the Year

REDEFINING
WHAT IS POSSIBLE

PERFORMANCES THAT SET WORLD & OLYMPIC RECORDS

Men's 400-meter sprint final

2016 SUMMER GAMES

RECORD FINALLY FALLS

Sprinter Wayde van Niekerk of South Africa set a new world record at the 2016 games in the 400-meter race, coming in at 43.03 seconds. The previous record of 43.18 had been set in 1999 by Michael Johnson of the U.S.

DOMINANCE

In cycling's men's team pursuit, Great Britain set four world records between 2008 and 2012. In 2016, Great Britain set new world and Olympic records twice—in the first round (3:50.570) and again in the final (3:50.265). With the 2016 gold medal, his seventh, Bradley Wiggins became his country's most decorated Olympic athlete.

PUSHING THE ENVELOPE

A single event saw three new world and Olympic records during the Rio games: women's team pursuit cycling, a four-person 4-kilometer race. Great Britain clocked in at 4:13.260 in the qualifying round, 4:12.152 in the first round, and 4:10.236 in the final.

STRONG SHOWING

In the women's 63 kg weightlifting competition, Deng Wei of China exceeded her own world record in the clean and jerk portion (147 kg, up from 2015's 146 kg) and set a world record with her final tally of 262 kg.

HAMMER TIME

Polish hammer thrower Anita Włodarczyk set four world records between 2009 and 2015. In Rio, she set a world and Olympic record with her 270.0-foot throw. Just two weeks later, she bested that with a 272.2-foot throw.

Women's hammer throw final

Men's 500-meter speed skating quarterfinals

AT THE 2018 WINTER OLYMPICS IN PYEONGCHANG, 25 OLYMPIC RECORDS AND 3 WORLD RECORDS WERE SET.

Women's team pursuit in speed skating

2018 WINTER GAMES

FIRE ON ICE

Chinese speed skater Wu Dajing broke the Olympic record in men's short track 500-meter speed skating in his heat and then went on to set two new world records in both the quarterfinal and final races (clocking in at 40.264, 39.800, and 39.584 seconds, respectively).

BESTS, NOT RECORDS

At the Pyeongchang Winter Games in 2018, only speed skating saw world and Olympic records broken at the same time. Performances at high elevations, as in Pyeongchang, tend to be better than those at sea level, so the latter may be designated world bests instead of world records. In the 2018 games, three world records and five world bests were recorded.

NO GOLD FOR FASTEST

In women's short track skating, the Netherlands' team set a new world record in the 3,000-meter relay, with a time of 4:03.471. But because they weren't among the top four teams competing for medals, they were almost sent home empty-handed. When other teams were disqualified, they ended up with the bronze medal—despite besting South Korea, the gold medal winners, by almost 4 seconds.

ONE AFTER ANOTHER

The Netherlands had another world best in the quarterfinals of the women's team pursuit with a time of 2:55.61, but two days later, Japan broke both records by finishing in 2:53.89. Japan also holds the world record for this event, set at the 2017 World Cup held in Salt Lake City, with a time of 2:50.87.

À LA CARTE

Jorien ter Mors of the Netherlands set world best and Olympic records for the women's 1,000-meter race with a time of 1:13.56. Ter Mors was also a member of the world-record-setting 3,000-meter relay team.

UNSTOPPABLE

In women's 500-meter speed skating, Japan's Nao Kodaira finished in 36.94 seconds, setting the world best and Olympic records—and earning her first gold medal. She also holds three world records, in the 500-meter x 2, 1,000-meter, and sprint combination events.

TRANSPORTATION
TIME LINE

PREHISTORY

- **ca 65,000 ya***
Modern humans reach New Guinea and Australia by boat.

- **ca 14,700 ya**
Humans are present in the Americas.

- **ca 10,000 ya**
Dugout canoes are in use in Europe.

- **ca 5500 BC**
Humans use bits and reins to manage horses for riding.

- **ca 3500 BC**
The wheel is invented in Mesopotamia.

- **ca 2500 BC**
Mesopotamians waterproof boats and buildings with tar.

* *years ago*

1700 to 1 BC

- **ca 1700 BC**
Horses and chariots are introduced to Egypt.

- **691 BC**
Assyrians build an aqueduct to carry water to their capital, Nineveh.

- **312 BC**
Rome builds its first major road, the Appian Way.

- **110 BC**
Romans use rudimentary horseshoes.

AD 1 to 1000

- **415**
In India, suspension bridges are built using iron chains.

- **ca 660**
Camel herds support a nomadic way of life among people living in the Sahara.

- **ca 700**
Europeans begin to adopt the use of stirrups for riding horses.

- **ca 800**
Roads in Baghdad, Iraq, are paved with tar extracted from nearby oil fields.

- **ca 860**
Viking longships venture as far west as Iceland.

1000 to 1700

- **ca 1088**
Shen Kuo first describes a magnetic compass used for navigation.

- **ca 1450**
The Inca construct a road system 20,000 miles long to unite their empire.

- **1457**
The first four-wheel passenger coach is built in Hungary.

- **1500**
Chinese scientist Wan Hu attempts to make a flying machine out of rockets tied to a chair.

- **1692**
In France, the 32-mile Canal du Midi, linking the Mediterranean Sea with the Atlantic Ocean, is completed.

1700 to 1900

1769
James Watt patents the modern steam engine.

1783
French brothers Joseph and Jacques Montgolfier first demonstrate the hot air balloon.

1869
The Suez Canal is completed in Egypt.

1869
The U.S. Transcontinental Railroad is completed.

1879
Karl Benz runs the first gas-powered automobile.

1891
Construction begins on the Trans-Siberian Railroad.

1900 to 1930

1903
Orville and Wilbur Wright fly a powered airplane at Kitty Hawk, North Carolina.

1904
The first portion of the New York City subway opens.

1908
The first Model T Ford comes off the assembly line.

1909
French aviator Louis Blériot flies across the English Channel.

1927
Charles Lindbergh flies the *Spirit of St. Louis* nonstop from New York to Paris.

1930 to 1960

1933
The first modern airliner, the Boeing 247, enters service.

1937
The *Hindenburg* dirigible bursts into flames when attempting to dock after a transatlantic flight.

1939
Inventor Igor Sikorsky builds the first helicopter.

1945
James Martin designs the ejector seat.

1947
American airman Charles "Chuck" Yeager makes the first supersonic flight.

1958
Australian engineer David Warren invents the "black box" flight data recorder.

1960 to PRESENT

1961
Soviet cosmonaut Yuri Gagarin becomes the first man in space.

1969
The British-French supersonic airliner Concorde takes its maiden flight.

1969
NASA's Apollo 11 makes the first piloted moon landing.

1998
English inventor David Baker patents the Land Shark, a high-speed amphibious car.

2010
Self-driving cars make their first test drives on public streets.

ICONIC
DESTINATIONS

JOURNEYS THAT SHOULD BE ON EVERY BUCKET LIST

NASHVILLE
U.S.
Immerse yourself in Americana at the Country Music Hall of Fame and Hatch Show Print. Then make a pilgrimage to the Ryman Auditorium and Music Row.

PACIFIC COAST HIGHWAY
U.S.
Savor the sweeping Pacific vistas and hairpin bends of the highway that clings to America's western edge. Cruise north from Hearst Castle to historic Monterey.

HANA HIGHWAY
U.S.
A restorative for mind and body, Maui's Hana coast—with black-sand beaches, plunging waterfalls, limpid pools, and rainbow eucalyptus—unspools for 52 miles.

TAHITI & BORA BORA
French Polynesia
A stroll along a black-sand beach, a dive into a translucent lagoon, or a visit to palm-shaded coral atolls will show you why these islands are considered paradise.

GALÁPAGOS
Ecuador
Visit for a day or more to see the lava fields, white-sand strands, and giant cliffs that are home to the abundant wildlife that inspired Charles Darwin.

DUTCH BULBFIELDS
Netherlands
In spring the famed bulbfields in South Holland become a blaze of color. Cycle around fields of brilliant hues, and then visit world-famous gardens.

PYRAMIDS OF GIZA
Egypt
The lone survivor of the original Seven Wonders of the World, these tombs have been astonishing visitors since they were first erected in the 26th century BC.

NORTH AMERICA

SOUTH AMERICA

PACIFIC OCEAN

ATLANTIC OCEAN

> " TRAVEL IS MORE THAN THE SEEING OF SIGHTS; IT IS A CHANGE THAT GOES ON, DEEP AND PERMANENT, IN THE IDEAS OF LIVING."
>
> —MIRIAM BEARD, HISTORIAN AND ACTIVIST

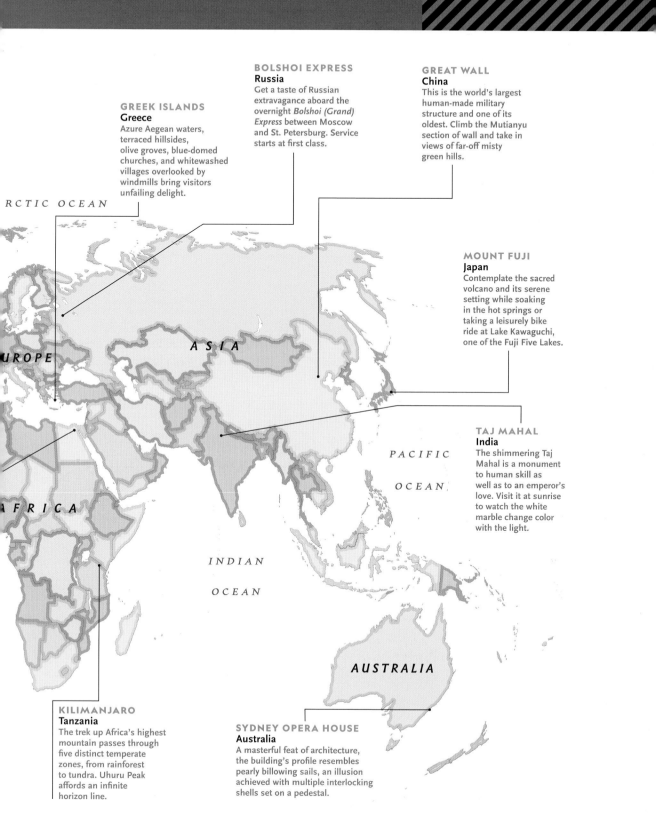

GREEK ISLANDS
Greece
Azure Aegean waters, terraced hillsides, olive groves, blue-domed churches, and whitewashed villages overlooked by windmills bring visitors unfailing delight.

BOLSHOI EXPRESS
Russia
Get a taste of Russian extravagance aboard the overnight *Bolshoi (Grand) Express* between Moscow and St. Petersburg. Service starts at first class.

GREAT WALL
China
This is the world's largest human-made military structure and one of its oldest. Climb the Mutianyu section of wall and take in views of far-off misty green hills.

MOUNT FUJI
Japan
Contemplate the sacred volcano and its serene setting while soaking in the hot springs or taking a leisurely bike ride at Lake Kawaguchi, one of the Fuji Five Lakes.

TAJ MAHAL
India
The shimmering Taj Mahal is a monument to human skill as well as to an emperor's love. Visit it at sunrise to watch the white marble change color with the light.

RCTIC OCEAN

UROPE

ASIA

AFRICA

PACIFIC

OCEAN

INDIAN

OCEAN

AUSTRALIA

KILIMANJARO
Tanzania
The trek up Africa's highest mountain passes through five distinct temperate zones, from rainforest to tundra. Uhuru Peak affords an infinite horizon line.

SYDNEY OPERA HOUSE
Australia
A masterful feat of architecture, the building's profile resembles pearly billowing sails, an illusion achieved with multiple interlocking shells set on a pedestal.

SAVOR THE WORLD'S
BEST CITIES

SEEKING OUT UNIQUE URBAN TREASURES

Puerto Madero, Buenos Aires

MARRAKECH

GREEN OASES
Marrakech is known for its gardens, particularly the Jardin Majorelle (Rue Yves Saint Laurent), a breathtaking landscape of exotic plants, trees, pools, and fountains. But few realize its haute couture legacy. Fashion legends Yves Saint Laurent and Pierre Berg bought and restored the garden in 1980, saving it from becoming part of a hotel complex.

READ AHEAD
Lords of the Atlas by Gavin Maxwell (1966), an account of the ruling Glaoua clan, who maintained a near-medieval fiefdom in southern Morocco from 1893 to 1956, is a must-read.

BUENOS AIRES

LIKE A LOCAL
Calle Florida in downtown Buenos Aires has been at least partly pedestrianized since 1913. Now totally off-limits for vehicles, it's one of the city's biggest tourist attractions, with shops and arcades selling leather, jewelry, and souvenirs.

READ AHEAD
The translated short stories of Argentina's most important writer, Jorge Luis Borges, are a great way to learn about the city, especially the tumultuous dark underworld of the *compadritos,* gangsters, of the 1920s and 1930s. Pick up his *Collected Fictions* (1999).

Jardin Majorelle in Marrakech

Aerial view of Paris at night

> **IF YOU ARE LUCKY ENOUGH TO HAVE LIVED IN PARIS AS A YOUNG MAN, THEN WHEREVER YOU GO FOR THE REST OF YOUR LIFE, IT STAYS WITH YOU, FOR PARIS IS A MOVEABLE FEAST."**
>
> **—ERNEST HEMINGWAY,**
> **AMERICAN AUTHOR AND PARIS RESIDENT**

Yu Garden in Shanghai

PARIS

LA TOUR MAGNIFIQUE

The Eiffel Tower—built as the centerpiece for the 1889 World's Fair—is France at its best: confident, brilliant, putting on a show for the world. Glass-roofed shopping arcades are another Paris invention, also from the 19th century. The ones that survive, mostly around the old Bibliothèque Nationale, are utterly charming; some are packed with old bookstores and curiosity shops, others with chic galleries and boutiques.

FLEA MARKETS

No trip to Paris is complete without a day at the 17-acre, 3,000-stall Marché aux Puces de Saint-Ouen on the city limits. You might score vintage French cookery or antique tomes at the centrally located Marché aux Puces d'Aligre. A visit to the intimate and friendly Marché aux Puces de Vanves is like rummaging through the attic of the French grandparents you never had.

READ AHEAD

All of Georges Simenon's Maigret detective stories are great for evoking Parisian life, both high and low. *Maigret at the Crossroads* (1931) is regarded as one of the best.

SHANGHAI

VISIT THE PAST

Take a break from the busy streets and glitzy skyscrapers and lose yourself in ancient China at the 400-year-old Yu Garden in the Huangpu District. The complex was a private garden in the Ming dynasty and has become one of Shanghai's most famous sites. See exquisite Chinese sculptures, carvings, garden pavilions, pagodas, and pools. Outside you'll find the bustling Yuyuan Bazaar with souvenir shops, teahouses, and restaurants.

READ AHEAD

Man's Fate (1933), which many consider to be André Malraux's best novel, follows two communist conspirators and two foreigners during the violent crackdown of the communist insurrection in 1927 Shanghai.

A TASTE OF ITALY

ABBONDANZA DELIZIOSA

Central Italy—its mountains, plains, valleys, and merry coastline—is both civilized and down to earth. Home of the Renaissance, this most visited part of Italy, along with its celebrated culture and cuisine, is what most travelers think of as "Italian." Indeed, the central Italian kitchen, which takes simplicity to a high level, characterizes much of what generally makes Italian food so special. That finesse is derived from two things: an ancient cosmopolitan heritage and a fidelity to high-quality ingredients that are locally grown or produced.

A WORD FROM

Traveling via Flavors The real Italy is so much more multifaceted, and so much more remarkable, than the Italy that lives on in popular imagination. For the traveler to Italy, this diversity means an incredible range of experiences and tastes, from heavenly white truffles in Alba to musky blood oranges in Sicily. These locally produced ingredients . . . shape the local cooking and produce the wide variety of regional cuisines . . . And 21st-century transport means these artisanal ingredients are likely available at your local market.

—**JACK BISHOP,** *chief creative officer of America's Test Kitchen*

Parmesan cheese and Bolognese sauce top homemade fettucine.

Traditional Dishes From
CENTRAL ITALY

■ **CHICKEN UNDER A BRICK**
(POLLO AL MATTONE)
This Tuscan technique ensures even cooking, speeds up the process, and maximizes contact with the cooking grate for perfectly crisp skin.

■ **FRIED STUFFED OLIVES**
(OLIVE ALL'ASCOLANA)
Crisp-coated, salty fried olives with a rich meat filling are a culinary marvel from the town of Ascoli Piceno in Le Marche.

■ **ORECCHIETTE WITH SAUSAGE AND CREAM**
(ORECCHIETTE ALLA NORCINA)
The black pigs of Umbria are prized for their superlative flavor, owing to their diet of plants, herbs, and truffles.

■ **ROMAN GNOCCHI**
(GNOCCHI ALLA ROMANA)
Semolina gnocchi—no potatoes here—is appealingly creamy and slightly dense, similar to polenta.

■ **SEAFOOD SOUP**
(BRODETTO ALL'ANCONETANA)
Ancona's trademark dish has long served as a way for fishermen to use the bycatch remaining after selling the day's haul.

■ **SPRING VEGETABLE STEW**
(VIGNOLE)
Spring vegetables abound in Abruzzo's inland, and *vignole* is a vibrant (and speedy) braise that celebrates them.

■ **TUSCAN TOMATO AND BREAD SOUP**
(PAPPA AL POMODORO)
This is a tomato-bread soup finished with basil. In the pot, the ingredients meld to form a fragrant porridge-like stew that's downright luxurious.

■ **VEGETABLE AND FARRO SOUP**
(MINESTRA DI FARRO)
Umbrians use coarsely ground farro, a staple of Umbria that predates common wheat, to thicken and flavor soups.

GREATEST EXPEDITIONS

FOLLOW HISTORY'S PATHWAYS AROUND THE WORLD

Passengers traverse Switzerland's Landwasser viaduct.

BY TRAIN

SWISS ALPS AND ITALIAN LAKE DISTRICT

Climb aboard the unhurried *Glacier Express* and savor the panorama of snowcapped peaks, dense forests, rushing rivers, Alpine meadows, and mountain villages near Switzerland's southern borders.

CANADIAN ROCKIES

Take the *Rocky Mountaineer*'s dramatic route through the Canadian Rockies—rocky gradients, soaring pine trees, spiraling tunnels—from Vancouver to Banff.

SHINKANSEN TRANS-SIBERIAN RAILWAY

A weeklong Moscow-Beijing route via Mongolia weaves though the Russian hinterlands of Siberia, the wilderness of Mongolia, and the wastes of the Gobi, within sight of Lake Baikal and the Great Wall.

ACROSS LAND

MOROCCO'S CITIES OF LEGEND

A journey along age-old trade routes—from Ceuta (officially part of Spain) to the tiny fishing port of Tarfaya—immerses you in ancient cultures, exotic markets, and imposing mountain and desert scenery.

NEW ZEALAND NORTH TO SOUTH

The unspoiled (but accessible) landscape between Karamea and Jackson Bay includes two glaciers, exceptional ocean vistas, and alpine scenery.

PILGRIMAGE TO BHUTAN

One enchanted tour includes a trek into Trashi-yangtse, a stunning "lost" valley, with a monastery, a wildlife sanctuary, a shrine, and welcoming locals.

Prayer flags frame Bhutan's mythic Taktsang Monastery.

Sea Cloud II approaches St. Lucia's Pitons.

BY SEA

CARIBBEAN DREAMING

These legendary islands are synonymous with paradise: idyllic beaches, water sports, and rum cocktails. A cruise through the breathtaking waters offers luxury, shopping, and outdoor fun.

EPIC POLYNESIA

During one seven-day excursion around Tahiti and nearby islands, guests can kayak, dive, snorkel, hike, or sunbathe. Inland spots to visit include an archaeological site and a vanilla plantation.

ANTARCTIC CRUISING

You'll be comfortable aboard an ice-reinforced vessel as icebergs float past, some of them as large as ships themselves. Time your trip right to catch sight of seals, whales, and penguins.

A WORD FROM

Overtourism According to figures from the United Nations World Tourism Organization, international tourism has grown 40-fold since commercial jet traffic began some six decades ago. The places that these people visit, however—the museums, the archaeological ruins, the natural attractions, the narrow medieval streets of historic cities—are still the same physical size.

—JONATHAN TOURTELLOT,
sustainable tourism expert

TOGETHER, TOURISTS FROM CHINA AND THE UNITED STATES SPEND ALMOST $400 BILLION A YEAR ON TRAVEL.

Zebras and wildebeests graze in Tanzania's Serengeti National Park.

ON SAFARI

TANZANIA'S GREAT MIGRATION

On the ground, in the trees, along rivers, and in the sky—more than 1,000 bird species can be found here, and it's possible to see 100 species in a day. Birding is good year-round, but fall migration is spectacular.

BOTSWANA GAME RESERVE

On a guided safari, guests of the national parks shoot the "big five" of African wildlife—lion, leopard, buffalo, rhino, and elephant—with cameras rather than guns.

VICTORIA FALLS

On a microlight aircraft, there's not much between you and the tree-covered islands that dot the Zambezi River as it approaches Victoria Falls. Want to see wildlife? Book a flight over the nearby national park.

U.S. NATIONAL PARKS

START PLANNING YOUR NEXT BIG OUTDOOR ADVENTURE

Olympic N.P.
• Seattle
WASHINGTON
North Cascades N.P.
Mt. Rainier N.P.
Glacier N.P.
Voyageurs N.P.

OREGON
Theodore Roosevelt N.P.
NORTH DAKOTA
MINNESOTA
WISCON
• St. Paul
MONTANA
• Billings

Crater Lake N.P.
IDAHO
Yellowstone N.P.
Grand Teton N.P.
Rapid City
SOUTH DAKOTA
Minneapolis

Redwood National and State Parks
Wind Cave N.P.
Badlands N.P.
IOWA

Lassen Volcanic N.P.
WYOMING

San Francisco
CALIFORNIA
NEVADA
Salt Lake City
NEBRASKA
U N I T E D   S T A T
Rocky Mountain N.P.
• Denver
Kansas City

Great Basin N.P.
UTAH
Capitol Reef N.P.
Arches N.P.
COLORADO

Yosemite N.P.
Kings Canyon N.P.
Bryce Canyon N.P.
Black Canyon of the Gunnison N.P.
KANSAS
MISSOURI

Pinnacles N.P.
Zion N.P.
Canyonlands N.P.

Sequoia N.P.
• Las Vegas
Grand Canyon N.P.
Mesa Verde N.P.
Great Sand Dunes N.P. & Pres.

Death Valley N.P.

Channel Islands N.P.
• Los Angeles
ARIZONA
Petrified Forest N.P.
NEW MEXICO
OKLAHOMA
ARKANSA
Lit
• Ro

Joshua Tree N.P.
• Phoenix
Hot Springs N.P.

San Diego

PACIFIC OCEAN
Saguaro N.P.
Tucson
Ft. Worth •   • Dallas

Carlsbad Caverns N.P.
El Paso
Guadalupe Mountains N.P.
TEXAS
LOUISI

ARCTIC OCEAN
RUSSIA
Big Bend N.P.
San Antonio
• Houston

Kobuk Valley N.P.
Gates of the Arctic N.P. & Preserve
ALASKA
Fairbanks •
CANADA

Denali N.P. & Pres.

Lake Clark N.P. & Pres.
Anchorage
Wrangell-St.Elias N.P. & Preserve
MEXICO

Kenai Fjords N.P.
Glacier Bay N.P. & Pres.
Juneau

0   400 MI
0   400 KM

Katmai N.P. & Pres.

PACIFIC OCEAN

" BREAK CLEAR AWAY, ONCE IN A WHILE, AND CLIMB A MOUNTAIN OR SPEND A WEEK IN THE WOODS. WASH YOUR SPIRIT CLEAN."

—JOHN MUIR, NATURALIST

KEY DESTINATIONS

Secret Gems Among the
U.S. PARKS

■ **SHENANDOAH**
Skyline Drive winds for 105 miles through this narrow park. Visitors can stroll to lookouts or hike to craggy summits, playful waterfalls, and watercolor vistas.

■ **WIND CAVE**
Above is a globally significant expanse of mixed-grass prairie; below is one of the world's most complex and unusual caves, sacred to indigenous peoples.

■ **BIG BEND**
This unusual habitat—the Chihuahuan Desert, the Rio Grande, and the Chisos Mountains—is home to more bird species than any other national park.

■ **SAGUARO**
This park, named for an iconic cactus, offers hikers, cyclists, mountain bike riders, and horseback riders desert, grassland, oak scrub, pine forest, and riparian zones.

■ **ROCKY MOUNTAIN**
Few other places make it so easy to traverse a true alpine environment, where rugged peaks rise above glacier-carved valleys, forested foothills, and the Continental Divide.

■ **JOSHUA TREE**
These wide-open desert spaces are rich with arid mountain ranges and fantastic boulder formations. Desert flora is surprisingly diverse and varies with season and elevation.

■ **CRATER LAKE**
This stunning sapphire lake, the country's deepest, is fed only by snowmelt. Many of the Cascade Range's neighboring volcanic mountains are visible from Rim Drive.

■ **KATMAI**
Accessible only by floatplane, this four-million-acre park offers opportunities for observing bears and experiencing the Valley of Ten Thousand Smokes, created after a 1912 eruption.

AUSTRALIA'S
BARRIER REEF

UNDERWATER WONDERS

You can spend a lifetime exploring the Great Barrier Reef and still not see it all. Sprawling off the east coast of Queensland, Australia, it stretches over 1,250 miles and covers some 135,000 square miles in total. The magnificent structures we see today—the largest structure on Earth built by living organisms—were produced by a slow process played out over millions of years. Home to a staggering diversity of plant and lower animal life, this colorful aquatic ecosystem is also frequented by larger species like dugongs, sea turtles, sharks, and dolphins.

Great Barrier's Opal Reef, shallow and easy to snorkel, can be a crowded destination.

THE GREAT BARRIER REEF MARINE PARK HOSTS 5,000 TYPES OF MOLLUSKS, 1,800 SPECIES OF FISH, 125 KINDS OF SHARKS, AND INNUMERABLE MINIATURE ORGANISMS.

Varieties of REEF LIFE

◼ DUGONG
These enormous vegetarians are related to manatees, yet with a tail fluked like a whale's. They graze on underwater grasses and can stay underwater as long as six minutes.

◼ CLOWNFISH
Bright orange with three white bars, just over four inches long, these are real-life Nemos. They nestle into colorful sea anemones, immune from their lethal sting.

◼ GREEN SEA TURTLE
Among the largest sea turtles in the world, these can weigh up to 700 pounds. Herbivorous as adults, the juveniles may also eat crabs, jellyfish, and sponges.

◼ SALTWATER CROCODILE
Opportunistic predators, these creatures can weigh as much as a ton. They lurk under the water, seeking prey at the water's edge, but also swim into open water.

◼ WHITE-BELLIED SEA EAGLE
One of the largest raptors in Australia, this bright white and ash-gray bird's wingspan may measure six feet as it soars over the coastline and inland as well.

◼ HUMPBACK WHALE
These legendary singers feed on krill, plankton, and small fish. Found near the poles in summer, they migrate toward the Equator in winter.

◼ BLACKTIP REEF SHARK
These small sharks glide through lagoons and in and out of coral reefs, their iconic black dorsal fin sticking up above the water.

◼ SMOOTH CAULIFLOWER CORAL
With colors ranging from cream and pink to yellow and green, this coral grows short branches from which tentacles extend at night.

BEST OF @NATGEO

TOP PHOTOS OF TRAVEL

@jenniferhayesig | JENNIFER HAYES
n the Philippines, a whale shark swims to the surface, drawn
by krill that a tour guide dropped into the water.

@irablockphoto | IRA BLOCK
A nun watches the sun set behind a statue of Buddha at the
Fo Guang Shan Buddha Museum in Kaohsiung, Taiwan.

@simonnorfolkstudio | SIMON NORFOLK
The Meidan Emam is a public square in Isfahan, Iran, originally built at the turn of the 17th century.

@stephenwilkes | STEPHEN WILKES
A composite photo shows Paris's Eiffel Tower and Trocadéro
transition from day into night.

@paolowoods @gabrielegalimbertiphoto
PAOLO WOODS & GABRIELE GALIMBERTI
A man floats in a rooftop swimming pool, Singapore.

@juanarre | **JUAN ARREDONDO**
Outside St. Peter's Basilica in the Vatican City, a line of visitors waits in the rain to enter the historic church.

@dguttenfelder | **DAVID GUTTENFELDER**
Costumed go-kart drivers prepare for a tour around the streets of Tokyo's Ginza district.

@renan_ozturk | **RENAN OZTURK**
Redwood trees like these hold a special place in the history of the Yurok people, the largest Native American tribe in California.

TOKYO

WHERE OLD MEETS NEW

All eyes will be on Tokyo for the 2020 Summer Olympics. Japan's capital—the world's largest city, population 37 million—can feel energetic one moment and calm the next, and that kind of mishmash is one of the city's endearing qualities. Plan to see some of the old and some of the new, some urban and some rural, and leave room in your itinerary for spontaneity so you can take part in a festival, sample street food, and explore alleyways.

A WORD FROM

Pace of Change Just 26 years—that's the average life span of a Tokyo building. As a result, there are fewer historical landmarks in Tokyo. In places like Kyoto, there are more traditional buildings, but everything that is really vital in Tokyo is so because of its newness and its sense of change. The environment here transforms constantly to make way for the future.

—**DARRYL JINGWEN WEE,** *lead consultant, Tokyo Tomo*

Pedestrians flood the streets of Tokyo's Shibuya shopping district.

What to Do in
TOKYO

1 **WILDLIFE** Off the Izu Islands, teeming with birds, you might see dolphins, humpback whales, and sperm whales.

2 **OFFBEAT** Trails wind through mountain scenery in Tanzawa-Oyama Quasi-National Park. Historical treasures await at the foot of Mount Oyama.

3 **HISTORY** The Edo-Tokyo Museum brings to life Edo-era Tokyo (1603–1868) with reconstructions of Edo housing and dioramas of the city.

4 **MOST ICONIC PLACE** Nothing else encapsulates modern Tokyo like the Shibuya Crossing at night: Crowds cross from six directions against a neon-lit high-rise backdrop.

5 **LATE NIGHT** Unleash your inner diva at karaoke. Rent a booth at a karaoke chain for a private space and order from the long menu of party food and drinks.

6 **NATURAL BEAUTY** Take the 26-hour ferry to the Ogasawara Islands, designated for their rich ecosystems, with 195 endangered bird species and over 400 native plant taxa.

7 **HIP NEIGHBORHOOD** Kichijoji has used clothing stores, record shops, craft breweries, street performers, and the acclaimed anime-themed Ghibli Museum.

8 **TIMELESS GARDEN** Founded in the 1600s, the Koishikawa Korakuen garden is an example of traditional landscaping, with paths, ponds, and gorgeous seasonal foliage.

9 **ART** The Tokyo Metropolitan Art Museum brings art from Japan and the rest of the world together in the heart of the capital.

10 **VIEWS** The Tokyo Skytree is the second tallest structure in the world, with a 360-degree view of the sprawling city from its upper observation deck.

SUSTAINABLE TRAVEL

RESPONSIBLE AND SPECTACULAR: UNIQUE LODGES OF THE WORLD

Topas Ecolodge's infinity pool and bungalows have unsurpassed views.

MOUNTAIN

SA PA, VIETNAM
Topas Ecolodge—a cluster of mountain bungalows north of Hanoi—organizes treks into Hoang Lien National Park, a global biodiversity hot spot.

ARISTI, GREECE
Crystal rivers, deep gorges, and soaring peaks combine with village life at Aristi Mountain Resort & Villas.

COCHRANE, CHILE
The Lodge at Valle Chacabuco, in Chile, sits in the heart of Patagonia Park, a conservation initiative protecting nearly 200,000 acres.

HIGH ATLAS MOUNTAINS, MOROCCO
Kasbah du Toubkal is a tribute to Berber culture and hospitality built upon the ruins of an ancient kasbah.

DESERT

NORTHERN TERRITORY, AUSTRALIA
The Longitude 131° lodge is built into the curve of a sand dune, isolated from everything but the raw beauty of Uluru-Kata Tjuta National Park.

GOBI, MONGOLIA
The Three Camel Lodge, a scattering of traditional felt-covered Mongolian tents, celebrates the traditions of Mongolia's nomads while seeking to preserve its awe-inspiring surroundings.

TRUTH OR CONSEQUENCES, NEW MEXICO
Ted Turner's Sierra Grande Lodge is on over half a million acres of private wilderness, part of the conservation crusader's efforts to rewild America.

The spa at Sierra Grande Lodge includes pools fed by hot springs.

Lapa Rios sits amid some of the last remaining lowland tropical rainforest in Central America.

SEASIDE

OSA PENINSULA, COSTA RICA
The Lapa Rios Lodge has long been a conservation icon in this lowland tropical rainforest, where guests are sure to spot plenty of local wildlife.

FÉLICITÉ, SEYCHELLES
Guests at the Six Senses Zil Pasyon can kayak to Cocos Island National Park. The resort is committed to habitat restoration, ridding the island of invasive species, and propagating rare local plants.

TETIAROA, FRENCH POLYNESIA
The Brando is late actor Marlon Brando's eco-dream brought to life: a private tropical island run on 100 percent renewable energy sources, including solar power and coconut oil.

KENAI PENINSULA BOROUGH, ALASKA
Nestled amid old-growth Sitka spruces at the mouth of a miles-long fjord, the Tutka Bay Lodge is a wilderness lodge with deep roots and a culinary twist.

MARVELS
OF THE MAYA

SATISFYING AN EXPLORER'S SPIRIT

The tip of the Yucatán Peninsula is best known for the resort city of Cancún. But the region has a wealth of natural and historic attractions away from the tourist traps, including two UNESCO World Heritage sites: Chichén Itzá and the Sian Ka'an Biosphere Reserve. Come for the picturesque beaches and the turquoise cenotes (pools formed by inland sinkholes) but stay for the history—grand ruins of the sprawling Maya Empire, which thrived here for centuries.

Built facing east, Tulum may have originally been called Zama, meaning "dawn."

LIDAR SCANNING TECHNOLOGY RECENTLY DISCOVERED MORE THAN 60,000 MAYA STRUCTURES, BEFORE UNKNOWN, SUGGESTING A CIVILIZATION AS COMPLEX AS ANCIENT GREECE.

KEY SPOTS

Exploring the RIVIERA MAYA

CHICHÉN ITZÁ
Vibrant urban center of the Maya Empire, with the Temple of Kukulkan

COBÁ
Largely unexcavated archaeological site with several Maya pyramids, including Nohoch Mul, the Yucatán Peninsula's tallest

DOS OJOS CENOTES
Part of the world's longest surveyed underwater cave system, irresistible for snorkeling and diving

EK BALAM
Sculpture-filled ruins (some from ca 100 BC) just a short bike ride from the tranquil Cenote Xcanche, a limestone sinkhole

ISLA BLANCA
Narrow peninsula north of Cancún, a favorite of kitesurfers, with quiet, pristine beaches and shallow lagoons

ISLA MUJERES
Island reached by ferry; popular for intimate snorkeling with whale sharks

PUNTA ALLEN
Quiet village on a remote peninsula, with a reef just offshore and opportunities for dolphin watching and lobster fishing

RIO SECRETO
Dramatic underground cave system with stalactites and stalagmites, accessible by hiking, biking, or swimming in a subterranean river

TULUM
Ruins of a 13th-century Maya walled seaport, including the Castillo and the Temple of the Frescoes

SIAN KA'AN
Biosphere Reserve Tropical forests, marshlands, mangroves, and a turquoise lagoon full of wildlife

VALLADOLID
Colorful town with colonial architecture, including the Convent de San Bernardino de Siena

OFF THE
BEATEN PATH

PUT ADVENTURE BACK IN YOUR TRAVEL PLANS

GREECE
Lousios Gorge
Traverse rugged hiking trails in this region of the Peloponnese peninsul amid towering cypress trees, olive groves, terra-cotta-rooftop towns, medieval villages, and mountaintop monasteries—like the Prodromos Monastery, built precariously into the rock face.

NORTH AMERICA

CANADA
British Columbia
In British Columbia's Yoho National Park, you can hike, snowshoe, spot wildlife and wild orchids, kayak on Emerald Lake, and explore the Burgess Shale fossil beds without bumping into busloads of tourists.

PACIFIC

OCEAN

ATLANTIC

OCEAN

SOUTH AMERICA

NICARAGUA
Lake Nicaragua
On a lake ringed by three volcanic peaks, the islets and lakeshores are shrouded in lush tropical forests that harbor myriad colorful bird and butterfly species. Nearby cities are awash with Spanish colonial splendor.

BRAZIL
Amazon Rainforest
Most of the action here takes place overhead. Eco tourism companies will take you climbing and pro vide the ropes, harnesses and hammocks you'll nee in the canopy, where you observe diverse, thriving flora and fauna.

> **" YOU THINK YOU ARE MAKING A TRIP, BUT SOON IT IS MAKING YOU—OR UNMAKING YOU."**
> **—NICOLAS BOUVIER, AUTHOR**

EGYPT
Sinai Peninsula
Curious about the life of a desert nomad? Book an expedition steeped in Bedouin culture along the Sinai Trail—from camels to desert dunes, slot canyons, and lush desert oases—ending at Mount Catherine, Egypt's highest peak.

MONGOLIA
Gobi Desert
Visit the protected Flaming Cliffs, the site of important paleontological discoveries, including the first nest of dinosaur eggs ever discovered. Hike up and slide down sand dunes, search out petroglyphs, photograph spectacular panoramas, and observe desert wildlife.

AUSTRALIA
Great Ocean Road
This scenic highway follows the coastline west of Melbourne for 151 miles through Victoria. You'll find coastal beauty like the magnificent Twelve Apostles rock formation, villages and lighthouses, and opportunities to learn about Aboriginal settlements.

MOZAMBIQUE
Vilankulo
After a coastal safari on horseback, sail out to the Bazaruto Archipelago—a 550-square-mile marine reserve recognized by the World Wildlife Fund as a "Gift to the Earth," home to coral reefs and rare manatee-like dugongs.

AMERICA'S BEST EATS

TASTY MEALS ARE ONE OF TRAVEL'S GREAT REWARDS

Vegetable and grain tortillas

MIDWEST

CINCINNATI CHILI

A heaping pile of spiced ground beef served atop spaghetti is a "two-way." Add shredded cheese for a three-way, beans or onions for a four-way.

ESKIMO PIES

Iowa folklore says a confectionary shop owner Christian Kent Nelson wrapped ice cream in a chocolate bar for a customer who wanted both treats.

CHEESE CURDS

Wisconsin leads the country in cheese production. Cheese curds, a byproduct of the cheddar-making process, are salty, but mild, with a springy texture. When you bite into one, it squeaks.

WEST COAST

BURRITOS

Californians agree a burrito is a tortilla filled with meat and sauce—but Northern Californians fill theirs to overflowing, whereas Southern Californians take a fusion approach.

DUNGENESS CRAB

Named for a small fishing village in Washington State, the ten-legged shellfish is found from Alaska down to the Gulf of Mexico.

RAINIER CHERRIES

A cross between the Bing and Van cultivars, Rainiers are extra sweet with succulent flesh that adds chewiness to each bite.

Beer-battered cheese curds

Ripe summer peaches

Blueberry pie with a lattice crust

SOUTH

PEACHES

Franciscan monks supposedly planted Georgia's first peach trees in 1571. Grower Samuel Henry Rumph invented the mother of all Georgia peaches, named Elberta after his wife.

GRITS

Grits are basically ground corn. Serve with butter and salt for breakfast; top with cheese and pair with shrimp; or bake with butter, egg, and cheese.

KING CAKE

To celebrate Three Kings' Day, bakers in New Orleans hide a tiny toy baby symbolizing the Christ Child in a cake. Whoever gets the slice with the toy must host next year's party.

NORTHEAST

BLUEBERRY PIE

The secret to this Maine treat is piles of tiny wild blueberries. The crust can use butter, shortening, or lard. It can have a lattice top or double crust.

NEW YORK-STYLE PIZZA

In New York, thin crust is the only proper pizza base. Order by the slice—the proper unit of New York pizza. Eat folded, and with your hands.

CRAB CAKES

For crab cakes, Maryland's favorite, mix crabmeat with bread crumbs, onions, eggs, mayonnaise, and seasoning, and then broil, sauté, or deep-fry the patties.

A WORD FROM

Try Something New There's nothing unsustainable about fishing. There's only unsustainable demand, and that's market pressure. That's why I think that we as consumers, we as chefs need to become more educated about the wealth of diversity of seafood that's available to us so that we are celebrating and placing our demand across a broad footprint on the ecosystem.

—**BARTON SEAVER,**
sustainable seafood chef

ICELAND'S
HOT SPRINGS

IMMERSIONS IN ICELAND

Escape the throngs of tourists and enjoy aquamarine-colored water at Mývatn Nature Baths in northern Iceland. Traveling farther afield means fewer people in the pools and increases your chances of witnessing the aurora borealis. More adventurous travelers will enjoy the challenge of reaching the geothermal pools inside the caves of Grjótagjá—a setting so magical it's appeared in *Game of Thrones*—or the hot stream at Reykjadalur, just an hour outside Reykjavík.

Bathers soak in the hot springs at Mývatn Nature Baths, where sulfur gives the water its blue tint.

ICELAND USES ITS GEOTHERMAL FEATURES FOR HEAT AND POWER GENERATION. IN REYKJAVÍK, 90% OF HOMES CONNECT DIRECTLY TO A GEOTHERMAL DISTRICT HEATING SYSTEM.

The World's Best
HOT SPRINGS

 1   **BEPPU, JAPAN** The ultimate *onsen*—Japanese for hot springs, here you'll find eight bathhouses.

2   **DECEPTION ISLAND, ANTARCTICA** An active underwater volcano offers a steamy caldera with penguins nearby.

 3   **PÚCON, CHILE** Waterfalls, plunge pools, and a red boardwalk distinguish the Termas Geometricas in the Villarrica National Park.

 4   **HOT SPRINGS, ARKANSAS, U.S.A.** Bathe your way into history on Bathhouse Row, the 19th-century main street now a national park.

 5   **DUNTON, COLORADO, U.S.A.** Hot springs steam up this luxury destination, a reconstructed ghost town in the Colorado Rockies.

 6   **BANFF, BRITISH COLUMBIA, CANADA** Gaze at the Canadian Rockies from the historic bathhouse, established in 1886.

7   **ROTORUA, NEW ZEALAND** The smell of sulfur infuses this region of the North Island, long deemed sacred by the Maori.

8   **PAMUKKALE, TURKEY** Naturally heated water cascades through 17 white limestone terraces, closed to bathers but still magnificent to view.

 9   **MAREMMA, ITALY** Soak in mineral springs that once comforted Roman generals in Tuscany's Terme di Saturnia.

  10   **BANJAR, BALI** Mineral-rich water spews from the mouths of intricately carved *naga*, mythical serpent demigods.

FURTHER

FOR A BETTER VIEW

Even earthbound spectators feel the frisson of triumph when an athlete like Pete Thompson accomplishes a feat like this, walking barefoot along a 411-foot-long highline off Mushroom Rock, a favorite lookout point above Carbondale, Colorado. Extreme sports—from classics like surfing and skateboarding to new high-tech ventures like wing suiting and zorbing—took off after ESPN's first Extreme Games in 1995. Now X Games happen all around the world, with millions of video viewers. Meanwhile, solitary achievers like Thompson push boundaries as well.

Highliner Pete Thompson appears to balance between the two peaks of Colorado's Mount Sopris.

> **"THERE IS NO 'MAYBE' WHEN YOU'RE 60 STORIES UP WITHOUT A ROPE."**
>
> **—JIMMY CHIN,**
> **PHOTOGRAPHER AND CO-DIRECTOR OF** *FREE SOLO*

THIS PLANET & BEYOND

PLANET EARTH | **EARTH, SEA & SKY**

Monsoon clouds hover above the Indian Ocean surrounding Madagascar.

| THE SOLAR SYSTEM | THE UNIVERSE & BEYOND

QUIZ MASTER

Planetary Genius? How much do you know about our planet—Earth, sea, and sky? How about the solar system, universe, and beyond? Test your knowledge, and then read on for answers and general amazement.

—CARA SANTA MARIA, *Our Favorite Nerd*

IN WHAT YEAR WAS THE **FIRST** KNOWN MAP OF **THE MOON** PUBLISHED?

p126

ABOUT HOW MANY YEARS AGO DID *HOMO SAPIENS* FIRST APPEAR ON EARTH?

p96

IN WHAT YEAR DID **MOUNT** ST. HELENS **ERUPT MOST** RECENTLY?

p124

THE BIG AND LITTLE DIPPER STAR PATTERNS ARE ALSO KNOWN BY NAMES THAT **TRANSLATE TO** WHICH ANIMAL?

p108

WHICH U.S. NATIONAL PARK **CONTAINS A** SUPERVOLCANO?

p108

HOW MANY DWARF PLANETS ARE ESTIMATED **IN OUR** SOLAR SYSTEM?

p130

IN WHAT YEAR **WAS THE** HUBBLE **SPACE** TELESCOPE LAUNCHED **INTO ORBIT?**

p127

WHICH OF THESE MINERALS IS HARDER: SERPENTINE **OR** QUARTZ?

p114

WHAT IS THE **PLANET** IN OUR **SOLAR** SYSTEM NEAREST TO THE SUN?

p128

ABOUT HOW FAR FROM **EARTH IS THE** SUPERMASSIVE **BLACK HOLE** AT THE CENTER OF THE **MILKY WAY?**

p147

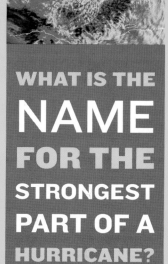

WHAT IS THE **NAME** FOR THE STRONGEST PART OF A HURRICANE?

p106

WHAT IS THE **NAME OF** THE TALLEST MOUNTAIN ON **MARS?**

p134

IN WHICH DECADE WAS THE THEORY OF **DARK MATTER FIRST** INTRODUCED?

p152

WHICH METEOROLOGICAL **PHENOMENA** IS TIM SAMARAS **FAMOUS FOR** STUDYING?

p110

EARTH SCIENCE
TIME LINE

| 4.6 to 2.3 BYA | 2.3 BYA to 400 MYA | 400 to 200 MYA | 200 MYA to 20,000 YA |

4.6 to 2.3 BYA

4.6 bya*
Planet Earth forms from the material that built the rest of the solar system.

4.5 bya
Earth's moon forms out of space debris.

4.3 bya
Liquid water appears on Earth.

3.8 bya
Single-celled life emerges on Earth.

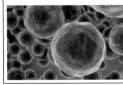

3 bya
Earth's continental masses form.

2.5–2.3 bya
Oxygen levels in the Earth's atmosphere rise.

* billion years ago

2.3 BYA to 400 MYA

2.1 bya
More complex multicellular organisms evolve.

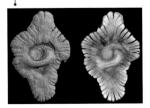

720–635 mya*
The temperature on Earth falls, and the entire planet is covered in ice.

541 mya
Most major animal groups evolve in an event known as the Cambrian explosion.

520 mya
Animals with bilateral symmetry first flourish on Earth.

470 mya
Plant life first appears on land.

* million years ago

400 to 200 MYA

360 mya
Amphibious life emerges from the water to live on land.

251 mya
Massive numbers of marine and land species die off in the Permian extinction, the largest mass extinction in history.

250 mya
A single supercontinent called Pangaea emerges.

240 mya
The first dinosaurs appear on Earth.

200 mya
The supercontinent Pangaea breaks up into separate landmasses.

200 MYA to 20,000 YA

130 mya
Flowering plants, the most diverse group of land plants, emerge.

65 mya
Dinosaurs go extinct in the aftermath of the Chicxulub asteroid impact.

2.6 mya
Continents arrive at roughly their modern positions and a pattern of glacial and interglacial periods emerges.

200,000 ya*
Homo sapiens first appear, and modern humans emerge.

* years ago

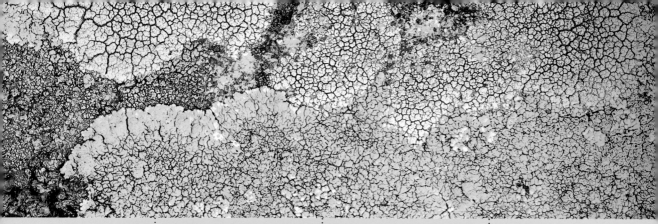

| 20,000 YA to AD 1 | AD 1 to 1800 | 1800 to 1920 | 1920 to PRESENT |

■ 11,700 ya
The Holocene,
the current geological
age, begins.

■ 10,000 ya
The last major
ice age ends.

■ ca 499 BC
Indian scientist Aryabhata
proposes that Earth
rotates on its axis.

■ 240 BC
Eratosthenes calculates
the circumference
of the Earth.

■ ca 1088
Chinese scientist
Shen Kuo first describes
a magnetic compass
used for navigation.

■ 1490s
Leonardo da Vinci begins
filling notebooks with
theories on astronomy,
Earth, physics, and more.

■ 1543
Copernicus publishes
ideas on heliocentrism.

■ 1595
Gerardus Mercator's
atlas of the world
is first published.

■ 1815
Explosion of Mount
Tambora temporarily
changes Earth's climate.

■ 1831
English explorer
James Ross locates
the position of the
north magnetic pole.

■ 1851
Léon Foucault constructs
Foucault's pendulum
to show Earth's rotation.

■ 1912
Alfred Wegener first
describes the theory
of continental drift.

■ 1913
Charles Fabry and Henri
Buisson discover
the ozone layer.

■ 1935
Charles Richter invents
the Richter scale
to measure earthquake
intensity.

■ 1960s
Scientists first describe
plate tectonics.

■ 1960
Jacques Piccard and Don
Walsh are first to visit
the deepest point in the
ocean, Challenger Deep.

■ 1970
The inaugural Earth Day
is held on April 22.

■ 2017
One of the largest
icebergs on record breaks
off from Antarctica's
Larsen C ice shelf.

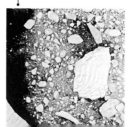

CLARIFYING CLIMATE

TO UNDERSTAND CLIMATE CHANGE, WE MUST UNDERSTAND CLIMATE

The climate of any location on Earth depends on latitude, elevation above sea level, proximity to the ocean, and the circulation patterns in the atmosphere and ocean. This map displays the Köppen-Geiger system of climate zones based on seasonal temperatures and precipitation.

WARMING ALPS
Climate change is expected to transform much of the European Alps from a snow to a warm temperate climate by the end of the 21st century.

ROCKY MOUNTAINS

NORTH AMERICA

TREES AT RISK
In the northern Rocky Mountains as summers get longer and hotter, trees at high altitudes will be especially vulnerable to drought, wildfire, and destructive insects.

CARIBBEAN HURRICANES
The Gulf Stream's warm ocean water intensifies the hurricanes that pass over it, often tracking the storms toward mainland North America.

ARCT

ATLANTIC OCEAN

PACIFIC OCEAN

RAIN SHADOWS
The Rocky Mountains and Andes form the spine of the Americas, influencing climate by stopping moist ocean air from reaching the interior.

SOUTH AMERICA

ANDES

EXPANDING DESERT
In Algeria, the desert has gradually expanded and displaced much of the warm temperate region where most people live.

DISAPPEARING ICE
Scientists expect the largest shifts in climate zones in the 21st century to replace about 1% of polar zones with warmer snow zones.

SOUTHERN AFRICA
The position of the island of Madagascar reduces the impact of wet trade winds on the mainland coast and lessens the chance of tropical cyclones land there.

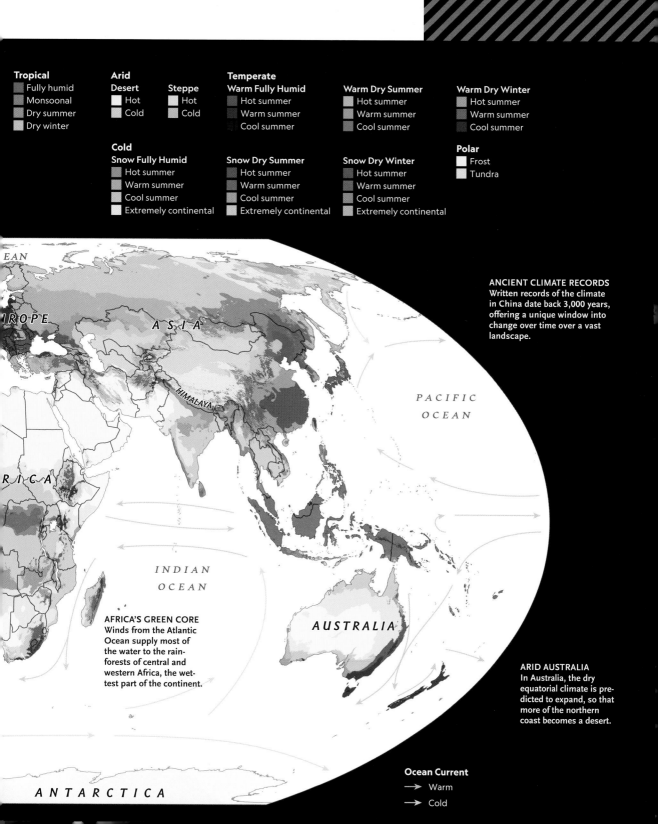

Tropical
- Fully humid
- Monsoonal
- Dry summer
- Dry winter

Arid

Desert
- Hot
- Cold

Steppe
- Hot
- Cold

Temperate

Warm Fully Humid
- Hot summer
- Warm summer
- Cool summer

Warm Dry Summer
- Hot summer
- Warm summer
- Cool summer

Warm Dry Winter
- Hot summer
- Warm summer
- Cool summer

Cold

Snow Fully Humid
- Hot summer
- Warm summer
- Cool summer
- Extremely continental

Snow Dry Summer
- Hot summer
- Warm summer
- Cool summer
- Extremely continental

Snow Dry Winter
- Hot summer
- Warm summer
- Cool summer
- Extremely continental

Polar
- Frost
- Tundra

EAN

IROPE

RICA

ASIA

HIMALAYA

ANCIENT CLIMATE RECORDS
Written records of the climate in China date back 3,000 years, offering a unique window into change over time over a vast landscape.

PACIFIC
OCEAN

INDIAN
OCEAN

AFRICA'S GREEN CORE
Winds from the Atlantic Ocean supply most of the water to the rainforests of central and western Africa, the wettest part of the continent.

AUSTRALIA

ARID AUSTRALIA
In Australia, the dry equatorial climate is predicted to expand, so that more of the northern coast becomes a desert.

Ocean Current
→ Warm
→ Cold

ANTARCTICA

DROUGHT

A WORLD WITHOUT WATER

Lake Mead and Hoover Dam

DEFINING DROUGHT

DISAPPEARING WATER

On a planet where water is life, drought can be deadly. On almost every continent, cities, states, and countries are struggling to find water. As climate change alters rain patterns, seasonal monsoons, and heat waves, water is becoming harder to find. Droughts are getting worse. At Lake Mead, along the Colorado River, the sprawling reservoir is ringed by a bleached line of barren rock marking how far its once flowing waters have fallen. In South America, Bolivia's second largest lake, Lake Poopó, disappeared completely, transformed into a barren salt flat. In Australia, vast reaches of the island continent fell under the worst drought in living memory.

LOSING RESOURCES

NOT A DROP TO DRINK

In Cape Town, South Africa, the drought is so intense and reservoirs have gotten so low the government is considering radical measures. They even predicted "Day Zero," saying that when the reservoirs reached 13.5 percent capacity, the city would severely limit water for its four million people. That day never came. For the time being, dam levels have risen in Cape Town, allowing the city to ease restrictions, but experts believe such rationing is now inevitable. And Cape Town is not alone: Sections of Mexico City limit water use to only part of the day, while Jakarta is literally sinking as it drains the freshwater aquifer beneath the city. Half the world could face similar stresses by 2030, according to UN estimates.

Aerial view of Mexico City

BY THE TIME THE COLORADO RIVER REACHES MEXICO, MOST OF ITS WATER HAS BEEN SIPHONED OFF TO SUPPLY THIRSTY U.S. CITIES OR TO BE USED FOR IRRIGATION OR HYDROPOWER.

The Colorado River Delta in Mexico is often too dry to flow into the Pacific Ocean.

CHANGING CLIMATE

CHANGING RAIN

Changing weather patterns mean that farmers can no longer rely on traditional wisdom. The once predictable wet and dry seasons powered by the tropical monsoon rains have become erratic. A warming atmosphere holds more water, which means storms can be more intense. Warming oceans power more intense storms and hurricanes. Record-long droughts are followed by record rains and snows, creating a weather whiplash that stresses natural and man-made systems even more. Estimates say that this whiplash will become more likely as the climate continues to warm. Water planners who have worked to solve the problems of the past are staring into an uncertain future.

GETTING READY

PREPARING FOR DROUGHT

In Cape Town, conservation efforts fended off "Day Zero" as the city cut back on its water consumption. The average family cut its consumption in half, and farmers and other growers cut their consumption as well. Desalination plants designed to create drinkable water from seawater also help reduce the threat from future droughts for the South African city. Another solution might be found in Israel, where new technology helps reuse 85 percent of wastewater and policies have helped shift the agricultural focus away from water-hungry crops like cotton. Whatever the metric, more droughts are coming, and Day Zero may not be far away.

READING THE CLOUDS

Looking Up Though we've always had clouds above, we are still coming up with new ways to categorize and name them. Changes in technology, especially the sharing of photos, is also leading to new identifications.

FAIR-WEATHER CUMULUS
Small, puffy, white

CUMULIFORM
Puffy, humid air condensing

ORTHOGRAPHIC
Precipitation near mountains

CIRRUS
Thin and transparent

CIRROCUMULUS
White patches of high clouds

CIRROSTRATUS
High and thin, hazy

ALTOCUMULUS
Puffy clouds with darker patches

LENTICULAR
Lens-shaped, over mountains

ALTOCUMULUS CASTELLANUS
Tall, narrow

STRATOCUMULUS
Spread across large areas

STRATUS
Featureless gray layers

ALTOSTRATUS
Thin, gray, highest sheet-type

NIMBOSTRATUS
Low, dark, gloomy

CUMULUS CONGESTUS
Cauliflower-like

CUMULONIMBUS
Anvil shape, brings thunderstorms

ALTOCUMULUS MAMMATUS
Hanging pouches

THE INTERNATIONAL CLOUD ATLAS RECOGNIZED A NEW CLOUD TYPE IN 2017: THE ASPERITAS, DAPPLED LIKE THE SEA SEEN FROM UNDERWATER.

Lightning begins as static charges in a rain cloud.

THUNDERSTRUCK

COUNTING THE FLASHES

Satellite data analyzed in 2016 identified 500 lightning "hot spots" around the world: the places where lightning flashes and strikes most often. Of those 500, more than half are in Africa, but the place that sees the most lightning—almost every night of the year—is Lake Maracaibo in Venezuela, South America's largest lake by area.

TOP TEN

Lightning HOT SPOTS

1   **LAKE MARACAIBO**
Venezuela

2   **KAHUZI-BIEGA NATIONAL PARK**
Democratic Republic of the Congo

3   **SHABUNDA**
Democratic Republic of the Congo

4   **CÁCERES**
Colombia

5   **WALIKALE**
Democratic Republic of the Congo

6   **DAGGAR**
Pakistan

7   **EL TARRA**
Colombia

8   **NGUTI**
Cameroon

9   **BUTEMBO**
Democratic Republic of the Congo

10   **BOENDE**
Democratic Republic of the Congo

COMBATING A BLAZE

THE COMPLICATED BATTLE AGAINST WILDFIRES

Fighting wildfire is often likened to a military campaign, with personnel deployed strategically on the ground and air support striking from above. Planning an attack, as here in the northern Rockies, firefighters weigh three factors that drive the course of any blaze: topography, weather, and the type of fuel in the line of fire.

1 Fires can spread especially rapidly up slopes and suddenly explode up canyons, which act as natural chimneys. Southern slopes, sunnier and drier, are more likely to burn than northern exposures.

2 Dramatic winds brought on by cold fronts and storms can shift a fire's direction or cause flare-ups. Low humidity and high temperatures make fuel, especially grass and accumulated underbrush, drier and quicker to burn.

3 Air tankers and helicopters, called in by coordinators on the ground, drop water or chemical fire retardant.

4 A fire crew's priority is to find a man-made or natural barrier to the fire's advance—a road or a stream—and from that anchor point dig a perimeter fire line to contain the blaze.

5 Long days are spent digging a fire line down to bare earth, even if a bulldozer is available to help. The line is banked to catch rolling debris.

6 Drip torches are used to burn out fuel between the fire line and the fire, halting its advance.

7 Felling dead trees prevents them from collapsing across the fire line or on firefighters and helps keep flames from climbing into the canopy.

8 Homes that have edged into forest fire territory can't be guaranteed protection. And even if fire is stopped before reaching a house, airborne embers can drift through vents and burn it down from the inside out.

A WORD FROM

Devastating Embers A fire acts like a living organism. The same way a plant spreads its seeds, a fire creates wind to spread its embers. A fire causes hot air and smoke to rise rapidly, pulling in air along the ground to replace it. This creates a wind that will push the fire along, which creates a self-perpetuating cycle of fire that is impossible to stop.

—**MARK THIESSEN,** *photographer and wildland firefighter*

HURRICANES

SWIRLING STORMS OF DESTRUCTION

Hurricanes are massive storm systems, sometimes broadening to more than a hundred miles across and packing damaging winds and intense amounts of water. In 2018, it was estimated that Hurricane Florence was carrying 18 trillion gallons of water in its rain bands, enough water to fill the Chesapeake Bay, and several North Carolina towns reported more than 30 inches of rain. Hurricane Harvey in 2017 held 25 trillion gallons. Like the ocean currents, hurricanes move heat from the warm tropics up toward the poles. They wreak chaos and can leave utter destruction in their wakes, but they also help maintain the thermal balance in tropical oceans.

ANTI-CYCLONE
High above the eye of the storm, an atmospheric anti-cyclone rotates in opposition to the hurricane below. This acts as an exhaust pipe for the warm winds spiraling up inside the eye wall.

EYE WALL
The eye wall is the strongest part of the storm; winds here can reach over 200 miles per hour.

NEGATIVE SURGE
Just as the winds push the ocean higher in a storm surge, they can also "blow away the ocean" in a negative surge, lowering tides when the winds aim seaward.

Tropical Storm Lowell strengthens into a hurricane in the Pacific Ocean.

HURRICANE WILMA IN 2005 IS THE MOST INTENSE ATLANTIC HURRICANE RECORDED SO FAR, WITH WIND SPEEDS REACHING 185 MILES AN HOUR. IT CAUSED AN ESTIMATED $34.4 BILLION IN DAMAGES.

SPIN
Hurricane spin depends on the Coriolis effect caused by Earth's rotation. Northern Hemisphere hurricanes rotate counterclockwise, and Southern Hemisphere hurricanes rotate clockwise.

EYE
The calm eye is the center of the storm, a central core of warm air that draws heat from the ocean to create intense low pressure that powers the devastating winds.

STORM SURGE
A hurricane's powerful winds can push the ocean over 10 feet higher than the highest tide, leading to devastating flooding, erosion, and property damage.

VOLCANOES

WHEN EARTH ERUPTS

When we talk about volcanoes in the continental U.S., we probably think of Mount St. Helens, the "Mount Fuji of America," which erupted spectacularly in May 1980. We are less likely to think of Yellowstone, even with its geysers and hot mud, because although it is surrounded by mountains, it is not one itself. But our most famous national park sits squarely atop one of Earth's biggest volcanoes—a supervolcano—and it is not extinct. Volcanoes, as we tend to imagine them, form mountains. Supervolcanoes erase them.

Sleeping Giants

Beneath Yellowstone is a hellish column of superheated rock—mostly solid, some viscous, some molten. Experts say three major blasts, bigger than most known prehistoric eruptions, have shaken Yellowstone in its two million years atop the plume. The smallest of these ejected 280 times the volume of what Mount St. Helens projected.

The U.S. Geological Survey's Yellowstone Volcano Observatory monitors sensors and satellites, looking for changes in activity. Despite rumors, a supereruption like the one illustrated on the facing page is not imminent. For its part, the USGS puts the rough yearly odds of another massive Yellowstone blast at one in 730,000.

CALDERA
Buoyed by an expanding magma chamber, the caldera, formed by the last major eruption, has risen as much as 2.8 inches a year over the past decade.

PLUME
Beneath the caldera, a vast rocky zone of primordial heat emanates from the mantle. This plume feeds a magma chamber brimming with volcanic fuel just a few miles below the surface.

HOT POCKETS
Current seismic data and geological conditions suggest there may be smaller pockets of hot rock associated with the Yellowstone plume.

POP!

MOVIES STARRING VOLCANOES

- *The Last Days of Pompeii* (1935)
- *Stromboli* (1950)
- *Krakatoa: East of Java* (1969)
- *St. Helens* (1981)
- *Joe Versus the Volcano* (1990)
- *Dante's Peak* (1997)
- *Volcano* (1997)
- *Supervolcano* (2005)
- *Disaster Zone: Volcano in New York* (2006)
- *Volcano Zombies* (2014)
- *Pompeii* (2014)
- *Ixcanul* (2015)

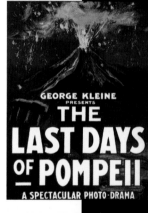

GEORGE KLEINE
PRESENTS
THE
LAST DAYS
OF POMPEII
A SPECTACULAR PHOTO-DRAMA

HOW DOES IT HAPPEN?

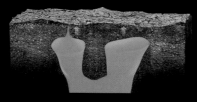

BEFORE THE ERUPTION Warning signs may appear years in advance. Pressure builds from below, driving seismic activity and doming of the land over the hot spot.

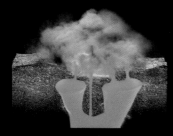

THE EARTH FRACTURES Gas-filled magma explodes upward; ash and debris soon rain down across hundreds of miles. Fiery ash flows clog rivers and carpet landscapes near and far.

ERUPTIONS CONTINUE Periodic blasts go on for weeks or even months, emitting pollutants and causing acid rain. Eventually, the land collapses and a new caldera is born.

World's Deadliest ERUPTIONS

 1 TAMBORA, INDONESIA
Apr. 10, 1815: 92,000 killed
Largest in recorded history, with ejecta volume of 12 mi^3

 2 KRAKATAU, INDONESIA
Aug. 26, 1883: 36,417 killed
Ash layer lowered temperatures and affected global climate.

 3 PELÉE, MARTINIQUE
May 8, 1902: 29,025 killed
Most deaths direct result of eruption and not tsunami, etc.

 4 RUIZ, COLOMBIA
Nov. 13, 1985: 25,000 killed
Mudflows caused by melting snow and ice buried thousands.

 5 UNZEN, JAPAN
May 21, 1792: 14,300 killed
Eruption followed by earthquake, landslide, and tsunami

 6 LAKI, ICELAND
June 8, 1783: 9,350 killed
Lava flows and explosions continued for eight months.

7 KELUD, INDONESIA
May 19, 1919: 5,110 killed
Still active with hundreds killed in 1951, 1966, 1990, and 2014

 8 GALUNGGUNG, INDONESIA
Oct. 8, 1882: 4,011 killed
Crater lake ejected boiling water and mud during eruptions.

 9 VESUVIUS, ITALY
Dec. 16, 1631: 3,500 killed
Fatal pyroclastic flows followed a 30-mile-high cloud.

 10 VESUVIUS, ITALY
79: 3,360 killed
Ash-covered Pompeii is famous for perfectly preserved victims.

TIM SAMARAS
STORM CHASER

HEAD FIRST INTO THE STORM

When tornadoes, one of nature's most powerful and least predictable disasters, come down from the sky, most people run away—but Tim Samaras went to work. Samaras faced the devastating force of a tornado more than 125 times in his life. But he wasn't a thrill seeker; he was a scientist. Under pelting hail and blinding rain, he braved the winds and flying debris to better understand the storm and, with that understanding, to save lives.

Tim Samaras deploys probes as a tornado approaches in South Dakota.

With winds almost 50 percent stronger than the strongest hurricanes, a tornado's power and potential to level towns and destroy lives is unmatched. The best hope for survival is to hide before it hits, but forecasters can give only 13 minutes' warning before a strike. Samaras's life goal was to increase the warning time for a tornado and, with it, the chance for survival. That meant he had to see into the heart of a twister and place himself in harm's way.

UNDERSTANDING TORNADOES

Storms were never far from Samaras's thoughts. He had a gift for reading the skies and understanding the behavior of storms. Despite never graduating from college, he was a gifted engineer. When the National Oceanic and Atmospheric Administration requested designs for a probe that could record data inside a tornado, Samaras combined his passions. After several failed attempts, he and his team succeeded when they deployed a hardened pressure sensor, nicknamed the "Turtle," in front of a tornado just 82 seconds before the twister struck. It was a meteorological milestone.

Samaras didn't take risk lightly. But for all his success, tornadoes remain unpredictable. On May 31, 2013, the tornado that Samaras was chasing suddenly doubled in size, stretching over 2.5 miles wide, the largest ever recorded. Samaras, his son, and their cameraman were caught inside, and all three perished. His life ended, but his work continues as storm chasers continue to travel across the plains every year to better understand these erratic, deadly storms.

> **" I'M NOT SURE EXACTLY WHY I CHASE STORMS. PERHAPS IT'S TO WITNESS THE INCREDIBLE BEAUTY OF WHAT MOTHER NATURE CAN CREATE."**

Tim Samaras stands over a tornado probe.

KEY DATES

Tim Samaras's
MILESTONES

■ **1980**
Begins selling storm footage to local news stations

■ **1997**
Builds first probe to gather data inside a tornado

■ **1998**
Founds the National Storm Chasers Convention

■ **2003**
First successful deployment of the tornado probe

■ **2005**
Named National Geographic Emerging Explorer

■ **2009**
Hosts *Storm Chasers* on the Discovery Channel

■ **2013**
Photographs lightning strike in slow motion at 150,000 frames per second

■ **2013**
Dies after being caught in the El Reno Tornado in Oklahoma

BEST OF @NATGEO

TOP PHOTOS OF EXTREME WEATHER

@ladzinski | KEITH LADZINSKI
A supercell thunderstorm gathers over a small town in Oklahoma. These powerful storms can reach nearly 70,000 feet tall.

@randyolson | RANDY OLSON
In the lower Omo River Valley in Ethiopia, water is scarce because of an upstream dam and periods of drought.

@franslanting | FRANS LANTING
Flames overtake mountains near Santa Barbara, California, in what was among the largest fires in the state's modern history.

@chamiltonjames | CHARLIE HAMILTON JAMES
A rainbow appears in airborne ice crystals over Jackson Hole, Wyoming, where below-zero temperatures are common in the winter.

> ## "A CHANGE IN THE WEATHER IS SUFFICIENT TO CREATE THE WORLD AND OURSELVES."
> —MARCEL PROUST, FRENCH NOVELIST

@yamashitaphoto | MICHAEL YAMASHITA
Heavy snowfall blankets a quiet forest on Hokkaido, the northernmost and coldest of Japan's main islands.

@franciscop777 | FRANCISCO J. PEREZ
A composite of long-exposure photographs shows a summer thunderstorm raging over the Grand Canyon.

@ladzinski | KEITH LADZINSKI
A tornado touches ground in Wyoming. Most twisters last for less than 10 minutes, but their destruction can be long lasting.

@carltonward | CARLTON WARD
A storm approaches Biscayne National Park in Florida. After-noon showers are common on humid summer afternoons.

MINERALS
REVEALED

How Hard Is It? More than 4,000 naturally occurring minerals have been found on Earth. Geologists classify them according to hardness, using the Mohs' scale (opposite). All rocks are made of mixtures of minerals.

JASPER
Hardness: 6–7

FELDSPAR
Hardness: 6–7

OLIVINE
Hardness: 6.5–7

GARNET
Hardness: 6.5–7.5

EPIDOTE
Hardness: 6–7

STAUROLITE
Hardness: 7–7.5

TOURMALINE
Hardness: 7–7.5

PYROXENE
Hardness: 5–6.5

TALC
Hardness: 1

HORNBLENDE
Hardness: 5–6

BIOTITE
Hardness: 2.5–3

MUSCOVITE
Hardness: 2–2.5

KAOLINITE
Hardness: 2–2.5

SERPENTINE
Hardness: 3–6

DOLOMITE
Hardness: 3.5–4

CALCITE
Hardness: 3

GYPSUM & ANHYDRITE
Hardness: 2 & 3–3.5

MALACHITE
Hardness: 3.5–4

CHALCOPYRITE
Hardness: 3.5–4

GALENA
Hardness: 2.5–3

PYRITE
Hardness: 6–6.5

FLUORITE
Hardness: 4

MAGNETITE
Hardness: 5.5

HEMATITE
Hardness: 5–6

QUARTZ
Hardness: 7

Marble rates between 3 and 5 on the Mohs' scale.

MARBLE

FROM ANCIENT SEAS TO KITCHEN COUNTERS

Marble countertops, statues, and columns dot the landscapes, filling our homes and museums. Every piece of the iconic stone, so common today, began in the fires and fissures of Earth's molten seams, or volcanic hot spots. Marble is a metamorphic rock. It begins as the crystallized calcium remnants of deep sea corals or other creatures. In the fiery seams of Earth's tectonic plates, or volcanic magma chambers, new crystals begin to form, and the metamorphosis begins. The more this crystallization spreads, the larger and stronger the marble becomes. Eventually vast marble beds form, containing millions of tons of the soft stone ready to be shaped. It comes in colors from pure white to pink, yellow, and black, depending on the mineral content.

IN ADDITION TO ITS FAMILIAR USES IN SCULPTING AND ARCHITECTURE, GROUND MARBLE IS SOMETIMES ADDED TO ANIMAL FEED AS A SOURCE OF CALCIUM.

Mohs' Mineral
HARDNESS SCALE

1 Easily scratched by fingernail, feels soapy or greasy
Example: talc

2 Can be scratched by fingernail Gold, 2.5–3.0.
Example: gypsum

3 Can be scratched by copper coin Copper penny, 3.2.
Example: calcite

4 Can be scratched by knife Platinum, 4–4.5; iron, 4–5.
Example: fluorite

5 Scratched by knife with difficulty Pocketknife, 5.1; plate glass, 5.5. *Example: apatite*

6 Can be scratched by steel file but not knife; scratches glass with difficulty Steel needle, 6.5.
Example: feldspar

7 Scratches window glass
Example: quartz

8 Scratches glass very easily Varieties of beryl, 7.5–8.
Example: topaz, cubic zirconia, emerald, aquamarine

9 Cuts glass *Example: corundum* (ruby and sapphire)

10 Cuts glass so easily that it is used as a glass cutter
Example: diamond

SAVING
PRISTINE SEAS

THERE ARE PLACES IN THE WORLD WHERE MARINE LIFE ABOUNDS

National Geographic Explorer-in-Residence Enric Sala launched the Pristine Seas project in 2008 to explore and help save the last wild places in the ocean. Since then, thanks to this effort, 21 marine reserves have been created and more than two million square miles of ocean have been protected.

THE OCEAN COVERS 70 PERCENT OF THE PLANET, YET ONLY 5 PERCENT OF THE OCEAN IS PROTECTED.

Manta rays glide through the pristine waters of Palau, in the South Pacific.

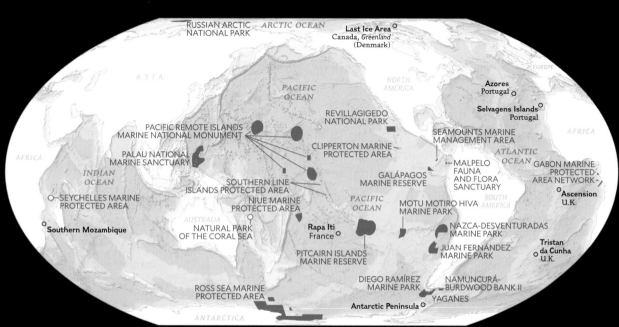

RUSSIAN ARCTIC NATIONAL PARK

ARCTIC OCEAN

Last Ice Area
Canada, *Greenland*
(Denmark)

ASIA

PACIFIC OCEAN

NORTH AMERICA

EUROPE

Azores
Portugal

Selvagens Islands
Portugal

REVILLAGIGEDO NATIONAL PARK

SEAMOUNTS MARINE MANAGEMENT AREA

AFRICA

PACIFIC REMOTE ISLANDS MARINE NATIONAL MONUMENT

CLIPPERTON MARINE PROTECTED AREA

ATLANTIC OCEAN

GABON MARINE PROTECTED AREA NETWORK

PALAU NATIONAL MARINE SANCTUARY

AFRICA

INDIAN OCEAN

MALPELO FAUNA AND FLORA SANCTUARY

Ascension
U.K.

SOUTHERN LINE ISLANDS PROTECTED AREA

GALÁPAGOS MARINE RESERVE

SEYCHELLES MARINE PROTECTED AREA

NIUE MARINE PROTECTED AREA

PACIFIC OCEAN

MOTU MOTIRO HIVA MARINE PARK

SOUTH AMERICA

Southern Mozambique

AUSTRALIA
NATURAL PARK OF THE CORAL SEA

Rapa Iti
France

NAZCA-DESVENTURADAS MARINE PARK

Tristan da Cunha
U.K.

PITCAIRN ISLANDS MARINE RESERVE

JUAN FERNÁNDEZ MARINE PARK

DIEGO RAMÍREZ MARINE PARK

NAMUNCURÁ-BURDWOOD BANK II

ROSS SEA MARINE PROTECTED AREA

YAGANES

Antarctic Peninsula

ANTARCTICA

Pristine Seas

■ Protected area
• Other expedition

A WORD FROM

A Spiritual Experience We go to the pristine places in the ocean to try to understand the ecosystems, to try to measure or count fish and sharks and see how these places are different from the places we know. But the best feeling is this biophilia that E. O. Wilson talks about, where humans have this sense of awe and wonder in front of untamed nature . . . If it were not for these places that show hope, I don't think I could continue doing this job.

—**ENRIC SALA,** *marine ecologist*

VOLCANIC ISLANDS

BORN FROM LAVA

Earth is constantly changing. Volcanic eruptions can reshape shorelines and create new islands, while ocean waves can erode and strip them away. In 2018, Hawaii briefly gained a new island as lava from the Kilauea volcano filled in over 700 acres of what used to be open ocean. Across the Pacific, the Polynesian island of Hunga Tonga-Hunga Ha'ipi, which erupted into existence in 2014, fought the slow erosion of the tides. NASA originally gave the island just six months to live before erosion stripped it below the waves, but new research estimates it may survive as long as 30 years.

The Kilauea eruption briefly formed a tiny islet in Hawaii.

The World's
VOLCANIC ISLANDS

■ HAWAII

Deep below the Pacific Ocean, submarine vents grew into volcanoes, building up the Hawaiian Islands over millions of years through continuous eruptions of lava. Today, the islands rise more than 10,000 feet above sea level.

■ TRISTAN DA CUNHA

This small island in the southern Atlantic Ocean measures just under 80 square miles; it may well be the most remote inhabited island in the world. The island is home to Queen Mary's Peak, which last erupted in 1961.

■ KRAKATAU

This massive volcano in Indonesia was the site of one of the largest and deadliest eruptions in recorded history in 1883. The sound of the eruption could be heard more than 2,800 miles away, and more than 34,000 people were killed.

■ SANTORINI

This well-known travel destination in the Aegean Sea is a volcanic lagoon, its rocky cliffs encircling a powerful shield volcano. The island's geological history is apparent in these cliffs, which show the layers of solidified lava built up over the course of many eruptions.

■ ICELAND

Located along a tectonic plate boundary, Iceland is one of the most active volcanic regions in the world. The island formed as the North American and Eurasian plates moved apart, and lava filled the gaps left between. The plates are still in motion, which means earthquakes and eruptions are common in Iceland today.

WINTER SKY

FINDING ORION

The winter sky hosts some of the brightest stars in the night sky, including the recognizable and popular constellation of Orion.

Orion: Hunter, Shepherd, Farmer
In the Northern Hemisphere, Orion is lord of the winter sky, his distinctive shape filled with bright stars and other astronomical sights. The constellation is named for a famed hunter of Greek mythology, but it is not the only story associated with this star pattern. Other cultures have seen the constellation as representing a shepherd or a harvesting scythe, because it first appears in the northern sky during harvest times.

Orion features two of the brightest stars in the sky. To the north, at the hunter's shoulder, is Betelgeuse, the ninth brightest star, with a diameter larger than the orbit of Earth and a mass of 20 suns. To the south Rigel, the sixth brightest, is also quite large (17 solar masses) and, thanks to its proximity to the Equator, was one of the "nautical stars" that sailors would use to locate themselves on the ocean. But the real action, astronomically speaking, is in Orion's belt and the "sword" that hangs from it. There you will find the Orion Nebula, one of the few easily seen with the naked eye.

> ❝ **IT OFTEN SEEMS TO ME THAT THE NIGHT IS MUCH MORE ALIVE AND RICHLY COLORED THAN THE DAY**
>
> —VINCENT VAN GOGH, POST-IMPRESSIONIST PAINTER

STELLAR MAGNITUDES

● −0.5 and brighter	● 2.1 to 2.5
● −0.4 to 0.0	● 2.6 to 3.0
● 0.1 to 0.5	● 3.1 to 3.5
● 0.6 to 1.0	● 3.6 to 4.0
● 1.1 to 1.5	· 4.1 to 4.5
● 1.6 to 2.0	· 4.6 to 5.0
	⊙ Variable star

DEEP SKY OBJECTS

- ⊙ Open star cluster
- ⊕ Globular star cluster
- □ Bright nebula
- ✧ Planetary nebula
- ⬭ Galaxy

A WORD FROM

Stars Being Born Dangling below Orion's belt, there is a line of fainter stars just visible to the naked eye. This special "gleam" in the sword is a colossal stellar nursery more than 1,200 light-years distant called the Great Orion Nebula . . . a glowing cloud in the shape of a blooming flower made of dust and gas, mostly hydrogen. It's amazing to think that you see it glowing from the light of dozens of newborn stars inside.

—**ANDREW FAZEKAS,** *"The Night Sky Guy"*

SUMMER SKY

WARM WEATHER SKIES

When you're outside enjoying a pleasant summer evening, see how easy it is to find the Summer Triangle overhead.

The Bright Summer Triangle

Just because all of the officially recognized constellations were in place by the 18th century doesn't mean that people aren't finding new pictures and patterns in the sky. The Summer Triangle—an asterism (or group of stars) featuring three bright stars in three separate constellations—is an example of this: Although the asterism itself was first noted in the 19th century, the name Summer Triangle was not popularized until the 1950s, when British broadcaster and astronomer Sir Patrick Moore used it and astronomer H. A. Rey (creator of Curious George) included it in his guidebook, *Find the Constellations.*

The stars that create the Summer Triangle are three of the brightest in the northern sky: Vega, in Lyra, is the second brightest star in the summer sky and the first (apart from the sun) to be photographed. Deneb, in Cygnus, is estimated to be 60,000 times more luminous than the sun. Altair, in Aquila, is just 16.7 light-years away. The grouping is visible to most in the Northern Hemisphere.

" THE STARS AWAKEN A CERTAIN REVERENCE, BECAUSE THOUGH ALWAYS PRESENT, THEY ARE INACCESSIBLE."

—RALPH WALDO EMERSON, POET

STELLAR MAGNITUDES

○	−0.5 and brighter	●	2.1 to 2.5
○	−0.4 to 0.0	●	2.6 to 3.0
○	0.1 to 0.5	●	3.1 to 3.5
○	0.6 to 1.0	•	3.6 to 4.0
○	1.1 to 1.5	•	4.1 to 4.5
○	1.6 to 2.0	·	4.6 to 5.0
		⊚	Variable star

DEEP SKY OBJECTS

- ◎ Open star cluster
- ⊕ Globular star cluster
- ☐ Bright nebula
- ✧ Planetary nebula
- ⬭ Galaxy

For Better Viewing
LIGHTS OUT

More than 80 percent of the planet's land areas—and 99 percent of the population of the United States and Europe—live under skies so blotted with man-made light that the Milky Way has become virtually invisible.

SHAPES IN THE STARS

Connecting the Dots Humans have an urge to order the heavens—whether for tracking seasons, navigating travel, or conveying history and myth. Here are 16 easily distinguished constellations in the Northern Hemisphere.

ANDROMEDA, the Chained Maiden
View in Oct.–Nov.;
contains galaxy visible to naked eye

AQUARIUS, the Water Bearer
Large constellation visible
in the SW U.S. during autumn

CANIS MAJOR, the Dog
Just southeast of Orion; contains
Sirius, brightest star in the night sky

CAPRICORNUS, the Sea Goat
Distinctive triangle of 12 faint stars;
visible in southern sky in late summer

CASSIOPEIA, the Queen
W-shape visible year-round
near North Pole

CYGNUS, the Swan
Shaped as if a bird, wings out, flying
south; also called the Northern Cross

DRACO, the Dragon
A long tail visible year-round
between Ursa Major and Ursa Minor

GEMINI, the Twins
From the twins originate
December's Geminid meteor showers

HYDRA, the Sea Serpent
Largest constellation of all; a serpentine
series of 17 stars visible in spring

ORION, the Hunter
Huge stars; famous Orion Nebula
easy to spot under belt

PERSEUS, the Hero
Double star cluster atop head; source
of August's Perseid meteor shower

SAGITTARIUS, the Archer
Prominent in midsummer; contains
eight high-magnitude stars

SCORPIO, the Scorpion
Bright star Antares known to the
Romans as the "heart of the scorpion"

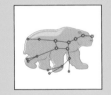

URSA MAJOR, the Great Bear
Includes the well-known Big Dipper;
points to the North Star

URSA MINOR, the Little Bear
Also called the Little Dipper;
includes Polaris, the North Star

VIRGO, the Virgin
Second largest constellation in the
sky; visible in the SE in late spring

> **"THE COSMOS IS ALSO WITHIN US. WE ARE MADE OF STAR STUFF. WE ARE A WAY FOR THE COSMOS TO KNOW ITSELF."**
>
> **—CARL SAGAN,** AUTHOR AND COSMOLOGIST

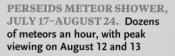
The annual Perseid meteor shower

PLANETARY CONJUNCTIONS

At the dawn of our solar system, a massive proto-planetary disk of gas and dust formed along the celestial equator. Virtually all the planets in our solar system formed along this invisible plane. As the planets orbit the sun, they will fall into natural alignments and oppositions along this plane. A planetary conjunction occurs when Earth, the sun, and a planet or planets occur in a straight line. Astrologers and mystics have often ascribed great importance to these alignments, because from Earth, the planets seem to group together in the sky. While the grouping is amazing to witness, it is an illusion, belying the immense distance between them.

TOP TEN

Skywatching Events
IN 2020

 1 — **TOTAL SOLAR ECLIPSE, DECEMBER 14.** Totality will be visible from southern Chile and Argentina.

 2 — **SUPERMOONS.** Full moons especially close to Earth will be visible on February 19, March 9, and April 7.

 3 — **CONJUNCTION OF JUPITER AND SATURN, DECEMBER 21.** For the first time since 2000, these two planets will appear at the same time.

4 — **MERCURY SIGHTINGS, FEBRUARY 10, JUNE 4, OCTOBER 1.** On these dates, Mercury will show above the horizon in the evening.

5 — **MARS SIGHTING, OCTOBER 13.** On this date, you may be able to pick out some surface details with a telescope.

 6 — **JUPITER SIGHTING, JULY 14.** Four moons may be visible with binoculars.

7 — **SATURN SIGHTING, JULY 20.** The ringed gas giant will be at its closest and brightest.

8 — **GEMINIDS METEOR SHOWER, DECEMBER 7–17.** The shower will peak on December 13 and 14, when a nearly new moon will ensure dark skies.

9 — **PERSEIDS METEOR SHOWER, JULY 17–AUGUST 24.** Dozens of meteors an hour, with peak viewing on August 12 and 13

 10 — **ETA AQUARIDS METEOR SHOWER, APRIL 19–MAY 28.** A smaller shower produced from dust particles left behind by Halley's comet, peaking on May 4 and 5

SPACE SCIENCE
TIME LINE

14 BYA to 1 BC	AD 1 to 1600	1600 to 1700	1700 to 1800

14 BYA to 1 BC

13.8 bya*
The universe forms in the big bang.

13.2 bya
Our home galaxy, the Milky Way, forms.

4.6 bya
Our solar system starts to emerge around the sun.

4.6 bya
Planet Earth forms.

4.5 bya
Earth's moon forms from debris.

240 BC
Chinese astronomers make the first record of what becomes known as Halley's comet.

* billion years ago

AD 1 to 1600

46
Roman emperor Julius Caesar introduces the Julian calendar.

ca 150
Ptolemy writes the *Almagest*, a standard guide to astronomy for over a thousand years.

310
Chinese astronomers produce a comprehensive star map.

1150
Astronomer Solomon Jarchus compiles the first celestial almanac.

1600 to 1700

1610
Galileo observes four of Jupiter's moons.

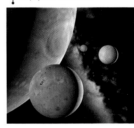

1645
Flemish cartographer Michael Langrenus publishes the first map of the moon.

1655
Dutch scientist Christiaan Huygens confirms that Saturn has rings.

1664
English scientist Robert Hooke describes Jupiter's red spot.

1676
Danish astronomer Ole Rømer makes the first quantitative measure of the speed of light.

1700 to 1800

1725
Catalog of over 3,000 stars compiled by England's first Astronomer Royal, Rev. John Flamsteed, is published.

1731
English astronomer John Bevis discovers the Crab Nebula.

1771
Charles Messier publishes catalog of astronomical objects including galaxies, star clusters, and nebulae.

1781
British astronomer William Herschel discovers the planet Uranus.

1783
English physicist John Michell predicts the existence of black holes.

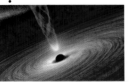

| 1800 to 1900 | 1900 to 1950 | 1950 to 1990 | 1990 to PRESENT |

1800 to 1900

1838
Friedrich Bessel uses stellar parallax to estimate the distance to the star 61 Cygni.

1846
German astronomer Johann Galle is first to observe Neptune.

1872
American astronomer Henry Draper first photographs the spectrum of a star (Vega).

1877
Two moons of Mars, Phobos and Deimos, discovered by American astronomer Asaph Hall.

1889
American astronomer Edward Barnard takes first pictures of the Milky Way.

1900 to 1950

1915
Scottish astronomer Robert Innes locates Proxima Centauri, the nearest star to the sun.

1916
Albert Einstein publishes his paper on the general theory of relativity.

1927
Georges Lemaître proposes the big bang theory.

1930
Clyde Tombaugh discovers Pluto.

1950 to 1990

1957
USSR launches Sputnik 1, first man-made satellite to orbit Earth.

1961
Russian astronaut Yuri Gagarin becomes first man in space.

1966
U.S.S.R. lands Luna 9, unmanned vehicle, on moon.

1969
U.S. Apollo 11 mission puts first men on moon.

1981
U.S. space shuttle *Columbia* completes maiden flight.

1990
Hubble Space Telescope launched into orbit.

1990 to PRESENT

2000
Two Russians and one American become the first crew to occupy the International Space Station.

2004
NASA lands two rovers, Spirit and Opportunity, on Mars.

2012
Mars Science Lab and Curiosity rover land on Mars.

2012
NASA's Voyager 1, launched in 1977, leaves the solar system and enters interstellar space.

2012
NASA's New Horizons probe passes close to Pluto and continues on to the Kuiper belt.

OUR
NEIGHBORHOOD

ONCE UPON A TIME

Many of us grew up with the idea of a static solar system, with well-behaved planets in their reliable orbits. But a more dramatic view has arisen among some scientists. Not only did the solar system go through a dramatic birth, but it also experienced a raucous adolescence: Hundreds of millions of years after they formed, the biggest planets were swept into new orbits, casting large rocks and comets every which way. The scarred surface of the moon is lingering testimony to a period of epic mayhem and gravitational instability.

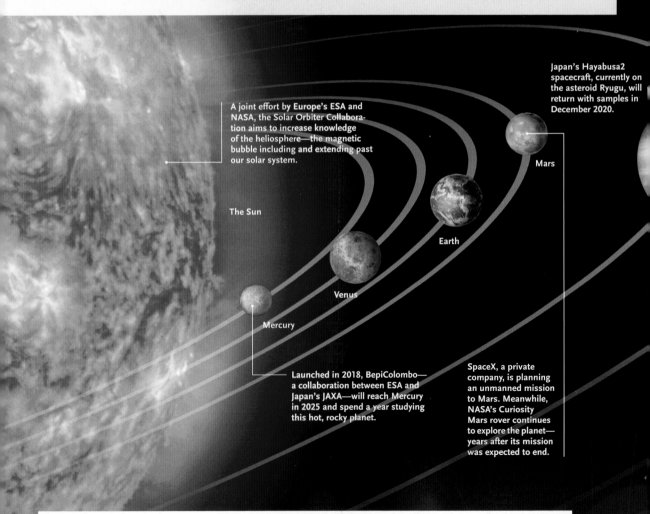

Japan's Hayabusa2 spacecraft, currently on the asteroid Ryugu, will return with samples in December 2020.

A joint effort by Europe's ESA and NASA, the Solar Orbiter Collaboration aims to increase knowledge of the heliosphere—the magnetic bubble including and extending past our solar system.

Mars

The Sun

Earth

Venus

Mercury

Launched in 2018, BepiColombo—a collaboration between ESA and Japan's JAXA—will reach Mercury in 2025 and spend a year studying this hot, rocky planet.

SpaceX, a private company, is planning an unmanned mission to Mars. Meanwhile, NASA's Curiosity Mars rover continues to explore the planet—years after its mission was expected to end.

A current theory is that our planets grew to full size by absorbing planetesimals, like rocky asteroids, icy comets, and larger objects.

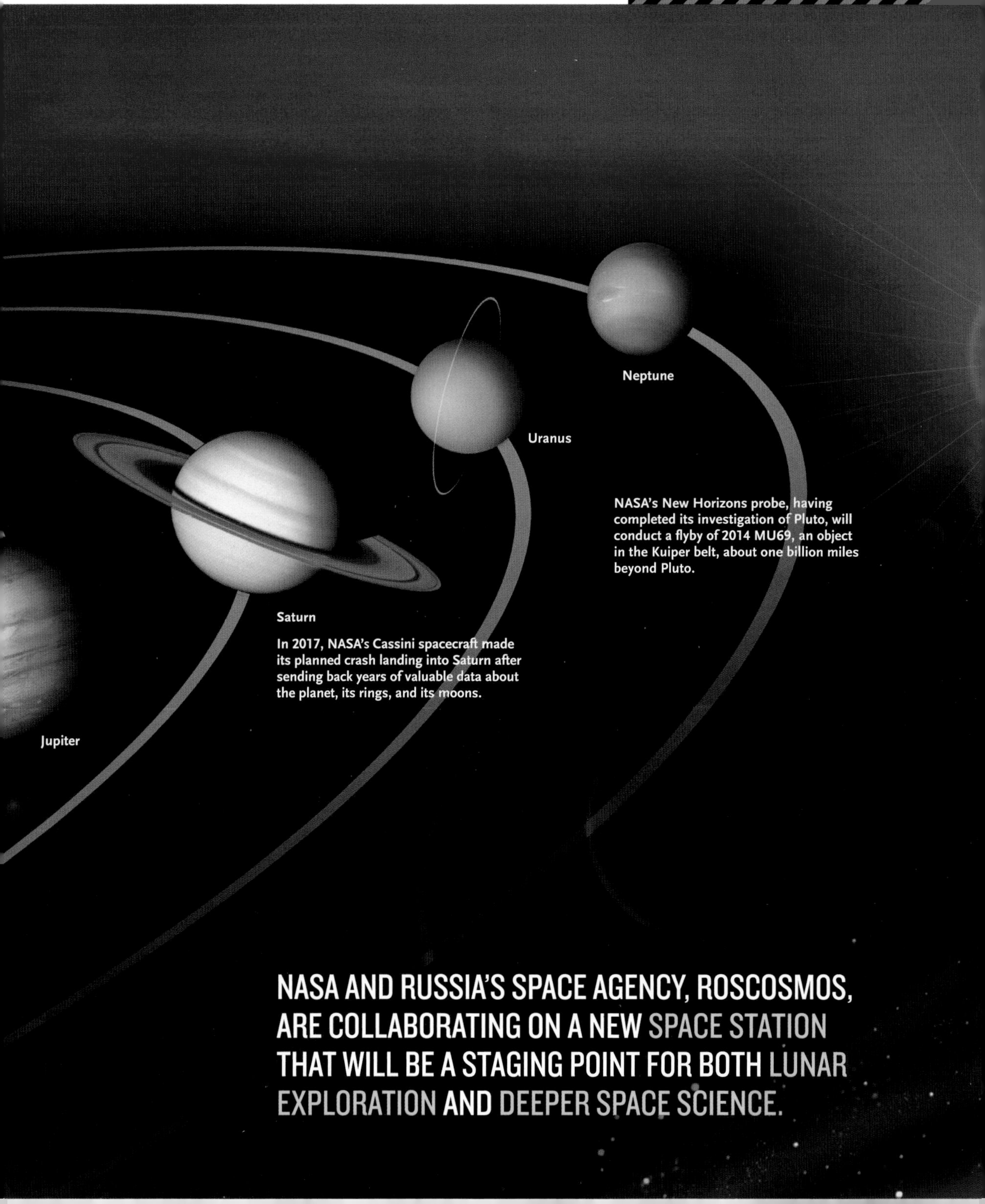

Neptune

Uranus

NASA's New Horizons probe, having completed its investigation of Pluto, will conduct a flyby of 2014 MU69, an object in the Kuiper belt, about one billion miles beyond Pluto.

Saturn

In 2017, NASA's Cassini spacecraft made its planned crash landing into Saturn after sending back years of valuable data about the planet, its rings, and its moons.

Jupiter

NASA AND RUSSIA'S SPACE AGENCY, ROSCOSMOS, ARE COLLABORATING ON A NEW SPACE STATION THAT WILL BE A STAGING POINT FOR BOTH LUNAR EXPLORATION AND DEEPER SPACE SCIENCE.

DWARF PLANETS

MEET THE NEW NEIGHBORS

An artist's rendering of Pluto

PLANETARY RULES

PLANET OR DWARF?

In 2006, scientists at the International Astronomers Union conference created three rules for a planet: It orbits the sun, has enough mass that gravitational forces shape it nearly round, and has cleared its orbit of all other material. If a heavenly body meets only the first two categories, it is called a dwarf planet. It was a great advance for science but the death knell for Pluto, which was demoted to a dwarf. Our solar system lost one planet but gained dozens or even hundreds of dwarf planets in the exchange.

PLUTO

THE FORMER PLANET

Pluto may be the ninth largest body in our solar system, but it's not a planet. It sits in the crowded asteroid field known as the Kuiper belt, violating the rules of planethood. While it is only one and a half times the size of Earth's moon, Pluto has five smaller moons of its own. The rocky world was visited by NASA's New Horizons probe in 2015 and found to have blue skies and red snow.

ERIS

THE HIDDEN GIANT

Pluto once marked the edge of our solar system, but today that honor belongs to Eris. The dwarf planet's orbit is three times as far out as Pluto's, nearly 9.5 billion miles from the sun. Eris has an unusual orbit: It doesn't follow the parallel rings of the inner planets but instead follows its own path at a nearly 45-degree angle to the others.

OUR SOLAR SYSTEM **MAY CONTAIN AS MANY AS** 200 DWARF PLANETS, **ACCORDING TO ASTRONOMERS' ESTIMATES.**

An illustration of Makemake

CERES

A ONCE WATERY WORLD

Although most dwarf planets lie beyond Pluto in the vast Kuiper belt, Ceres can be found in the asteroid belt between Mars and Jupiter. It used to have vast oceans, but today all that remain are salts such as sodium carbonate. How Ceres got to the asteroid belt is perhaps one of its most intriguing mysteries. Some scientists think Ceres may have been a planetary wanderer, moving into the inner asteroid belt from beyond the solar system.

MAKEMAKE

MINIATURE WORLD

Makemake (pronounced MAH-keh MAH-keh) is the second brightest object in the Kuiper belt after Pluto. It's a small world, just 888 miles across, with the same red-brown shading as Pluto. But this is an airless place, with no atmosphere at all. Little is known about its makeup and structure, but its discovery changed history. The discovery of Eris in 2003 and Makemake in 2005 led astronomers to redefine what makes a planet.

HAUMEA

BATTERED PLANET

At some point in its distant past, the dwarf planet Haumea slammed into another world at 7,000 miles per hour. The collision blasted huge chunks of Haumea into space and sent the celestial body spinning. Haumea spins so rapidly that a day there is equivalent to four hours on Earth. This super-speed of its rotation has even shaped the dwarf planet into an elongated football. Two moons and faint rings, also remnants of ancient disaster, circle the planet.

EARTH'S MOON

MAGNIFICENT DESOLATION

The topography of the moon is varied. Collisions with meteors over its 4.5-billion-year life have created a surface of pulverized rock, called regolith. Craters are as wide as 1,600 miles across, with mountainous walls as high as 4.8 miles. Its distinctive "seas" are actually areas given a smooth sheen by molten lava brought to the surface after major impacts that occurred around 3.8 to 3.9 billion years ago.

OCEANUS PROCELLARUM
This large, dark "ocean of storms," easily visible from Earth, is probably rift valleys formed by emerging magma. Apollo 12 landed here in 1969.

MONTES APENNINUS
Apollo 15 landed at the base of this mountain range in 1971. Formed by the impact of an asteroid, comet, or other object almost four billion years ago, it includes the tallest lunar mountain, Mons Huygens.

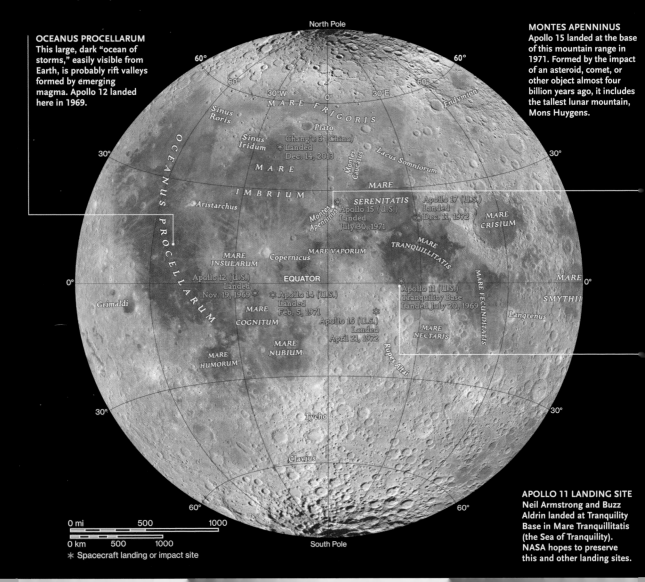

North Pole

OCEANUS PROCELLARUM

MARE FRIGORIS

Sinus Roris

Sinus Iridum

Plato

Chang'e 3 (China)
✳ Landed
Dec. 14, 2013

Montes Caucasus

Lacus Somniorum

Endymion

MARE IMBRIUM

Aristarchus

Montes Apenninus

MARE SERENITATIS
✳ Apollo 15 (U.S.)
Landed
July 30, 1971

Apollo 17 (U.S.)
✳ Landed
Dec. 11, 1972

MARE CRISIUM

MARE VAPORUM

MARE TRANQUILLITATIS

MARE INSULARUM

Copernicus

EQUATOR

Grimaldi

Apollo 12 (U.S.)
Landed
Nov. 19, 1969

✳ ✳ Apollo 14 (U.S.)
Landed
Feb. 5, 1971

Apollo 11 (U.S.)
✳ Tranquility Base
Landed July 20, 1969

MARE FECUNDITATIS

MARE SMYTHII

Langrenus

MARE COGNITUM

✳ Apollo 16 (U.S.)
Landed
April 21, 1972

MARE NECTARIS

MARE NUBIUM

MARE HUMORUM

Rupes Altai

Tycho

Clavius

South Pole

0 mi   500   1000
0 km   500   1000
✳ Spacecraft landing or impact site

APOLLO 11 LANDING SITE
Neil Armstrong and Buzz Aldrin landed at Tranquility Base in Mare Tranquillitatis (the Sea of Tranquility). NASA hopes to preserve this and other landing sites.

IN 2019 CHINA'S CHANG'E 4 BECAME THE FIRST CRAFT EVER TO LAND ON THE MOON'S FAR SIDE. IT BOUNCED IMAGES BACK TO EARTH VIA RELAY SATELLITE QUEQIAO.

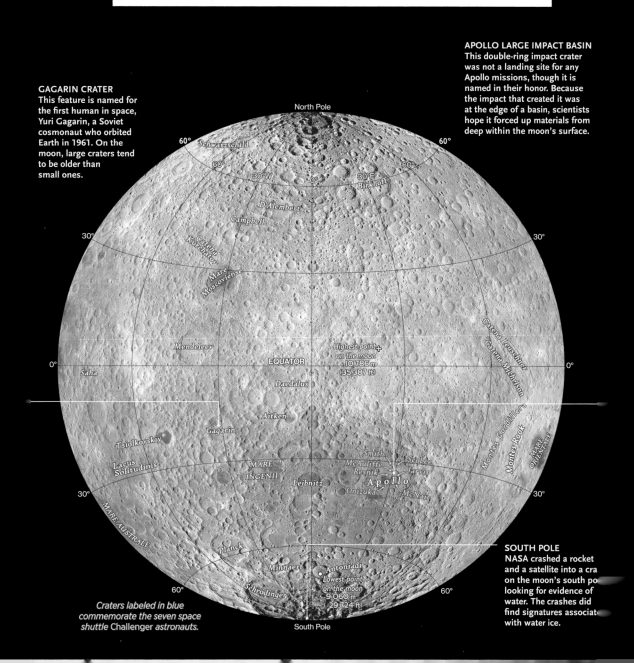

APOLLO LARGE IMPACT BASIN
This double-ring impact crater was not a landing site for any Apollo missions, though it is named in their honor. Because the impact that created it was at the edge of a basin, scientists hope it forced up materials from deep within the moon's surface.

GAGARIN CRATER
This feature is named for the first human in space, Yuri Gagarin, a Soviet cosmonaut who orbited Earth in 1961. On the moon, large craters tend to be older than small ones.

SOUTH POLE
NASA crashed a rocket and a satellite into a cra on the moon's south po looking for evidence of water. The crashes did find signatures associat with water ice.

Craters labeled in blue commemorate the seven space shuttle Challenger *astronauts.*

North Pole

Schwarzschild

Birkhoff

D'Alembert

Campbell

Catena Kurchatov

Mare Moscoviense

Mendeleev

Highest point
on the moon
10,786 m
(35,387 ft)

EQUATOR

Saha

Daedalus

Catena Leuschner

Catena Michelson

Aitken

Gagarin

Montes Cordillera

Montes Rook

MARE ORIENTALE

Tsiolkovskiy

Lacus Solitudinis

Smith

MARE INGENII

McAuliffe
Resnik

Scobee
Jarvis

Apollo

Leibnitz

Onizuka

McNair

MARE AUSTRALE

Planck

Minnaert

Antoniadi
Lowest point
on the moon
9,060 m
(29,724 ft)

Schrödinger

South Pole

ON TO MARS

WATER ON THE FOURTH PLANET

Astronomers using some of the world's most powerful telescopes have determined that an ocean at least a mile deep covered a significant fraction of the Martian surface four billion years ago. The research reinforces earlier evidence that water once existed on the surface of the red planet, leaving traces such as stream pebbles, ancient shorelines, river deltas, minerals that must have formed in a watery environment, and more.

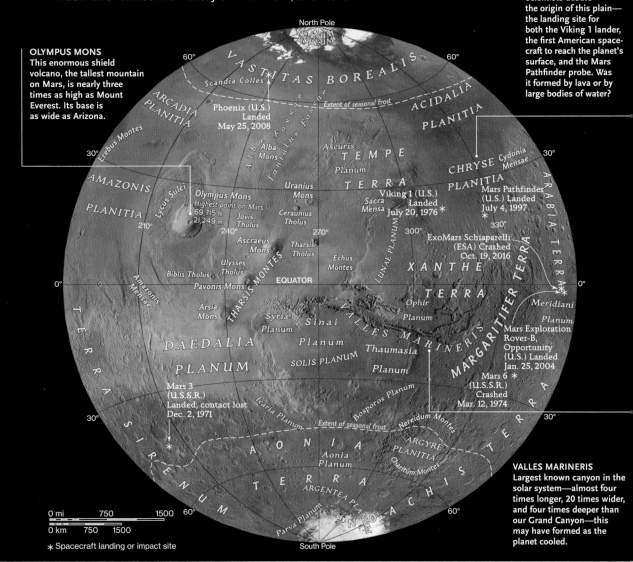

OLYMPUS MONS
This enormous shield volcano, the tallest mountain on Mars, is nearly three times as high as Mount Everest. Its base is as wide as Arizona.

CHRYSE PLANITIA
Scientists debate the origin of this plain—the landing site for both the Viking 1 lander, the first American spacecraft to reach the planet's surface, and the Mars Pathfinder probe. Was it formed by lava or by large bodies of water?

VALLES MARINERIS
Largest known canyon in the solar system—almost four times longer, 20 times wider, and four times deeper than our Grand Canyon—this may have formed as the planet cooled.

North Pole

South Pole

VASTITAS BOREALIS

ARCADIA PLANITIA

Scandia Colles

Extent of seasonal frost

ACIDALIA PLANITIA

Phoenix (U.S.) Landed May 25, 2008

Alba Fossae

Alba Mons

Tantalus Fossae

Ascuris

TEMPE Planum

TERRA

CHRYSE PLANITIA

Cydonia Mensae

ARABIA TERRA

AMAZONIS PLANITIA

Erebus Montes

Lycus Sulci

Olympus Mons
Highest point on Mars
69,715 ft
21,249 m

Uranius Mons

Jovis Tholus

Ceraunius Tholus

Viking 1 (U.S.) Landed July 20, 1976

Sacra Mensa

Mars Pathfinder (U.S.) Landed July 4, 1997

ExoMars Schiaparelli (ESA) Crashed Oct. 19, 2016

Ascraeus Mons

Tharsis Tholus

Echus Montes

XANTHE TERRA

Ulysses Tholus

Biblis Tholus

Pavonis Mons

EQUATOR

Lunae Planum

Amazonis Mensae

Arsia Mons

THARSIS MONTES

Syria Planum

Sinai Planum

VALLES MARINERIS

Ophir Planum

Meridiani Planum

MARGARITIFER TERRA

TERRA

DAEDALIA PLANUM

Solis Planum

Thaumasia Planum

Mars Exploration Rover-B, Opportunity (U.S.) Landed Jan. 25, 2004

Mars 6 (U.S.S.R.) Crashed Mar. 12, 1974

Mars 3 (U.S.S.R.) Landed, contact lost Dec. 2, 1971

Icaria Planum

Bosporos Planum

Extent of seasonal frost

Nereidum Montes

ARGYRE PLANITIA

Charitum Montes

SIRENUM TERRA

AONIA TERRA

Aonia Planum

Argentea Planum

Parva Planum

ACHISTER TERRA

0 mi 750 1500
0 km 750 1500

* Spacecraft landing or impact site

CHEMICAL DISCOVERIES MADE IN 2019 BY NASA'S CURIOSITY ROVER SUGGEST THAT MICROSCOPIC LIFE MAY HAVE LIVED ON MARS—AND MAY LIVE THERE STILL.

VASTITAS BOREALIS
This region, which surrounds and includes Mars's north pole, had a visitor in 2008: NASA's Phoenix lander, which processed samples of soil and ice for evidence of life or indications that it could support life.

SYRTIS MAJOR PLANUM
Visible from Earth, this feature was included in depictions of Mars as far back as 1659. Its appearance has some variability, once thought to be caused by vegetation or a body of water.

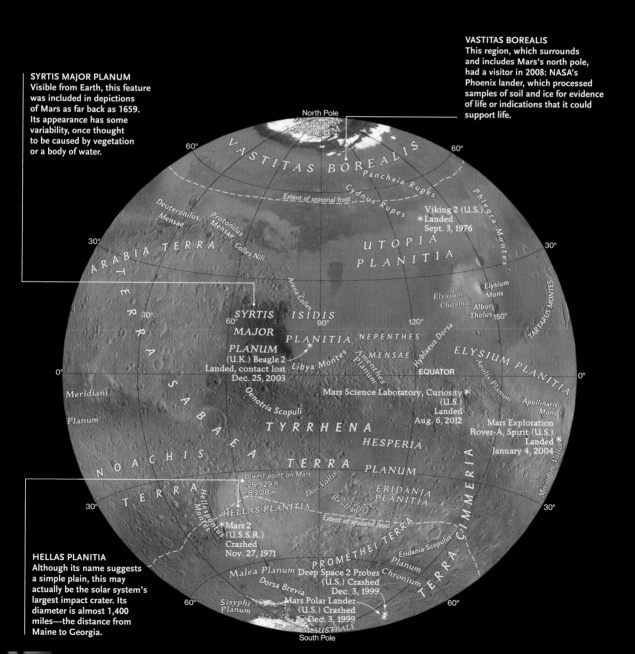

HELLAS PLANITIA
Although its name suggests a simple plain, this may actually be the solar system's largest impact crater. Its diameter is almost 1,400 miles—the distance from Maine to Georgia.

MARTIAN
PROBES

MISSIONS TO MARS

Each line below is color-coded to represent one mission that reached Mars, or failed in the attempt, the type of mission, and the county of origin.

Flyby   Lander   Orbiter

HOW WE STUDY
THE RED PLANET

Even before humans landed on Earth's moon, we'd been sending spacecraft to our closest planetary neighbor, Mars. As these craft have flown past, orbited around, landed on, and driven over the surface of Mars, there have been utter failures and spectacular successes. As NASA sets its sights on a manned Mars mission in the 2030s, we look back on mission history.

1960   Marsnik 1 Launched 1960

        Mariner 4 1964

1970

        Mars 3 1971

        Mars 6 1973
        Viking 1, Viking 2 1975
1980   Phobos 2 1988
1990

        Mars Pathfinder 1996

2000   Mars Odyssey 2001
        Mars Express 2003
        Spirit, Opportunity 2003

2010   MSL Curiosity 2011
        Mars Orbiter Mission 2013
        ExoMars 2016

43 TOTAL MISSIONS*

SUCCESS		FAILURE
	Russia/U.S.S.R.	
	United States	
	European Space Agency	
	Japan	
	China-Russia	
	India	

MARINER 4
U.S. 1964
This flyby provided the first close-up photos of Mars.

MARS 3
U.S.S.R. 1971
This was the first successful lander, though it stopped transmitting after 20 seconds.

VIKING 1 & 2
U.S. 1975
The first U.S. landers on Mars returned color images from the surface.

2001 MARS ODYSSEY
U.S. 2001
The orbiter is the longest
serving Mars spacecraft.

MARS EXPRESS
ESA 2003
The lander was lost,
but the orbiter keeps
making images.

MARS ORBITER MISSION
INDIA 2013
India's first Mars probe
carries imaging and
scientific instruments.

JUPITER & ITS MOONS

LEARNING FROM JUNO'S OBSERVATIONS

According to NASA, Jupiter is "a physics lab of sorts," and one of the phenomena under study is the Jovian magnetosphere, using data and images collected by the Juno spacecraft, which spent a few years in orbit around our largest planet. For example, scientists are working to understand Jupiter's radiation belts, in part because protecting spacecraft and astronauts from radiation is a constant concern. And unlike auroras in our atmosphere (triggered by extraplanetary particles), Jupiter's most intense auroras are the result of an as-yet unknown acceleration process.

POP!

TOP 10 SPACE FLICKS

- *Metropolis* (1927)
- *Star Wars, Episode IV: A New Hope* (1977)
- *Alien* (1979)
- *E.T. The Extra-Terrestrial* (1982)
- *Aliens* (1986)
- *WALL-E* (2008)
- *Star Trek* (2009)
- *Gravity* (2013)
- *Star Wars, Episode VII: The Force Awakens* (2015)
- *Arrival* (2016)

Jupiter's Great Red Spot is 1.3 times as wide as Earth.

> ## " I LOVE EUROPA, WHO DOESN'T? IT HAS TWICE AS MUCH SEAWATER AS THE EARTH. LET'S GO!"
>
> —BILL NYE, THE SCIENCE GUY

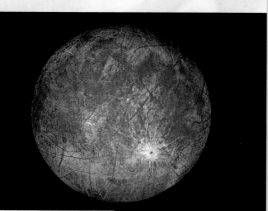

Europa, one of Jupiter's 69 moons

OTHER MOON LANDINGS

For obvious reasons, investigating a gas giant needs to be done from some distance, but we may be able to get a vessel on or near Jupiter's four Galilean moons—the largest among its 69—instead. Here's why Europa seems to be the most likely destination.

Great Amenities and Quite a View

Although this moon has an outer crust of solid ice, cracks in its surface indicate that the crust sits on top of liquid water. Because little warmth from the sun reaches Europa, it's likely that its ocean is kept from freezing by hydrothermal vents. Hubble telescope images from 2013 show plumes of liquid water at Europa's south pole, too. All of this—water! heat! nutrients!—makes Europa a compelling candidate for life.

Because it will be years before a spacecraft (already being referred to as the Europa Clipper) reaches Europa, scientists are investigating life found in Earth's extreme environments to feed their imagination of what life on other planets might look like.

KEY DATES

Getting to Know
JUPITER

■ **1610: GALILEO SEES THE MOONS**
When astronomer Galileo Galilei observed four satellites orbiting Jupiter through his improved telescope, he also identified the key to Copernicus's sun-centered model, displacing the Earth-centered Ptolemaic system.

■ **1831: RED SPOT SPOTTED**
Although several stargazers had noted Jupiter's spotted appearance, Samuel Heinrich Schwabe, a German amateur astronomer studying sunspots, first described the planet's distinctive Great Red Spot (a cyclone).

■ **1955: JUPITER SPEAKS TO US**
While collecting radio signals to map the spring sky, astronomers Bernard Burke and Kenneth Franklin captured interference eventually revealed as coming from Jupiter—and that helped find the planet's rotation speed.

■ **1979: PUT A COUPLE RINGS ON IT**
Saturn's always been the one with flashy rings, but Jupiter's dusty, beautiful rings were photographed by the paparazzi known as Voyager 1 and 2 (and, later, Galileo).

■ **1995: AN EXTENDED STAY**
When the Galileo spacecraft arrived in Jupiter's neighborhood for a four-year visit to the planet and its moons, it brought along a probe that entered the planet's atmosphere.

■ **2016: JUNO CALLING**
Data from the Juno orbiter will be analyzed by pros and citizen scientists studying structure, composition, and magnetic and gravitational fields. Highlights include the stunning, mysterious auroras at the north pole.

■ **2018: DISCOVERY OF NEW MOONS**
While searching for a hypothetical planet on the outskirts of the solar system, researchers found 12 small, previously unknown moons around Jupiter. They range in size from about one to three miles across, and their discovery brings the total number of Jupiter's moons to 79.

BEST OF @NATGEO

TOP PHOTOS OF THE NIGHT SKY

@renan_ozturk | RENAN OZTURK
Ice and snow reflect the aurora borealis on the Vatnajökull glacier in Iceland.

@geosteinmetz | GEORGE STEINMETZ
Rock sculptures shaped by strong winds in Egypt's White Desert shine on a moonlit night.

@salvarezphoto | STEPHEN ALVAREZ
Petroglyphs on the Butler Wash panel in southeastern Utah date back to approximately 1500 BC.

@jimmy_chin | JIMMY CHIN
The Kamchatka Peninsula in Russia is home to the planet's highest concentration of active volcanoes.

@pedromcbride | PETE MCBRIDE
A six-hour exposure captures the movement of the stars in the Andean Altiplano in Argentina.

@lucalocatelliphoto | LUCA LOCATELLI
Telescopes at the Deimos Sky Survey in southern Spain collect about 50,000 images every night.

@renan_ozturk | RENAN OZTURK
Climbers scale an ice wall under the glow of the northern lights in Iceland.

@johnstanmeyer | JOHN STANMEYER
Explorer Paul Salopek stands under the Milky Way, visible in the darkness of the Kyzylkum Desert in Uzbekistan.

BIRTH OF THE UNIVERSE

A HISTORY SHAPED BY DARK FORCES

Cosmologists have determined that the universe was born 13.8 billion years ago. But they've also concluded that what we see in the sky makes up only 5 percent of the observable universe. The invisible majority consists of 27 percent dark matter and 68 percent dark energy.

What's Dark Matter?

We can't see dark matter, but we can see the effects of its gravity. And dark matter can't just be inconspicuous normal matter—in no plausible scenario would it add up to five times the mass of the bright stuff—hence scientists think it must be made of more exotic materials.

What's Dark Energy?

Dark energy, even more mysterious, refers to whatever is accelerating the rate at which the cosmos expands. It has been called a "general label for what we do not know about the large-scale properties of our universe."

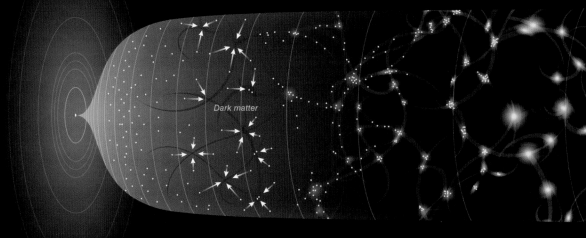

Dark matter

The big bang
13.8 billion years ago

Our universe blossoms from a hot, dense state smaller than an atom. Within milliseconds it inflates enormously.

Dark matter forms
First seconds of the universe

Dark matter also emerges in the first second. Interacting with particles of normal matter only through gravity, it begins to pull them together.

Stars light up
100 million years after the big bang

Clouds of hydrogen assembled by the gravity of dark matter collapse to form the first scattered stars. Nuclear fusion inside them creates heavier elements—and lights space.

Composition of the universe

Dark energy <1%   ┌Dark matter <1%
                                                          86%
Matter <1%   Radiation 99%*   <1%   <1%
                                                          13%

A BELGIAN PRIEST NAMED GEORGES LEMAÎTRE FIRST SUGGESTED THE BIG BANG THEORY IN THE 1920S WHEN HE THEORIZED THAT THE UNIVERSE BEGAN FROM A SINGLE PRIMORDIAL ATOM.

Dark energy

e expansion slows
llion years after the big bang

rs clump into galaxies and
axies into clusters along a scaffold-
of dark matter. The mass of all
tter, most of it dark, is so great that
gravity slows cosmic expansion.

Dark energy rises
4–8 billion years after the big bang

After slowing for billions of years,
the expansion accelerates again.
Why? A mysterious repulsive force,
dubbed dark energy, has begun to
counteract the pull of dark matter.

Ever outward
Today

The universe hurtles
outward toward an
uncertain future.

84%		
%		<1%
	15%	

75%		
13%		<1%
	12%	

Dark energy	Dark matter 27%	Radiation
68%		<1%
	Matter 4%	

* Percentages do not add up to 100 due to rounding.

ANN DRUYAN
SCIENCE COMMUNICATOR

A LIFE OF WONDERMENT

The wonders of the cosmos have fascinated Ann Druyan since her childhood. Though girls were not encouraged to explore science in the 1950s, Druyan prevailed, finding ways to share her fascination with science.

Ann Druyan and Carl Sagan in Los Angeles in 1980, during the production of *Cosmos: A Personal Voyage*

In 1977, Ann was chosen by Carl Sagan to be the creative director of the iconic NASA Voyager Interstellar Message, better known as the Golden Record, a repository of 118 pictures, greetings in 54 languages and one dialect of humpback whales, 27 pieces of world music, and a sound essay with everything from the chirping of crickets to the brain waves of a young woman newly fallen in love. "We all looked upon it as something sacred," Druyan says of the Golden Record: "a cultural Noah's Ark of human culture with a shelf life of billions of years." The record was affixed to the two Voyagers, which launched in 1977 and have been traveling ever since—the most distant objects ever touched by human hands.

THE COSMOS PHENOMENON

Druyan and Sagan fell in love while working on Voyager, and they soon went on to create their legendary collaboration, *Cosmos*. Together with Steven Soter they wrote the television series that first aired on PBS in 1980, won two Emmys and a Peabody Award, and went on to be broadcast in 60 countries. The beloved companion book, dedicated to Druyan, became one of the top-selling science books of all time and paved the way for six more *New York Times* best sellers on the importance of scientific knowledge in our world and to our future, all co-written by Sagan and Druyan.

Druyan's work as author and television producer has continued beyond Carl Sagan's untimely death in 1996. She has been creating sequels to *Cosmos*. The first, *Cosmos: A Spacetime Odyssey*, aired in 2014 and won four Emmys and a Peabody. The second, *Cosmos: Possible Worlds*, will debut in 2020.

> **" SCIENCE IS NOTHING MORE THAN A NEVER-ENDING SEARCH FOR TRUTH. WHAT COULD BE MORE PROFOUNDLY SACRED THAN THAT?"**

Ann Druyan today

KEY DATES

Anne Druyan's
ACCOMPLISHMENTS

■ **1979**
With Carl Sagan, co-creates *Contact*, which became a movie starring Jodie Foster

■ **1980**
With Carl Sagan, writes the landmark TV series *Cosmos*

■ **2000**
Founds Cosmos Studios, dedicated to creating science-based entertainment

■ **2005**
Serves as program director of the deep space solar sail mission COSMOS 1

■ **2014**
Serves as executive producer, writer, and director of *Cosmos: A Spacetime Odyssey*

■ **2019**
Performs the same roles on her third series, *Cosmos: Possible Worlds*

WHEN A STAR EXPLODES

THE LIFE CYCLE OF A STAR

Every star begins as a collapsing cloud of interstellar dust. Stars stabilize when the temperature in the core is hot enough to begin nuclear fusion: turning hydrogen into helium. From there, a star grows and changes, using the hydrogen at its core as fuel along the way. Eventually, there's nothing left to burn, and some of the star's mass flows into its core. Once the core reaches critical mass—becoming too heavy to withstand its own gravitational force—the star collapses in on itself, producing massive shock waves and the giant explosion of a supernova.

A WORD FROM

The Cosmic Dawn The Giant Magellan Telescope will have 10 times the resolution of the Hubble Space Telescope. It will be 20 million times more sensitive than the human eye. And it may, for the first time ever, be capable of finding life on planets outside of our solar system. It's going to allow us to look back at the first light in the universe—literally, the dawn of the cosmos.

—WENDY FREEDMAN, *astronomer*

The next supernova visible from Earth—as bright as Polaris—will be in Cygnus around 2022 and will last a year.

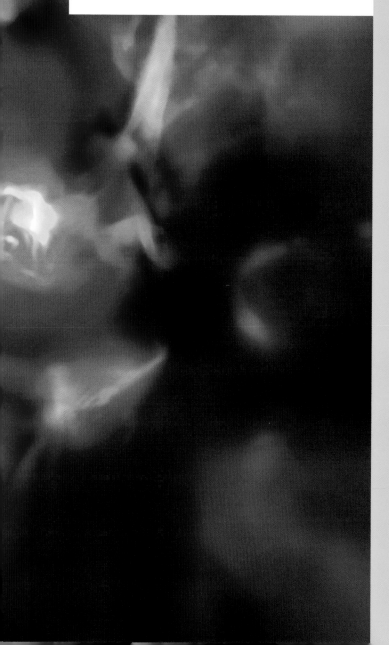

IN THE SPACE OF JUST A FEW YEARS A SUPERNOVA, A SPECIAL KIND OF EXPLODED STAR, RADIATES MORE ENERGY THAN OUR SUN DOES IN ITS ENTIRE LIFETIME.

Distances Out Into THE UNIVERSE

ASTEROID: 26,000 MILES
A tiny asteroid, just 50–100 feet long and known as 2012 TC4, flew very close to Earth on Oct. 12, 2017, just above the orbit of communications satellites.

COMET: 1.4 MILLION MILES
Appearing about four times as large as a full moon to the naked eye in July 1770, comet Lexell (aka D/1770 L1) was six times as far away as the moon.

NEXT STAR: 4.25 LIGHT-YEARS (LY)
Proxima Centauri, our second nearest star (the sun is closer, obviously), is in the constellation of Centaurus. It is part of a three-star system with Alpha Centauri A and B.

HABITABLE EXOPLANET: 4.25 LY
Our nearest star has in its orbit an exoplanet (Proxima Centauri B) that could, based on its size and location, have liquid water.

SUPERNOVA CANDIDATE: 150 LY
The most likely star to become a supernova is the smaller partner in a binary system known as IK Pegasi at a not insignificant distance from Earth—but by the time it explodes, millions of years from now, the distance will be much greater.

PLANETARY NEBULA: 650 LY
Not actually home to planets, this celestial object is the glowing remnants of a sunlike star. The Helix Nebula, in the constellation of Aquarius, is likely the closest to us.

BLACK HOLE: 3,000 LY
Almost every galaxy has a supermassive black hole in its center. Ours is 27,000 ly from Earth. A stellar-mass black hole, V616 Monocerotis, is about 3,000 ly away.

GALAXY: 25,000 LY
The Canis Major dwarf galaxy, closest to us and to the center of the Milky Way (42,000 ly), is being unraveled by our galaxy's gravity.

SPACE RADIATION

FOLLOWING COSMIC RAYS THROUGH THE UNIVERSE

Pulsars emit particles along their two magnetic poles.

TRACING A PATH

WHERE DO THEY COME FROM?

By the time most cosmic rays reach Earth, many have been traveling for thousands or millions of years across the cosmos. But even when traveling near the speed of light, the universe is a big place. For scientists, the distance is less of a problem than the direction. Most cosmic radiation carries an electrical charge, which can be significantly affected by magnetic fields. A cosmic ray passing too close to a sun or large planet can find its path altered by its magnetic field. By the time the particle gets to Earth, it could be coming from a completely different direction than it started from, which means scientists can't necessarily match a cosmic ray to its cosmic source. Generating the ability to follow these pathways would give scientists new tools to explore and understand the universe.

UNDER SIEGE

HIGH-ENERGY INVASION

Earth is pelted with high-energy particles from outer space every second. These high-energy projectiles are atomic particles born in distant stars, many traveling near the speed of light. Cosmic radiation is a danger for astronauts, but for scientists, these aren't threats but atomic ambassadors from across the universe. Cosmic radiation helped science unlock the world beyond the atom, and understanding it better can help astronomers radically advance our understanding of the cosmos.

Particles of plasma lead to the aurora borealis.

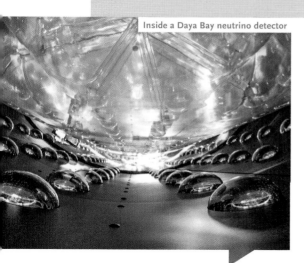
Inside a Daya Bay neutrino detector

SOLAR WEATHER **AFFECTS LEVELS OF RADIATION IN SPACE. EVERY** 11 YEARS, **THE SUN CYCLES THROUGH PERIODS OF HIGHER AND LOWER ACTIVITY, AND** RADIATION LEVELS **RISE WITH LEVELS OF SOLAR ACTIVITY.**

An illustration of Earth's radiation belts

NEUTRINOS

A PECULIAR PARTICLE

One type of subatomic particle, the neutrino, rarely interacts with matter. Neutrinos can fly through magnetic fields, asteroids, and even planets without ever altering course. To catch a neutrino, scientists have buried storage tanks deep beneath lead mines or the Antarctic ice sheets and waited for the brief flash when a neutrino interacts with their contents. If scientists can find a way to successfully trace neutrinos, they will open up a new way of searching the universe for supernovae, black holes, and other wonders of the cosmos.

A WORD FROM

The Human Body in Space On my previous flight to the space station, a mission of 159 days, I lost bone mass, my muscles atrophied, and my blood redistributed itself in my body, which strained and shrank the walls of my heart. More troubling, I experienced problems with my vision, as many other astronauts had. I had been exposed to more than 30 times the radiation of a person on Earth, equivalent to about 10 chest x-rays every day. This exposure would increase my risk of a fatal cancer for the rest of my life.

—SCOTT KELLY, *astronaut*

BLOCKING RADIATION

BEYOND THE SPHERE

Earth's magnetic field blocks 99.9 percent of space radiation , but humanity is safe only as long as we stay within our protective magnetic bubble. Beyond that layer, the radiation level rises, and so do health concerns for astronauts. High-energy cosmic rays can damage sensitive electronics, but even normal radiation could dramatically increase the risk of cancer. A single trip to Mars would be like undergoing an x-ray or MRI scan every week of the journey, and that covers only the voyage. Whether on the surface of Mars, the moon, or even the International Space Station, there is nowhere to hide from the cosmic storm. If humanity leaves the planet, understanding the cosmic storm will be vital.

EXOPLANETS
IS THERE LIFE?

IN SEARCH OF GOLDILOCKS

When astronomers discuss planets that might support life, they refer to Goldilocks: Conditions have to be just right for life to happen. Once an exoplanet (a planet outside our solar system) is identified, astronomers assess its distance from the star it orbits and determine whether it is too close or too far to keep surface water in a liquid state. Size also matters: A planet that's too small cannot maintain an atmosphere; one that's too large will have a crushing atmosphere. "Goldilocks" planets have the right atmospheric pressure and the right temperature.

POP!

PLANETARY PLAYLIST

- "Aquarius (Let the Sunshine In)," The 5th Dimension
- "Fly Me to the Moon," Frank Sinatra
- "From Here to the Moon and Back," Dolly Parton
- "Gagarin," Public Service Broadcasting
- "Here Comes the Sun," The Beatles
- "Kuiper Belt," Sufjan Stevens, Bryce Dessner, Nico Muhly & James McAlister
- "Man on the Moon," R.E.M.
- "Pluto," Clare & the Reasons
- "Rocket Man," Elton John
- "Space Oddity," David Bowie
- "Stars Align," Lindsey Stirling
- "Supermassive Black Hole," Muse
- "We Are All Made of Stars," Moby

Imagine a planet with two nearby moons, visible day and night.

ONE IN FIVE SUNLIKE STARS HARBORS AN EARTH-SIZE WORLD THAT ORBITS IN A "HABITABLE ZONE" FRIENDLY TO OCEANS AND PERHAPS LIFE.

Earth Kepler-62e Kepler-62f

IN SEARCH OF EARTHS

For nine years NASA's Kepler spacecraft stared from its perch in space toward a patch of sky studded with 156,000 stars. Its goal? To find the frequency of Earthlike planets in the habitable zones of stars. The spacecraft did this by watching for the periodic blips in starlight produced when a planet passed between its star and Kepler's unblinking eye. Of the 2,600 planets discovered, some are relatively nearby, which makes them obvious targets in the search for life.

DARK MATTER

A MYSTERY AS BIG AS THE UNIVERSE

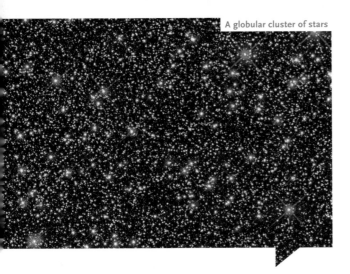

A globular cluster of stars

THE MISSING PIECE

A SEARCH FOR INVISIBLE MATTER

Astrophysics has a problem: The visible universe doesn't have enough stuff in it. Every star we see, every exoplanet and black hole we measure, every nebula we survey, is only 5 percent of what gravity tells us should be present in our universe. Hidden out in the vast reaches of space is a new type of matter—a new particle that neither emits nor reflects light but still makes up most of the universe. We can detect it only through its gravitational pushes and pulls on the visible universe we're familiar with. Scientists refer to it as the dark universe, a massive intergalactic web of dark matter and dark energy. A name is not an explanation, however, and scientists are still stumped for details.

DEFINING DARK MATTER

FILLING THE EMPTY SPACE

The idea of dark matter first appeared in the 1930s, when Swiss astronomer Fritz Zwicky focused on two galaxies orbiting each other in a distant stellar cluster. Without the galaxies containing much more mass than was seen, the galaxies should have spun away from each other. Zwicky theorized that galaxies must contain massive amounts of dark matter, many times greater than the visible matter we can detect. Other observations have only confirmed that hypothesis. In his planetary musings, Isaac Newton couldn't understand how gravity could pull Earth around the sun if the space between was totally empty. It turns out that empty space is far from empty. Our galaxy, and all the others, are filled with dark matter.

The Pinwheel galaxy

The Alpha Magnetic Spectrometer

SCIENTISTS HAVE OBSERVED A GALAXY ABOUT 65 MILLION LIGHT-YEARS AWAY. CALLED NGC 1052-DF2, IT APPEARS TO HAVE ALMOST NO DARK MATTER.

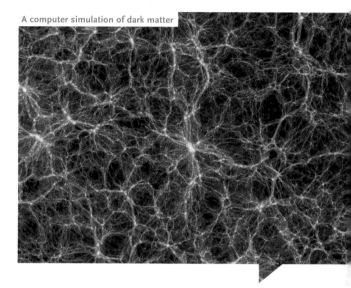
A computer simulation of dark matter

THEORETICAL PARTICLES

PICKING ON WIMPS

Scientists aren't certain what exactly dark matter is or where it comes from. Numerous theories have been formulated, but so far each one has been disputed. For decades scientists focused on a class of particles are known as WIMPs—weakly interacting massive particles. Some researchers are using ever more powerful colliders to search for these elusive entities; some seek evidence of dark matter collisions in sunken tanks containing various chemicals; a third approach is to study cosmic rays for evidence of dark matter. Some of the biggest and most expensive science experiments, both on and off the planet, are dedicated to searching out this mysterious form of matter. From the two-billion-dollar alpha magnetic spectrometer mounted on the International Space Station, to the Axion Dark Matter eXperiment (ADMX) in Seattle, Washington, the search is on.

SHINE A LIGHT

A NEW UNDERSTANDING

To reveal the secrets of dark matter would do more than unveil a new particle. It could rewrite our understanding of the universe. Dark matter is vital to create the universe around us; it is the soil where stars are born and the strings that connect galaxies. A simulated map of the dark universe we've identified reveals strands of the mystery material connecting stars, planets, and nebula in a vast intergalactic web. Some telescopes are able to study dark matter through its impact on light itself. Since dark matter affects gravity and gravity bends light, scientists have been able to literally "see" its effect. We can see it, but we do not know it. Not yet. So our universe is still literally held together by dark matter and mystery.

FURTHER

PATHWAY TO AN ICY FUTURE

We look to the icebound regions of the Poles—the lands above the Arctic Circle to the north and the frigid continent of Antarctica to the south—for signs that our human efforts to stave off global climate change might be making a difference. Cracks in the ice sheet and calving bergs cause concern. The Antarctic Peninsula, which stretches up toward South America, shows alarming signs of warming, despite eerily beautiful and frigid shades of aqua.

Sea-worn stones form a path to beached and broken sea ice on the Antarctic Peninsula.

> “WHAT HAPPENS IN THE ANTARCTIC DOES NOT STAY IN THE ANTARCTIC.”
>
> —FRANK PATTYN, GLACIOLOGIST

LIFE ON EARTH

ALL LIVING THINGS | **OF THE EARTH**

Endangered golden snub-nosed monkeys inhabit the Qinling Mountains in China.

OF THE SEA | OF THE SKY | CARE FOR ALL LIFE

QUIZ MASTER

Know Your Biosphere? Ever wonder what's the meaning of life? Start here for answers by exploring the many forms of life, from microbes to megafauna, from rarely seen life-forms to the plants and animals we know and love.

—CARA SANTA MARIA, *Our Favorite Nerd*

WHAT WAS THE **NAME** OF THE **SHEEP CLONED** IN 1996?
p161

p181
WHAT IS THE ONLY GREAT APE NATIVE TO A COUNTRY OUTSIDE OF **AFRICA?**

HOW MANY HEARTS DOES AN **OCTOPUS** **HAVE?**

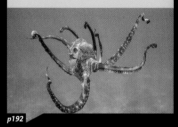
p192

IN WHAT YEAR DID NATURALIST **CARL LINNAEUS INTRODUCE THE BINOMIAL NAMING SYSTEM FOR PLANTS AND ANIMALS?**
p160

IN WHICH CANADIAN **PROVINCE WAS A** WELL-PRESERVED **SPECIMEN OF** NODOSAUR FOUND?

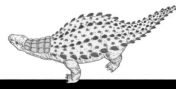
p170

NAME THE THREE **DOMAINS** OF LIFE.
p162

WHICH SPECIES OF **BUTTERFLY** IS THE OFFICIAL **STATE INSECT OF SEVEN** U.S. STATES?

p203

AN ANCIENT CREATURE KNOWN AS **PAKICETUS** WAS AN **ANCESTOR** TO WHICH **MODERN ANIMALS?**

p189

p183

ABOUT **HOW** LONG AGO **WERE** **DOGS** **FIRST** DOMESTICATED?

p176

IN WHAT **LANGUAGE DID** **KOKO THE** **GORILLA** **COMMUNICATE** WITH HUMANS?

HOW MANY **KNOWN** SPECIES OF HUMMINGBIRDS ARE THERE?

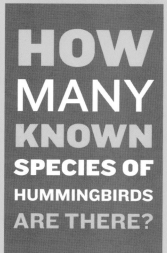

p198

p174

WHAT TYPE OF **INSECT** IS OUR MOST **VALUABLE** **POLLINATOR?**

p204

ABOUT HOW FAR **CAN A** NORTHERN **FLYING** SQUIRREL **GLIDE?**

ON WHICH CONTINENT WILL YOU FIND A SMALL **MARSUPIAL** KNOWN AS A QUOLL?

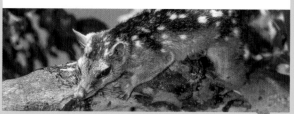

p178

LIFE SCIENCE
TIME LINE

900 to 1 BC

ca 900 BC
Neolithic farmers use fertilizer and irrigation.

ca 800 BC
Egyptians use artificially heated incubators to hatch eggs.

ca 400 BC
Hippocrates of Kos describes human anatomy.

ca 350 BC
Aristotle draws up a classification scheme for plants and animals.

300 BC
Diocles of Carystus is credited with writing the first text on anatomy.

AD 1 to 1100

77
Roman scholar Pliny the Elder summarizes natural history as known to the Romans in his *Naturalis Historia*.

752
Chinese physician Wang Tao describes ailments including diabetes and malaria, along with remedies.

ca 900
Arab physician Rhazes distinguishes between measles and smallpox.

ca 1075
Female physician Trotula of Salerno writes about hygiene and women's disorders.

1100 to 1600

ca 1260
Arab physician Ibn al-Nafis describes the pulmonary circulation of the blood.

1276
Giles of Rome discusses the role of both parents in procreation in his work, *De Formatione Corporis*.

1410
Italian physician Benedetto Rinio catalogs more than 500 medicinal plants.

1517
Girolamo Fracastoro proposes that fossils are the petrified remains of once living organisms.

1583
Italian botanist Andrea Cesalpino devises a system of classifying plants by their structure.

1600 to 1800

1658
Dutch naturalist Jan Swammerdam describes red blood cells.

1665
Robert Hooke coins the word "cell" to describe individual units in plant tissues.

1677
Dutch scientist Antonie van Leeuwenhoek reports on his observations of bacteria.

1735
Swedish naturalist Carl Linnaeus introduces the binomial naming system.

1796
Georges Cuvier identifies "elephant" remains from Siberia as a separate and extinct species: "mammoth."

1800 to 1900

1822
Englishwoman Mary Ann Mantell discovers teeth from one of the first fossils to be recognized as a dinosaur.

1831–1836
Darwin completes a five-year voyage on the H.M.S. *Beagle,* during which he conducted studies that lead to his theory of evolution.

1860
The first fossil of *Archaeopteryx,* a birdlike prehistoric flying reptile, is found.

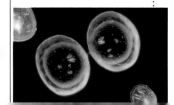

1865
Gregor Mendel presents his ideas on inheritance.

1876
Mitosis, the process of cell replication, is first described by Eduard Strasburger.

1900 to 1925

1900
Cuban-American physiologist Aristides Agramonte y Simoni discovers that yellow fever is transmitted through mosquitoes.

1901
Russian scientist Élie Metchnikoff determines the role of white blood cells in fighting infection.

1913
Alfred Sturtevant introduces the technique of chromosome mapping to record positions of genes.

1919
Karl von Frisch describes the "bee's dance," the way in which honeybees communicate.

1924
Fossils of human ancestor *Australopithecus* are discovered, helping establish Africa as the site of humankind's origins.

1925 to 1960

1926
Walter Cannon introduces the concept of homeostasis, in which the body's systems work together to maintain balance.

1944
Oswald Avery shows that nearly all organisms have DNA as their hereditary material.

1953
Francis Crick, James Watson, and Rosalind Franklin determine the double-helix structure of DNA.

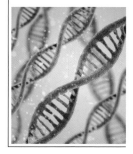

1960
Jane Goodall begins her studies of chimpanzees in Gombe, Tanzania.

1960 to PRESENT

1969
The first human eggs are fertilized using in vitro fertilization.

1996
Scottish scientists clone a sheep named Dolly.

2000
The Human Genome Project produces a rough draft of the human genome sequence.

2006
Analysis of a 375-million-year-old fossil shows it to be a "missing link" between fish and four-legged vertebrates.

2010
Genetic evidence shows that interbreeding between humans and Neanderthals took place and that some modern humans have Neanderthal genes.

DOMAINS OF LIFE

AN INVISIBLE WORLD

We share this planet with more than eight million other species, and each of them falls into one of only three types: Archaea, the ancient line; bacteria, the microbial line; and Eukarya, which includes plants, animals, fungus, and others.

ARCHAEA

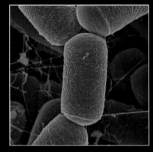

METHANOSARCINA SP.
A type of archaea
that produces methane

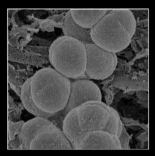

METHANOBREVIBACTER SP.
One of the archaea found
in the human gut

SULFOLOBUS SP.
Thrives in hot springs
>176°F (80°C)

ARCHAEA & BACTERIA

MILLIONS OF MICROORGANISMS

Archaea are so difficult to detect that they were unknown until the 1970s. They resemble bacteria in their simple shape and lack of complex cellular organs, but they are as genetically distinct from bacteria as humans are. Their ancient genetic markers suggest that life may have started in the hydrothermal vents of the deep ocean.

Despite their microscopic size, bacteria make up most of the mass of life on Earth. There are as many bacteria on your skin and inside your body as there are human cells making it up. Although the battle against bacterial infection has been common for centuries, this microbial world represents an ecosystem scientists are only starting to approach cohesively.

BACTERIA

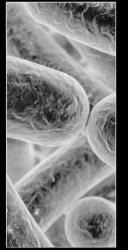

MYCOBACTERIUM SP.
This bacterium
causes tuberculosis.

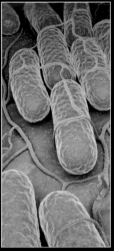

SALMONELLA SP.
Infected food causes
gastric disease.

FUNGI

POLYPORUS SP.
Shelf fungus, grows
on dead or dying trees

COOKEINA SP.
Tropical toadstool,
grows on trees

PLANTS

MAMMILLARIA SP.
Twin-spined cactus,
from Mexico

COSMOS
Annual seed-
bearing flower

POACEAE SP.
One of 8,000 species
of grasses

QUERCUS SP.
Southern live oak,
North America

EUKARYA

FROM FUNGI TO PRIMATES

Eukarya, which contain every complex multicellular organism on the planet, are divided into four taxonomic kingdoms: Plants, Animals, Fungi, and Protoctista. Despite their seeming diversity, Eukarya share a single set of characteristics: multicellular organisms with clearly defined cellular structures, such as a nucleus, mitochondria, and other organelles.

ANIMALS

TANGARA SP.
Golden-hooded tanager,
from Costa Rica

CHAETODON SP.
Masked butterfly fish,
from Asia

ELEPHANT
Two species,
Indian and African

CHIMPANZEE
In African rainforests,
woods, and grasslands

PLANTS UP CLOSE

A WHOLE NEW LOOK AT ROSEMARY

When it comes to evolution, plants are anything but placid. At a microscopic scale, plants are dazzlingly varied and have astonishing structural complexity. Modern imaging reveals the incredible structures plants use to transform sunlight into energy and energy into everything else. Inside the cellular walls, chemical kitchens create oils, acids, and toxins that plants use to attract allies or keep away predators. If you've ever thought the kingdom of plants is boring, take a closer look. Here is a colorized microscopic look at a leaf of rosemary, a beloved kitchen herb.

A WORD FROM

Forests as Families In a single forest, a mother tree can be connected to hundreds of other trees. Using our isotope tracers, we have found that mother trees will send their excess carbon through the mycorrhizal network to the understory seedlings—and we've associated this with increased seedling survival.

—SUZANNE SIMARD, *ecologist*

A microscopic view of a rosemary leaf reveals a functional coat of hair.

THROUGH PHOTOSYNTHESIS, PLANTS TURN SUNLIGHT, WATER, AND CARBON DIOXIDE INTO OXYGEN AND SUGARS. THIS NATURAL TURNAROUND RETURNS 100 BILLION NET TONS OF CARBON ANNUALLY TO THE PLANETWIDE SYSTEM AND GENERATES 40% OF THE PRECIPITATION THAT FALLS ON LAND.

Tiny repositories of oily essences help to fend off predators and give rosemary its distinctive flavor.

Under a microscope, the slight furriness of a rosemary leaf looks like a tangle of uncombed hairs.

Plant cells are mostly green because chlorophyll, the pigment central to photosynthesis, reflects green light and absorbs red and blue.

Talking Trees

THE SECRETS WAYS OUR FORESTS ARE COMMUNICATING

Beneath a single patch of forest soil lies a vast interconnected web of life. Forest ecologist Suzanne Simard likens it to a kind of hidden intelligence. By tracking specific chemicals, she and other scientists observed how trees in the Douglas fir forests of Canada "talk," forming underground symbiotic relationships, called mycorrhizae, with fungi to relay stress signals and share resources.

Douglas fir
(hub tree)

Douglas fir
(younger tree)

Excess sugar from photosynthesis

Understory nursery
Douglas fir trees use the network to identify and nurture related seedlings.

Douglas fir
(seedling)

Symbiotic
fungal network

Resource pathways

→ Sugar from trees
→ Nutrients from soil
→ Mixed resources from network: nutrients and carbon (from sugar)
→ Chemical stress signals

Nitrogen, potassium, phosphorus, and other nutrients

Enlarged section of tree root tip

Resource-exchange pathway

Fungal thread

Tree root cell

1.

Excess production
Taller, older trees, called hub trees, often have more access to sunlight and produce more sugar through photosynthesis than they need.

2.

Exchange of goods
A mass of fungal threads, or mycelium, envelops the root tips of a hub tree, feeding it nutrients from the soil in exchange for sugar, which the fungus lacks.

Western spruce
budworm

Paper
birch

Douglas fir
(hub tree)

Pine preparation
Fir trees infected with
budworms send stress
signals to nearby pines.

Chemical stress signals

Ponderosa
pine

In spring and fall, firs share
sugar with leafless birches.

In summer, birches return
the favor to shaded firs.

Symbiotic
fungal network

▶ FOREST IN
DISTRESS

3.

Deep connections
Weaker firs in the shaded understory tap
into the network as it swells with
resources. Firs can also share with other
species, such as birch.

WARNING SIGNS
Through the network, trees under stress can
transfer resources, such as water, and can
send chemical signals that trigger defensive
mechanisms in other trees. Threats like insect
infestation and drought are expected to
increase as the climate changes.

FOSSILS
PAST LIVES

LASTING IMPRESSIONS Fossils are the preserved remains or imprints of ancient living things. They offer clues about past life-forms and environments and are keys to understanding the evolution of life on Earth.

> **"** I WANT YOU TO SEE THE WORLD THROUGH THE EYES OF TRILOBITES ... MAKE A JOURNEY BACK THROUGH HUNDREDS OF MILLIONS OF YEARS.**"**
>
> **—RICHARD FORTEY, PALEONTOLOGIST**

PLANT PARTS
Leaves, spores, pollen from as far back as 450 mya

PETRIFIED WOOD
Preserved when minerals fill pores in organic material

GRAPTOLITES
Wormlike marine animals from 500–315 mya

BRYOZOANS
Aquatic colonies in shallow limestone formations

CORALS
Main component of reefs; some date to 500 mya

TRILOBITES
Extinct animals that once dominated Earth's oceans

BRACHIOPODS
Tens of thousands of species of these once flourished.

BIVALVES
Ancestors of today's clams, mussels, oysters, and scallops

GASTROPODS
Remains of ancient snails and sea slugs

AMMONITES
Spiral-shelled creatures once prolific, extinct about 65 mya

ECHINODERMS
Five-point symmetry, like sand dollars of today

CRINOIDS
Marine animals: flexible stalk, head of waving filaments

FISH
First vertebrates in fossil record, starting 500 mya

SHARK TEETH
One ancient species left behind teeth 7 inches long.

INSECTS
Amber, fossilized tree resin, has preserved whole bodies.

A fossil from the Burgess Shale in Canada shows a trilobite's flattened, segmented shape.

TRILOBITES

ANCESTORS OF THE HORSESHOE CRAB

In Earth's early seas, trilobites roamed, only known to us now through their distinctive shapes in the fossil record. Though paleontologists have identified more than 20,000 species of trilobite, we know very little about their behavior, diet, or even how they moved. A particularly well-preserved specimen found in Morocco in 2017 gave scientists some insight into their diets, which likely consisted of a mix of sediment feeding and scavenging.

TRILOBITES FIRST APPEARED MORE THAN 500 MILLION YEARS AGO DURING THE CAMBRIAN PERIOD.

NODOSAUR

AN ARMORED WONDER

This astonishing creature is a nodosaur, an armored dinosaur we know now better than ever thanks to fossils found in Alberta, Canada, in 2017. Traces of red pigment found on its body and the armor plates that scattered during decomposition remain preserved, though the fossil is around 110 million years old. The process of fossilization often distorts the core shape of living things, but this nodosaur was well preserved. Paleobiologist Jakob Vinther noted the specimen was so complete that it "might have been walking around a couple of weeks ago." The new discovery could reveal how dinosaur armor functioned and provide new windows into dinosaur evolution and behavior.

Fossilized remains were so complete, illustrators and sculptors could envision the nodosaur in all its detail.

THE WORD "FOSSIL" COMES FROM THE LATIN WORD *FOSSUS,* MEANING "HAVING BEEN DUG UP." FOSSILS ARE OFTEN FOUND IN ROCK FORMATIONS DEEP IN THE EARTH.

BEST OF @NATGEO

TOP PHOTOS OF LIFE ON LAND

@ronandonovan | RONAN DONOVAN
Mr. Blue, a well-known wolf in Yellowstone National Park, stands alert over a drowned bison.

@franslanting | FRANS LANTING
This tiny primate is a tarsier. Found in the rainforests of Borneo, they're about the size of a mouse.

@kengeiger | KEN GEIGER
With distinct spots called rosettes helping it blend in, a leopard rests in the shade at Kenya's Maasai Mara National Reserve.

@argonautphoto | AARON HUEY
A herd of African elephants drink from their trunks, which are actually long noses used for smelling, breathing, and grabbing things.

@stefanounterthiner | STEFANO UNTERTHINER
A crested black macaque cradles her baby while grooming another macaque, a way of maintaining relationships within their groups.

@franslanting | FRANS LANTING
Yet to become a fierce predator, a baby crocodile emerges from its egg in the Okavango Delta, Botswana.

@amivitale | AMI VITALE
A 16-year-old giant panda finds a perch in the Wolong Nature Reserve's panda center in China.

@florianschulzvisuals | FLORIAN SCHULZ
A mother polar bear nurses her cubs on an ice floe in the Arctic Circle, keeping them close for warmth.

TELLTALE TRACKS

Who Goes There? There is a hidden world all around you: Animals you do not see may still leave traces of their lives behind. By studying animal tracks, scientists and guides can estimate population size, ages, and even what the animal was doing as it left the marks.

VIRGINIA OPOSSUM
North America's only marsupial

BLACK-TAILED PRAIRIE DOG
Complex tunnel town dwellers

NORTHERN FLYING SQUIRREL
Can glide up to 300 feet

EASTERN GRAY SQUIRREL
Tail serves as umbrella or wrap.

GROUNDHOG
Also called woodchuck

EASTERN CHIPMUNK
Caches food underground for winter

AMERICAN BEAVER
Incisors fell trees to build dams.

NORTH AMERICAN PORCUPINE
Sharp quills fend off predators.

MUSKRAT
Still trapped for fur

NORTH AMERICAN DEER MOUSE
Huddles together in cold weather

HOUSE MOUSE
Can have up to 14 litters a year

NORWAY RAT
Prefers to live near humans

ANTELOPE JACKRABBIT
Huge ears help cool off.

EASTERN COTTONTAIL
Named for its powder-puff tail

NORTHERN SHORT-TAILED SHREW
Preys with poisonous bite

EASTERN MOLE
Flat, clawed forefeet dig tunnels

BOBCAT
Most widespread cat in North America

MOUNTAIN LION
Solitary unless mating

COYOTE
So adaptable, now in cities

RED FOX
Imported from Europe for sport

AMERICAN BLACK BEAR
Males weigh up to 900 pounds.

NORTH AMERICAN RIVER OTTER
Playful swimmer

BLACK FOOTED FERRET
Nearly extinct; takes over prairie dog dens

STRIPED SKUNK
Spray can be smelled half mile away.

RACCOON
Handy thanks to dexterous fingers

Black bear cubs follow their mother along water's edge in Alaska.

BLACK BEAR CUBS ARE GENERALLY BORN IN WINTER AND SPEND THEIR FIRST 18 MONTHS OF LIFE WITH THEIR MOTHERS.

BLACK BEARS

MAMMAL MODEL OF ADAPTABILITY

You can find the American black bear in forests across North America. As the smallest of the three American bears, the black bear may lack the massive size of polar bears or brown bears (better known as grizzlies), but it makes up for it in adaptability. There are estimated to be as many as 950,000 black bears living in North America—in Mexico, Canada, and 40 of the 50 states. They also aren't all black. Black bears' coats can come in red, brown, blond, and, rarely, blue and white. The secret to their success is adaptability. Black bears happily eat berries, insects, fish, mammals—almost anything they can get their paws on, even human trash.

A WORD FROM

Among the Bears There's only so much you can learn by measuring a tranquilized bear and putting dots on a map . . . Because if you want to learn about their habitat use, social organization, language—everything that makes a bear a bear—you have to at least see the animal that you're studying, and it can't be tranquilized. I knew I had to get close, and do more of a Jane Goodall kind of research.

—**LYNN ROGERS,** *biologist*

DOMESTICATION
TRANSFORMATION

ONCE WILD, NOW OUR FAITHFUL COMPANIONS

Playtime in a park

SHAPING DOGS

FROM WOLF TO WOOF

The process of domesticating dogs began at least 10,000 years ago, and it may have happened simultaneously in different parts of the world. It likely began by accident, as wolves followed human hunters, scavenging their kills or eating scraps. While no one is certain exactly what the early relationship looked like, the transformation from fearful antagonist to companion and guardian happened remarkably quickly. Social transformation led to genetic change as humans began selecting for preferential traits. Some dogs were bred for strength, others for speed, but virtually all of them were chosen based on their behavior toward humans—survival of the friendliest. It was a genetic experiment that we're now seeing in the DNA and behavior of modern dogs around the world.

SHAPING EVOLUTION

MAKING OUR BEST FRIENDS

Today they're our best friends, but we are still unraveling the process that transformed wild cats into house cats and wolves into springer spaniels. Domestication isn't just about behavior or tameness; the friendliest wild animal is still wild in ways our pets can never be again. As humans worked with animals, our domesticated friends underwent a remarkable transformation, human-led evolution that changed behavior, size, and coloration. Cats and dogs, cows and mice—dozens of species have undergone domestication, each one with a suite of physical changes. A puppy's floppy ears and curly tail, a cow's white spots and massive size, and the orange coat of a tabby cat are all physical manifestations of this transformation.

A wolf and a Maltese

Loving foxes

HOW TO MAKE A PET

EFFORTS TO REENACT EVOLUTION

In 1959, Russian geneticist Dmitry Belyaev began to study 130 silver foxes, breeding together the tamest individuals and those most responsive to humans. The goal was to re-create in miniature the long journey from wolves to dogs.

After six generations, the foxes were eager for human contact and attention. Physical changes also occurred. The foxes' tails shrank, the pups' ears stayed floppy, their tails began to wag, they began to lick their humans' faces, and they acted more like trusting young kits than wary adult foxes: a suite of genetic changes that have become known as the domestication phenotype.

EARTH DAY EVERY DAY

House Cats and
WILD BIRDS

According to the American Bird Conservancy, domesticated cats allowed to roam outdoors kill some 2.4 billion birds each year. The World Conservation Union (IUCN) includes house cats on their list of the world's 100 worst invasive species. By keeping pet cats indoors, you can help save biodiversity and beloved songbird species.

STUDIES HAVE FOUND THAT MANY DOGS CAN RECOGNIZE DIFFERENT EMOTIONS, AND MAY EVEN MIMIC THE EMOTIONAL STATE OF HUMANS THAT THEY'RE CLOSE TO.

A few genes govern breed variability.

PET GENETICS

UNRAVELING THE DNA

When Belyaev's experiment began, genetic sequencing was a distant dream. But he believed that genetic changes could contain the answers he sought. Because dog breeds have almost always been governed by human selection, the deliberate creation and cultivation of traits has left clues in the genome that can be traced. Just a single gene can change a dog's size from Dachshund scale to Rottweiler scale. Hair length, ear shape, coat color, even fur type are all controlled by about 50 genetic switches. The diversity of dogs and their domestication is not a natural wonder. We have shaped our animal companions to be as amazing as they are. They are our perfect companions because we made them that way.

MEET THE
QUOLL

A MARSUPIAL ON THE MEND

This cat-size marsupial is a quoll, once native to Australia. Depleted habitat and introduced predators including cats drove them to the edge of extinction. Three subspecies survive in Australia, but one, the eastern quoll, persisted only in Tasmania. In 2017, 20 eastern quolls were released into southeastern Australia in the hope that these creatures will reestablish themselves in their original homeland.

TOXIC CANE TOADS, UNWITTINGLY INTRODUCED TO AUSTRALIA IN 1935, ACCOUNT FOR RECENT QUOLL DEATHS, BUT CARETAKERS HAVE BEEN TRAINING TASTE AVERSION IN SOME OF THE QUOLLS BEFORE REINTRODUCING THEM INTO THE WILD.

Quolls usually spend daytime in their dens, but sometimes they venture out to forage.

Wildlife Found Only in
AUSTRALIA

■ SOUTHERN CASSOWARY
Cassowaries are large, flightless birds—relatives to emus, ostriches, and kiwis. The southern cassowary is the largest of three species, standing up to six feet tall and weighing up to 160 pounds.

■ TASMANIAN DEVIL
These feisty mammals have one of the most powerful bites relative to their size in the animal kingdom. They were once common across the continent of Australia, but now their range is limited to the island of Tasmania.

■ KOALA
Though they're often called koala bears, these small gray animals are actually marsupials. Their diet is almost exclusively made of leaves from eucalyptus trees—a single koala can eat up to three pounds of leaves in a single day.

■ RED KANGAROO
One of the most recognizable Australian species, the red kangaroo is the largest marsupial in the world. With their powerful hind legs, they can jump up to six feet high and cover 25 feet in a single leap.

■ PLATYPUS
One of the few egg-laying mammals in the world, platypuses look like a mixture of a duck and a beaver. They're amphibious creatures that feed on frogs and fish and burrow into muddy riverbanks.

■ LAUGHING KOOKABURRA
Found in the eastern forests, the laughing kookaburra has a distinctive call that sounds a bit like manic laughter. Their long, distinctive beaks help them catch the small lizards, snakes, and insects that their diet comprises.

PRIMATE FAMILY TREE

OUR DISTANT COUSINS

Humans have many characteristics that make each of us unique, but biologically, we're not a class unto ourselves. Among the more than 500 different species of primate, we humans are just one. And these days, our family could use some help: Most of our cousins live in the shrinking tropical rainforest, and two-thirds of us are at risk of extinction.

SPECTRAL TARSIER

One of the smallest primates in the world is a scant three and a half inches in length. Although they may look adorable, tarsiers are the only truly carnivorous primates, grabbing beetles, bats, and even snakes—often in midair—before devouring them.

GOLDEN LION TAMARIN

These iconic creatures live in the forests of Brazil. Tamarin juveniles, which are raised by the entire community, are sometimes twins—rare among primates. Once on the edge of extinction, tamarins have been saved by intensive conservation efforts.

HAMADRYAS BABOON

These amazingly social creatures can often be seen in troops numbering in the hundreds. Though found across northeast Africa and the Arabian Peninsula, they are locally extinct in Egypt, where they were once revered as favorites of Thoth, the ancient Egyptian god of learning.

ORANGUTAN

Orangutans are the only great apes found outside of Africa: They live in the forests of Borneo and Sumatra, where they spend almost all of their time aloft. Like many primates, they have been seen creating and using simple tools when hunting and are chimpanzees' closest genetic relatives.

GORILLA

The largest of the primates, gorillas may look intimidating, but these herbivorous apes are more Curious George than King Kong. They spend most of their day wandering about, eating plants, and building new nests every night. A group of gorillas, called a "troop," can be as large as 30 individuals.

CHIMPANZEE

One of our closest genetic relatives, chimps live in tightly bonded families, use tools, and even eat medicinal plants when injured. Generally fruit and plant eaters, they also consume insects, eggs, and meat, including carrion. With such a varied diet, they can habituate themselves to African rainforests, woodlands, and grasslands. They are known to make weapons, commit murder, and even coordinate attacks on other tribes.

> " WE ARE, INDEED, UNIQUE PRIMATES, WE HUMANS, BUT WE'RE SIMPLY NOT AS DIFFERENT FROM THE REST OF THE ANIMAL KINGDOM AS WE USED TO THINK."
>
> —JANE GOODALL, PRIMATOLOGIST

A WORD FROM

Compassionate Conservation
Working with the gorillas taught me how readily our emotions, our sense of compassion, and our humanity influence conservation decisions. I finally understood that conservation is more than a science. I realized it was time to shift gears in my career and start teaching. I no longer wanted to work to save the last of a species or focus just on the science of veterinary medicine. I wanted to help inspire the next generation of conservationists.

—LUCY SPELMAN, *wildlife biologist*

KOKO
THE SIGNING GORILLA

ANIMAL AMBASSADOR

By the time of her death in 2018, Koko knew over 2,000 words in American Sign Language and held extended conversations with journalists, scientists, and entertainers. Her gentleness, playfulness, and humor led to a new imagining of animals' mental and emotional lives.

As Koko signals "eat" by moving her fingertips to her mouth, Francine Patterson rewards her with a treat.

Koko was born on July 4, 1971, at the San Francisco Zoo. When she was just one year old, she started working with Francine Patterson, then a graduate student in psychology at Stanford University. Earlier experiments had focused on primates' mimicking human speech, but Project Koko focused instead on sign language. The outcome seemed incredible. Koko made tremendous progress "talking" about her world. She showed interest in books, painting, and small animals, especially kittens, picking them up to pet or nurture. Her ability and seeming willingness to talk captured public attention.

Koko appeared in numerous documentaries and television shows, and twice on the cover of *National Geographic*. She became a celebrity in her own right, appearing with Mister Rogers and Robin Williams. Her adoption of the kitten All Ball became an image for animal empathy and inspired multiple children's books. She was an icon and ambassador but, despite many attempts, never a parent.

A LASTING LEGACY

Some scientists are skeptical of Koko's abilities. They see trained behaviors and anthropomorphism rather than independent speech, and some argue that her trainers and the public saw in Koko what they wanted to see. While Koko's fame has lasted, the idea of primate-speech studies has not, and few are ongoing. Even after her death in 2018, Koko offers hope for the possibility of interspecies communication.

> **" UNCONTAMINATED BY HUMANS, [GORILLAS] ARE DEFINITELY CLOSER TO LIVING IN THE NOW . . . THEY ARE SO MUCH IN HARMONY WITH NATURE, WE SURELY COULD USE THEM AS A MODEL."**
>
> **—FRANCINE PATTERSON,** PSYCHOLOGIST AND KOKO'S TEACHER

A western lowland gorilla, Koko lived to age 46.

KEY FACTS

Other Famous TALKING ANIMALS

ALEX, GRAY PARROT In 1977, Irene Pepperberg bought an African gray parrot from a pet shop. Over the next 30 years Alex learned over 100 English words and simple math skills.

HECTOR AND HAN, BOTTLENOSE DOLPHINS These two young male dolphins seem to understand a request to innovate, responding by not performing the same trick twice in a given session.

CHANTEK, ORANGUTAN While living with anthropologist Lyn Miles, Chantek learned to communicate using American Sign Language, clean his room, and use a toilet.

BEST OF @NATGEO

TOP PHOTOS OF SEA LIFE

@brianskerry | BRIAN SKERRY
Green sea turtles mate off the coast of St. Croix in the U.S. Virgin Islands. These endangered turtles can weigh up to 700 pounds.

@cristinamittermeier | CRISTINA MITTERMEIER
With its tail fin poised, a humpback whale dives into ocean off the Antarctic Peninsula.

@brianskerry | BRIAN SKERRY
A spinner dolphin—known for its aerial maneuvers—jumps from calm waters after a morning storm in Oahu, Hawaii.

@carltonward | CARLTON WARD
Manatees breathe air above surface, but this mother and calf dip underwater during a rain shower in King's Bay, Florida.

@mattiasklumofficial | MATTIAS KLUM
Clownfish have a symbiotic relationship with a stinging anemone; in exchange for safe shelter, the fish cleans and defends the anemone.

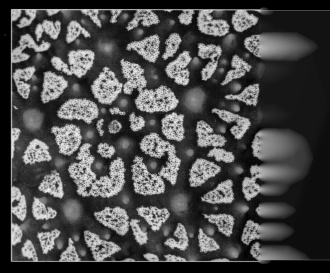

@timlaman | TIM LAMAN
Up close, the bright colors and intricate details of a sea star's skin are revealed.

@enricsala | ENRIC SALA
A Galápagos sea lion searches for its next meal in a large school of salema fish off the coast of Isabela Island.

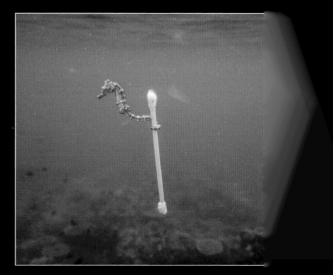

@justinhofman | JUSTIN HOFMAN
Using its tail like a finger, a seahorse snatches trash caught in the current around the Indonesian islands.

SAVE THE REEFS

PARADISE ALMOST LOST

Coral reefs may seem like an explosion of color, but coral themselves are translucent. Reefs get their radiant hues by hosting billions of colorful algae, which they use for food. Unfortunately, when waters warm, reefs expel these algae, leaving the reefs bleached and damaged. Back-to-back bleaching events in 2016 and 2017 damaged or destroyed over half of the Great Barrier Reef. A quarter of all marine species live on the reefs and rely on these algae. Without them, the whole ecosystem crumbles.

Color abounds at the Great Detached Reef on the Northern Great Barrier Reef.

> **"NOT SO LONG AGO, A CORAL REEF WAS JUST IN THE WAY OF A** HOUSING DEVELOPMENT. **YOU CAN DREDGE IT AND FILL IT AND PUT HOTELS ON TOP. NOW WE HAVE A** BETTER PERSPECTIVE **ON WHAT** CORAL REEFS **GIVE US."** —SYLVIA EARLE, OCEANOGRAPHER

EARTH DAY EVERY DAY

Protecting
CORAL LIFE

Diving a coral reef can be the experience of a lifetime, but it can also be a threat to the ecosystem you're observing. Keep the corals safe by only using eco-conscious operators, never touching the reef with any part of a body or boat, and wearing sun-protective clothes instead of applying sunscreen, which has harsh chemicals that can promote coral bleaching.

WHALES

LEARNING FROM THESE GIANTS OF THE SEA

A sperm whale tail

OCEAN ELDERS

A SPECTACLE OF SIZE AND LONGEVITY

Whales are some of the largest animals in the history of Earth, and some of the most graceful. Blue whales, which can weigh up to 150 tons and measure as long as the boats sent to watch them, glide with seemingly no effort. They leap from the water, spin, and dive with casual elegance.

Some whales can dive more than 10,000 feet into the darkest depths, going hours between breaths. The rewards for these astonishing dives are squid, krill, and crustaceans. The whale's massive size comes with a long life span. Baby whales can take a decade to reach adulthood, and even the shortest lived whales can live for 40 years, the longest for more than 200.

WHALE SONG

SOUNDS OF THE SEA

In the deep sound channel of the open ocean, the clicks and songs of whales filter in from thousands of miles away. For many, it is the song of the sea, and all whales are part of its chorus. These animals, including the blue whale, the largest mammal on Earth, fill the ocean with their haunting melody.

Like bats or dolphins, some whales can echolocate, using their calls to "see" objects through reflected soundwaves. Other whale songs are used to show off for mates or rivals, while mothers and calves whisper to each other to avoid aquatic eavesdroppers. Sometimes whale pods sing in something near conversation across hundreds of miles. Still, evolutionarily, this is a recent soundtrack, and the song of the whales wasn't always aquatic.

A humpback whale calf

A mother blue whale and her calf

SPERM WHALES HAVE THE LARGEST BRAINS EVER KNOWN TO EXIST ON EARTH, MEASURING NEARLY 500 CUBIC INCHES. A HUMAN BRAIN IS ABOUT 80 CUBIC INCHES.

A pod of sperm whales

EVOLUTIONARY HISTORY

THE EARLIEST WHALES

Pakicetus was an ancient ancestor of the massive blue whales and all other cetaceans, a group of marine mammals that includes dolphins and porpoises. With a hairy coat, four legs, a long tail, and a long, narrow mouth, this distant relative looked more like a German shepherd than a cetacean. It lived alongside the ocean, not in it, but over millions of years it evolved into more and more of an ocean dweller. Archaeologists have reconstructed the story piece by piece, watching the slow transformation of ankles to fins, and long snouts to massive mouths.

PROTECTING WHALES

KEEPING MARINE MAMMALS SAFE

They may be titans in the sea, but whales are under threat. Commercial whaling continues in countries like Iceland, Norway, and Japan, and traditional indigenous spear hunting continues as well. Whales often meet with accidental threats as well— entanglement in fishing lines or nets, strikes by oceangoing vessels. Changes in the temperature and water quality of the ocean affect their survival as well.

Climate change, the threat for most animals, hits some species harder than others. Some whales like the vaquita live in specialized climates, with no escape, while global wanderers like the gray whales are thriving in warmer waters and venturing into new regions.

A WORD FROM

Creating Crittercam I conceived of Crittercam as a scientific tool, a way of studying animal behavior in places people access. What I didn't expect was the tremendous attraction the resulting images hold for people. Every time we deploy, Crittercam brings home the animal's point of view . . . a perspective that allows people to connect with the animal and its struggles to survive. It's this empathic experience that I didn't necessarily expect when I invented Crittercam.

—**GREG MARSHALL,** *biologist and cinematographer*

SEA SHELLS

A Home in the Sea Creatures started building shells around 500 million years ago. Since then, they have evolved spirals, spines, and ridges, but the purpose is still the same: to protect the delicate animal living inside it.

FLORIDA FIGHTING CONCH
Spurred foot for defense, burrowing

FRILLED DOGWINKLE
Preys with tongue and poison

KNOBBED WHELK
Like conch, can be made into a horn

LETTERED OLIVE
Used by Native Americans for jewelry

ATLANTIC PLATE LIMPET
Attaches to rocks by suction

ATLANTIC SLIPPER SHELL
Shells stack for reproduction

BAY SCALLOP
Senses predators with 18 pairs of eyes

PACIFIC LITTLENECK CLAM
Abundant in U.S. West Coast shallows

EASTERN OYSTER
Must attach to hard surface to mature

PACIFIC RAZOR CLAM
Meaty edible bivalve

ATLANTIC JACKKNIFE CLAM
Digs itself down into sand or mud

ATLANTIC AUGER
Stuns prey with poisonous barb

PACIFIC GEODUCK
Can age to more than 150 years

NORTHERN QUAHOG
Harvested for clam chowder

MARINE MUSSEL
One of many edible mussel species

BLACK TURBAN SNAIL
Feeds on algae, has many predators

COMMON MARSH SNAIL
Breathes air, feeds on marsh grasses

COMMON PERIWINKLE
Two antennae, one foot

RED ABALONE
Long valued for pearlescent colors

VIOLET SEA SNAIL
Churns bubbles and floats to survive

> **" NATURE IS THE MOST BEAUTIFUL ENGINEER AND IT ALWAYS HAS A REASON FOR CHOOSING ANY SHAPE."**
>
> **—DR. CHANDRA TIWARY,** INDIAN INSTITUTE OF SCIENCE

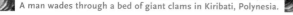

A man wades through a bed of giant clams in Kiribati, Polynesia.

CLAMMING UP

MARINE MARVELS

Clams, snails, and giant squids all are mollusks, one of the most diverse groups of life on Earth. There are more than 100,000 known species, but the number may be twice that, found in every aquatic environment from freshwater lakes to deep-sea trenches. Mollusks are invertebrates, with a mantle covering the soft body. Some possess a biological glue stronger than any other substance in nature, and some can survive briefly outside their aquatic environment. Their abundance and versatility has made them desirable food. In fact, early American waters had so many oysters, they were considered peasant food. Today they are an expensive gourmet treat.

THE AMAZING
OCTOPUS

UNDERWATER GENIUSES

The octopus is a strange animal. Its three hearts pump blue blood through a boneless frame. Some can compress their bodies from three feet across to the size of a quarter. Other species mimic textures and shapes like ridges, bumps, or spines. It takes a common octopus approximately two seconds to fully camouflage itself with its surroundings. Octopuses may have been the first intelligent creature on Earth, yet of their 500 million neurons, two-thirds are located in their arms, not their heads.

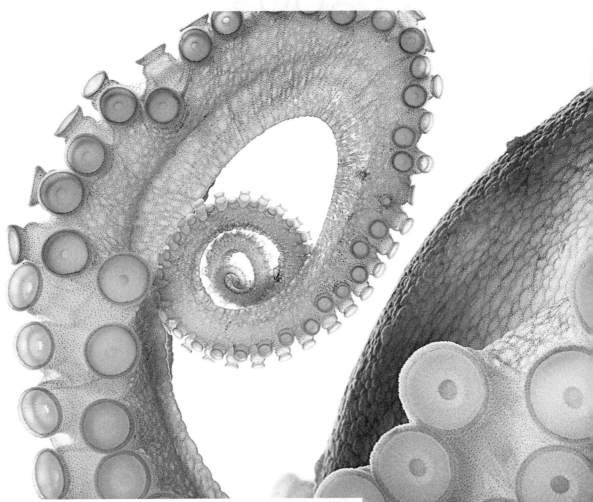

The common octopus's pigment cells and special muscles give it unique camouflage abilities.

THE LARGEST OCTOPUS EVER RECORDED WAS A GIANT PACIFIC OCTOPUS THAT MEASURED 30 FEET ACROSS AND WEIGHED MORE THAN 600 POUNDS.

BEST OF @NATGEO

TOP PHOTOS OF LIFE ON THE WING

@franslanting | FRANS LANTING
n addition to their large, colorful bills, toucans have bright
blue and orange skin surrounding their eyes.

@timlaman | TIM LAMAN
A male red bird-of-paradise begins an elaborate courtship display. The species is found only in the West Papuan Islands.

@carltonward | CARLTON WARD
Common in eastern North America, barred owls make a
range of calls and are more likely to be heard during the day
than other owls.

@joelsartore | JOEL SARTORE
These bright colors actually help the red-winged parrot
blend into its native rainforest environment.

@jasperdoest | JASPER DOEST
Flamingos are often seen in flocks gathered on mudflats, but his arthritic Caribbean flamingo favors water.

@stephenwilkes | STEPHEN WILKES
A group of migrating sandhill cranes take wing in Nebraska against the setting sun.

@brianskerry | BRIAN SKERRY
A mother gentoo penguin and her chick stick close together. Hatchling gentoos stay in the nest for up to a month.

@argonautphoto | AARON HUEY
A lone bird soars above the roofline in the old city of Kabul, Afghanistan.

BACKYARD
BIRDS

Flights of Fascination Birds wing their way through everyone's landscape, on every continent, whether hot or cold, rural or urban. Birding is about more than checking lists: Birders turn their love of these avians into real science.

AMERICAN GOLDFINCH
One of the few vegan birds

HOUSE FINCH
Males have rose-colored breast.

BALTIMORE ORIOLE
Weaves hanging nest of fibers

AMERICAN ROBIN
Traditional sign of spring

BLACK-CAPPED CHICKADEE
Chirps its own name

WESTERN BLUEBIRD
Nests in knotholes or birdhouses

EASTERN BLUEBIRD
Eats primarily insects and grubs

SONG SPARROW
May raise two or more broods a year

TUFTED TITMOUSE
Hoards food for winter

WARBLING VIREO
Melodious, recognizable song

NORTHERN CARDINAL
Males bright red, females olive

HOUSE SPARROW
Prefers to live near to humans

NORTHERN FLICKER
Digs in soil for ants and beetles

HOUSE WREN
Wide range, Canada through S. America

RED-WINGED BLACKBIRD
Winter flocks in the millions

RUBY-THROATED HUMMINGBIRD
Sips from red and orange flowers

GREAT HORNED OWL
Head swivels to look in all directions.

EASTERN PHOEBE
Perching, tail wags up and down

EUROPEAN STARLING
Mimics calls of other birds

CLIFF SWALLOW
Creates gourd-shaped nest of mud

AMERICAN CROW
Crafts tools to get at food

PURPLE MARTIN
Will move into erected nesting boxes

NORTHERN MOCKINGBIRD
May learn 200 different songs

WHITE-BREASTED NUTHATCH
Creeps along tree trunks, often head down

BLUE JAY
Throat pouch can hold 2–3 acorns.

Common ravens are the largest perching birds in North America.

CORVIDS

A family that includes ravens, crows, and magpies, corvids are often recognized as some of the most intelligent birds in the world. Their abilities run the gamut from mimicking other animal sounds to using tools and other problem-solving skills. Researchers studying animal cognition have found that ravens are able to preplan tasks, a skill once thought to be unique to humans and great apes. The Eurasian magpie, with its distinct black and white plumage, recognizes its own reflection in a mirror. Some species of crow recognize human faces, and sometimes they are more comfortable with humans they have interacted with before than with strangers.

MYTHICAL BIRDS

Corvids feature prominently in folklore across cultures and religions. In the Old Testament, it is said that Noah sent out both a raven and a dove to see if floodwaters had receded. In some Native American traditions, a raven swallowed the sun out of jealousy. The Norse God Odin had two ravens, named Huginn and Muninn— thought and memory.

> **"IF YOU TAKE CARE OF BIRDS, YOU TAKE CARE OF MOST OF THE ENVIRONMENTAL PROBLEMS IN THE WORLD."**
>
> **—THOMAS E. LOVEJOY,**
> **CONSERVATION BIOLOGIST**

A WORD FROM

Better Together [Crows] have this family unit, but they also have a neighborhood that they have some allegiance to as well. You keep your territory and you don't let the neighbors in, but if a predator is attacking them, you go help. They all know everybody in the neighborhood; they know what's happening by what everybody else is saying.

—KEVIN MCGOWAN, *ornithologist*

HUMMINGBIRDS
WINGED WONDERS

FIREWORKS IN FLIGHT

Hummingbirds fly like magical fairies and shimmer like jewels in the sky, but scientists have never fully understood these glorious birds. The hummingbird can fly backward, hover, and even fly sideways—all at incredible speed. But how? The answer comes in unique biological adaptations only recently discovered: larger brains to process information, symmetrical wing strokes, and longer "hands" for greater flexibility and movement. Despite their diminutive size—the smallest of 340 species weighs less than two grams—their brain represents 4.2 percent of their body weight, making it proportionally one of the largest in the animal kingdom.

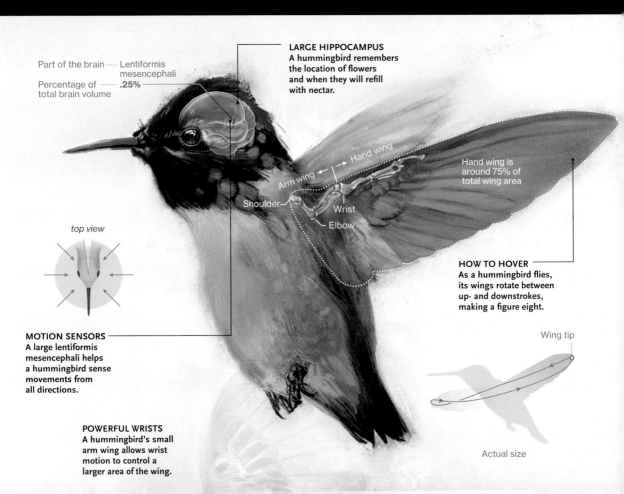

Part of the brain ···· Lentiformis mesencephali

Percentage of ······· .25% total brain volume

LARGE HIPPOCAMPUS
A hummingbird remembers the location of flowers and when they will refill with nectar.

Hand wing

Arm wing

Shoulder

Wrist

Elbow

Hand wing is around 75% of total wing area

top view

MOTION SENSORS
A large lentiformis mesencephali helps a hummingbird sense movements from all directions.

HOW TO HOVER
As a hummingbird flies, its wings rotate between up- and downstrokes, making a figure eight.

Wing tip

POWERFUL WRISTS
A hummingbird's small arm wing allows wrist motion to control a larger area of the wing.

Actual size

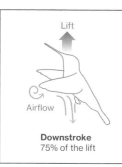

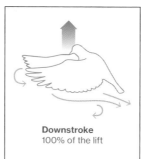

| **Downstroke**
75% of the lift | **Upstroke**
25% of the lift | **Downstroke**
100% of the lift | **Upstroke**
0% of the lift |

DOWNSTROKE
Hummingbirds produce lift with both upward and downward wing strokes.

UPSTROKE
They can beat their wings up to 100 times a second.

PROPULSION
In larger birds, all the propulsion comes from downward wing strokes.

FORWARD
Larger birds tend to fly forward rather than hovering.

> ## " THE HUMMINGBIRD IN FLIGHT IS A WATER-SPARK, AN INCANDESCENT DRIP OF AMERICAN FIRE."
> **—PABLO NERUDA, POET**

SEEING EVERY MOVE

FLIGHT OF HANDS

By using super-high-speed cameras to slow down time, scientists are finally unlocking the secrets of the world's smallest bird. Hummingbirds have, proportionally, the longest hands and shortest arms of any bird. Arm wings are often used for gliding, while hand wings provide the lift. With a larger hand wing, hummingbirds can rotate the shape of their wing on every stroke, generating precise and constant lift, at the cost of constant flapping. Moving at this speed and control takes massive brainpower. Here too, the hummingbird is unique, having proportionally the second largest brain in the animal kingdom. Speed, smarts, and control are vital for the birds to access the nectar they so desperately need.

TOP FIVE

Best Flowers for
HUMMINGBIRDS

1 **SCARLET BEE BALM**
Hummingbirds love this hardy perennial. Its red, pink, or lavender petals catch a wandering bird's eye.

2 **CARDINAL FLOWER** This 48-inch-tall flower is loaded with long-lasting deep-red blossoms providing nectar and height to any garden.

3 **TRUMPET VINE** The bright orange flowers on this creeping vine delight hummingbirds and other avians but can take over small areas.

4 **LUPINE** This early blooming flower attracts the first hummingbirds of the season.

5 **BUTTERFLY BUSH** True to its name, the thick clusters of flowers on this bountiful bush attract insects as well as hummingbirds.

PARROTS

MORE THAN JUST POLLY AND HER CRACKER

A row of macaws

SUCH DIVERSITY

A PLETHORA OF PARROTS

From the streets of San Francisco to the tip of South Africa, the Peruvian Amazon to the jungles of New Guinea, you can find parrots on five of the seven continents. The extensive range of these birds has led to incredible biodiversity. There are over 350 kinds of parrot scattered across the globe, appearing in all sizes: A tiny pygmy parrot measures just three inches across, while the hyacinth macaw's wingspan stretches more than three feet when fully spread.

Most are a riot of colors—pale greens and teal blues, deep blacks and violent reds—though others, like the African grays, are more muted. These birds aren't just beautiful flashes in the wilderness. Some of the larger species of parrots can live for over 80 years.

SOCIAL CREATURES

FLOCKING TOGETHER

At night in the tropics, the oldest, tallest trees in the forest resound with the singsong conversation of flocks of parrots. Tree canopies form the heart of a parrot's social life, and parrot parents often nest in the hollowed-out core of the tree below. Lorikeets, lovebirds, and cockatoos gather in flocks of hundreds or even thousands.

Unfortunately, this socialization has made them a prime target of trappers, who often gather numerous birds at once. In Mexico alone, up to 75,000 birds were harvested in a single year, and more than 75 percent of the birds harvested die before they even make it into trade. In the pet market, they often face a life of stress and isolation and develop symptoms of anxiety and depression.

Scarlet macaws

A crimson-fronted parakeet

LANGUAGE LEARNERS

AN INSTINCT FOR IMITATION

While many birdcalls are biologically hardwired, parrots learn language from their flock. Some flocks develop unique accents and dialects. Certain calls can act as passwords, with parrot calls identifying outsiders to the flock. While parrots are famous for their mimicry—several species can accurately mimic other birdcalls, fire alarms, and even human speech—it's not limited to copying. Parrots have shown complex reasoning skills on the same scale as chimpanzees or small children.

PARROTS HAVE TASTE BUDS ON THE INSIDE OF THEIR BEAKS AS WELL AS ON THEIR TONGUES.

Australian king parrots

WILDLIFE TRADE

A WILDLIFE DISASTER

No order of birds has been more exploited in the wild than the parrot, and no individual bird more than the African gray parrot. More than 1.3 million African grays were removed from the continent legally, and it's unknown how many others were smuggled out or died in transit. In Ghana, the population of African grays has been reduced by 99 percent, and a bird once as common as a pigeon is now exceedingly rare. Australian palm cockatoos can fetch up to $30,000 per bird and have attracted the types of organized crime usually associated with elephant and rhino poaching. The international pet trade means we may be loving these animals to death.

WHOSE CATERPILLAR?

MIRACULOUS TRANSFORMATION

The famous transformation from caterpillar to butterfly looks a little different to scientists studying the creatures than to poets writing about them. To change their structure so completely, caterpillars almost completely dissolve themselves into a stem cell soup inside the cocoon. They rebuild themselves from scratch using pockets of specialized imaginal cells before emerging in their new form.

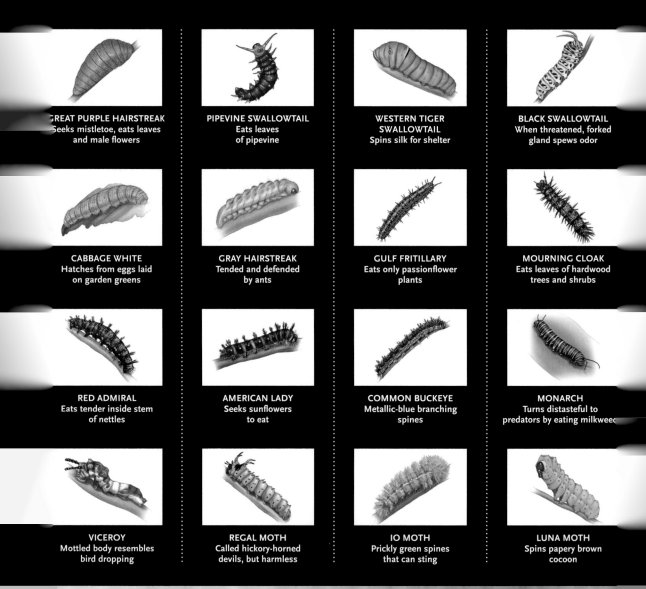

GREAT PURPLE HAIRSTREAK
Seeks mistletoe, eats leaves and male flowers

PIPEVINE SWALLOWTAIL
Eats leaves of pipevine

WESTERN TIGER SWALLOWTAIL
Spins silk for shelter

BLACK SWALLOWTAIL
When threatened, forked gland spews odor

CABBAGE WHITE
Hatches from eggs laid on garden greens

GRAY HAIRSTREAK
Tended and defended by ants

GULF FRITILLARY
Eats only passionflower plants

MOURNING CLOAK
Eats leaves of hardwood trees and shrubs

RED ADMIRAL
Eats tender inside stem of nettles

AMERICAN LADY
Seeks sunflowers to eat

COMMON BUCKEYE
Metallic-blue branching spines

MONARCH
Turns distasteful to predators by eating milkweed

VICEROY
Mottled body resembles bird dropping

REGAL MOTH
Called hickory-horned devils, but harmless

IO MOTH
Prickly green spines that can sting

LUNA MOTH
Spins papery brown cocoon

BUTTERFLIES SIP WATER, NECTAR, AND EVEN ANIMAL BLOOD USING A LONG, THIN PROBOSCIS. ALTHOUGH IT LOOKS LIKE A STRAW, BUTTERFLIES DO NOT SUCK THROUGH IT. INSTEAD, THE ORGAN SOAKS UP FLUID BY CAPILLARY ACTION, AS IF IT WERE A TUBE MADE OUT OF PAPER TOWEL.

GREAT PURPLE HAIRSTREAK
Brilliant blue on upper wing

PIPEVINE SWALLOWTAIL
Poisons from pipevine deter predators.

WESTERN TIGER SWALLOWTAIL
Clusters in mud puddles

BLACK SWALLOWTAIL
Courting pairs flutter before landing.

CABBAGE WHITE
One of spring's first butterflies

GRAY HAIRSTREAK
3–4 generations a year in the southern U.S.

GULF FRITILLARY
Migrates south to escape cold

MOURNING CLOAK
Long life span of 11–12 months

RED ADMIRAL
Prefers dung and carrion to nectar

AMERICAN LADY
Males are territorial.

COMMON BUCKEYE
Wing eyespots may scare predators.

MONARCH
State insect or butterfly in seven U.S. states

VICEROY
Mirrors bitter-tasting monarch as defense

REGAL MOTH
Adults do not eat at all.

IO MOTH
When disturbed, spreads wings to show eyespots

LUNA MOTH
Wing tails distract bats from preying on body.

PLIGHT OF
THE HONEYBEE

POLLINATOR IN PERIL

One of tens of thousands of pollinating species, honeybees do more than their share: It's estimated that one out of eight nonagricultural plants around the world was pollinated by honeybees. But honeybees face many threats: habitat loss, monoculture farming, pesticides, and parasitic mites, to name several. Since wild bees often don't produce honey, commercial honeybees are imported, but these nonnative bees can spread disease to wild populations or turn invasive. Wild bees are suffering as a result, some seeing population drops of 70 percent and others going completely extinct. The humble workers of the bee world can't seem to catch a break.

Worker bees forage for pollen and nectar; they are the only bees that most people see.

IN SUMMER, A HONEYBEE QUEEN LAYS UP TO 2,500 EGGS A DAY.

How to Help
HONEYBEES

■ **PLANT A POLLINATOR GARDEN**
Green lawns are deserts for bees. Add flowering plants and gardens to your yard.

■ **BUY LOCAL RAW HONEY**
Local honey supports local bees and promotes local beekeeping.

■ **DON'T REMOVE NATURAL WEEDS AND LOCAL PLANTS**
A field of dandelions is a feast for the bees. Let the weeds live!

■ **AVOID PESTICIDES ON LAWNS AND PLANTS**
These chemicals kill off insects and bugs, already at risk.

■ **PROVIDE A SMALL, SHALLOW WATER BASIN**
Bees can get thirsty too. Offering water helps them stay productive.

CONSERVATION
TIME LINE

8000 to 1 BC	AD 1 to 1850	1850 to 1900	1900 to 1950

8000 to 1 BC

■ 8000 BC
Organized agriculture begins: cultivated plants and herded animals.

■ 6000 BC
Animal manure is used as fertilizer.

■ 6000 BC
Maize is domesticated in the Americas.

■ ca 1500 BC
Aztecs build chinampas, floating gardens, on edges of Mexican lakes.

AD 1 to 1850

■ 1661
London's Vauxhall Gardens open to the public.

■ 1701–1731
Jethro Tull invents seed drill, improves plow, and makes other farming innovations.

■ 1730
British statesman-farmer Charles Townshend develops four-year crop rotation.

■ 1789
Englischer Garten opens in Munich, Germany.

■ 1849
The U.S. Department of Interior is established.

1850 to 1900

■ 1854
Henry David Thoreau's *Walden* is published.

■ 1858
Construction of New York City's Central Park, the first major urban park in the U.S., is under way.

■ 1863
Britain's Alkali Act curbs acid gas emissions.

■ 1872
Yellowstone National Park, the first legislated national park, is established.

■ 1892
The Sierra Club is founded, with John Muir as its first president.

1900 to 1950

■ 1913
German People's Park Association (Deutscher Volksparkbund) is founded in Germany.

■ 1916
U.S. and Canada sign Migratory Birds Treaty, first international conservation effort.

■ 1916
The U.S. National Park Service is established.

■ 1918
Fritz Haber receives Nobel Prize for synthesizing ammonia, used for fertilizer.

■ 1940s
High-yield wheat is introduced in Mexico, starting "green revolution."

1950 to 1970

1962
Rachel Carson's *Silent Spring* is published.

1964
U.S. legislates Wilderness Act, protecting lands from development.

1968
Apollo 8 astronauts create "Earthrise" photo.

1968
First edition of the *Whole Earth Catalog* is published.

1968
Paul R. Ehrlich's *The Population Bomb* is published.

1970 to 1980

1970
About 20 million participate in first Earth Day, April 22.

1970
The U.S. Environmental Protection Agency is established.

1970
Monsanto develops glyphosate herbicide, soon known as Roundup.

1971
Greenpeace begins as protest against nuclear testing in Alaska.

1972
Apollo 17 astronauts create "Blue Marble" photo.

1973
U.S. Congress approves Endangered Species Act.

1979
An accident occurs at Three Mile Island nuclear power plant.

1980 to 2000

1980
Green Party is established in West Germany.

1987
Montreal Protocol, which reduces emissions that deplete the ozone layer, is signed by 140 nations.

1988
First GMO crops, Roundup-resistant soybeans, developed.

1992
United Nations convenes Earth Summit in Rio de Janeiro, Brazil.

2000 to PRESENT

2000
In U.S., Green Party presidential candidate Ralph Nader receives 2.7% of vote.

2008
Svalbard Global Seed Vault is established in Norwegian Arctic.

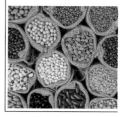

2011
The population of humans on Earth reaches 7 billion, according to estimates from the United Nations.

2016
Paris Agreement is ratified, joining nations in combating climate change.

PHOTO ARK

USING HIS ART TO SAVE ENDANGERED SPECIES

The number of animals going extinct is growing exponentially, warn the experts. Witnessing the problem firsthand, photographer Joel Sartore wanted to make a difference. Now he and his team are creating the National Geographic Photo Ark, collecting portraits of every animal species under human care—he figures the total could be as high as 13,000. In late 2018, the number of species in the Photo Ark reached 9,000 as Sartore photographed the bandula barb, a red-and-turquoise freshwater fish found in the wild in one protected stream in rural Sri Lanka.

Rarely seen in the wild, clouded leopards are listed as vulnerable species.

> **"** WITH EVERY PHOTO ARK TRIP, I MEET PEOPLE WHO ARE TRUE CONSERVATION HEROES ... THEY'RE DOING ALL THEY CAN, RIGHT THIS MINUTE, TO ENSURE BIODIVERSITY SURVIVES."
>
> **—JOEL SARTORE,** PHOTOGRAPHER AND CREATOR OF THE PHOTO ARK

Joel Sartore meets black flying foxes at the Australian Bat Clinic.

KEY NUMBERS

Species and Subspecies
PHOTOGRAPHED

■ **AMPHIBIANS**
807 species

■ **BIRDS**
2,464 species

■ **FISH**
1,243 species

■ **INVERTEBRATES**
(TERRESTRIAL AND AQUATIC)
2,312 species

■ **MAMMALS**
1,177 species

■ **REPTILES**
1,582 species

■ **TOTAL**
9,585 species and subspecies
photographed as of April 2019

BIODIVERSITY

THE WORLD'S CREATURES ARE UNDER SIEGE

A polar bear in the Arctic

SIXTH EXTINCTION?

THE NEXT APOCALYPSE

There have been five mass extinction events in the history of Earth, when over half of all the species present on the planet died off. Today, we may be in the middle of a new extinction. Earth may have as many as two billion species, from bacteria to elephants, but that number is falling rapidly. Past extinctions resulted from volcanic eruptions and asteroid impacts, but the current extinction is caused by humans.

Since the agricultural revolution 12,000 years ago, humanity has reshaped the planet for farms and food. So many creatures have died that it would take an estimated three million to five million years to restore what has already been lost. From the mastodons hunted during the last ice age to massive coral fields bleaching in warming seas, the planet's life is under threat—but it is not too late to turn the tide.

KEYSTONE SPECIES

WHY BIODIVERSITY MATTERS

Like any other complex mechanism, the life of ecosystems depends on every element within them. Certain species can help protect or even enhance biodiversity. Sharks and otters are keystone species representing thriving and healthy ecosystems. Beavers, wolves, and kelp act as ecosystem engineers, creating specialized climates for other animals.

Coral reefs support billions of people, dependent on fishing for food and livelihood, as well as global populations of sharks and other animals. Our oxygen is generated by phytoplankton and plants, our water filtered through natural purification in swamps, and dunes and mangroves protect our cities from storms. Respecting these processes is part of the solution.

A wolf pack

The Atlantic Forest in Brazil

MORE THAN 26,000 SPECIES **OF PLANTS AND ANIMALS ARE CURRENTLY AT RISK OF** EXTINCTION, **ACCORDING TO THE INTERNATIONAL UNION FOR CONSERVATION OF NATURE.**

ESSENTIAL FORESTS

CHANGING CLIMATE, CHANGING WORLD
Tropical rainforests contain about 80 percent of the world's documented species: a riotous diversity of plants, insects, birds, and other animals. A changing climate, clear-cutting for agriculture, and timber harvesting all threaten this lush ecosystem and its biodiversity.

Halting biodiversity loss in the tropics requires a mix of solutions, from small to global. Improving and increasing protected areas can renew habitat and rescue fragile ecosystems. International actions such as the Paris Climate Agreement and zero deforestation commitments by multinationals can influence progress on a larger scale. At home, here's one thing you can do: Eat less meat, which reduces the demand to clear forests for grazing.

Clouds over the Amazon Basin

UNITED EFFORT

A WORLD PROTECTED
In 2010, the United Nations passed a Strategic Plan for Biodiversity, 2011–2020, with ambitious goals including halving the rate of habitat loss and increasing protection of wild places by at least 17 percent on land and 10 percent in the ocean and along coastlines. So how have we done? "Despite numerous efforts on countless fronts in practically all the corners of the world," says Cristiana Paşca Palmer, executive secretary of the UN Convention on Biological Diversity, "we are losing too many ecosystems, too many species, too many genes and their combinations far too quickly." She invites people and nations around the world to seek to live "in harmony with nature," so that "by 2050, biodiversity is valued, conserved, restored, and wisely used, . . . sustaining a healthy planet and delivering benefits essential for all people."

A WORD FROM

Marketplace of Life Extinction is not evolution's driver; survival is . . . Competition among living species drives proliferation into diversified specialties . . . We can think of this as a marketplace of life, where little competition necessitates little specialization, thus little proliferation. An area with many types of trees, for instance, directly causes the evolution of many types of highly specialized pollinating insects, hummingbirds, and pollinating bats, who visit only the "right" trees. Many flowering plants are pollinated by just one specialized species.

—CARL SAFINA, *ecologist*

PLASTIC IN OUR WORLD

AN ENDURING THREAT

Since it was first mass-produced in the 1940s, plastic has made its way into every corner of life, from soda bottles and IV bags, to car parts and insulation, and even soaps and shampoos. It has revolutionized our society—but at a cost. Plastic takes more than 400 years to degrade, so most of it still exists in some form. Only 12 percent has been incinerated, and only 9 percent has been recycled. Of the 8.3 billion metric tons produced to date, 6.3 billion has become plastic waste.

The vast majority of plastic waste—79 percent—is accumulating in landfills or sloughing off in the natural environment as litter.

NEARLY HALF OF ALL PLASTIC EVER MANUFACTURED HAS BEEN MADE SINCE 2000.

Do Your Part to Minimize
POLLUTION

When it comes to pollution, simple acts can make a difference—especially when finding alternatives to single-use plastics. One million shopping bags are used every minute, but each one lasts 1,000 years—so bring reusable bags to the store. Reuse glass containers for spices or bulk goods instead of tossing your empties. And decline plastic straws, which are uniquely dangerous to marine life and among the most common items found on beaches.

HEATHER KOLDEWEY
MARINE BIOLOGIST

THE GHOST NET BUSTER

Originally a research scientist, now Heather Koldewey has turned activist, finding ways to help communities balance conservation with their own human needs. In one of her many projects, she hunts ghosts—deadly, virtually invisible, abandoned fishing nets that are threatening species around the world. "Ghost nets" account for almost 10 percent of all plastic in the ocean and have killed millions of creatures, from whales, sea lions, and seals to shorebirds and smaller fish. Koldewey works with fishing villages to remove these nets from the ocean, and transform them into something useful.

Heather Koldewey wants to see the end of single-use plastic water bottles as part of a more ocean-friendly society.

The Philippines' Danajon Bank was Koldewey's proving ground. A rare double barrier reef, where a second reef formed over subsiding shoals, Danajon Bank once teemed with fish. Overfishing devastated the area. As catch rates declined, fisheries used more nets, caught fewer and smaller fish, and often left remnants of their efforts behind. Ghost nets still haunt the reef, devastating the ecosystem.

Today, these fisheries, part of Net-Works, hunt down and gather the very nets they once used. The nets represent massive amounts of recyclable plastics and a new economy for the local villages. Now these communities have an incentive to remove these harmful waste nets. The nets are locally gathered and bailed and then shipped into the global market for recycled plastic, protecting the livelihood of the community and the lives in the marine environment at the same time.

SEARCHING FOR A SAFER OCEAN

Globally, nearly 650,000 tons of fishing nets are lost every year, part of the eight million tons of plastic pollution that enter our oceans annually, creating a sea filled with deadly traps. Whether broken, lost, or abandoned, ghost nets kill until they are trapped on the ocean floor. So far, Koldewey and the Net-Works team have pulled out more than 200 metric tons of plastic. The program's success is even changing the minds of local fishers, who now track and recycle their old nets rather than abandoning them. This slow exorcism of the seas will take time, but Koldewey envisions an ocean where fish swim free, unhaunted by these ghosts.

> **" WE NEED TO RETHINK PLASTIC, VALUE IT AND THE WAY WE USE IT, AND ENSURE IT NEVER GETS INTO THE OCEAN IN THE FIRST PLACE."**

Heather Koldewey looks for conservation solutions that benefit both people and the planet.

KEY DATES

Milestones in
OCEAN PLASTIC

■ 1907
The first fully artificial plastic created.

■ 1960s
First plastic debris observed in ocean.

■ 1979
Plastic grocery bags introduced in the U.S.

■ 1990s
Plastic microbeads now used in cosmetics.

■ 1997
The Great Pacific Garbage Patch discovered.

■ 2007
San Francisco bans plastic bags.

■ 2014
The Netherlands bans microbeads.

■ 2015
Some 448 million tons of plastic produced globally.

EARTH DAY
50 YEARS LATER

KEEPING THE PROMISE

"Why haven't we seen a picture of the whole earth yet?" Stewart Brand scribbled in his notebook. "There it would be for all to see, the earth complete, tiny, adrift, and no one would ever perceive things the same way." That was 1966. In 1968, Apollo 8 astronauts circled the moon and sent back the famous photo of "Earthrise." In 1969, Brand and friends began publishing the era-defining *Whole Earth Catalog.* In 1970, the first Earth Day was celebrated. Fifty years later, it's worth seeing how far we have come.

The famed Earthrise photo taken from the Apollo 8 mission in 1968 changed the way we see our planet.

EARTH DAY EVERY DAY

In 1970, Earth Day was a grassroots explosion across the United States, driven by Wisconsin senator Gaylord Nelson. The celebration and environmental teach-in spread across 12,000 schools, colleges, and universities. Twenty million people—nearly 10 percent of the U.S. population at that time—took part. The success drove immediate legislative and political actions, and the years following that first Earth Day led to the creation of the Environmental Protection Agency, the National Oceanic and Atmospheric Administration, the Clean Air and Clean Water Acts, and a new spirit of environmental awareness.

Today, Earth Day is an annual reminder for us to renew our commitment to protecting the planet's environment. Particularly as we celebrate the 50th anniversary of Earth Day, it's time to revive the determination, vision, and joy that was felt in its first celebration. Let's make a promise from now on that every day is Earth Day!

Crowds gather outside the U.S. Capitol on Earth Day.

EARTH DAY EVERY DAY

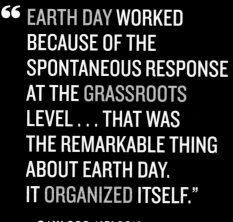

" EARTH DAY WORKED BECAUSE OF THE SPONTANEOUS RESPONSE AT THE GRASSROOTS LEVEL . . . THAT WAS THE REMARKABLE THING ABOUT EARTH DAY. IT ORGANIZED ITSELF."

—GAYLORD NELSON, GOVERNOR, SENATOR, AND FOUNDER OF EARTH DAY

Contributing to a HEALTHIER PLANET

1 CALL YOUR LEGISLATORS
Make your voice heard on environmental issues.

2 COMMUNITY CLEANUPS
Pollution starts at home; cleaning it up does too.

3 TAKE THE PLASTICS PLEDGE
Single-use plastics take centuries to dissolve. Using less reduces waste and protects the ocean.

4 REDUCE WASTE
Hundreds of millions of tons of waste end up in landfills where it cannot be recycled. Use less, waste less.

5 RETHINK TRAVEL
Use human-powered methods (e.g., biking, walking) where possible.

FURTHER

THE SECRET TO LIFE EVERLASTING

Throbbing through Earth's oceans for hundreds of millions of years, dating back to way before the dinosaurs, jellyfish must have some secret formula for prevailing. Today there are about 2,000 known species, every one of them surviving without bones, brains, eyes, or hearts. This golden jellyfish *(Mastigias papua etpisonii)* lives in one saltwater lake on an uninhabited island of Palau, closed for a while to protect the species but now reopened to divers, who must take special precautions: no sunscreen, no scuba tanks, no kicks, no touching.

Jellyfish throng a saltwater lake on Palau's Mecherchar, or Eil Malk.

"I HAVE VISITED SOME OF THE MOST REMOTE PLACES IN THE OCEAN, FULL OF SHARKS AND HUGE FISH SCHOOLS, BUT THESE LITTLE ANIMALS, VIRTUALLY WATER INSIDE A LIVING BAG, MADE ME FEEL CLOSER TO NATURE THAN ANYTHING EVER HAD BEFORE."

—ENRIC SALA, MARINE ECOLOGIST, ON SWIMMING IN JELLYFISH LAKE, PALAU

THE SCIENCE OF US

ORIGINS | THE HUMAN JOURNEY

Marcia and Millie, fraternal twins, share a mother from England and a father of Jamaican descent.

BODY & BRAIN | HEALTH & MEDICINE

QUIZ MASTER

Expert on You and Me? There's a lot to know about the world of us humans, from our earliest ancestors to our cities today, from the microbes in our gut to the neurons in our brain. And you don't have to leave home to do the exploring!

—**CARA SANTA MARIA,** *Our Favorite Nerd*

SCIENTISTS **USED A** SPINACH LEAF **TO BUILD A MUSCLE** FOR WHAT **HUMAN ORGAN?**

p267

IN WHAT YEAR DID THE FIRST **SUCCESSFUL** HEART **TRANSPLANT** TAKE PLACE?

FOR WHAT **PURPOSE DID ANCIENT** EGYPTIANS **CHEW ON** CARDAMOM **PODS?**

p272

WHAT IS THE LARGEST CITY IN SOUTH AMERICA?

p244

p277

WHAT IS THE LEADING **CAUSE OF BLINDNESS** IN THE WORLD?

ABOUT HOW MANY **YEARS AGO** DID ANIMALS **START WALKING** UPRIGHT **AND ON** TWO LEGS?

p267

WHO INVENTED **THE** VACCINE **FOR POLIO?**

p224

p265

WHICH ENGLISH NATURALIST PUT FORTH HIS THEORY OF EVOLUTION IN A BOOK CALLED *ON THE ORIGIN OF SPECIES*?

p225

WHICH RIVER IN INDIA IS SACRED TO THE HINDU RELIGION?

p249

IN WHAT COUNTRY DO CELEBRATIONS OF DÍA DE LOS MUERTOS ORIGINATE?

p235

IN WHAT REGION OF THE WORLD ARE QUECHUA-SPEAKING PEOPLE FOUND?

p234

ON AVERAGE, HOW MANY SPECIES OF BACTERIA LIVE ON THE HUMAN FOREARM?

p274

WHAT HERB IS A TRADITIONAL REMEDY TO SOOTHE AN UPSET STOMACH?

p276

APPROXIMATELY HOW MANY PEOPLE ON EARTH ARE BLIND?

p268

HUMAN EVOLUTION
TIME LINE

4 MYA to 80,000 YA	80,000 YA to 8000 BC	8000 to 1500 BC	1500 to 1 BC

3.5 mya*
Upright bipedalism—walking on two legs—evolves.

ca 1.75 mya
Homo erectus, an early ancestor of modern humans, uses stone tools.

ca 400,000 ya**
Neanderthals use fire as a tool in some areas.

ca 160,000 ya
Homo sapiens, the modern human race, first appears.

ca 120,000 ya
Neanderthals live in modern-day Europe.

ca 80,000 ya
Early humans begin moving out of Africa onto other continents.

* million years ago
** years ago

ca 80,000 ya
Modern humans move into Europe and live alongside Neanderthals.

ca 65,000 ya
Modern humans reach the Australian continent.

ca 40,000 ya
Neanderthals die out.

ca 25,000 ya
A small figurine called the Venus of Willendorf is crafted. It is the oldest known art in Europe.

ca 15,000 ya
The first human settlements appear in North America.

ca 11,000 ya
Agricultural systems begin to emerge in the Middle East, as humans cultivate plants and domesticate animals.

ca 6500 BC
Farming begins in the Indus Valley in modern-day Pakistan and western India.

ca 5000 BC
Rice is cultivated as a crop in central and eastern China.

ca 3500 BC
First wheels appear in Mesopotamia, used for pottery and later for vehicular use.

2630 BC
The Egyptians begin building pyramids.

ca 2300 BC
The earliest known maps are produced in Mesopotamia.

ca 2000 BC
Austronesians settle on islands in the South Pacific.

ca 1550 BC
The Mesopotamian empire begins to grow from the city of Mittani.

ca 1050 BC
Ironworking is introduced to Greece.

1000 BC
The Phoenicians develop an alphabet.

ca 600 BC
The Maya use cacao to make a chocolate drink.

ca 400 BC
Hippocrates of Kos describes human anatomy and various diseases.

ca 300 BC
The Maya build pyramids in modern-day Mexico.

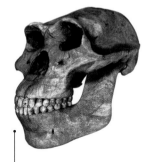

| **AD 1 to 1850** | **1850 to 1900** | **1900 to 1975** | **1975 to PRESENT** |

AD 1 to 1850

■ **1677**
Dutch scientist Antonie
van Leeuwenhoek
observes and describes
both bacteria and human
sperm cells.

■ **1691**
John Ray suggests that
fossils are the remains
of creatures from the
distant past.

■ **1735**
Swedish naturalist
Carolus Linnaeus
introduces the binomial
naming system.

■ **1836**
English naturalist Charles
Darwin completes his
five-year voyage on
the H.M.S. *Beagle*.

1850 to 1900

■ **1856**
Workmen digging in the
valley of the Neander River
near Düsseldorf, Germany,
discover remains of
Neanderthal man.

■ **1859**
Charles Darwin publishes
On the Origin of Species,
the book in which he
puts forward his theory
of evolution.

■ **1865**
Austrian monk Gregor
Mendel presents his
research on inheritance.

■ **1868**
French paleontologist
Louis Lartet excavates
fossils of Cro-Magnon man
in southwestern France.

■ **1891**
Dutch anthropologist
Eugene Dubois discovers
fossils of the human
ancestor "Java man," now
known as *Homo erectus*.

1900 to 1975

■ **1924**
Raymond Dart discovers
the first fossils of human
ancestor *Australopithecus*
in Africa.

■ **1933**
Anthropologists discover
a 92,000-year-old fossil of
Homo sapiens in Israel.

■ **1948**
English anthropologist
Mary Leakey discovers fossils
of possible ape ancestor
Proconsul africanus in Africa.

■ **1960**
Anthropologist Jonathan
Leakey discovers the remains
of *Homo habilis* in Tanzania.

■ **1972**
Anthropologist Richard
Leakey finds an intact
skull of *Homo habilis*.

1975 to PRESENT

■ **1974**
Donald Johanson
unearths "Lucy," a fossil
of *Australopithecus
afarensis*, in Ethiopia.

■ **1993**
Anthropologists
from Berkeley discover
remains of oldest known
hominoid, *Ardipithecus
ramidus*.

■ **2004**
An 80,000-year-old skele-
ton of a small humanoid
called *Homo floresiensis* is
found in Indonesia.

■ **2008**
Fossil of a new hominid,
Australopithecus sediba, is
discovered by Lee Berger
in South Africa.

■ **2013**
Multiple remains of a
newly discovered species,
Homo naledi, are found in
a cave in South Africa.

MEET OUR HUMAN ANCESTORS

HOW WE GOT TO WHERE WE ARE NOW

Scientists no longer use a family tree to depict relationships among early humans. It is now understood that several lines of early humans evolved at the same time. We also know that chimpanzees (or other apes) didn't evolve into humans. Instead, both lineages descended from a common ancestor and went their separate ways.

ARDIPITHECUS RAMIDUS (4.4 MYA)

Found in northeastern Ethiopia in 1992–1994, the partial skeleton of a female *Ar. ramidus* (nicknamed "Ardi") is more like a human—and less like a chimpanzee—than was expected in the human-ape record. For example, some believe foot and pelvis characteristics indicate that *Ar. ramidus* walked upright when on the ground. It is not clear yet whether it is an ancestor of *H. sapiens*.

AUSTRALOPITHECUS AFARENSIS (3.85–2.95 MYA)

"Lucy" *(Au. afarensis),* the most famous of our fossilized ancestors, was discovered in 1974 in eastern Africa. Scientists have concluded that *Au. afarensis* climbed trees, though it was mostly bipedal. Despite having a brain about one-third of modern humans', this tenacious species lived for over 900,000 years.

PARANTHROPUS BOISEI (2.3–1.2 MYA)

P. boisei, discovered in 1955, was immediately distinctive, because of its large jaw. This indicates a diet that required heavy chewing, though other evidence that it consumed hard substances (like nuts) is lacking. A recent report identified another exceptional characteristic: It may have carried HSV2, the virus causing genital herpes.

HOMO HABILIS (2.4–1.4 MYA)

H. habilis (aka "handy man") was discovered in 1960 at Tanzania's Olduvai Gorge at the same site and by the same team that found *P. boisei*. Its appearance reoriented the search for human origins from Asia, where *H. erectus* had been found, to Africa. A prominent researcher recently argued that it is different enough from other *Australopithecus* and *Homo* specimens to merit its own genus.

HOMO ERECTUS (1.89 MYA–143,000 YA)

H. erectus has proportions similar to modern humans', including shorter arms and longer legs in relation to the torso. Tools such as hand axes have been found near to and in the same sediment layers as *H. erectus,* marking an important moment in evolution. *H. erectus* was also migratory. In fact, it was first discovered in Indonesia in 1891.

HOMO SAPIENS IS NOW THE ONLY SPECIES OF HUMAN ON EARTH. BUT THAT'S BEEN TRUE FOR LESS THAN 30,000 YEARS.

PREHISTORY ON-SCREEN

- *One Million Years B.C.* (1966)
- *The Land That Time Forgot* (1974)
- *At the Earth's Core* (1976)
- *Quest for Fire* (1981)
- *Iceman* (1984)
- *The Clan of the Cave Bear* (1986)
- *Encino Man* (1992)
- *10,000 B.C.* (2008)
- *The Croods* (2013)
- *Early Man* (2018)

SHARED TIME ON EARTH?

These hand bones are among thousands recently found by paleoanthropologist Lee Berger and his team in South Africa. They belong to an all-new hominid species, *Homo naledi*, which likely lived alongside *Homo sapiens* less than 500,000 years ago.

PAUL SALOPEK
IMMERSIVE JOURNALIST

FOLLOWING ANCIENT PATHS

Over the course of several years, Pulitzer Prize–winning journalist and National Geographic Fellow Paul Salopek is retracing the path, as best we know it, taken by our *Homo sapiens* ancestors over millennia: from the Rift Valley in Ethiopia, through the Holy Lands of the Middle East, onto the Silk Road, into Pakistan and India, north to the Russian Far East, over the Bering Sea into North America, and down to the tip of South America—ETA 2023.

Paul Salopek waits for water to boil at his campsite in the Kyzylkum Desert, Uzbekistan, during his years-long trek.

P aul Salopek's 21,000-mile odyssey is a decade-long experiment in slow journalism. Along the way he is covering modern stories—from climate change to technological innovation, from mass migration to cultural survival—by giving voice to the people who inhabit them every day. His words, as well as his photographs, video, and audio, create a global record of human life at the start of a new millennium as told by villagers, nomads, traders, farmers, soldiers, and artists who rarely make the news.

He has walked alongside Syrian refugees and was detained by security forces in Pakistan. He is joined by local walking partners, including nature photographer Arati Kumar-Rao and environmentalist Siddharth Agarwal while in India. A cargo animal—sometimes a camel, sometimes a donkey—is also a constant companion.

GROUND-LEVEL INSIGHT

In his second dispatch of 2019, Salopek shared two impressions from his journey so far. First, he witnesses migration everywhere. "Even at the utterest ends of the Earth," he wrote, "I've found myself walking among striving people on the move." Second, he sees the world orienting toward China: "I have seen societies transformed by Chinese economic power: new highways, pipelines, communications grids, railroads."

"All roads may yet lead to Rome. But there are new Romes now," he writes. "Whatever the case, there is no need for fear. The key is to stop and talk, and then to keep moving. To cross the next river. To look around the next mountain. Humankind's ancestors did this, and they gave us the world."

" BREAKING BREAD IS THE UNIVERSAL BONDING MECHANISM OF HUMANITY. AT A TABLE, OVER FOOD, ONE HAS NO ENEMIES. AT LEAST NOT FOR THE DURATION OF THAT MEAL. WARS TAUGHT ME THIS."

Paul Salopek enjoys a cup of Arabian coffee in the desert of Jericho, West Bank.

KEY DATES

Salopek's Out of Eden
MILESTONES

■ **JAN. 21, 2013**
Day 1, mile 0, elev. 1,809 ft.
Began walk in Ethiopia

■ **NOV. 23, 2015**
Day 1,049, mile 3,000, elev. 2,566 ft.
Gabala, Azerbaijan

■ **SEPT. 7, 2017**
Day 1,703, mile 5,000, elev. 10,217 ft.
Chapursan Valley, Pakistan

■ **FEB. 28, 2019**
Day 2,160, mile 6,200, elev. 252 ft.
Near Varanasi, Uttar Pradesh, India

■ **2023**
Projected to complete the 21,000-mile journey

OUR DEEP ANCESTRY

STAGES OF HUMAN MIGRATION

The character of a person's mitochondrial DNA (passed down intact from mother to child) and, in each male, of the Y chromosome (passed intact from father to son) are only two threads in the vast tapestry of genetic information in any individual's genome. Studies like the years-long National Geographic Genographic Project now allow us to map human migration over tens of thousands of years by comparing the mtDNA and Y chromosomes of people from various populations.

What Stories Do Our Genes Tell?

Between 70,000 and 50,000 years ago, a small group of *Homo sapiens*—perhaps as few as 1,000, to whom all modern non-Africans are related—emigrated from Africa. One group continued along the coast to southern Asia, reaching a supercontinent made up of Tasmania, Australia, and New Guinea. Recent DNA research confirms that Aboriginal civilization is one of the longest continuous human occupations outside Africa.

EARLY HUMAN MIGRATIONS

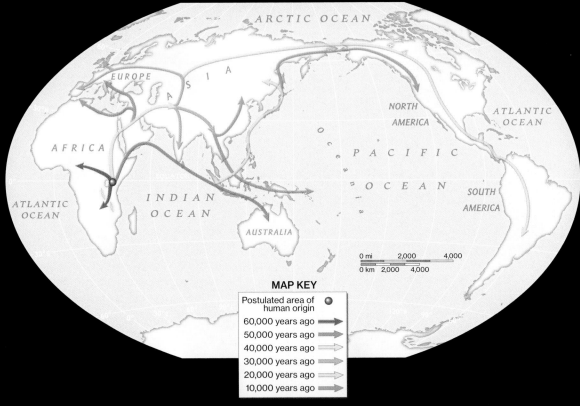

MAP KEY

Postulated area of human origin ●

60,000 years ago ➤
50,000 years ago ➤
40,000 years ago ➤
30,000 years ago ➤
20,000 years ago ➤
10,000 years ago ➤

FINDING YOUR ROOTS

TRACKING THE HUMAN JOURNEY
These days it's possible to learn more about your own deep ancestry through projects like National Geographic Genographic Project or commercial offerings from companies like Ancestry.com or 23andMe. A swab of cells from inside your cheek provides enough to learn what your genetic makeup tells about the path your long-ago ancestors took in the massive human migrations over tens of thousands of years. You may find your ancestors coming from one of several directions.

AFRICA
The diversity of genetic markers is greatest in the African continent, the earliest home of modern humans. "The genetic makeup of the rest of the world is a subset of what's in Africa," says Yale geneticist Kenneth Kidd.

ASIA
As some modern humans pushed into Central Asia, others traveled through Southeast Asia and China, eventually reaching Japan and Siberia. Humans in northern Asia eventually migrated to the Americas.

EUROPE
Genetic data show that the DNA of today's western Eurasians resembles that of people in India. It's possible that an inland migration from Asia seeded Europe between 40,000 and 30,000 years ago.

THE AMERICAS
When sea levels were low and the first humans crossed the land bridge between Siberia and Alaska, ice sheets covered the interior of North America, forcing the new arrivals to travel down the west coast.

> **" I THINK [EARLY HUMANS] WERE MAINLY MOTIVATED BY CURIOSITY AND THE DESIRE FOR EXPLORATION."**
>
> —ELENI PANAGOPOULOU, ARCHAEOLOGIST

Immigrants gather at a Sikh festival in Barcelona.

KEY FACTS

Natural Reasons for
MIGRATION

CLIMATE CHANGE Modern humans' departure from Africa around 60,000 years ago was likely in response to a deteriorating climate, growing cooler and drier and less hospitable to human life.

LAND BRIDGES Climate changes can determine access between regions, such as the sea-level drop about 40,000 years ago that exposed a lowland area connecting Australia to Tasmania.

COMPETITION Despite arriving in Europe hundreds of thousands of years before their modern relatives, Neanderthals went extinct not long after modern humans' arrival.

SEAFARING Axes found on Crete in 2010 may be evidence that early humans had the knowledge and technology to sail across the Mediterranean to the island.

AGRICULTURE Farming and herding developed around 12,000 years ago in the Near East and then, as farmers migrated to Europe and elsewhere, quickly replaced the hunter-gatherer lifestyle.

NEANDERTHALS
JOIN THE FAMILY

NOT-SO-DISTANT RELATIVES

When our ancestors emerged from Africa into Eurasia around 45,000 years ago, they found the landscape already inhabited. Neanderthals were 99.5 percent genetically identical to modern humans *(Homo sapiens)* but had evolved distinctive anatomy—such as wide bodies to conserve heat—during hundreds of thousands of years in the cold Eurasian climate.

NEANDERTHAL FEATURES

A form of the gene *MC1R* would have endowed its carriers with red hair and pale skin.

Large browridges combined with a receding forehead gave Neanderthals a beetle-browed look.

Neanderthal skulls were long and low, but they held brains slightly larger than those of living humans.

Neanderthal faces projected farther forward in the middle than do those of modern humans.

Large, conical rib cages housed big lungs needed for high levels of activity.

Neanderthals carried a version of the *FOXP2* gene, associated with language ability.

Neanderthal mandibles lacked chins.

DIVERGENT LINES REUNITE

Neanderthals, our closest prehistoric relatives, dominated Eurasia for the better part of 200,000 years. During that time, they poked their famously large and protruding noses into every corner of Europe and beyond. But climate swings and competition with newcomers may have combined to push Neanderthals into a few outposts before they went extinct, mysteriously dying out about 30,000 years ago.

Friend or Foe?

Scientists posit that the lineages of Neanderthals and their European successors diverged long before modern humans migrated out of Africa, as far back as 370,000 years ago. But until recently, questions lingered: Did modern humans replace Neanderthals, or did they interbreed with them?

Then, in 2010, scientists uncovered the first solid genetic evidence that "modern" humans interbred with their Neanderthal neighbors. Today, we know that genomes of people currently living outside Africa are composed of 1.8 to 2.6 percent Neanderthal DNA. Some parts of non-African genomes are totally devoid of Neanderthal DNA, but other regions abound with it, including those containing genes that affect our skin and hair. This hints that those Neanderthal gene versions conferred some benefit and were retained during evolution. Other genes, however, match segments now closely associated with various health concerns, including blood cholesterol levels and rheumatoid arthritis.

250,000–45,000 YEARS AGO
Neanderthals before the arrival of modern humans in Eurasia

Neanderthal range
0 mi 800
0 km 800

45,000–28,000 YEARS AGO
Period of Neanderthal and modern human overlap in Eurasia

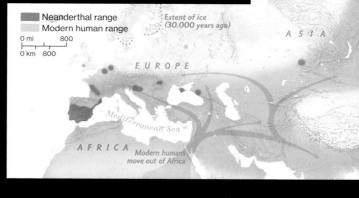

Neanderthal range
Modern human range
Extent of ice (30,000 years ago)
0 mi 800
0 km 800

Mediterranean Sea

Modern humans move out of Africa

DIGGING DEEPER

At-Home
DNA TESTING

Today it is possible to collect a DNA sample, send it in, and have it analyzed for ancestry markers. Some organizations will link you up with other contemporary individuals who are a match and have a good probability of being related to you. National Geographic's Genographic Project, which has more than 800,000 participants, probes further, providing regional and deep ancestry going back hundreds of generations— even identifying two hominin species, Neanderthals and Denisovans. The project has found that most non-Africans are about 2 percent Neanderthal and slightly less than 2 percent Denisovan.

INTANGIBLE CULTURE

MORE THAN MONUMENTS AND ARTIFACTS

Communities worldwide are working to identify and preserve practices, events, skills, and knowledge—intangibles—passed down by ancestors.

Dancers perform the *Ramayana*.

PERFORMING ARTS

THE RAMLILA, INDIA

An epic poem recounting the eventful life of Rama, an important Hindu god, the *Ramayana* is reenacted each fall in northern India. During Ramlila ("Rama's play"), which can last up to a month, seasoned storytellers are joined on stage by audience members—who also help create masks, costumes, and sets.

SHADOW PUPPETS, SYRIA

In these performances, a puppeteer voices characters in traditional stories and situations depicting current social issues with humor, satire, and music. Shadows of two-dimensional handmade puppets enact scenarios starring two characters—one clever, the other naive. As of 2018, only one puppeteer remained active in the country.

CULTURAL PRACTICES

SACRED KAYA FORESTS, KENYA

The Mijikenda of coastal Kenya believe that their ancestors reside in sacred forest *kayas*—village sites that date back to the 16th century, uninhabited but still tended and protected. Stories and ritual ceremonies honor and maintain the forest even as urban development encroaches.

Q'ESWACHAKA ROPE BRIDGE, PERU

Beyond facilitating transportation, the Q'eswachaka bridge serves as a sacred connection for Quechua-speaking people in the southern Andes. They congregate to restore the rope suspension bridge over a three-day gathering that includes ritual ceremonies and a festival. Families make ropes that bridge builders attach to ancient stone pillars.

A Quechua woman crosses the Q'eswachaka bridge.

Celebrants dress up for Día de los Muertos.

TO SAFEGUARD THE WORLD'S INTANGIBLE HERITAGE, UNESCO CURRENTLY RECOGNIZES 508 PRACTICES, ARTS, AND CULTURAL EXPRESSIONS FROM 122 COUNTRIES.

CELEBRATIONS

DÍA DE LOS MUERTOS, MEXICO
Flower petals strewn from homes to cemeteries, ancestors' favorite foods placed at tombs—these are part of Day of the Dead celebrations, combining precolonial religious rites and Catholic practices.

CATALAN HUMAN TOWERS, SPAIN
Costumed men and young children—surrounded by a base of tightly packed adults (the *pinya*)—rise up into human towers. Music featuring the *gralla,* a traditional Catalonian reed instrument, tells *castellers* how far a tower has progressed.

A woman extracts scents from processed flowers.

ARTS & CRAFTS

PERFUME, FRANCE
For over 400 years, the community of Pays de Grasse in southern France has cultivated plants and created fragrances. This artisanal, community-based approach stands in contrast to more commercial enterprises, which import oils and create synthetic perfumes.

WASHI PAPER, JAPAN
Just three communities produce authentic washi—paper used as stationery and in iconic Japanese room dividers, doors, and screens. Washi is made by hand using fibers from mulberry plants, clear river water, and bamboo screens. Members of the community participate at every stage, strengthening community bonds.

EARTH DAY EVERY DAY

The Ancient Arts of
PLANTS

Ethnobotanists are trying to preserve the indigenous knowledge about medicinal plants that is disappearing along with plant species and habitats. They interview practitioners to learn their treatments for everything from infections and heart disease to mental illness and cancer.

SEEKING REFUGE

ON THE MOVE TO SAFETY AND A BETTER LIFE

In 2010, the United Nations identified more than 15 million refugees; 2017 saw more than 25 million. In that same time period, the number of asylum seekers more than tripled. The United Nations estimates that in 2017, 44,000 people per day were forcibly displaced from their homes.

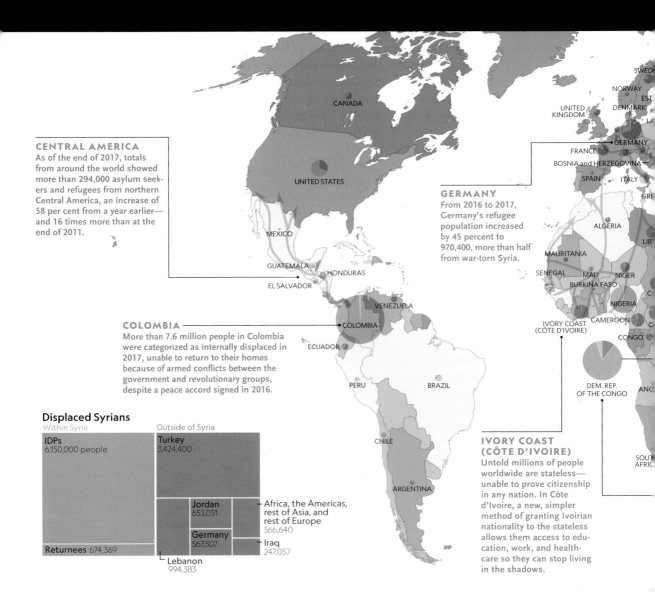

CENTRAL AMERICA
As of the end of 2017, totals from around the world showed more than 294,000 asylum seekers and refugees from northern Central America, an increase of 58 per cent from a year earlier—and 16 times more than at the end of 2011.

GERMANY
From 2016 to 2017, Germany's refugee population increased by 45 percent to 970,400, more than half from war-torn Syria.

COLOMBIA
More than 7.6 million people in Colombia were categorized as internally displaced in 2017, unable to return to their homes because of armed conflicts between the government and revolutionary groups, despite a peace accord signed in 2016.

IVORY COAST (CÔTE D'IVOIRE)
Untold millions of people worldwide are stateless—unable to prove citizenship in any nation. In Côte d'Ivoire, a new, simpler method of granting Ivoirian nationality to the stateless allows them access to education, work, and healthcare so they can stop living in the shadows.

Displaced Syrians

Within Syria
IDPs
6,150,000 people

Returnees 674,369

Outside of Syria
Turkey
3,424,400

Jordan
653,031

Germany
567,507

Lebanon
994,383

Africa, the Americas, rest of Asia, and rest of Europe
566,640

Iraq
247,057

Map labels: CANADA, UNITED STATES, MEXICO, GUATEMALA, HONDURAS, EL SALVADOR, VENEZUELA, COLOMBIA, ECUADOR, PERU, BRAZIL, CHILE, ARGENTINA, SWEDEN, NORWAY, EST, DENMARK, UNITED KINGDOM, GERMANY, FRANCE, BOSNIA and HERZEGOVINA, SPAIN, ITALY, ALGERIA, LIB, MAURITANIA, SENEGAL, MALI, NIGER, BURKINA FASO, NIGERIA, CAMEROON, IVORY COAST (CÔTE D'IVOIRE), CONGO, DEM. REP. OF THE CONGO, ANG, SOUTH AFRICA

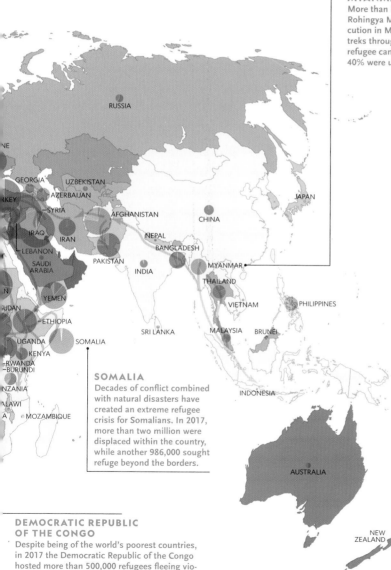

MYANMAR

More than half a million stateless Rohingya Muslims have fled brutal persecution in Myanmar, making dangerous treks through forests and by sea to reach refugee camps in Bangladesh. More than 40% were under age 12.

FORCED TO FLEE

The United Nations counted 68.5 million people of concern in 2017 who were fleeing their homes because of conflict, violence, or natural disaster. This includes internally displaced people (IDPs) migrating within their own countries and refugees and asylum seekers who have crossed national borders.

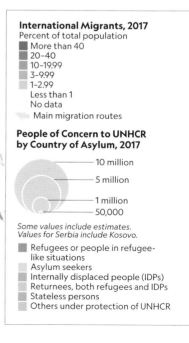

International Migrants, 2017
Percent of total population
- More than 40
- 20–40
- 10–19.99
- 3–9.99
- 1–2.99
- Less than 1
- No data
- Main migration routes

People of Concern to UNHCR by Country of Asylum, 2017
- 10 million
- 5 million
- 1 million
- 50,000

Some values include estimates.
Values for Serbia include Kosovo.

- Refugees or people in refugee-like situations
- Asylum seekers
- Internally displaced people (IDPs)
- Returnees, both refugees and IDPs
- Stateless persons
- Others under protection of UNHCR

SOMALIA

Decades of conflict combined with natural disasters have created an extreme refugee crisis for Somalians. In 2017, more than two million were displaced within the country, while another 986,000 sought refuge beyond the borders.

DEMOCRATIC REPUBLIC OF THE CONGO

Despite being of the world's poorest countries, in 2017 the Democratic Republic of the Congo hosted more than 500,000 refugees fleeing violence in neighboring countries, while 4.4 million native Congolese were internally displaced.

BEST OF @NATGEO

TOP PHOTOS OF WORLD TRADITIONS

@cristinamittermeier | CRISTINA MITTERMEIER
A tribeswoman in Papua New Guinea gazes from beneath a generations-old headdress.

@johnstanmeyer | JOHN STANMEYER
A group of boys watch as pilgrims at the Ganges make their offerings to the sacred river.

@irablockphoto | IRA BLOCK
An irresistible salesgirl wears and sells peanuts on the Maeklong train in Thailand.

@amivitale | AMI VITALE
A woman roasts coffee in her home in the village of Choche, Ethiopia, where the drink is a cultural mainstay.

> **"CULTURE IS ALL THE** THINGS AND IDEAS **EVER DEVISED BY** HUMANS **WORKING AND LIVING TOGETHER."**
>
> **—PETER FARB,** WRITER

@ciriljazbec | CIRIL JAZBEC
Samburu warriors in customarily bright adornments pose on the Samburu Reserve in Kenya.

@chancellordavid | DAVID CHANCELLOR
A gamekeeper at Scotland's Cairngorms National Park gives his tired companion a lift.

@kitracahana | KITRA CAHANA
A young girl in traditional Mexican dress celebrates the Day of the Virgin of Guadalupe in Tijuana.

@paleyphoto | MATTHIEU PALEY
Honoring a centuries-old practice, Kazakh eagle hunters ride to a festival in western Mongolia.

DISAPPEARING
LANGUAGES

WE MAY LOSE OVER HALF OF OUR 7,000 LANGUAGES BY 2100

Language defines a culture, through the people who speak it and what it allows speakers to say. Words that describe a particular cultural practice or idea may not translate precisely into another language. To lose those words is to lose those treasures.

HAIDA
100 speakers
Northern and southern versions spoken on the Haida Gwaii (Queen Charlotte Islands) off the coast of British Columbia

RESIGARO
Nearly extinct
Language of the Peruvian Amazon that has blended in with those of other tribes in this rainforest region

CHOROTE
Few speak only this language
More than 2,000 speakers of two related languages in Argentina, Paraguay, and Chile, 750 of whom speak only this language

DOLGAN
About 1,000 speakers
Spoken in the far north of Central Russia; few speak it, although those who do still teach this language to their children.

BOBOT
Threatened with extinction
In 1989, about 4,500 spoke Bobot, linguistically related to three other Indonesian languages. Bobot is purely oral; it is not a written language.

THAYORE
May have disappeared
Indigenous to Australia's Cape York Peninsula, only 29 speakers in 2006, although some children were learning it in 2011

Language Location and Endangerment Level
× Extinct
● High
● Medium
○ Low
○ Minimal
▨ Language hot spot
(Regions with high linguistic density, severe endangerment, and lack of documentation)

ASIA

AUSTRALIA

KATE ORFF
LANDSCAPE ARCHITECT

RESTORATION AND ADAPTATION

Making places beautiful is not enough for Kate Orff. The landscape architect also wants to make them adaptable to climate change and its extreme effects. "Every square inch of the planet has been impacted, intentionally or not, by human agency," she says. "My goal is to translate that into something positive."

Kate Orff approaches landscape design with an eye to the challenges of climate change and social issues.

URBAN NATURE

MAKING METRO MEAN HEALTHY

Cities around the world are striving to improve air quality and provide better transit options to their citizens by embracing environmentally friendly practices such as creating bike lanes, using alternative fuels, and offering incentives for electric vehicles. A recent survey of a hundred international cities ranks how well municipal governments are doing at helping people get where they need to go while also making cities more livable and attractive—and sustainable.

A jogger and a bike rider enjoy Manhattan's Central Park in the fall.

IN 2000, THE WORLD COUNTED 19 CITIES OVER 10 MILLION, 10 OF WHICH WERE IN ASIA. BY 2018, THERE WERE 33 MEGACITIES—HOME TO ONE IN EIGHT PEOPLE ON THE PLANET.

WHERE WE LIVE

The world's urban population passed 55% in 2018, but the size and location of population centers varies. North Americans and Europeans tend to spread out among small and medium-size cities, with relatively few migrating to megacities of more than 10 million people. Nations as diverse as Iceland, Kuwait, and Uruguay are more than 90% urban, while Liechtenstein, Burundi, and Papua New Guinea are among the most rural.

Moscow
12,410,000

A S I A

Tianjin
13,215,000

Beijing
19,618,000

ROPE

Istanbul
14,751,000

Lahore
11,738,000

Delhi
28,514,000

Chongqing
14,838,000

Tokyo
37,468,000

Osaka
19,281,000

Karachi
15,400,000

Kolkata
14,681,000

Cairo
20,076,000

C A

Dhaka
19,578,000

Shenzhen
11,908,000

Shanghai
25,582,000

SHRINKING CITIES
Japan's low population growth affects its cities: Osaka is the only megacity with a declining population, and Delhi will displace Tokyo as the world's largest by 2030.

Mumbai
19,980,000

Manila
13,482,000

Kinshasa
13,171,000

Bangalore
11,440,000

Bangkok
10,156,000

Guangzhou
12,638,000

Chennai
10,456,000

RURAL-URBAN BALANCE
India has the world's largest rural population—at almost 900 million—and the most rapidly growing urban population, adding over 400 million city dwellers by 2050.

Jakarta
10,517,000

AUSTRALIA

URBAN ISLANDS
Indonesia is urbanizing at lightning speed, and it expects to see over 60% of its people living in cities by 2025—including the new megacity of Jakarta.

MOST RURAL
In 2018, 57% of Africa's population was still rural, but some cities are growing rapidly, including Kinshasa, which may be the most populous African city by 2030.

URBANIZATION

MOVING TO THE CITY

By 2050, almost 70 percent of the global population will live in cities. As recently as 1950, these figures were reversed, and 70 percent lived in rural areas. The number of people living in rural areas has changed little, however, indicating that cities have been absorbing the world's exponential population growth since the mid-20th century—from 2.5 billion in 1950 to almost eight billion today.

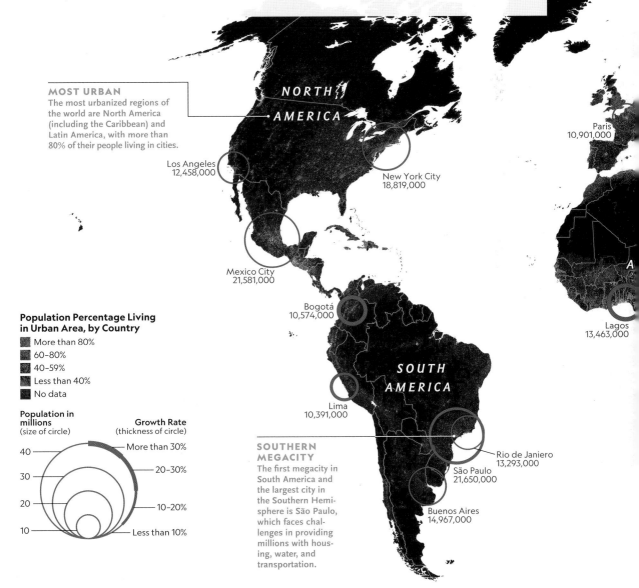

MOST URBAN
The most urbanized regions of the world are North America (including the Caribbean) and Latin America, with more than 80% of their people living in cities.

NORTH AMERICA

Paris
10,901,000

Los Angeles
12,458,000

New York City
18,819,000

Mexico City
21,581,000

Bogotá
10,574,000

Lagos
13,463,000

Population Percentage Living in Urban Area, by Country
- More than 80%
- 60–80%
- 40–59%
- Less than 40%
- No data

Population in millions
(size of circle)

Growth Rate
(thickness of circle)

- 40
- 30
- 20
- 10

- More than 30%
- 20–30%
- 10–20%
- Less than 10%

SOUTH AMERICA

Lima
10,391,000

SOUTHERN MEGACITY
The first megacity in South America and the largest city in the Southern Hemisphere is São Paulo, which faces challenges in providing millions with housing, water, and transportation.

Rio de Janiero
13,293,000

São Paulo
21,650,000

Buenos Aires
14,967,000

As director of Columbia University's Urban Design Program, Orff approaches landscape design from what she calls "a stance of activism." One of her current efforts is the Living Breakwaters project along the south shore of Staten Island, which was pummeled by Hurricane Sandy in 2012. Breakwaters protect the coastline from storm damage and erosion, help restore marine habitat, and provide places along the shore for residents to learn about the ecosystem and to engage with it. Behind it, throughout the harbor, dozens of artificial reefs built from stone, rope, and wood pilings will be seeded with oysters and other shellfish.

NATURAL BREAKWATERS

Living Breakwaters is part of the vision cast by Orff and SCAPE (her landscape architecture and urban design studio), which is informed by New York's past—before islands and shallows were demolished by harbor-dredging and landfill projects to add new real estate. It conceives of a living reef that would grow as sea levels rose, helping to buffer storm waves; resident shellfish, being filter feeders, would also help clean the harbor.

Along with her colleagues, Orff—the first MacArthur Fellow in landscape architecture—works to both restore shorelines' original profiles and make them responsive to rising sea levels, warmer temperatures, and escalating carbon levels. Other adaptive SCAPE projects include the Gowanus Lowlands in Brooklyn; Town Branch Commons in Lexington, Kentucky; and Alameda Creek in the San Francisco Bay Area—all of which also provide recreation space and opportunities for education and activism.

> " THERE IS A WAY THAT DESIGN AND PLANNING CAN PLAY A ROLE TO PRESERVE AND PROTECT ECOSYSTEMS AND ECOLOGIES, BUT ALSO A WAY THAT HUMAN SETTLEMENT CAN PERSIST AND STILL BE STRONGLY CONNECTED TO THE COAST."

A model of "oyster-tecture," a plan to develop oyster beds as ecological breakwaters.

KEY DATES

Orff's ACCOMPLISHMENTS

■ **2010**
Gives TED Talk, "Reviving New York's Rivers— With Oysters!"

■ **2011**
Co-edits *Gateway: Visions for an Urban National Park*

■ **2012**
Publishes, with photographer Richard Misrach, *Petrochemical America*

■ **2016**
Publishes *Toward an Urban Ecology*

■ **2018**
Named director of the Center for Resilient Cities and Landscapes at Columbia University's Graduate School of Architecture, Planning, and Preservation

TOWARD GREENER CITIES

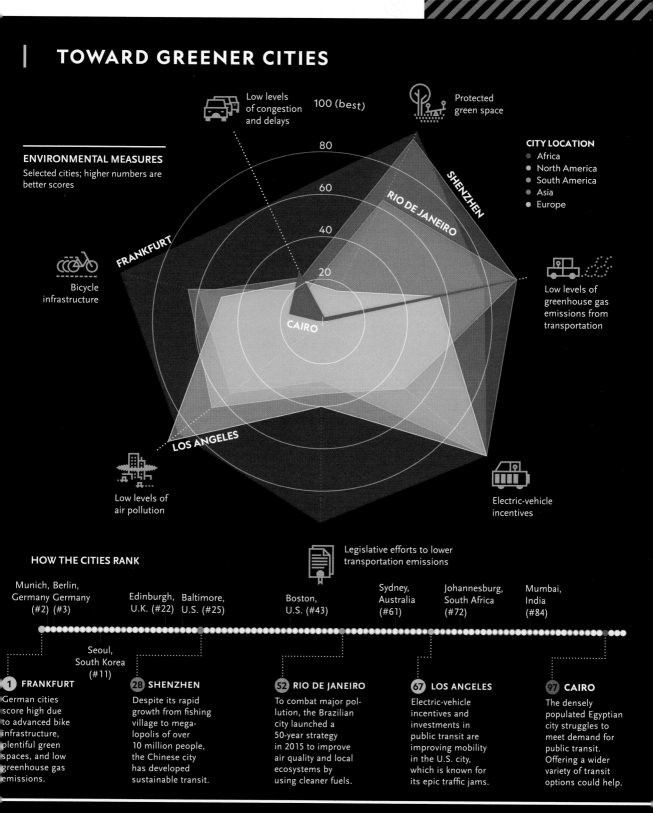

ENVIRONMENTAL MEASURES
Selected cities; higher numbers are better scores

Low levels of congestion and delays

100 (best)

Protected green space

80

60

40

20

CITY LOCATION
- Africa
- North America
- South America
- Asia
- Europe

SHENZHEN

RIO DE JANEIRO

FRANKFURT

Bicycle infrastructure

CAIRO

Low levels of greenhouse gas emissions from transportation

LOS ANGELES

Low levels of air pollution

Electric-vehicle incentives

Legislative efforts to lower transportation emissions

HOW THE CITIES RANK

Munich, Berlin, Germany Germany (#2) (#3)

Edinburgh, U.K. (#22)

Baltimore, U.S. (#25)

Boston, U.S. (#43)

Sydney, Australia (#61)

Johannesburg, South Africa (#72)

Mumbai, India (#84)

Seoul, South Korea (#11)

1 FRANKFURT
German cities score high due to advanced bike infrastructure, plentiful green spaces, and low greenhouse gas emissions.

28 SHENZHEN
Despite its rapid growth from fishing village to megalopolis of over 10 million people, the Chinese city has developed sustainable transit.

52 RIO DE JANEIRO
To combat major pollution, the Brazilian city launched a 50-year strategy in 2015 to improve air quality and local ecosystems by using cleaner fuels.

67 LOS ANGELES
Electric-vehicle incentives and investments in public transit are improving mobility in the U.S. city, which is known for its epic traffic jams.

97 CAIRO
The densely populated Egyptian city struggles to meet demand for public transit. Offering a wider variety of transit options could help.

RELIGION
AROUND THE WORLD

CULTURE AND MEANING

Religion's great power comes from its ability to speak to the heart and longings of individuals and societies. In time, an untold number of local religious practices yielded to just a few widespread traditions.

CHACO CANYON
A ceremonial site for the Pueblo peoples between AD 850 and 1250, the complex remains here are protected as a U.S. National Historical Park and a UNESCO World Heritage site.

MEXICO CITY
The Basilica of Our Lady of Guadalupe in Mexico City is the most visited Catholic pilgrimage site in the world. Accounts state that a vision of the Virgin Mary appeared there in 1531.

GUYANA
Although most of South America is predominantly Christian, Guyana is predominantly Hindu; nearby Suriname includes both Christian and Hindu adherents, yet neither represents the majority religion

NORTH AMERICA

SOUTH AMERICA

EARTH DAY EVERY DAY

When Beliefs Drive
ACTION

Many find their religious faith fueling conservation efforts. For example, A Rocha is an international network of environmental projects—from freshwater filtration in Africa to bird-watching tours in Australia, meadow assessment in Switzerland to tree planting in Lebanon—consciously linked to principles of Christianity.

Predominant Religion by State/Province

- Buddhism
- Christianity
- Ethnic religion
- Hinduism
- Islam
- Judaism
- Other

ASIA

GANGES RIVER
In Hinduism, the Ganges is regarded as a sacred river. Multiple pilgrimage sites are found along the river, and some Hindus cast the ashes of the dead into the waters of the Ganges.

BODH GAYA
One of the holiest sites in Buddhism, Bodh Gaya is said to be where Siddhartha Gautama achieved enlightenment and became the Buddha.

MECCA
Non-Muslims are not allowed to enter Mecca, the holiest city in Islam. Making a pilgrimage to the city at least once is obligatory to all Muslims who are able.

AUSTRALIA

JERUSALEM
All three Abrahamic religions—Judaism, Christianity, and Islam— consider Jerusalem a holy place. The city is a destination for religious pilgrims from all over the world.

Religious Holidays

SOMEWHERE IN THE WORLD, a meal, ritual, or offering is being prepared in religious observance — most likely by the busy adherents of Roman Catholicism or Hinduism. If Catholics celebrated every saint's day or Hindus commemorated each deity's birthday, nearly the entire year would be accounted for.

WHO CELEBRATES THE MOST?

With feasts, fasts, and prayers, the world's nine largest religions can collectively observe more than a hundred holidays in a year.

HINDUS LEAD THE FESTIVITIES

Hinduism recognizes the birthdays and milestones of hundreds of deities. It also commemorates the changing of the seasons, the harvest, and lunar phases.

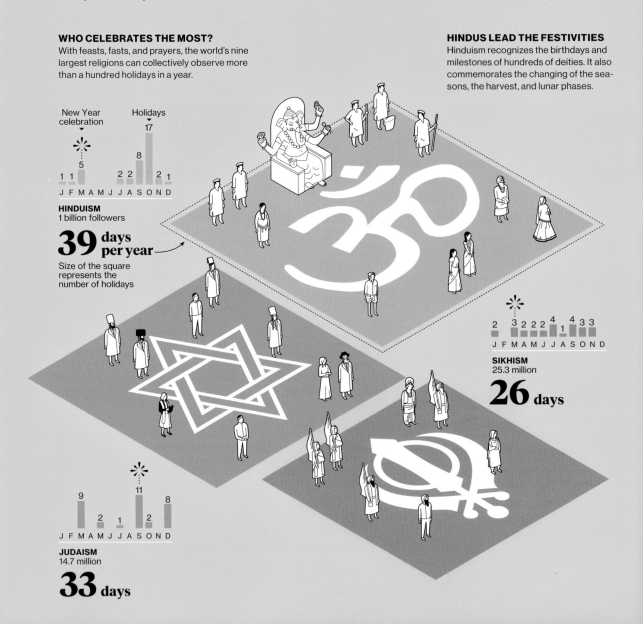

New Year celebration ▼
Holidays
17
8
5
1 1   2 2   2 1
J F M A M J J A S O N D

HINDUISM
1 billion followers

39 days per year

Size of the square represents the number of holidays

2   3 2 2 2   4   4 3 3
              1
J F M A M J J A S O N D

SIKHISM
25.3 million

26 days

9   2   1   11   2   8
J F M A M J J A S O N D

JUDAISM
14.7 million

33 days

The Jewish calendar has dozens of holidays — but the Torah only mandates strict observance of the five holiest. Muslims, too, are holiday minimalists. In Islam the biggest celebrations are saved for the last days of its two major holidays: Id al-Fitr for Ramadan and Id al-Adha to end the hajj pilgrimage.

Compiling a schedule of the holidays most widely observed by the world's nine largest religions is no simple task. Different countries and regions, as well as denominations, celebrate their own versions of the holidays, and some religions follow a unique calendar.

China's lunar calendar runs on a 60-year cycle; India uses several types of calendars.

The establishment of the international date line in 1884 pushed holidays that used to begin at sunset to the next day in many countries. Today holiday scheduling can be influenced by things like economic productivity, which is the reason some celebrations move around each year to bookend a weekend.

NEW YEARS ALL YEAR ROUND
While Christians follow the Gregorian calendar, many traditions follow other calendar systems and celebrate the New Year during different months.

3 4 1 1   1 2
J F M A M J J A S O N D

CHRISTIANITY
2.4 billion

12 days

1 1 2 2 1
J F M A M J J A S O N D

ISLAM
1.7 billion

7 days

1 2 3 1   4
J F M A M J J A S O N D

BAHA'I FAITH
7.9 million

11 days

1 1 1 1
J F M A M J J A S O N D

TAOISM
8.6 million

4 days

1 1 1
J F M A M J J A S O N D

BUDDHISM
516 million

3 days

1 1   1
J F M A M J J A S O N D

CONFUCIANISM
8.5 million

3 days

INDIA OUT-CELEBRATES THE U.S.
Some religiously diverse countries like India formally recognize the holidays of both majority and minority religions.

INDIA
HOLIDAYS
A YEAR
48

SECULAR
5

U.S.
10

SECULAR
9

BEST OF @NATGEO

TOP PHOTOS OF PEOPLE

@renan_ozturk | RENAN OZTURK
A village elder from the shamanistic Kulung culture in Nepal draws wisdom from the forest.

@cristinamittermeier | CRISTINA MITTERMEIER
Feathers of Amazonian parrots and macaws make a beautiful headdress for a Kayapó man.

@brianfinke | BRIAN FINKE
A competitor eyes the open water in a nearly 3,000-mile rowing race from the Canary Islands to Barbados.

@salvarezphoto | STEPHEN ALVAREZ
Wearing bright woven textiles, a young Peruvian woman honors the Andean weaving tradition.

> ❝ **CULTURE DOES NOT MAKE** PEOPLE. PEOPLE **MAKE CULTURE.**❞
>
> —**CHIMAMANDA NGOZI ADICHIE,** WRITER

@mmuheisen | **MUHAMMED MUHEISEN**
A nine-year-old Afghan girl adapts to life as a refugee at a camp north of Athens, Greece.

@stephsinclairpix | **STEPHANIE SINCLAIR**
American trapeze artist Kristin Finley prepares to fly in a circus performance.

@paleyphoto | **MATTHIEU PALEY**
A mother and son pose in front of a mud wall in their home in Afghanistan.

@chamiltonjames | **CHARLIE HAMILTON JAMES**
A boy in the Amazon gives a capuchin monkey a ride on his head.

THE SCIENCE
OF SLEEP

Listeners relax during a performance by the Philharmonie de Paris designed to ease its audience into rest.

THE NECESSITY OF SLEEP

Everything we've learned about sleep has emphasized its importance to our mental and physical health. Our sleep-wake pattern is a central feature of human biology—an adaptation to life on a spinning planet, with its endless wheel of day and night. The 2017 Nobel Prize in medicine was awarded to three scientists who, in the 1980s and 1990s, identified the molecular clock inside our cells that aims to keep us in sync with the sun. When this circadian rhythm breaks down, recent research has shown, we are at increased risk for illnesses such as diabetes, heart disease, and dementia.

There is evidence that sleep is essential for maintaining a healthy immune system, body temperature, and blood pressure. Without enough of it, we can't regulate our moods well or recover swiftly from injuries. Sleep may be more essential to us than food. Animals will die of sleep deprivation before starvation.

Good sleep likely also reduces one's risk of developing dementia. It appears that while we're awake, our neurons are packed tightly together, but when we're asleep, some brain cells deflate by up to 60 percent, widening the spaces between them. These intercellular spaces are dumping grounds for the cells' metabolic waste—notably a substance called beta-amyloid, which disrupts communication between neurons and is closely linked to Alzheimer's. Only during sleep can spinal fluid slosh like detergent through these broader hallways of our brain, washing beta-amyloid away.

HOW LIGHT AFFECTS US

How perky we're feeling at any moment depends on the interaction of two processes: "sleep pressure," which is thought to be created by sleep-promoting substances that accumulate in the brain during waking hours, and our circadian rhythm, the internal clock that keeps brain and body in sync with the sun. The clock can be set backward or forward by light. We're particularly sensitive to blue (short-wavelength) light, the kind that brightens midday sunlight and our computer screens, but can disrupt our cycle—especially at night, when we need the dark to cue us to sleep.

A seven-year-old falls asleep watching cartoons on his iPad.

SLEEP LITERALLY MAKES CONNECTIONS YOU MIGHT NEVER HAVE CONSCIOUSLY FORMED, AN IDEA WE'VE ALL INTUITIVELY REALIZED. NO ONE SAYS, "I'M GOING TO EAT ON A PROBLEM." WE ALWAYS SLEEP ON IT.

Eating Insects

As incomes rise in developing countries, so too does the demand for meat. But raising livestock uses a lot of resources. Eating insects—already common in many tropical countries—could be an alternative. Beetles and crickets, for example, are packed with nutrients and provide protein at a low environmental cost.

Palatability poses a problem. "People have an emotional response to bugs—it's the yuck factor," says Arnold van Huis of Wageningen University in the Netherlands. To disguise their form, insects can be processed into powders or pastes. What's next? Protein-rich "bug flours" that are part flour and part ground insect are starting to appear on the market.

ON THE MENU

2 billion

MORE THAN A FOURTH OF THE WORLD'S PEOPLE EAT INSECTS.
The popularity of Western diets is reducing insect consumption in developing countries.

2,000

NUMBER OF KNOWN EDIBLE SPECIES

EFFICIENT PROTEIN

Edible insects provide a sustainable alternative to meat. They are a healthy food source with a high protein and fat content, but their nutritional value varies by species.

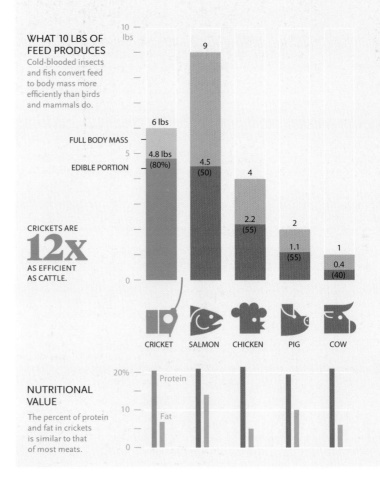

WHAT 10 LBS OF FEED PRODUCES
Cold-blooded insects and fish convert feed to body mass more efficiently than birds and mammals do.

FULL BODY MASS
EDIBLE PORTION

CRICKETS ARE

12x

AS EFFICIENT AS CATTLE.

- CRICKET: 6 lbs / 4.8 lbs (80%)
- SALMON: 9 / 4.5 (50)
- CHICKEN: 4 / 2.2 (55)
- PIG: 2 / 1.1 (55)
- COW: 1 / 0.4 (40)

NUTRITIONAL VALUE
The percent of protein and fat in crickets is similar to that of most meats.

Protein
Fat

MOST COMMONLY CONSUMED
Beetles are the most consumed species; mealworms are beetle larvae.

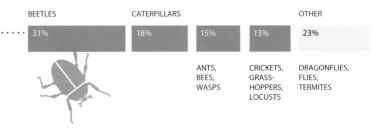

- BEETLES 31%
- CATERPILLARS 18%
- 15% ANTS, BEES, WASPS
- 13% CRICKETS, GRASSHOPPERS, LOCUSTS
- OTHER 23% DRAGONFLIES, FLIES, TERMITES

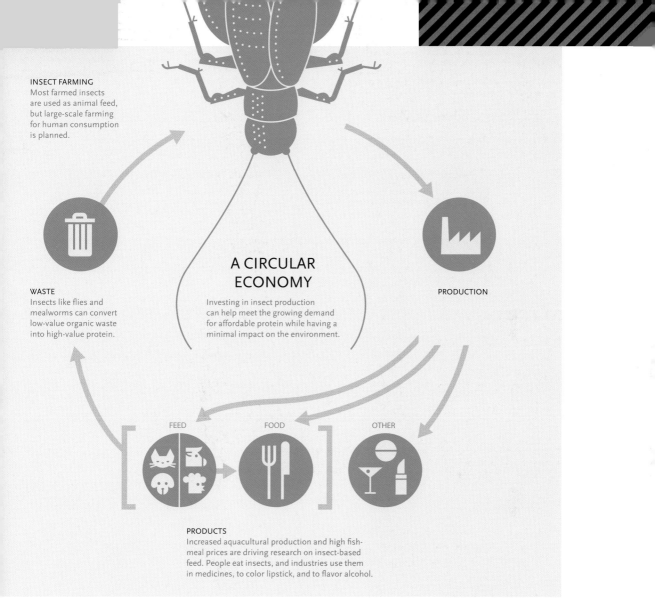

INSECT FARMING
Most farmed insects are used as animal feed, but large-scale farming for human consumption is planned.

A CIRCULAR ECONOMY

Investing in insect production can help meet the growing demand for affordable protein while having a minimal impact on the environment.

WASTE
Insects like flies and mealworms can convert low-value organic waste into high-value protein.

PRODUCTION

FEED

FOOD

OTHER

PRODUCTS
Increased aquacultural production and high fish-meal prices are driving research on insect-based feed. People eat insects, and industries use them in medicines, to color lipstick, and to flavor alcohol.

ENVIRONMENTAL IMPACT

Insects emit fewer greenhouse gases and require less land to produce than livestock such as pigs and cattle.

GREENHOUSE GAS PRODUCTION
Pounds of CO_2-eq* generated from producing a pound of protein

14
MEALWORM

38
PIG

LAND USE
Square feet needed to produce a pound of protein

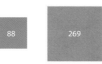

88
MEALWORM

269
PIG

A DELICACY

IN UGANDA A POUND OF GRASSHOPPERS COSTS

40%

MORE THAN
A POUND OF BEEF

* CO_2-equivalents: the sum of carbon dioxide, methane, and nitrous oxide emissions

How the World Gives Birth

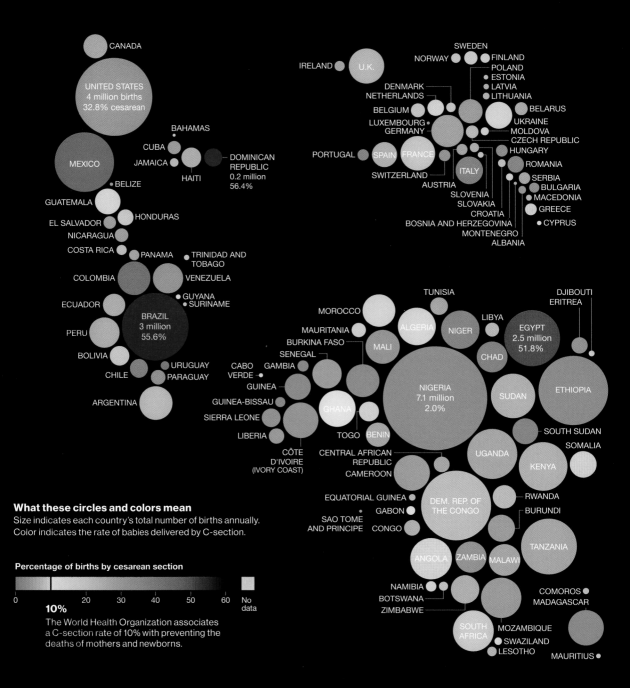

What these circles and colors mean
Size indicates each country's total number of births annually.
Color indicates the rate of babies delivered by C-section.

Percentage of births by cesarean section

| 0 | 20 | 30 | 40 | 50 | 60 | No data |

10%
The World Health Organization associates
a C-section rate of 10% with preventing the
deaths of mothers and newborns.

BRAZIL
The country with one of the highest C-section rates (55.6%) launched a public health campaign in 2015 to promote natural births.

FINLAND
The lowest rate among developed countries (14.7%) is likely a product of midwife-led deliveries and strict clinical protocols.

EGYPT
Its rate (51.8%) is growing fast, as more women ask for C-sections and doctors try to avoid medical and legal complications.

AFRICAN NATIONS
Less than 1.6% of babies in Niger, Chad, and Ethiopia are delivered via C-section, largely owing to a shortage of care facilities.

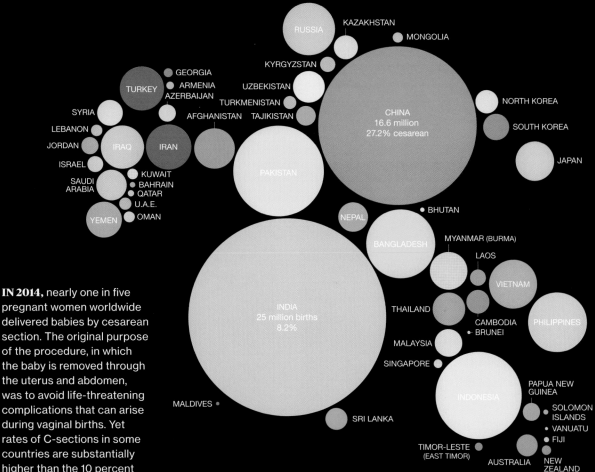

IN 2014, nearly one in five pregnant women worldwide delivered babies by cesarean section. The original purpose of the procedure, in which the baby is removed through the uterus and abdomen, was to avoid life-threatening complications that can arise during vaginal births. Yet rates of C-sections in some countries are substantially higher than the 10 percent rate the World Health Organization associates with preventing the deaths of mothers and newborns.

Why do some countries see so many C-sections? According to the WHO, factors favoring the procedure include families' and doctors' expectations of achieving safer outcomes and avoiding long or painful labors. High rates, such as those seen in Brazil, also can reflect a desire to time births more predictably, while low rates can indicate reduced access to medical care.

As doctors and expectant mothers evaluate the benefits of delivering through the birth canal, C-section rates could decline.

THE TERM "CESAREAN SECTION" HAS NOTHING TO DO WITH JULIUS CAESAR. MORE LIKELY IT COMES FROM THE LATIN WORD *CAEDARE,* **MEANING "TO CUT."**

UNDERSTANDING
GENDER

NO LONGER SIMPLY MALE OR FEMALE

Our society is in the midst of a conversation about gender issues, with evolving notions about what it means to be a woman or a man. At the same time, scientists are uncovering new complexities in the biological understanding of sex. Whereas genital differentiation takes place in the first two months of fetal development, sexual differentiation of the brain comes months later.

IN A SURVEY OF A THOUSAND MILLENNIALS AGES 18 TO 34, HALF AGREED THAT "GENDER IS A SPECTRUM, AND SOME PEOPLE FALL OUTSIDE CONVENTIONAL CATEGORIES."

More children are opting for new gender identities, like this young transgender artist.

Glossary of Terms for
GENDER

CISGENDER A term describing one whose gender identity matches the biological sex assigned at birth.

GENDER BINARY The idea that gender is strictly either male/man/masculine or female/woman/feminine based on sex assigned at birth, rather than a continuum or spectrum of gender identities and expressions.

GENDER CONFORMING One whose gender expression is consistent with cultural norms expected for that gender.

GENDER DYSPHORIA The medical diagnosis for being transgender. It is controversial because it implies that being transgender is a mental illness, rather than a valid identity.

GENDER EXPRESSION One's outward gender presentation: clothing, hairstyle, makeup, vocal inflection, body language.

GENDERFLUID One whose gender identity or expression shifts between man/masculine and woman/feminine or falls somewhere along this spectrum.

GENDER IDENTITY One's deep-seated, internal sense of who one is as a gendered being; the gender with which one identifies.

INTERSEX Any mix of male and female chromosomes, testicular and ovarian tissue, genitals, or other sexual characteristics.

NONBINARY A spectrum of gender identities and expressions. Terms include genderqueer, genderfluid, and pangender.

QUEER An umbrella term for a range of people who are not heterosexual and/or cisgender. Some consider the term derogatory.

TRANSGENDER: An adjective describing one whose gender identity does not match the biological sex assigned at birth. Sometimes abbreviated as trans.

CHINESE
TRADITIONS

TREATMENT EXTREMES

Wasp nests for itching skin and rashes, earthworms for asthma and convulsions: Traditional Chinese healers have turned to many items, not just plants, as remedies. Even scales from the pangolin, an African anteater, have been claimed to be a cancer treatment —a notion driving this rare animal to extinction.

BAIKAL SKULLCAP

CITRUS PEEL

CUTTLEFISH BONE

CITRON DAYLILY

CHINESE DATE

EPIMEDIUM LEAF

PANGOLIN SCALE

SWEET WORMWOOD

LICORICE ROOT

ROSEBUD

PAPER WASP NEST

MOLTED CICADA SHELL

TUCKAHOE

NIGHT-BLOOMING CEREUS

FRANKINCENSE

TRICHOSANTHES FRUIT

CHINESE FOXGLOVE ROOT

MONK FRUIT

EARTHWORM

JENNIFER DOUDNA
BIOCHEMIST

STARTING A REVOLUTION

Crispr-Cas9, the gene-editing technique that biochemist Jennifer Doudna has pioneered, is one that organisms already use on their own. The thrilling discovery is that we can employ it strategically—in specific places in the genome to achieve certain ends. "We uncovered the workings of an incredible molecular machine that could slice apart viral DNA with exquisite precision," Doudna says.

Jennifer Doudna in her lab at the Li Ka Shing Center, University of California, Berkeley

Doudna first heard about Crispr (clustered regularly interspaced short palindromic repeats) in 2006 when discussing immunological adaptations made by bacteria with geomicrobiologist Jill Banfield. When bacteria battle a virus, they place an excerpt of the virus's DNA into their own genome.

In 2011, Doudna, microbiologist Emmanuelle Charpentier, and their team used the Cas9 enzyme from common *Streptococcus* bacteria—and discovered what has been celebrated as "the cheapest, simplest, most effective way of manipulating DNA." With Crispr-Cas9, scientists can dispatch a synthetic replacement part to any location in a genome made of billions of nucleotides. After the enzyme snips out the unwanted DNA sequence, the cell inserts the chain of nucleotides delivered in the Crispr package.

THE PROMISE AND PERIL OF CRISPR

Crispr has transformed biology. For example, one could edit genes of crops to resist pests, eliminating the need for pesticides. Crispr could even be used to find and treat mutations that lead to cancer.

No scientific discovery of the past century holds more promise—or raises more ethical questions. If Crispr were used to edit a human embryo's germ line, the change would be passed on in perpetuity. "Application of the technology with the intention to establish a pregnancy or birth should not occur," says Doudna, "until we fully understand the scientific risks and ethical issues surrounding such profound use."

" AT ITS CORE, THE CRISPR GENE-EDITING **TECHNOLOGY IS NOW GIVING HUMAN BEINGS THE** OPPORTUNITY **TO CHANGE THE COURSE OF EVOLUTION."**

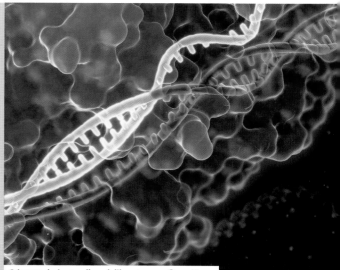

Crispr techniques allow deliberate reconfiguration of bits of DNA's double helix.

KEY DATES

Doudna's Crispr
ACHIEVEMENTS

■ **2012**
Co-authors an article announcing the Crispr-Cas9 technique

■ **2015**
Calls for a moratorium on human genome editing

■ **2015**
Receives Breakthrough Prize in life sciences, awarded by Silicon Valley notables

■ **2017**
Publishes *A Crack in Creation: Gene Editing and the Unthinkable Power to Control Evolution* with co-author Samuel H. Sternberg

■ **2018**
Receives patents for Crispr-Cas9 compositions

MEDICINE
TIME LINE

6500 to 1 BC

■ ca 6500 BC
The first known surgery is completed.

■ ca 3000 BC
The Ayurveda, a Hindu medical treatise, establishes a holistic medical system still in use today.

■ ca 2500 BC
Chinese doctors use acupuncture to heal ailments.

■ ca 2000 BC
In Syria and Babylon, medicine becomes an important practice; recipes for ointments and poultices are recorded on clay tablets.

■ ca 1550 BC
Egyptians have about 700 drugs and medications in use.

■ 440 BC
The Hippocratic Corpus, a collection of medical treatises from ancient Greece, is compiled.

AD 1 to 1500

■ ca 30
Roman doctors use splints and bandages stiffened with starch to set broken bones.

■ 77
Pedanius Dioscorides writes a guide to medicinal herbs and drugs that remains authoritative until the 15th century.

■ 1012
Persian physician Ibn Sina publishes an influential medical text, *The Canon of Medicine*.

■ ca 1286
Eyeglasses are invented in Italy.

■ 1347–1351
The Black Death spreads across Europe and Asia in one of the most devastating pandemics in history.

1500 to 1850

■ 1628
English physician William Harvey explains the circulation of blood in the body.

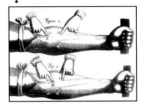

■ 1796
English physician Edward Jenner introduces the smallpox vaccination in Europe.

■ 1805
Japanese physician Hanaoka Seishu performs the first surgery on a patient using general anesthesia.

■ 1824
Louis Braille invents the Braille alphabet to aid blind people in reading and writing.

■ 1840
Jakob Henle proposes the germ theory of disease.

1850 to 1900

■ 1854
English physician John Snow connects cholera and contaminated water.

■ 1863
Louis Pasteur invents a sterilization process now known as pasteurization.

■ 1867
Joseph Lister publishes a paper on the use of antiseptic surgical methods.

■ 1885
Sigmund Freud begins developing his theories of psychoanalysis.

■ 1893
Surgeon Daniel Hale Williams performs the first heart surgery.

■ 1895
German physicist Wilhelm Röntgen takes the first x-ray.

| 1900 to 1930 | 1930 to 1970 | 1970 to 1985 | 1985 to PRESENT |

1900 to 1930

■ 1917
Margaret Sanger opens a birth control clinic in the United States.

■ 1921
Psychiatrist Hermann Rorschach introduces his inkblot test for studying personality.

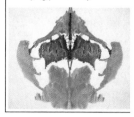

■ 1922
Vitamins D and E are first discovered.

■ 1925
Biologist Ernest Just demonstrates that UV radiation can cause cancer.

■ 1928
Scottish bacteriologist Alexander Fleming discovers penicillin.

1930 to 1970

■ 1937
Italian scientist Daniel Bovet identifies the first antihistamine effective in treating allergies.

■ 1948
The World Health Organization is founded.

■ 1950
Link between smoking and lung cancer is shown.

■ 1952
Jonas Salk develops the first polio vaccine.

■ 1953
Francis Crick, James Watson, and Rosalind Franklin determine the double-helix structure of DNA.

■ 1967
South African surgeon Christiaan Barnard performs the first successful heart transplant.

1970 to 1985

■ 1973
American and English physicians begin to develop magnetic resonance imaging (MRI) scanning.

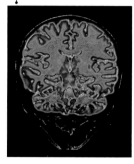

■ 1976
The Ebola virus is first identified after outbreaks in Africa.

■ 1978
The first "test tube" baby is born in England.

■ 1982
The first genetically engineered insulin is produced.

■ 1983
Luc Montagnier and Robert Gallo discover the human immuno-deficiency virus (HIV).

1985 to PRESENT

■ 1998
Researchers at Johns Hopkins University successfully grow human stem cells in a lab.

■ 2001
American researchers successfully clone a human embryo.

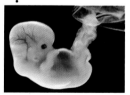

■ 2007
Geneticist J. Craig Venter publishes his entire genetic sequence—the first genome published of a single person.

■ 2010
World's first all-robotic surgery takes place in Canada.

■ 2013
Researchers develop a 3-D printed prosthetic hand that can be produced at a low cost.

EYES ON THE PRIZE

SEEING THE WAY TO NEW PATHS IN MEDICINE

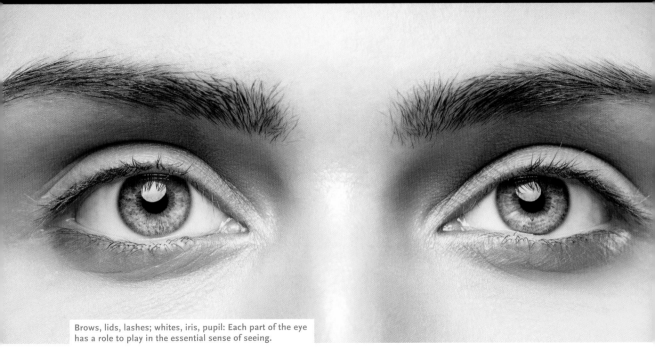

Brows, lids, lashes; whites, iris, pupil: Each part of the eye has a role to play in the essential sense of seeing.

LOOKING DEEPER INTO OUR EYES

The eyes are windows to the soul, lamp of the body—literature is full of such metaphors, which are today taking on new meaning. Yet roughly one in every 200 people on Earth—39 million of us—can't see. Another 246 million have low vision to degrees that impose moderate or severe limits. These burdens alone justify the search for new treatments. Yet the eye is also getting increased attention because it provides a safe, accessible spot to test treatments that might also be used elsewhere in the body.

To start with, researchers can look directly into the eye to see what's wrong and whether a treatment is working. Likewise, the eye's owner can see out of it (or not), providing a quick, vital measure of function. The eye is also tough, so doctors can more safely try a remedy in the eye, such as gene therapy, that might wreak havoc elsewhere. The eye is becoming a window not just to the soul, but also to the possibilities—and limits—of therapeutic approaches on which medicine is betting its future.

Eyes Under Threat

Multiple diseases can afflict the same eye. Three common and treatable diseases occur in the front of the eye. There currently is no cure for age-related macular degeneration, which occurs in the back of the eye near the retina.

Normal vision

GLAUCOMA

Glaucoma is caused by fluid buildup in the eye, resulting in pressure that can damage the optic nerve. If it's caught early enough, surgery and medication may slow its advance.

CATARACTS

The world's leading cause of blindness, cataracts are caused when proteins in the lens clump together, blocking and distorting light to the retina. Surgery can restore sight.

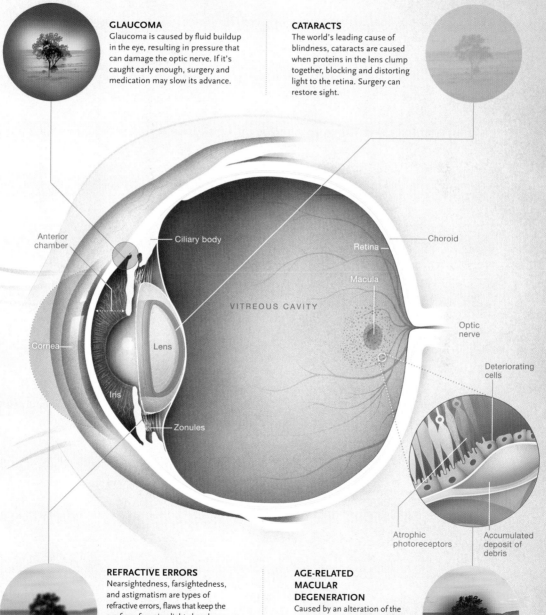

Anterior chamber

Ciliary body

Retina

Choroid

Macula

VITREOUS CAVITY

Optic nerve

Cornea

Lens

Iris

Zonules

Deteriorating cells

Atrophic photoreceptors

Accumulated deposit of debris

REFRACTIVE ERRORS

Nearsightedness, farsightedness, and astigmatism are types of refractive errors, flaws that keep the eye from focusing light sharply on the retina. They're the most common causes of impairment yet easily corrected with lenses or surgery.

AGE-RELATED MACULAR DEGENERATION

Caused by an alteration of the underlying layers of the retina's macular area, AMD affects photoreceptors that process images. There is no cure.

Antibiotic Resistance

THE POULTRY CASE STUDY

Americans today eat three times as much poultry as they did in 1960. Since most U.S. chickens are raised in large, crowded facilities, farmers feed them antibiotics to prevent disease as well as speed their growth.

Decades of Antibiotics

Since the 1950s, farmers have fed antibiotic growth promoters (AGPs) to livestock. Overusing these substances can create superbugs, pathogens that are resistant to multiple drugs and could be passed along to humans. Mindful of that, companies such as Perdue Farms have stopped using the drugs to make chickens gain weight faster. Since Denmark banned AGPs in the 1990s, the major pork exporter says it's producing more pigs— and the animals get fewer diseases. Says Centers for Disease Control and Prevention epidemiologist Tom Chiller, "Antibiotics are miracle drugs that should only be used to treat diseases."

MEAT CONSUMPTION IN THE U.S.

100 pounds per person per year

Beef

Pork

Chicken

Turkey

80

60

40

20

0

1930 1940 1950 1960 1970 1980 1990 2000 2010

Antibiotics as Growth Promoters

They help chickens grow bigger faster, making the meat . . .

. . . cheaper for the consumer.

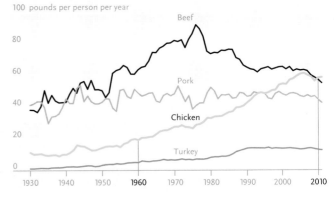

In 1960 it took 63 days to grow a 3.4-pound broiler.

$3.24 * a pound

In 2011 it took 47 days to grow a 5.4-pound one.

$1.29 a pound

* 2011 dollars, adjusted for inflation

IN 2015, ANTIBIOTICS GIVEN TO MEAT ANIMALS AROUND THE WORLD TOTALED 126 MILLION POUNDS.

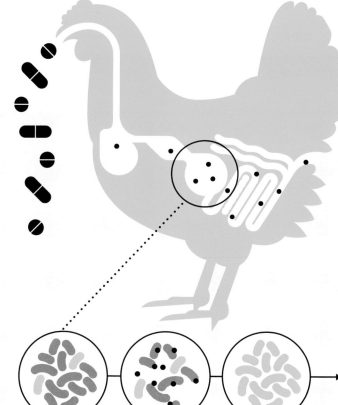

How Resistance Develops and Spreads

1.

Antibiotics can be given to livestock in their feed or sprayed on them, to be ingested when the animals groom themselves.

2.

The bacteria causing an infection are usually not resistant to drugs.

But some of them can be naturally drug resistant.

When antibiotics kill the nonresistant bacteria . . .

. . . the resistant ones, the superbugs, can flourish.

53%

of grocery store chicken sampled in a 2013 study had resistant *E. coli.*

3.

Superbugs can be passed to humans in many ways.

Farmworkers often have direct contact with animals.

Drug-resistant bacteria can linger on improperly cooked meat.

Fertilizer or water containing animal feces can spread superbugs to food crops.

FUTURE PROSTHETICS

TECHNOLOGY THAT CAN MAKE US MORE HUMAN

A spinach leaf models human heart tissue.

GROWING A HEART

POPEYE WAS RIGHT

One of the defining traits of a leaf is the branching network of thin veins that delivers water and nutrients to its cells. Now, scientists have used plant veins to replicate the way blood moves through human tissue.

Plant cells were removed from a spinach leaf, leaving behind a frame of cellulose. The remaining plant frame was bathed in live human cells, so that the human tissue grew on the spinach scaffolding and surrounded the tiny veins. Then the team sent fluids and microbeads through its veins to show that blood cells can flow through this system. The goal is to eventually be able to replace damaged tissue in patients who have had heart attacks or who have suffered other cardiac issues.

FEELINGS

SENSATIONAL

Scientists have made great strides toward making prosthetics that are part of the patients themselves, not just tools. One team in Europe wired pressure sensors in the fingers of an artificial hand to sensory nerves in an amputee's upper arm, allowing him to feel textures, pressure, and vibrations. In Chicago, a group of researchers created a thought-controlled leg that can climb stairs and go from sitting to standing in response to signals from nerves in a patient's stump. Another group, also in Chicago, developed pattern recognition, in which the prosthetic limbs interpret nerve signals from patients in real time, responding directly to intentions.

A boy tries on a 3-D–printed hand.

A man who is an amputee stretches before a run.

USING 3-D PRINTERS, POLYMER SCAFFOLDING, AND HUMAN CELLS AS INK, RESEARCHERS ARE ON THE VERGE OF CREATING LIVING LIMBS AND ORGANS.

Eyes gleam in a robot at the AI for Good Global Summit.

ACCESSIBILITY

MAKERS MAKING A DIFFERENCE

Traditional prosthetics can cost thousands of dollars and need to be replaced as children grow. But over the last few years, with the help of an organization called e-NABLE, volunteers across the globe have been using open-source technology and 3-D printers to provide free prosthetic hands and below-elbow devices for children and adults who need them. These simple, mechanical prosthetics—which have no motors, sensors, or batteries—are individualized to meet each individual's physical needs.

Often made in bold colors with visible working parts, these prosthetics have a different appeal from those intended to resemble missing limbs. The attention the devices draw is not necessarily unwelcome, especially when it gives children wearing them a chance to talk to their peers about how they work.

Organizers estimate that volunteers, which number in the tens of thousands and span more than 100 countries, have designed and created over 5,000 devices. E-NABLE, which sees itself as part of a "connected humanitarianism" movement, is looking to help volunteers create additional 3-D printed devices and assistive technologies.

ROBOTICS

MUSCULAR ROBOTS

Researchers in Tokyo have developed a new method for using living rat muscle tissue in robotics. The "biohybrid" design simulates the look and movements of a human finger. The research group modeled their work on living muscle tissue. To grow their robot's muscles, they layered hydrogel sheets filled with myoblasts—rat muscle cells—on a robotic skeleton. The grown muscle is then stimulated with an electric current that forces it to contract.

The research team thinks that future versions of muscle-driven robots could help engineers create more nimble prosthetics. The human-like muscle system could also one day help scientists test drugs and toxins, reducing the need for animal testing.

PSYCHOBIOME

THE BRAIN-GUT CONNECTION

The human body contains as many microbes as it does cells—nearly 30 trillion of them. Several ecosystems are found on our skin: Your forearm has the richest community, with an average of 44 species. The human gut teems with bacteria, which help us digest food, absorb nutrients, and protect our intestinal walls. The more we learn about our microbes, the more we realize their profound effect on mental health, attitudes, and emotions—which is why many now call that population inside us our "psychobiome."

OUR LANGUAGE ALREADY HINTS AT HOW THE MICROBIOME INFLUENCES OUR FEELINGS, WHEN WE TALK ABOUT GUT FEELINGS, GUT INSTINCTS, GUTSY MOVES.

An illustration colorized to emphasize the variety of microbes in the human microbiome

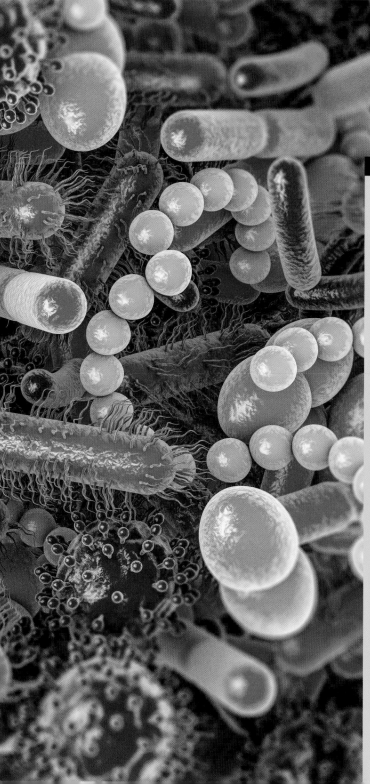

Five Ways the Gut Affects
WELL-BEING

INFECTIONS AND DEPRESSION In 2000, following a contamination of the water supply, an infection spread among 5,000 residents of a single town, Walkerton, Ohio. In addition to causing gastrointestinal illness, the related inflammation resulted in widespread depression and anxiety.

STRESS AND INFLAMMATION Stress hormones are part of our fight-or-flight response. But they also quiet the immune system, allowing gut pathogens such as *Salmonella* and *E. coli* to flourish, which means people who are stressed become more susceptible to infection and inflammation.

TEENAGE HABITS AND DECISION-MAKING The sheathing of the brain's nerve fibers (myelination), a process governed by the microbiome, spreads to the frontal lobes in our teen years. This means executive function and thought processes are shaped in part by youthful eating habits and stressors.

FERMENTED FOODS AND MEMORY The psychobiotic *Lactobacillus plantarum*, found in foods such as kimchi and sauerkraut, has anti-inflammatory properties. Evidence from animal studies indicates that it improves memory even in cases of memory loss related to aging.

JUNK FOOD AND ANXIETY Foods with added sugars boost harmful bacteria in the gut and have been shown to bring on depression. In a study involving 23,000 mothers and children, junk food in a mother's diet while pregnant or in a child's own diet was a predictor of psychological problems in the children.

HERBS & SPICES
FOR HEALTH

BASIL
Fragrant annual
native to India

BAY
Aromatic shrub leaf
flavors soups.

CHERVIL
Delicate relative
of parsley

CHIVES
Tender stalks
in onion family

CILANTRO
Leaves of plant whose
seeds are coriander

DILL
Ancient cure
for indigestion

FENNEL
Seeds, leaves, stalks,
bulbs all tasty

LEMONGRASS
Southeast Asian native,
citrus flavor

MARJORAM
Sweet herb, makes
a calming tea

OREGANO
Classic herb in
Mediterranean cuisines

PARSLEY
Edible garnish high
in antioxidants

PEPPERMINT
Tea is a favorite
stomach soother.

ROSEMARY
Research affirms
tradition as pain reliever.

SAGE
Honeybees love
sage flowers.

TARRAGON
Fragile flavor best captured
in vinegar

THYME
Good in cooking;
tea also calms a cough.

ALLSPICE
Ground from dried berries, Caribbean native

BLACK PEPPER
Native to India, spurred spice trade in 1600s

CARDAMOM
Ancient Egyptians chewed it for clean breath.

CAYENNE
Powdered hot peppers, rich in vitamins and minerals

CINNAMON
Inner bark of tropical tree, lowers blood sugar

CLOVES
Ground tree buds, antioxidant and mildly anesthetic

CORIANDER
Seed of cilantro plant, often used in curries

CUMIN
Aromatic seed essential to Mexican and Indian cuisines

GINGER
Ground root, traditional remedy for seasickness

MACE
Outer covering of nutmeg; both appetite stimulants

PAPRIKA
Bright red, made of dried peppers, typical in Hungary

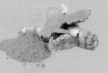

TURMERIC
Related to ginger, provides many health benefits

ANCIENT WISDOM

Herbs and spices add flavor, aroma, color, texture, and nutrients to food—and many improve health as well. Herbs are leaves or stems of plants from temperate zones, used fresh or dried. Spices come from many parts of tropical plants—dried seeds, flowers, fruit, bark, or roots—and are used either whole or ground fine. Most of these provide vitamins and minerals, and many have healing properties.

A WORD FROM

Passing on Knowledge Interviewing people is a standard method in ethnobotanical research. Through individual interviews with several people in the community who self-medicate with "bush medicines," I am hoping to develop a database of locally useful plants and to understand the myriad of ways in which these plants are used . . . The ultimate goal is to give back that information to the community, so that these precious oral traditions do not disappear.

—**INA VANDEBROEK,** *ethnobotanist*

MINDFULNESS

THE SCIENCE OF PAYING ATTENTION

Even just one generation ago, traits like compassion and focus were thought to be inherent and predetermined. But scientists have come to understand that mental patterns are malleable: Through practice and repetition, the brain's circuitry can be rerouted, and one's reactions and habits can be intentionally redirected. This is known as neuroplasticity.

Meditation is a deliberate approach to mindfulness in which one remains present and reflects on internal thoughts, physical responses, and external stimuli. Practitioners have been found to have better control of their attention and emotions. Meditation also appears to slow loss of the brain's gray matter and age-related cognitive decline.

A woman sits mindfully at the edge of the Trolltunga rock formation in Norway.

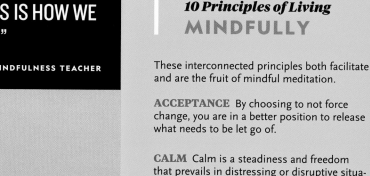

> ## " THE BEST WAY TO CAPTURE MOMENTS IS TO PAY ATTENTION. THIS IS HOW WE CULTIVATE MINDFULNESS."
>
> **—JON KABAT-ZINN, AUTHOR AND MINDFULNESS TEACHER**

10 Principles of Living
MINDFULLY

These interconnected principles both facilitate and are the fruit of mindful meditation.

ACCEPTANCE By choosing to not force change, you are in a better position to release what needs to be let go of.

CALM Calm is a steadiness and freedom that prevails in distressing or disruptive situations, regardless of the emotions involved.

CLARITY Consistent habits of observation and openness yield deep wisdom and the ability to see yourself rightly.

COMPASSION When you're able to identify suffering and to have empathy with those in pain—whether yourself or others—you can act compassionately to bring relief.

CONNECTEDNESS We are connected to everything around us. Consider and celebrate the ways we need one another and the natural world.

CONSCIOUSNESS Practice being aware of what is immediately present and of what you're experiencing in the moment. Do not need to judge it as right or wrong. Just name it.

GRATEFULNESS Acknowledge the world's goodness and beauty and be receptive to these gifts. By cultivating gratitude, you reap great connection and joy.

IMPERMANENCE Being present in each moment is key in a changing, temporary world, where grasping at what is passing brings only grief and regret.

JOY Deep-seated bliss transcends the situations in which we find ourselves and guides us toward truth and health.

NEWCOMER'S EYES Observe yourself and what's around you with curiosity, wonder, and openness, as if seeing it for the first time—setting aside presumptions and previous experiences.

FURTHER

PERPETUATING THE SPECIES

These babies, born in 2010, will grow up to see a world populated by more than 10 billion. Earth's population reached 7 billion in 2011, more than doubling since 1960, and it has already jumped beyond 7.7 billion today, with people living longer and healthier lives in many regions of the world. Countries in the Middle East and Africa show the fastest rate of population increase; Europe and the United States show generally declining fertility.

Nurses cluster swaddled newborns for a group portrait at Winnie Palmer Hospital in Orlando, Florida.

"I AM ONE OF 7 BILLION. YOU ARE ALSO ONE OF 7 BILLION. TOGETHER, WE CAN BE 7 BILLION STRONG—BY WORKING IN SOLIDARITY FOR A BETTER WORLD FOR ALL."

—BAN KI-MOON, FORMER SECRETARY-GENERAL OF THE UNITED NATIONS

YESTERDAY TO TOMORROW

WORLD HISTORY | U.S. HISTORY

Built some 4,500 years ago, the Giza Pyramids hold clues to life—and the afterlife—in Egypt's Old Kingdom.

QUIZ MASTER

Looking Back For some, the definition of nerdy is being able to recite little-known facts about history. Truth is, understanding our past helps us shape our future. Here's a chapter that looks out over millennia and dives deep into a few special stories.

—**CARA SANTA MARIA,** *Our Favorite Nerd*

p288

IN WHAT YEAR WAS THE CITY OF ROME FOUNDED?

p 286

WHICH GERMAN BROTHERS COLLECTED VOLUMES OF FOLKTALES IN THE 19TH CENTURY?

p291

HOW OLD WAS KING TUT WHEN HE BECAME PHARAOH?

p302

IN WHAT YEAR DID THE PANAMA CANAL OPEN?

p290

IN WHAT YEAR DID THE INTERNATIONAL SPACE STATION BEGIN OPERATING WITH A CREW?

p305

ON WHAT CONTINENT DID THE ASANTE KINGDOM RULE IN THE 18TH CENTURY?

WHAT TYPE OF TREE DOES WASHINGTON, D.C., CELEBRATE EACH SPRING?

p314

WHAT CHARTER, ENACTED IN 1215, ENSURED INDIVIDUAL RIGHTS AND JUSTICE TO CITIZENS OF ENGLAND?

p294

IN WHAT CENTURY DID QUEEN SEMIRAMIS RULE THE ANCIENT KINGDOM OF BABYLON?

p292

p304

WHAT CITY, LOCATED IN MODERN-DAY TURKEY, WAS THE FIRST TO HAVE A SYSTEM OF STREET LIGHTING?

WHICH THREE RIGHTS WERE SPELLED OUT IN THE DECLARATION OF INDEPENDENCE?

p295

WHO WAS THE FIRST AFRICAN-AMERICAN WOMAN ELECTED TO THE U.S. CONGRESS?

p313

p305

WHO SENT THE FIRST TELEGRAPH MESSAGE IN THE U.S.?

WHICH AMENDMENT TO THE U.S. CONSTITUTION GAVE AMERICAN WOMEN THE RIGHT TO VOTE?

p309

PREHISTORY TO 1600
TIME LINE

PREHISTORY	3000 to 1000 BC	1000 to 500 BC	500 to 1 BC

PREHISTORY

ca 100,000 ya*
Early humans migrate from Africa to other continents.

ca 80,000 ya
Neanderthals and modern humans live alongside each other in Europe.

ca 14,500 ya
Human populations are present in North and South America.

ca 10,000 ya
Agriculture develops in the Yellow River Valley and other places in China.

ca 3200 BC
Sumer, the first known civilization, emerges in modern-day Iraq.

* years ago

3000 to 1000 BC

ca 2575 BC
Ancient Egypt's Old Kingdom begins.

ca 2500–1900 BC
The Indus civilization thrives in modern-day Pakistan and northwest India.

ca 1766–1122 BC
The Shang dynasty rules in ancient China.

ca 1500 BC
Olmec culture develops in modern-day Mexico.

ca 1200 BC
Proto-Celtic people of Indo-European origin settle in central Europe.

1000 to 500 BC

753 BC
Rome is founded by Romulus and Remus, according to legend.

ca 700 BC
Athens and other Greek city-states become centers of learning and maritime trade.

ca 560 BC
Siddhartha Gautama is born in the Himalayan foothills; he is later known as the Buddha.

509 BC
The Roman Republic is established.

500 to 1 BC

ca 500 BC
Iron tool technology spreads across Africa.

334 BC
Alexander the Great invades Persia and carves out an empire stretching from Greece to northwestern India.

ca 100 BC
Buddhism spreads into Central Asia along the Silk Road.

27 BC
Augustus becomes the first emperor of Rome.

| AD 1 to 500 | 500 to 1090 | 1090 to 1400 | 1400 to 1600 |

■ 79

Mount Vesuvius erupts, destroying Pompeii and Herculaneum.

■ ca 300

Maya in South America develop a script and a calendar.

■ 312

Constantine I becomes the emperor of Rome and expands legal rights for religions.

■ 441

Attila the Hun launches a massive attack on the Eastern Roman Empire.

■ ca 500

The empire of Ghana gains prominence in West Africa.

■ 570

Muhammad, the Prophet and future messenger of Islam, is born in Mecca.

■ 800

Charlemagne is crowned the Holy Roman Emperor.

■ 960

The Song dynasty reunifies China and ushers in economic, social, and cultural change.

■ ca 1000

Leif Eriksson sails to North America.

■ 1054

The schism between the Roman and Eastern Christian churches becomes permanent.

■ 1095

The First Crusade begins, inaugurating a series of religious wars that would last for hundreds of years.

■ 1206

Genghis Khan becomes leader of the Mongol confederation.

■ 1337

The Hundred Years' War begins between England and France.

■ 1368

Zhu Yuanzhang founds the Ming dynasty in China.

■ 1440

Moctezuma I becomes ruler of the Aztec.

■ 1478

The Spanish Inquisition begins.

■ 1517

Martin Luther instigates the Protestant Reformation.

■ 1519–1521

Spain conquers the Aztec Empire, beginning a century-long colonial period.

■ 1560s

The transatlantic slave trade grows in West Africa.

■ 1577–1580

English explorer Sir Francis Drake circumnavigates the globe.

TALES OLDER
THAN THE HILLS

A BOY STEALS THE OGRE'S TREASURE
4,500 years old
A boy trespasses into a giant's house to steal his treasure. When the giant comes home, the boy hides and then manages to evade the giant's pursuit. Finally the boy kills the giant and takes his treasure.

THE SMITH AND THE DEVIL
6,000 years old
A blacksmith trades his soul to the devil for the power to weld any materials together. With his wish granted, the man traps the devil, sticking him to the ground until the evil spirit releases him from the bargain.

THE ANIMAL BRIDEGROOM
3,000 years old
Picking a rose lands a father in debt to a beast. In exchange for his freedom, his daughter is taken prisoner. After falling in love with the beast, she must overcome a curse to transform him into a prince.

FAIRY TALES—OLDER THAN YOU MIGHT THINK

As Wilhelm and Jacob Grimm collected Germanic folktales in the 19th century, they realized that many were similar to stories told in distant parts of the world. The brothers wondered whether similarities indicated a shared ancestry thousands of years old.

To test the Grimms' theory, anthropologist Jamie Tehrani and literary scholar Sara Graça da Silva traced 76 basic plots back to their oldest linguistic ancestor. If a similar tale was told in German and Hindi, the researchers concluded its roots lay in the languages' last common ancestor. "The Smith and the Devil," a story about a man who trades his soul for blacksmith skills, was first told some 6,000 years ago in Proto-Indo-European. In the United States, we tell a similar tale about blues guitarist Robert Johnson.

FRIENDS IN LIFE AND DEATH
2,000 years old
A man invites his dead friend to his wedding. When the groom accompanies his friend to the underworld, 400 years pass and he misses his own nuptials.

THE SUPERNATURAL HELPER
2,500 years old
A peasant falsely tells the king his daughter can spin gold out of straw. An elfin creature appears, offering the real skill in exchange for her firstborn child. The only way out is to guess his name—which she does.

MODERN TAKES

FRIENDS IN LIFE AND DEATH
A dead man accepts Don Juan's invitation to a banquet in exchange for Don Juan's attendance at another event—in the underworld.

THE ANIMAL BRIDEGROOM
In Disney's *Beauty and the Beast,* a witch's curse traps the prince in a beast's body until Belle's love breaks the spell.

THE SMITH AND THE DEVIL
Fictional scholar Faust and blues guitarist Robert Johnson are among the modern figures said to have sold their souls to the devil for knowledge.

A BOY STEALS THE OGRE'S TREASURE
Magic beans grow to great heights in "Jack and the Beanstalk," allowing Jack to climb up into a giant's lair and steal his treasures.

THE SUPERNATURAL HELPER
Trapped in an agreement to give Rumpelstiltskin her first child, a young queen overhears him chanting his name and gets out of the deal.

FOLKTALES ARE PASSED DOWN ORALLY, OBSCURING THEIR AGE AND ORIGIN.

1600 TO RECENT PAST
TIME LINE

1600 to 1700	1700 to 1800	1800 to 1860	1860 to 1900

1600s
European powers expand their colonization around the world.

ca 1600
Algonquin tribes unite to form the Powhatan Confederacy in North America.

1633
For his theory that Earth circles the sun, Galileo goes on trial for heresy.

1649
Civil war in England results in the execution of King Charles I.

1661
Swedish banknotes become the first paper currency in use in Europe.

1701
The Asante kingdom expands in West Africa under the reign of Osei Tutu.

1762
Catherine II proclaims herself empress of Russia.

1770
Aboard the *Endeavour*, James Cook claims Australia for Britain.

1776
Americans post their Declaration of Independence.

1789
A mob storms the Bastille, marking the beginning of the French Revolution.

1801
A slave rebellion succeeds, leading to Haiti's independence from France three years later.

1815
Simón Bolívar writes his "Letter From Jamaica," outlining his vision of South America freed of colonial rule.

1833
Slavery is abolished throughout the British Empire.

1837
Queen Victoria begins her 63-year reign.

1845–1851
Irish potato famine causes poverty and mass starvation; millions emigrate to North America.

1861
Tsar Alexander II frees serfs in Russia.

1863
Abraham Lincoln issues the Emancipation Proclamation, freeing slaves in 10 states.

FREEDOM TO SLAVES!

1867
Provinces in Canada unite into a single country.

1884–1885
The Berlin Conference divides Africa among various European powers.

1897
First Zionist Congress convenes in Basel, Switzerland.

| 1900 to 1925 | 1925 to 1950 | 1950 to 1975 | 1975 to 2000 |

1900 to 1925

■ 1914
The Panama Canal opens, enabling faster transoceanic shipping.

■ 1914
Assassination of Archduke Ferdinand sparks years-long World War I.

■ 1917
Lenin and the Bolsheviks overthrow the tsar in Russian Revolution.

■ 1920
Mohandas Gandhi becomes India's leader in its struggle for independence.

1925 to 1950

■ 1929
Wall Street stock market crashes, beginning the Great Depression.

■ 1933
Adolf Hitler is appointed chancellor of Germany.

■ 1939–1945
In World War II, Allied powers (including U.K., U.S., Soviet Union, France, and China) battle Axis powers (Germany, Italy, and Japan).

■ 1945
United Nations is founded.

■ 1949
Marxist leader Mao Zedong transforms China into Communist People's Republic of China.

1950 to 1975

■ 1955
Rosa Parks's arrest in Alabama sets the American civil rights movement in motion.

■ 1957
European Economic Community, precursor to the European Union, is established.

■ 1959
Fidel Castro takes over Cuba after leading a Marxist revolution.

■ 1973
Organization of Petroleum-Exporting Countries (OPEC) embargoes oil supplies, causing a worldwide energy crisis.

1975 to 2000

■ 1979
Muslim cleric Ayatollah Ruhollah Khomeini seizes power in Iran.

■ 1986
Disastrous accident at Chernobyl nuclear power plant in Ukraine forces massive resettlement.

■ 1989
Thousands of students occupy Beijing's Tian'anmen Square, advocating democracy in China.

■ 1989
Built in 1961 to encircle Germany's West Berlin, the Berlin Wall falls, a sign of the end of the Cold War.

■ 1990
Nelson Mandela is released after 27 years in prison, signifying end of apartheid in South Africa.

SEMIRAMIS
QUEEN OF BABYLON

THE ASSYRIAN EMPIRE'S ONLY WOMAN RULER

In the Neo-Assyrian regime of the ninth century BC, one woman commanded an entire empire—stretching from Asia Minor to today's western Iran. She was Sammu-ramat, thought to mean "high heaven," and she inspired universal respect. Centuries after her brief five-year reign, Greeks wrote about Semiramis, as they called her, and her achievements. From there, the Assyrian queen passed into the realm of legend. What stands out is how both the woman and the myth were celebrated for things traditionally associated with male rulers: scoring military triumphs, building architectural wonders, and ruling with wisdom.

> **" AS FOR SEMIRAMIS, APART FROM HER WORKS AT BABYLON, MANY OTHERS ARE ALSO TO BE SEEN THROUGHOUT ALMOST THE WHOLE OF THE CONTINENT OF ASIA."**
>
> **—FROM *THE GEOGRAPHY OF STRABO*, WRITTEN AROUND 10 BC**

Queen Sammu-ramat of history begat Queen Semiramis of legend, whose civic accomplishments are lauded on the same level as her beauty.

Semiramis's
LIFE AND LEGEND

■ **MARRIAGE**
According to artifacts, Queen Sammu-ramat was married to King Shamshi-Adad V, who reigned 823–811 BC, and was the mother of King Adad-nirari III.

■ **INHERITING THE THRONE**
When the king died, his son, Adad-nirari III, was too young to rule, leaving Queen Sammu-ramat to govern Assyria through her regency.

■ **BATTLE**
One monument mentions that the queen accompanied her son into battle, which indicates her actions were honored and respected.

■ **EARNING RESPECT**
Another monument bears this exceptional dedication: "Sammu-ramat, Queen of Shamshi-Adad, King of the Universe, King of Assyria; Mother of Adad-nirari, King of the Universe, King of Assyria."

■ **A PLACE IN HISTORY**
In the fifth century BC, the historian Herodotus perpetuated memory of Sammu-ramat using the Greek form of her name, Semiramis, by which she is best known today.

■ **MYTHIC ORIGINS**
In the account perpetuated by Diodorus Siculus in the first century BC, Semiramis was the child of a Syrian goddess and a young Syrian man.

■ **ANCIENT WONDERS**
Greek historians said the queen ordered a new city, with fabulous hanging gardens, to be built on the banks of the Euphrates—Babylon. No historical evidence supports their claims.

■ **CIRCLES OF HELL**
She inspired the Italian medieval poet Dante, who placed her in his *Inferno,* where she is punished for her "sensual vices."

■ **A LASTING LEGACY**
The French Enlightenment writer Voltaire wrote a tragedy about her, which was later made into Rossini's 1823 opera, *Semiramide.*

A HISTORY OF DEMOCRACY

THE QUEST FOR EQUAL RIGHTS

Raphael's "School of Athens"

ANCIENT HISTORY

FIRST GRANTING OF RIGHTS, CA 594 BC

Solon of Athens institutes economic and political reforms, including granting all citizens the right to participate in the ecclesia (general assembly), which has legislative and judicial powers.

REFORMING POWER STRUCTURE, 508 BC

Athenian statesman Cleisthenes encourages participation in government by extending the right to participate to all free adult men born in townships—and becomes the father of democracy.

COMMON GOOD, 4TH CENTURY BC

Aristotle describes a "polity" as government by consent and for the common good—which resembles what comes to be known as a constitutional democracy.

EARLY TIMES

OLDEST PARLIAMENT, 930

During the Viking era and predating Iceland's written language, the first parliament, Althing, is established at Thingvellir, a place-name literally meaning "parliament plains." It has become the world's longest-running representative democracy.

LEVELS OF REPRESENTATION, CA 11TH TO 15TH CENTURIES

The Igbo society in what is now Nigeria has representative bodies at the village level that seek consensus under the leadership of elders. This decentralized, chiefless system endures until colonialism.

INDIVIDUAL FREEDOM, 1215

The Magna Carta—"Great Charter"—is issued in Latin by England's King John in the context of power struggles between the pope and the king of England. Reaffirmed by John's successors, it ensures basic individual rights and guarantees justice and the right to a fair trial, thus granting protection to individuals from higher authorities.

SELF-GOVERNANCE, 1620

Most of the men arriving on the *Mayflower* sign a compact that will influence governance in the Plymouth colony. The Mayflower Compact has inclinations toward democratic values of self-government and common consent.

The U.S. Constitution

> ❝ DEMOCRACY ALONE, OF ALL FORMS OF GOVERNMENT, ENLISTS THE FULL FORCE OF MEN'S ENLIGHTENED WILL.❞
>
> —**FRANKLIN DELANO ROOSEVELT, THIRD INAUGURAL ADDRESS, 1941**

Tunisian demonstrators during election, 2011

REVOLUTIONARY ERA

ALL CREATED EQUAL, 1776

Colonists in the Americas draft the Declaration of Independence—asserting "that all men are created equal, that they are endowed by their Creator with certain unalienable Rights, that among these are Life, Liberty and the pursuit of Happiness." This becomes a globally recognized document of self-governance and the fundamental rights of human beings.

BALANCE OF POWER, 1787

The U.S. Constitution is presented to the states for ratification. It outlines the workings of a federal democratic government, including the balance of power in a tripartite government, individual rights versus the state, and the limits of centralized government versus the state sovereignty. Amendments known as the Bill of Rights are added in 1789.

RIGHTS OF THE CITIZEN, 1789

As the French Revolution begins, France's National Assembly adopts the Declaration of the Rights of Man and of the Citizen, which is later revised and incorporated into subsequent constitutions.

MODERN TIMES

END TO COLONIALISM, 1950

India becomes a democratic republic when its new constitution takes effect—the world's largest democracy.

CIVIL PROTEST, 1989

Hundreds of thousands occupy China's Tiananmen Square to demand democratic reform. After a tense few months, the government responds with violence, martial law, and criminal prosecutions.

BRINGING DOWN APARTHEID, 1996

Following centuries of occupation by the Dutch and British, including decades of apartheid, the government of South Africa transitions to majority rule.

ARAB SPRING, 2010

The first of several pro-democracy protests takes place in Tunisia, inspiring uprisings across North Africa and the Middle East. Some countries suppress the movement; others, like Morocco, implement reforms.

ADA LOVELACE
EARLY PROGRAMMER

THE ENCHANTRESS OF NUMBERS

Augusta Ada Byron, who later became the Countess of Lovelace, was born in Britain in 1815—not a time known for women scientists. Her father, Lord Byron, was one of the most popular poets in Europe, and she herself was a celebrity of sorts. Ada Lovelace, as she was known, became the world's first programmer a century before computers were invented.

The visionary Ada Lovelace was the daughter of Romantic poet Lord Byron and Annabelle Byron, who encouraged her education in mathematics.

Educated in math and science—part of her mother's efforts to tamp down any dangerous creative tendencies she may have inherited from her infamous father—Lovelace followed her scientific and technological passions, much a scandal at the time. But as her collaborator, Charles Babbage, wrote, Lovelace's "taste for mathematics is so decided that it ought not to be checked."

SEEING COMPUTERS' POTENTIAL

In 1833, the teenage Lovelace began to work with Babbage, a mathematician and engineer. They collaborated on his Analytical Engine, a precursor to the modern computer that could calculate complex mathematical problems.

Lovelace wrote a series of notes about the device for publication and included an algorithm for using the Analytical Engine to calculate a sequence of numbers called Bernoulli numbers. Her algorithm—which told the Analytical Engine exactly which functions to calculate and in what order—was the first computer program. Her mastery of abstract ideas and the science of operations anticipated computers' being able to process any information represented by numbers. It was a full century later, in the 1940s, that Alan Turing built the first modern computer.

Today Lovelace is honored as a pioneer in computer science. The second Tuesday of October is Ada Lovelace Day. A programming language bears her name. A medal named after her is awarded by the British Computer Society. She stands as a model and inspiration for girls interested in engineering and science.

> **" THIS SCIENCE CONSTITUTES THE LANGUAGE THROUGH WHICH ALONE WE CAN ADEQUATELY EXPRESS THE GREAT FACTS OF THE NATURAL WORLD."**

A model of Lovelace and Babbage's proto-computer

KEY DATES

Imagining and Inventing MODERN COMPUTERS

1833
Meets Babbage and hears of his hand-cranked calculator, the Difference Engine

1835
Marries, at age 19, William King, age 30, eighth Baron King and first Earl of Lovelace

1843
Publishes her translation of a French paper on Babbage's Analytical Engine

1852
Dies from cancer, age 36

2009
Ada Lovelace Day celebrated internationally for the first time

BEST OF @NATGEO

TOP PHOTOS OF HISTORIC PLACES

@yamashitaphoto | MICHAEL YAMASHITA
A restored section of the Great Wall of China at Jinshanling s part of a fortification system whose construction began in the third century BC.

@salvarezphoto | STEPHEN ALVAREZ
A Bedouin man leads camels past an intricately carved mausoleum facade in Petra, an ancient city in what is now Jordan.

@simonnorfolkstudio | SIMON NORFOLK
Lights shine in the streets of Matera, a city built out from what s thought to be one of the earliest human settlements in Italy.

@salvarezphoto | STEPHEN ALVAREZ
The massive moai statues of Easter Island, erected between 1250 and 1500 AD, can weigh up to 86 tons.

@dguttenfelder | **DAVID GUTTENFELDER**
Grass carpets the site of a Viking ring fortress in Trelleborg, Denmark. These structures are remarkable for their symmetry and uniformity.

@irablockphoto | **IRA BLOCK**
A sacred destination for Buddhists, the Golden Rock gleams at the top of Mount Kyaiktiyo in Myanmar.

@argonautphoto | **AARON HUEY**
A pilgrim embraces the outside of the shrine of the Sufi saint Shah Yusuf Gardezi in Multan, Pakistan.

@simonnorfolkstudio | **SIMON NORFOLK**
Peaking during the Maya Classic period, Tikal in Guatemala maintains its wondrous temples, palaces, and plazas.

TERRA-COTTA
WARRIORS

A LEGION FOR ETERNITY

Workers digging a well outside the city of Xi'an, China, in 1974 struck upon one of the greatest archaeological discoveries in the world: a life-size clay soldier poised for battle. Government archaeologists arrived to find not one but thousands of clay soldiers, each with unique facial expressions and positioned according to rank, in trenchlike underground corridors. In some of the corridors, clay horses are aligned four abreast; behind them are wooden chariots. The terra-cotta army, we now know, was part of an elaborate mausoleum created to accompany the first emperor of China, Qin Shi Huang Di, into the afterlife.

THE AVERAGE TERRA-COTTA SOLDIER STANDS ABOUT FIVE FEET, EIGHT INCHES TALL.

Ranks of life-size clay soldiers, buried with the first emperor of China more than 2,000 years ago, were rediscovered in 1974.

The Emperor's ARMY FOR THE AFTERLIFE

■ **FIRST EMPEROR**
Ying Zheng took the throne in 246 BC at the age of 13. By 221 BC, he had unified a collection of warring kingdoms and took the name of Qin Shi Huang Di—the First Emperor of Qin.

■ **LABOR**
Court historian Sima Qian of the following Han dynasty claims that more than 700,000 laborers worked on the project, though modern scholars doubt that figure.

■ **BURIAL GUARDS**
An estimated 8,000 statues of warriors were buried in three pits less than a mile from the emperor's tomb.

■ **TOMB**
The burial complex covers almost 38 square miles.

■ **BURIED ALONGSIDE**
Artisans, craftsmen, and laborers—likely including shackled convicts—who died during the 36 years it took to build this complex were buried here.

■ **BURSTS OF COLOR**
Qin's army of soldiers and horses was a supernatural display swathed in a riot of bold colors: red and green, purple and yellow.

■ **PRESERVING EARTH**
The original paint degrades on exposure but adheres to dirt, so preservationists are now trying to preserve the earth itself.

■ **OTHER CULTURES**
Terra-cotta acrobats and bronze figures of ducks, swans, and cranes uncovered at the grand funerary complex may show evidence of Greek influence.

■ **EXCAVATION**
Archaeologists have no plans to unearth the first emperor's tomb, waiting instead for new conservation technologies.

GENOME CLUES IN EGYPT

An ornate gold coffin preserves the body of the pharaoh Tutankhamun.

ANCIENT RIDDLES, MODERN SCIENCE

Tutankhamun was a pharaoh during ancient Egypt's New Kingdom era, about 3,300 years ago. He ascended to the throne at the age of nine but ruled for only 10 years before dying at 19, around 1324 BC. Despite his brief reign, King Tut is perhaps Egypt's best known pharaoh because of the treasures—including a solid gold death mask—found in his tomb in 1922.

Yet while King Tut may be seen as the golden boy of ancient Egypt today, he wasn't exactly a strapping sun god during his reign. Instead, a DNA study says, King Tut was a frail pharaoh, beset by malaria and a bone disorder—his health possibly compromised by his incestuous origins.

The study could be conducted on ancient Egyptian royal mummies because the embalming method the ancient Egyptians used seems to have protected DNA as well as flesh. Using DNA samples taken from the mummies' bones, scientists were able to create a five-generation family tree for the boy pharaoh.

One genealogical mystery lingers: Some Egyptologists have speculated that King Tut's mother was Akhenaten's chief wife, Queen Nefertiti, who was also Akhenaten's cousin. Others claim that DNA shows his mother was the daughter of Amenhotep III and Tiye and thus the sister of her husband, Akhenaten.

LASTING LEGACIES

In addition to using DNA to identify royalty, scientists are evaluating the genetic makeup of mummies spanning 1,300 years. One surprising finding is that modern Egyptians have sub-Saharan ancestry not found in the ancient population, which was similar genetically to people from the Levant.

It had been thought that Egyptians acquired European and Middle Eastern ancestry over time, following conquests and contact with those populations. But scientists have determined that about 700 years ago, the amount of sub-Saharan DNA in Egyptians' makeup population increased. What facilitated this change is not clear. What is clear, however, is that Europeans are more closely related to ancient Egyptians than are modern Egyptians.

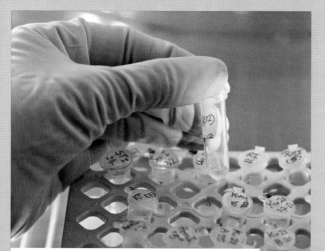

DNA samples from King Tut shed light on the royal lineage.

KEY FACTS

Ancient Egypt
THEN AND NOW

■ **DUSTING FOR PRINTS**
To dust for prints at a crime scene, modern investigators use Egyptian blue, a pigment formulated some 5,250 years ago—in the time of the pharaohs.

■ **EMBALMING**
A decade-long investigation of prehistoric mummy wrappings roughly 6,600 years old established that Egyptians embalmed their dead thousands of years earlier than previously thought.

■ **FEMALE FIGURE**
Historians had speculated that Akhenaten's feminine features—such as wide hips, a potbelly, and female-like breasts—were caused by a genetic disorder, but none has been found. It is now believed that these features, evident in statues, were created for religious and political reasons.

■ **ANCIENT BEERS**
Archaeologists have excavated a tomb belonging to Khonso Im-Heb, who was head of granaries and beer brewing for the worship of the Egyptian mother goddess, Mut.

■ **METEORIC METAL**
Researchers have confirmed that the iron of a dagger placed on King Tutankhamun's mummified body has meteoric origins. This follows an earlier identification of 5,000-year-old Egyptian beads made of meteoric iron—the earliest known sign of metalwork.

■ **SATELLITE**
Using high-resolution satellite images near Lisht, at the edge of the Sahara, archaeologists identified looted pits that turned out to be an interlocking mortuary system housing at least 4,000 individuals in the afterlife.

INNOVATIONS
TIME LINE

| 6000 to 1500 BC | 1500 to 1 BC | AD 1 to 1000 | 1000 to 1600 |

ca 6000 BC
The world's first known city, Çatalhöyük, is built in Anatolia.

ca 3500 BC
Wheeled vehicles are in use in the Middle East.

ca 3000 BC
Egyptians have developed a process for making paper from the papyrus plant.

ca 2500 BC
The Great Pyramids and the Sphinx are completed in Egypt.

ca 2500 BC
Peruvians use a canal system to irrigate crops.

ca 1525 BC
Stonehenge is completed in England.

ca 1400 BC
Iron weapons are in use by the Hittites of modern-day Turkey.

ca 500 BC
The abacus, earliest calculating tool, is in use in China.

ca 300 BC
The Maya begin constructing their monumental pyramids in Mexico and Central America.

214 BC
The main section of the Great Wall of China is completed.

ca 120 BC
Romans use concrete to create paved streets, aqueducts, and bridges.

ca 200
Porcelain is being produced in Han dynasty China.

350
Antioch, in today's Turkey, becomes the first city to have a system of street lighting.

ca 600
Chatrang, an early version of chess, is popular in parts of Central Asia.

607
Japan's Horyuji Temple, the world's oldest wooden building, is completed.

ca 800
Islamic scientists use the astrolabe for celestial observation.

ca 1000
Fireworks, made of a bamboo tube filled with gunpowder, are invented in China.

ca 1040
Chinese explorers use magnetic compasses to navigate.

ca 1286
In Italy, the first known eyeglasses are manufactured to correct vision.

ca 1450
The Inca construct a 20,000-mile-long roadway to unite their empire.

1455
Johannes Gutenberg prints the Bible on a movable type press.

| 1600 to 1800 | 1800 to 1900 | 1900 to 1950 | 1950 to PRESENT |

1600 to 1800

1609–1610
Galileo first observes Earth's moon and four moons of Jupiter with a telescope.

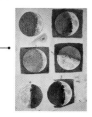

1626
St. Peter's Basilica is completed in Rome after 120 years of construction.

1716
The first lighthouse in North America is built, in Boston Harbor.

1752
After demonstrating the electrical nature of lightning, Benjamin Franklin invents the lightning rod.

1775
Inventor Alexander Cummings patents the first flushing toilet.

1800 to 1900

1843
Ada Lovelace and Charles Babbage collaborate on the world's first computer.

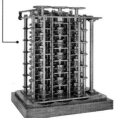

1844
Samuel Morse sends the first telegraph message in the United States.

1867
Alfred Nobel patents dynamite in Britain.

1876
Alexander Graham Bell invents the telephone and makes the first long-distance call.

1898
German chemist Hans von Pechmann synthesizes polyethylene, the world's first plastic.

1900 to 1950

1901
Italian scientist Guglielmo Marconi makes the first transatlantic radio broadcast.

1904
German engineer Christian Hülsmeyer patents the first radar system, used to prevent collisions among shipping vessels.

1931
The Empire State Building in New York City becomes the world's tallest building.

1943
Jacques Cousteau begins using the Aqua-Lung, which he designed with engineer Émile Gagnan, for underwater diving.

1945
Americans manufacture, test, and deploy the atom bomb.

1950 to PRESENT

1954
The first solar cells, converting sunlight to electricity, are developed.

1959
Unimate #001, the first industrial robot, is deployed in a General Motors engine plant.

1959
The microchip, key component of computers, is invented.

1989
The World Wide Web is initiated by British computer scientist Tim Berners-Lee.

2000
The International Space Station begins operating with a crew.

WAR IN OUR TIMES

THE EVOLUTION OF WEAPONS OF WAR

Strategies of war often pivot on newly available technologies, such as chemical weapons amid trenches in WWI and coordinated ground, naval, and air attacks in both theaters of WWII. By the late 20th century, the U.S. military was deploying surveillance drones (remotely piloted aerial systems). Unmanned weaponized drones soon followed and have been key in efforts against non-state actors such as al Qaeda and ISIS, which often embed militants among civilians in cities. Future conflicts will use multiple stealth vehicles, weapons systems, and cyberweapons.

SOME SOLDIERS NOW USE NANO-DRONES, MINIATURE CAMERA-EQUIPPED HELICOPTERS THAT WEIGH AN OUNCE OR TWO AND FIT INTO A POCKET.

The Global Hawk, an unmanned surveillance aircraft, images large areas from high altitudes for more than 30 hours at a time: one of many ways in which remotely piloted drones characterize military actions today.

KEEPING THE PEACE

Since its founding in 1948, the United Nations has operated 71 peacekeeping missions—almost two-thirds of those in the last 30 years. Today, over 110,000 peacekeepers are part of more than a dozen ongoing missions.

MAY 1948, MIDDLE EAST

The UN's first and longest-running peacekeeping mission continues to promote stability to the Middle East.

JANUARY 1949, INDIA AND PAKISTAN

This mission has been in place for decades to observe the cease-fire in the disputed region of Kashmir.

MARCH 1964, CYPRUS

With no political settlement between the Greek and Turkish communities, this mission maintains buffer zones, among other responsibilities.

MAY 1974, SYRIA

Originally in place to maintain the cease-fire between Israeli and Syrian forces, peacekeepers seek to de-escalate armed conflicts in the area.

MARCH 1978, LEBANON

Started to confirm Israel's withdrawal from Lebanon, the mission continues to monitor hostilities and ensure humanitarian access to civilians.

APRIL 1991, WESTERN SAHARA

This mission aims to help the people of Western Sahara choose independence or integration with Morocco.

JUNE 1999, KOSOVO

Having helped this republic (claimed by Serbia) gain autonomy, the mission now provides security and stability.

JULY 2007, DARFUR

Along with the African Union, this mission is in place to protect civilians, facilitate humanitarian aid, and help the political process.

JULY 2010, DEMOCRATIC REPUBLIC OF THE CONGO

Armed peacekeepers are deployed to protect civilians under imminent threat of physical violence and to support stabilization efforts.

JUNE 2011, ABYEI

The armed mission in this volatile region, claimed by Sudan and South Sudan, monitors the border, facilitates delivery of aid, and protects civilians.

JULY 2011, SOUTH SUDAN

In South Sudan, the world's newest country, peacekeepers work to protect civilians, reduce hostilities, and deliver humanitarian assistance.

APRIL 2013, MALI

Alongside Mali's transitional authorities, this mission focuses on civilian security and the reestablishment of government after regional conflicts.

APRIL 2014, CENTRAL AFRICAN REPUBLIC

Created amid political crisis, this mission is tasked with protecting civilians and supporting transition processes.

OCTOBER 2017, HAITI

This nonmilitary mission, which follows successful elections, helps develop the National Police, strengthen justice institutions, and protect human rights.

U.S. armored vehicles approach the Syria-Turkey border, April 2017.

KEY DATES

U.S. War in the MIDDLE EAST

■ **1990–1991**
The U.S. deploys troops to Kuwait to repel the invading Iraqi army, joining the first Gulf War (aka Operation Desert Storm).

■ **2001 ON**
In pursuit of Osama bin Laden, mastermind of the 9/11 attacks, U.S. troops invade and occupy Afghanistan (and, later, parts of northwestern Pakistan). The Taliban-led government is replaced by a U.S.-backed administration, though insurgencies and instability continue.

■ **2003–2011**
The U.S. declares war on Iraq, alleging state-sponsored terrorism and development of weapons of mass destruction (later disproven). Known as the Second Persian Gulf War, this mission evolves into years of occupation and insurgency.

■ **2014 ON**
U.S. military deploys troops to and plays supporting roles in civil wars in Syria and Yemen; it also assists and participates in battles to expel ISIS from the region.

UNITED STATES
TIME LINE

1500 to 1650	**1650 to 1770**	**1770 to 1800**	**1800 to 1850**

1500 to 1650

1587
English colonists settle briefly at Roanoke Island.

1607
Capt. John Smith founds the Jamestown settlement on behalf of England.

1619
The Virginia Assembly, the oldest governing body in the modern United States, first meets.

1620
The *Mayflower* lands in modern-day Massachusetts.

1625–1643
The colonies of New Hampshire, Massachusetts, Rhode Island, Connecticut, Maryland, and Delaware are established.

1636
Harvard College is founded.

1650 to 1770

1692
The Salem witch trials occur in Massachusetts.

1720s–1740s
A religious revival, the Great Awakening, sweeps through the British colonies.

1754
The French and Indian War breaks out between Britain and France.

1763
Chief Pontiac leads a Native American rebellion against British settlers near Detroit.

1763–1767
Surveyors Charles Mason and Jeremiah Dixon lay out the boundary between Pennsylvania, Maryland, and Delaware.

1770 to 1800

1775
Fighting at Lexington and Concord begins the American Revolution; the next year, the Continental Congress adopts the Declaration of Independence.

1781
At the Battle of Yorktown, American and French forces defeat the British Army.

1783
By the Treaty of Paris, Britain accepts American independence.

1789
George Washington becomes the first president of the United States of America.

1800
Washington, D.C., becomes the seat of the U.S. government.

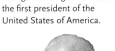

1800 to 1850

1803
Napoleon sells the lands between the Mississippi River and the Rocky Mountains to the U.S. for $15 million in the Louisiana Purchase.

1812–1814
The War of 1812 is fought between the U.S. and the British; British forces burn down the White House.

1825
The Erie Canal opens, allowing boats to travel from the Great Lakes to the Atlantic.

1830s
The Cherokee, Chickasaw, Chocktaw, Creek, and Seminole tribes are forced west on the Trail of Tears.

1841
The first wagon trains to cross the Rocky Mountains arrive in California.

1850 to 1900

1850
Harriet Tubman returns to Maryland after escaping from slavery.

1857
The Dred Scott decision makes the Missouri Compromise unconstitutional, increasing tension over slavery between the North and the South.

1861
The American Civil War begins when Confederates fire on Fort Sumter.

1863
President Abraham Lincoln signs the Emancipation Proclamation, freeing slaves in the Confederate states.

1865
Robert E. Lee surrenders at Appomattox Court House, ending the Civil War.

1900 to 1940

1903
Orville and Wilbur Wright fly a powered airplane at Kitty Hawk, North Carolina.

1908
Teddy Roosevelt undertakes the first inventories of public lands and their resources in the United States.

1917
The U.S. enters World War I.

1920
The 19th Amendment gives women the right to vote.

1929
The Wall Street stock market crash signals the beginning of the Great Depression.

1940 to 1970

1941
Japanese planes bomb the American base at Pearl Harbor; the following day the U.S. joins the Allies in World War II.

1945
The U.S. drops atomic bombs on Hiroshima and Nagasaki; World War II ends soon after.

1963
President John F. Kennedy is assassinated in Dallas, Texas.

1968
Martin Luther King, Jr., is assassinated in Memphis, Tennessee.

1969
Apollo 11 lands the first men on the moon.

1970 to PRESENT

1973
The U.S. and South Vietnam sign a cease-fire agreement with North Vietnam and the last U.S. troops are withdrawn.

1974
The Watergate scandal forces Richard Nixon to resign.

2001
Planes hijacked by al Qaeda terrorists crash into the World Trade Center and Pentagon, sparking the current U.S. conflict in the Middle East.

2008
Barack Obama is the first African American to be elected president of the United States.

AMERICA'S OTHER
LOST COLONIES

EARLY COLONIAL PURSUITS

Archaeologists continue to seek clues about European colonies established before Jamestown on the east coast of North America. Many early ventures ended in failure, but some staked claims that ultimately developed into cities we know today, such as St. Augustine, Florida, and Charleston, South Carolina.

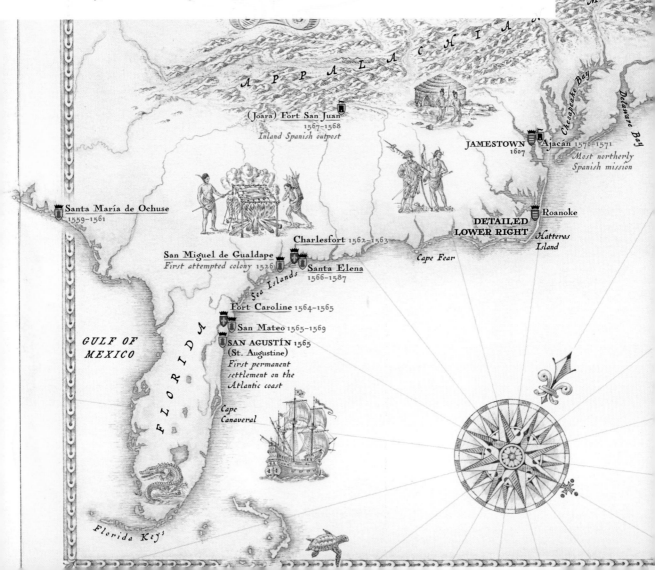

Lake Ontario

APPALACHIA

(Joara) Fort San Juan
1567–1568
Inland Spanish outpost

JAMESTOWN 1607

Ajacán 1570–1571
Most northerly Spanish mission

Chesapeake Bay

Delaware Bay

Santa María de Ochuse
1559–1561

Charlesfort 1562–1563

San Miguel de Gualdape
First attempted colony 1526

Santa Elena
1566–1587

Roanoke

DETAILED
LOWER RIGHT

Hatteras Island

Cape Fear

Sea Islands

Fort Caroline 1564–1565

San Mateo 1565–1569

SAN AGUSTÍN 1565
(St. Augustine)
First permanent settlement on the Atlantic coast

GULF OF
MEXICO

FLORIDA

Cape Canaveral

Florida Keys

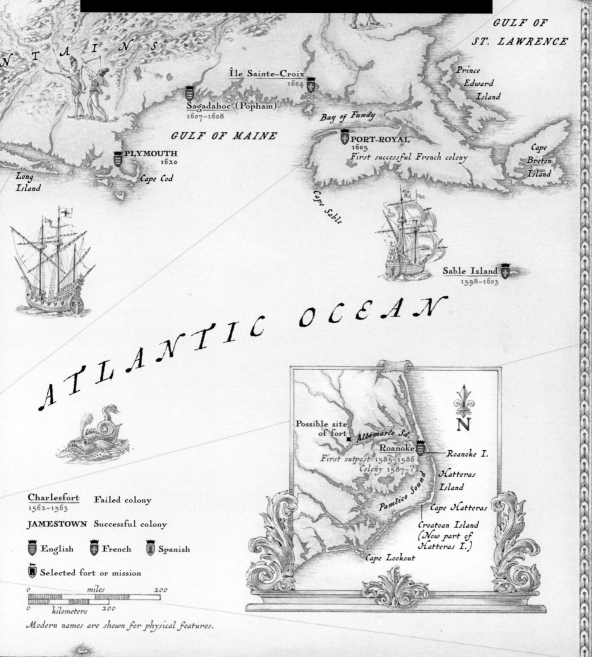

THE ROANOKE COLONY WAS, IN ESSENCE, THE APOLLO PROGRAM OF ELIZABETHAN ENGLAND, SPANNING THREE YEARS AND THREE MAJOR VOYAGES, STARTING IN 1584.

Île d'Anticosti

GULF OF ST. LAWRENCE

Prince Edward Island

Île Sainte-Croix
1604

Sagadahoc (Popham)
1607–1608

Bay of Fundy

Cape Breton Island

GULF OF MAINE

PORT-ROYAL
1605
First successful French colony

PLYMOUTH
1620

Cape Cod

Long Island

Cape Sable

N T A I N S

Sable Island
1598–1603

ATLANTIC OCEAN

Possible site of fort

Albemarle Sd.
Roanoke
First outpost 1585–1586
Colony 1587–?

N

Roanoke I.

Hatteras Island

Pamlico Sound

Cape Hatteras

Croatoan Island
(Now part of
Hatteras I.)

Cape Lookout

Charlesfort
1562–1563   Failed colony

JAMESTOWN Successful colony

English   French   Spanish

Selected fort or mission

0   miles   200

0   kilometers   200

Modern names are shown for physical features.

WOMAN SUFFRAGE

FIGHTING FOR GENDER EQUALITY IN POLITICS

The Sewall-Belmont House, now a National Park Service property

THE HOUSE THAT SUFFRAGE BUILT

In 1929, suffragist Alice Paul moved the National Woman's Party (NWP) to a brick house on Constitution Avenue in Washington, D.C. Its members were political participants and needed—in the words of suffragist Elsie Hill—"a vantage point from which they may keep Congress under perpetual observation." The house, located near Capitol Hill, was just that place.

The women of the NWP campaigned for female candidates and legislation that addressed issues like property rights, divorce, and the ability for women to keep their birth name after marriage. Alice Paul herself drafted the Equal Rights Amendment, which activists have been trying to pass since 1923.

THE EQUALITY STATE

Leading the way, Wyoming gave women the right to vote on December 10, 1869. A few months before, Congress had proposed the 15th Amendment (ratified in 1870), giving all men the right to vote. The Wyoming Territory's woman suffrage bill—granting women the rights to vote, sit on juries, and run for political office—was introduced in the legislature's first session and quickly signed by the governor, hoping to increase the territory's population. "We now expect at once quite an immigration of ladies to Wyoming," wrote the *Cheyenne Leader,* a local newspaper. This is how Wyoming earned its nickname—the Equality State—and why the state seal includes a banner bearing the words "Equal Rights."

Women voting in 1869

Suffragettes campaign in New Jersey, 1915.

THINK GLOBALLY, VOTE LOCALLY

Around the world, women have won suffrage only because they demanded it. The first country to grant the full right to vote was New Zealand, in 1893. In 2015, Saudi Arabia, the last holdout, finally enfranchised women—though they still cannot move about freely.

Challenges to participating in the political process remain. In many countries, women lack access to the institutions, experiences, and resources needed to hold office. Even more frequently, they face discrimination and intimidation. To address this problem, the United Nations set goals for women's inclusion. It also offers training to candidates and runs campaigns urging voters to elect qualified women.

As of 2017, the head of government or head of state was a woman in 15 countries, and Bolivia and Rwanda were the only countries in which at least 50 percent of the members of parliament were women. The worldwide average was just 23 percent.

KEY DATES

Political Firsts for WOMEN IN THE U.S.

■ **1916**
Jeannette Rankin becomes the first woman elected to Congress.

■ **1968**
Shirley Chisholm becomes the first black woman elected to the U.S. Congress.

■ **1981**
Sandra Day O'Connor becomes the first woman justice on the Supreme Court.

■ **2007**
Nancy Pelosi becomes the first woman speaker of the House.

■ **2009**
Sonia Sotomayor becomes the first justice of Hispanic descent on the Supreme Court.

■ **2016**
Hillary Clinton becomes the first woman to be a national party's candidate for president.

THE POLITICS OF
CHERRY BLOSSOMS

THE CAPITAL IN BLOOM

Washington, D.C., has celebrated its Cherry Blossom Festival each spring since 1935. Its origins reach back more than 100 years. In 1909, the idea of bringing cherry trees to the District—championed by a food explorer with the Department of Agriculture—was gaining traction. When America's new First Lady, Helen Taft, marveled over the trees' beauty, President William Howard Taft saw a diplomatic tool to build up international relations with Japan. On March 27, 1912, Mrs. Taft broke ground near the banks of the Potomac River. The wife of the Japanese ambassador was invited to plant the second tree. It took only two springs for the trees to become universally adored by the American public.

Cherry blossoms adorn the Tidal Basin in Washington, D.C.

WASHINGTON'S CHERRY BLOSSOM BLOOM LASTS ABOUT TWO WEEKS, AND EACH YEAR SOME MILLION AND A HALF PEOPLE COME TO ENJOY IT.

History of
DIPLOMATIC GIFTS

1860
After Japan signs a treaty with the U.S., the emperor sends, for the first time, a delegation to the U.S. They bring President James Buchanan a saddle and accessories decorated with gold and pearls.

1862
President Abraham Lincoln declines a gift of elephants offered by the king of Siam, who had proposed establishing a population of them in the U.S.

1871
Mexican officials present a finished piece of meteorite to President Ulysses S. Grant.

1880
The *Resolute* desk, made with wood from a British vessel that explored the Arctic, is given to President Rutherford B. Hayes by Queen Victoria, who has an identical one made for her own use.

1886
Perhaps the world's most famous diplomatic gift, the Statue of Liberty (originally called "Liberty Enlightening the World"), is presented to the U.S. by France.

1972
China gives two pandas, the hugely popular Ling-Ling and Hsing-Hsing, to President Richard Nixon following his visit to the country; the president donates them to the National Zoo.

1984
Sri Lankan president Junius R. Jayewardene presents an orphaned baby elephant to President Ronald Reagan at the White House.

1990
The government of Indonesia gives President George H. W. Bush a Komodo dragon, which lives out its days at the Cincinnati Zoo.

2018
An oak sapling from Belleau Wood, where thousands of American Marines died in a World War I battle, is given to President Donald Trump by President Emmanuel Macron of France.

STARS AND STRIPES
THROUGH THE CENTURIES

NO COUNTRY HAS CHANGED ITS FLAG AS MUCH AS THE UNITED STATES

The Continental Colors (below, top left) represented the colonies during the early years of the American Revolution. Its British Union Jack, which signified loyalty to the crown, was replaced on June 14, 1777, by a flag designed by New Jersey Congressman Francis Hopkinson to include 13 stars for the 13 colonies, "representing a new constellation," as was said at the time. In 1817, Congressman Peter Wendover of New York wrote the current flag law, which retains 13 stripes permanently but adds stars as new states join the union. The original "Star-Spangled Banner," which inspired Francis Scott Key during the War of 1812 to write what became our national anthem, is elegantly preserved at the Smithsonian's National Museum of American History in Washington, D.C.

/1/1776–6/14/1777

6/15/1777–4/30/1795

5/1/1795–7/3/1818

7/4/1818–7/3/1819

7/4/1822–7/3/1836

7/4/1836–7/3/1837

7/4/1837–7/3/1845

/4/1847–7/3/1848

7/4/1848–7/3/1851

7/4/1851–7/3/1858

7/4/1858–7/3/1859

7/4/1859–7/3/1861

/4/1865–7/3/1867

7/4/1867–7/3/1877

7/4/1877–7/3/1890

7/4/1890–7/3/1891

7/4/1891–7/3/1896

/4/1896–7/3/1908

7/4/1908–7/3/1912

7/4/1912–7/3/1959

7/4/1959–7/3/1960

FUTURE (51-STAR)?

"THIS FLAG, WHICH WE HONOR AND UNDER WHICH WE SERVE, IS THE EMBLEM OF OUR UNITY, OUR POWER, OUR THOUGHT AND PURPOSE AS A NATION. IT HAS NO OTHER CHARACTER THAN THAT WHICH WE GIVE IT FROM GENERATION TO GENERATION."

—PRESIDENT WOODROW WILSON, 1917

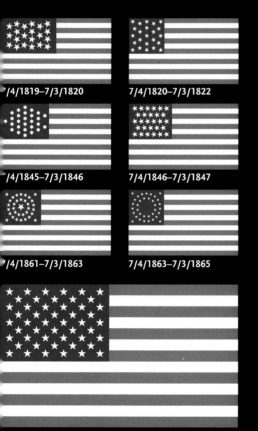

7/4/1819–7/3/1820

7/4/1820–7/3/1822

7/4/1845–7/3/1846

7/4/1846–7/3/1847

7/4/1861–7/3/1863

7/4/1863–7/3/1865

7/4/1960–PRESENT

KEY DATES

The Evolution of the
U.S. FLAG

1776
The Grand Union Flag is replaced by the first true American flag, said to have been sewn by Betsy Ross.

1779
According to tradition, with stars now in rows, the Serapis flag or John Paul Jones flag flew through the War of 1812.

1821
Missouri joined the Union as the 24th state, and the 24-star flag lasted for 14 years and through three presidencies.

1837
Many versions of a Great Star Flag, with a star made of stars, flew in the 19th century.

1847
When Iowa joined the United States, it was time to design a 29-star flag. It lasted only one year.

1863
During the Civil War, the 34 stars were arranged in several designs: rows, circles, stars, even a flower.

1876
A centennial flag arranged 80 stars to spell out the numerals 1776 and 1876.

1892
The Pledge of Allegiance, written by Francis Bellamy, first appears in a magazine called *The Youth's Companion*.

1912
President Howard Taft signs an executive order specifying proportions and design of the U.S. flag.

1960
The addition of Alaska and Hawaii gives the U.S. flag the design we know today, with 50 stars for 50 states and 13 stripes for the 13 original colonies.

FLAGS OF THE
UNITED STATES

ALABAMA
Became a state in 1819
A simple design, crimson cross
field of white; until 1987 it could
be either square or rectangular.

ALASKA
Became a state in 1959
Against the blue of sea and sky,
the Big Dipper and Polaris,
signifying Alaska's northernmost position;
designed by a 13-year-old Alaskan.

ARIZONA
Became a state in 1912
A copper star, signifying Arizona's copper
industry, on a blue field in the face of
a setting sun with 13 rays
for the original colonies.

ARKANSAS
Became a state in 1836
Diamond signifies its status
the sole diamond-producing state;
ring of 25 stars since it was
the 25th state to join the union.

CALIFORNIA
Became a state in 1850
Grizzly bear, also the state animal,
on red and white for bravery and purity;
first flown by settlers resisting
Mexican rule in 1846.

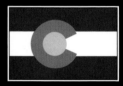

COLORADO
Became a state in 1876
White for snow-covered mountains, gold
for sunshine, red for red soil,
blue for clear blue skies,
and a C for the state's name.

CONNECTICUT
Became a state in 1788
Three fruiting grapevines and
ate motto, "*Qui transtulit sustinet*
who transplanted still sustains."

DELAWARE
Became a state in 1787
Coat of arms with a ship, farmer,
militiaman, and ox; below, the date
when Delaware ratified the Constitution
and became the first state.

FLORIDA
Became a state in 1845
Red cross on white, in the center
the state seal: Seminole woman,
palmetto pine, and steamboat
in nearby water.

GEORGIA
Became a state in 1788
Thick red and white stripes,
blue square on which 13 stars
circle the state seal; three pillars
ent three branches of government.

HAWAII
Became a state in 1959
Eight horizontal stripes representing
the eight major islands; a Union Jack
in the upper left, reflecting past
British rule.

IDAHO
Became a state in 1890
A robed woman represents liberty
and justice; a miner holds a pick
and shovel; wheat sheaves and cornucopia
represent plentiful harvests.

ILLINOIS
Became a state in 1818
State seal centered on white
includes bald eagle holding banner
with motto, "State Sovereignty,
National Union."

INDIANA
Became a state in 1816
Torch of enlightenment circled
by stars: 13 for the first states,
five for the next, and a large one
for Indiana, 19th state.

IOWA
Became a state in 1846
An eagle flies amid red, white,
and blue, carrying a banner:
"Our liberties we prize and
our rights we will maintain."

KANSAS
Became a state in 1861
A sunflower atop the state seal,
with scenes of farming, a wagon train,
Native Americans, buffalo, steamboat,
and the rising sun.

KENTUCKY
Became a state in 1792
A pioneer and a statesman
shake hands, surrounded
by the motto "United we stand,
divided we fall."

LOUISIANA
Became a state in 1812
White pelican nurtures her
nestling young with her own blood;
beneath them, the motto
"Union Justice Confidence."

MAINE
Became a state in 1820
Farmer and sailor flank a crest
with an evergreen and a moose;
above, the North Star atop the motto
"*Dirigo*—I lead."

MARYLAND
Became a state in 1788
Checkerboard of two family arms:
Calvert, state founders, and Crossland,
mother of George Calvert,
the first Lord Baltimore.

MASSACHUSETTS
Became a state in 1788
Native American holds bow and
arrow pointing down, symbolizing peace;
star at his shoulder means this was
one of the first 13 states.

MICHIGAN
Became a state in 1837
Moose, elk, and bald eagle surround
crest with explorer at water's edge,
sun rising, topped with word
"*Tuebor*—I will defend."

MINNESOTA
Became a state in 1858
Native American and farmer,
tree stump for timber industry,
waterfall for wilderness.
"*L'Etoile du Nord*—the North Star State."

MISSISSIPPI
Became a state in 1817
In upper left, square canton
containing 13 stars for 13 colonies;
three broad stripes in red,
white, and blue.

MISSOURI
Became a state in 1821

Stars circle grizzlies clasping seal
with American eagle, crescent moon,
and grizzly within; above,
another 24 stars, since 24th state.

MONTANA
Became a state in 1889

Mountains, cliffs, trees, and river
represent the landscape; tools represent
farming and mining, as does motto:
"*Oro y plata*—gold and silver."

NEBRASKA
Became a state in 1867

On blue, state seal with
blacksmith in foreground, steamboat
and train in background,
farm and homestead in between.

NEVADA
Became a state in 1864

Bright blue and in corner, silver star,
sprigs of sagebrush, with banner reading
"Battle Born," since state entered
union during Civil War.

NEW HAMPSHIRE
Became a state in 1788

On blue field, seal portraying frigate
Raleigh, one of the first American
Revolutionary warships,
built in Portsmouth.

NEW JERSEY
Became a state in 1787

On a buff background, seal including
plows for agriculture, helmet
for courage, and figures of Liberty
and Ceres, harvest goddess.

NEW MEXICO
Became a state in 1912

Red symbol for the sun,
sacred to the Zia Indians,
on a bright yellow background.

NEW YORK
Became a state in 1788

On blue, the seal portrays ships
of commerce flanked by the figures
of Liberty and Justice. Below,
the motto "*Excelsior*—ever upward."

NORTH CAROLINA
Became a state in 1789

Broad stripes—top red, bottom white—
alongside a blue bar with "NC,"
a star, and two key dates as
the colony declared independence.

NORTH DAKOTA
Became a state in 1889

A bald eagle, wings spread, holds
an olive branch and arrows in its talons;
stars for 13 colonies spread
out into sun rays.

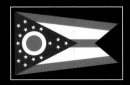

OHIO
Became a state in 1803

Swallowtail burgee with
red and white stripes, blue triangle
with 17 stars, since the 17th state
to join the Union.

OKLAHOMA
Became a state in 1907

An Osage warrior's rawhide
shield hung with eagle feathers,
across which sit an olive branch
and a peace pipe.

OREGON
Became a state in 1859

Blue flag with yellow insignia.
On front, state seal including
wagon train, ships, and setting sun.
On back, the state animal: a beaver.

PENNSYLVANIA
Became a state in 1787

An eagle and two horses surround
a crest with a ship, a plow, and wheat
sheaves; below, the motto "Virtue Liberty
and Independence."

RHODE ISLAND
Became a state in 1790

White flag bearing a golden
anchor, circled by 13 gold stars,
and beneath it a blue banner
with the simple motto "Hope."

SOUTH CAROLINA
Became a state in 1788
A crescent, from local Revolutionary
War uniforms, and a palmetto
tree—white designs against
deep blue.

SOUTH DAKOTA
Became a state in 1889
Farmer, livestock, factory,
and steamboat on the state seal,
circled by yellow sun rays
on a field of bright blue.

TENNESSEE
Became a state in 1796
A circle containing three white stars
representing East, Middle,
and West, all against red,
with blue and white edge.

TEXAS
Became a state in 1845
The famous "Lone Star"
in white against a blue background
with broad horizontal panels
of white and red.

UTAH
Became a state in 1896
Beehive, symbol of industry,
surrounded by U.S. flags and a spread eagle.
Two dates: 1847, Mormons arrived,
and 1896, statehood.

VERMONT
Became a state in 1791
A field with sheaves, pine,
and cow stretches back to mountains;
pine boughs on either side,
antlered buck atop.

VIRGINIA
Became a state in 1788
Female Virtus (Virtue) stands over
a fallen man, his crown toppled;
beneath, the motto "Sic semper tyrannis—
Thus always to tyrants."

WASHINGTON
Became a state in 1889
Portrait of George Washington
circled by yellow on a field of green—
the only U.S. flag with a
historical figure on it.

WEST VIRGINIA
Became a state in 1863
A farmer and a miner lean against
a rock inscribed with the date
of gaining statehood;
rhododendrons drape the seal.

WISCONSIN
Became a state in 1848
Against a bright blue background,
sailor and miner dominate the state seal,
topped by a badger
and the motto "Forward."

WYOMING
Became a state in 1890
State seal in blue against
the silhouette of a bison in white,
background blue with red,
and white borders top and bottom.

> **"I SALUTE THE FLAG OF THE STATE OF
> NEW MEXICO, THE ZIA SYMBOL OF PERFECT
> FRIENDSHIP AMONG UNITED CULTURES."**
>
> —OFFICIAL PLEDGE TO NEW MEXICO'S FLAG

TERRITORIES OF
THE UNITED STATES

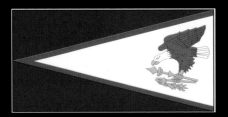

AMERICAN SAMOA
Became a U.S. territory in 1900
Blue with red-edged white triangle;
bald eagle gripping native symbols of authority:
war club and coconut fiber whisk.

GUAM
Became a U.S. territory in 1898
Dark blue flag with red border; central emblem,
shaped like native sling stone, encloses palm tree,
outrigger canoe, and beach.

PUERTO RICO
Became a U.S. territory in 1898
Five bands of red and white; triangle of blue,
for sky and waters, with central white star,
which symbolizes Puerto Rico.

NORTHERN MARIANA ISLANDS
Became a U.S. territory in 1976
Blue flag containing gray foundation stones,
white star, and floral head wreath
representing native Chamorro culture.

U.S. INTEREST IN PACIFIC ISLANDS DATES BACK TO THE 1856 GUANO ISLANDS ACT, BY WHICH CONGRESS CLAIMED RIGHTS TO UNINHABITED ISLANDS IN ORDER TO MINE GUANO— BIRD DROPPINGS—FOR GUNPOWDER AND FERTILIZER.

U.S. VIRGIN ISLANDS
Became a U.S. territory in 1917
On field of white, yellow eagle holds olive
branch and arrows; modified U.S. coat of arms
in center, initials "V" and "I" on either side.

NOT QUITE STATES

BUT STILL PART OF THE U.S.

The U.S. Constitution gives Congress the power to incorporate new federal territories, organize them, and admit them as new states. The most recent territories to become states were Alaska and Hawaii, in 1959. Present-day U.S. territories range from uninhabited specks in the Pacific Ocean to the organized Caribbean island of Puerto Rico. Some of the small islands in the Pacific were once military bases, but many now function as wildlife refuges. American Samoa, Puerto Rico, and the Northern Mariana Islands all possess their own constitutions. The people living in these territories are U.S. citizens, but they are not allowed to vote in presidential elections.

DISTRICT OF COLUMBIA

NATION'S CAPITAL

"End Taxation Without Representation" reads the license plates of those who live in the District of Columbia, created in 1790 as a federal district for the new nation's capital city. Residents of the District have voted in presidential elections since 1964, but they do not have any representatives in Congress. Since the 1970s, many have been pushing for D.C. statehood.

The Other U.S.
TERRITORIES

■ **BAKER ISLAND**
A treeless atoll midway between Hawaii and Australia, this is a home to sea turtles and a migratory resting point for numerous bird species.

■ **HOWLAND ISLAND**
This is famous as the island toward which Amelia Earhart was flying when she disappeared.

■ **JARVIS ISLAND**
This national wildlife refuge, found just 22 miles south of the Equator, was expanded in 2009 to include about 430,000 submerged acres around it.

■ **JOHNSTON ATOLL**
Named a federal bird refuge in 1926, the atoll was later used as a nuclear test and chemical weapons storage site, prompting recent cleanup efforts.

■ **KINGMAN REEF**
Now a national wildlife refuge, this triangle of coral was once called Danger Reef, because it is treacherous for vessels.

■ **MIDWAY ISLANDS**
The position of these islands and an atoll fringe—equidistant from North America and Asia—made them a Pacific battleground during World War II.

■ **NAVASSA ISLAND**
Off the west coast of Haiti, this has hosted eight native species of reptile, although some may now be extinct.

■ **PALMYRA ATOLL**
A national wildlife refuge since 2001, its protection efforts are a partnership between U.S. and the Nature Conservancy.

■ **WAKE ISLAND**
Life-and-death battles were fought here during WWII, and its airfield is a refueling station.

FURTHER

ARS LONGA: ART LIVES ON TO TELL THE TALE

All history is a story, and artists tell the stories best. Here schoolchildren sit before Pablo Picasso's legendary "Guernica," painted in 1937 in response to the agonies of the Spanish Civil War. Some look down, some look away, some stare transfixed, but all come away from the experience with a deeper sense of connection with the people and events of the past.

Children visit the Reina Sofía Museum in Madrid, encouraged by their teacher to pause and take some time to understand Picasso's "Guernica."

"THERE ARE TWO LANGUAGES . . . THESE ARE VERBAL—WHICH SEPARATES PEOPLE—[AND] VISUAL, WHICH IS UNDERSTOOD BY EVERYBODY." —YAACOV AGAM, ARTIST

OUR
WORLD

WORLD VIEWS | CONTINENTS & OCEANS

The moon and stars enhance a spectacular sunrise over New Mexico.

COUNTRIES OF THE WORLD | THE FUTURE

QUIZ MASTER

Geographical Wizard? Places to know and forces to understand—geography sits at the heart of all knowledge. Here are maps galore, but they can only hint at the diversity of features that make Earth such a fascinating place to study.

—CARA SANTA MARIA, *Our Favorite Nerd*

THE UNITED NATIONS BEGAN IN 1945 WITH HOW MANY MEMBER STATES?

P357

AT **63.8 MILLION** SQUARE MILES, WHAT IS THE LARGEST OCEAN ON THE PLANET?

WHAT PERCENT OF THE EARTH'S SURFACE IS COVERED WITH LANDMASSES?

p331

p372

p330

IN WHAT COUNTRY HAVE THE **WORLD'S OLDEST** ROCKS BEEN FOUND?

WHAT SPECIES OF BIRD CALLS THE SALAR DE ATACAMA IN CHILE HOME?

p361

WHAT IS THE SMALLEST OCEAN ON THE PLANET?

WHICH BODY OF WATER DOES THE MISSISSIPPI RIVER EMPTY INTO?

p340

p338

p332

FOR WHAT MINERAL DOES THE CHILEAN GOVERNMENT CONTROL ABOUT 20 PERCENT OF THE WORLD'S RESERVES?

IN WHICH CANADIAN PROVINCE CAN YOU FIND THE GREAT BEAR RAINFOREST?

p338

p342

WHAT IS THE NAME OF THE SMALL COUNTRY LOCATED IN THE PYRENEES MOUNTAINS BETWEEN FRANCE AND SPAIN?

p344

ON WHICH CONTINENT IS TOURISM GROWING MOST RAPIDLY?

p333

WHAT IS THE OLDEST FRESHWATER LAKE ON EARTH, LOCATED IN RUSSIA?

p344

HOW MANY YEARS AGO DID THE TIBETAN PLATEAU FORM?

WHICH BODY OF WATER CONTAINS THE MOST OFFSHORE DRILLING RIGS?

p358

OUR PHYSICAL
WORLD

CANADA
Oldest rocks

An area of exposed bed-rock discovered in northern Quebec is estimated to be as much as 2.28 billion years old. At more than 250 million years older than any rocks previously dated, the Nuvvuagittuq greenstone belt is one of the oldest pieces of the planet's crust known.

ANDES
Longest mountain system

Measuring about 4,700 miles, the Andes are the world's longest mountain system on land. The range stretches the full length of the continent, through seven countries. Its highest peak, at 22,841 feet, is Argentina's Aconcagua.

ABOUT 29.1%—57 MILLION SQUARE MILES—OF EARTH'S SURFACE IS NOT COVERED BY WATER.

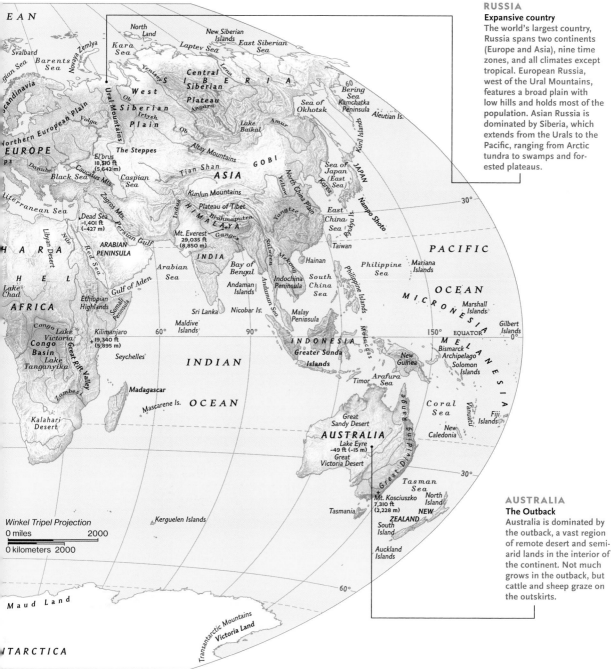

RUSSIA

Expansive country

The world's largest country, Russia spans two continents (Europe and Asia), nine time zones, and all climates except tropical. European Russia, west of the Ural Mountains, features a broad plain with low hills and holds most of the population. Asian Russia is dominated by Siberia, which extends from the Urals to the Pacific, ranging from Arctic tundra to swamps and forested plateaus.

AUSTRALIA

The Outback

Australia is dominated by the outback, a vast region of remote desert and semi-arid lands in the interior of the continent. Not much grows in the outback, but cattle and sheep graze on the outskirts.

Winkel Tripel Projection

0 miles 2000
0 kilometers 2000

OUR POLITICAL
WORLD

UNITED STATES

Growing Cities

People are increasingly moving to urban areas, creating mega-cities—cities with populations of at least 10 million. The U.S. has two megacities: New York–Newark–Jersey City (20.3 million) and Los Angeles (13.4 million).

CHILE

National Copper Mines

In 1971, Chile national-ized the country's cop-per mines and later grouped them under a single company known as the National Copper Corporation of Chile (CODELCO). Today, Chile is the largest cop-per producer in the world, with about 20 percent of all copper reserves under its purview.

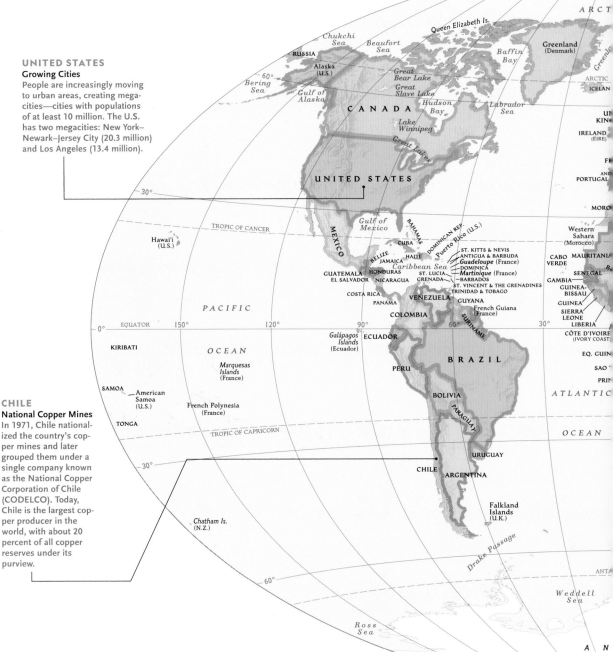

JAPAN

Aging Population

As the planet's human population continues to grow, some countries are seeing an aging population instead of a booming one. Japan's low birthrate has led to a population that is growing smaller and older over time. By 2065, it's projected that 38 percent of Japan's population will be over the age of 65.

TAIWAN
The People's Republic of China claims Taiwan as its 23rd province. Taiwan's government (Republic of China) maintains that there are two political entities.

Winkel Tripel Projection
0 miles   2000
0 kilometers 2000

NORTH AFRICA

Rising Tourism

The global tourism market is massive, with some 1.4 billion people traveling internationally every year. In recent years, African tourism—especially to northern countries such as Morocco and Tunisia—has grown at a faster rate than that in the rest of the world.

BEST OF @NATGEO

TOP PHOTOS OF LANDSCAPES

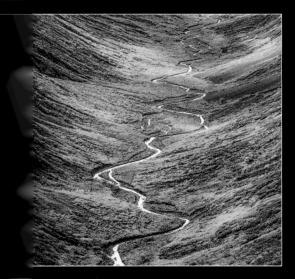

@franslanting | FRANS LANTING
A river winds through a golden-hued valley in Wrangell–St. Elias National Park & Preserve, Alaska.

@renan_ozturk | RENAN OZTURK
Climbers celebrate their ascent on a red rock peak in Bears Ears National Monument, Utah.

@GEOSTEINMETZ | GEORGE STEINMETZ
Summer rain pools amid white sand dunes at Lençóis Maranhenses National Park in Brazil.

@simonnorfolkstudio | SIMON NORFOLK
Socotra in the Arabian Sea is the only native habitat for dragon blood trees, named for their red resin.

@ladzinski | KEITH LADZINSKI
Triple waterfalls plunge into a lagoon at the foot of Kirkjufell Mountain in Iceland.

@pedromcbride | PETE MCBRIDE
Lights accentuate architecture and activity in Manhattan, home to more than 1.6 million people.

@irablockphoto | IRA BLOCK
Daylight fades from the Diomede Islands, separated by the U.S.-Russian boundary in the Bering Strait.

@paleyphoto | MATTHIEU PALEY
Spring turns the hills around Song Köl lake a soft green in Kyrgyzstan in Central Asia.

THE CONTINENTS

LANDFORMS CHANGE SHAPE OVER MILLENNIA

With the unceasing movement of Earth's tectonic plates, continents "drift" over geologic time—breaking apart, reassembling, and again fragmenting to repeat the process. Three times during the past billion years, Earth's drifting landmasses have merged to form so-called supercontinents. Rodinia, the earliest known supercontinent, began breaking apart in the late Precambrian, about 750 million years ago (mya).

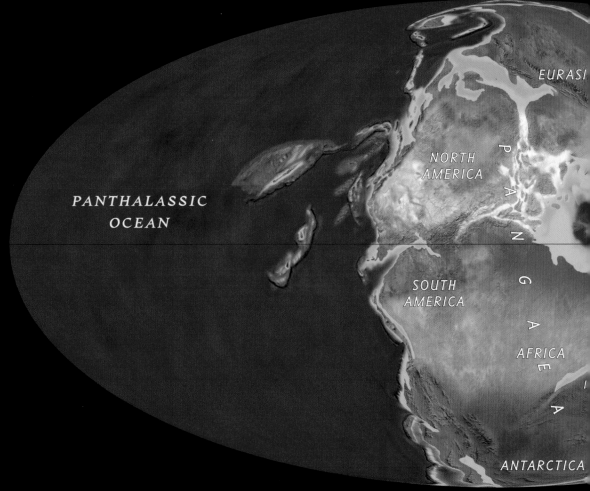

PANGAEA, 240 MILLION YEARS AGO
Even when most of Earth's landmass was a single continent, named Pangaea,
surrounded by a single ocean, the Panthalassic (predecessor to the Pacific),
configurations began taking shape that presaged the continents of today.
The Tethys Ocean ultimately became the Mediterranean.

DINOSAURS ROAMED POLE TO POLE ON PANGAEA, BUT OVER TIME THE CONTINENTS SPLIT AND DISTINCT DINOSAUR SPECIES EVOLVED SEPARATELY IN DIFFERENT LOCATIONS.

China

TETHYS OCEAN

AUSTRALIA

Stages in Earth's EVOLUTION

■ **PRECAMBRIAN TIME (4,500–542 MYA)**
Archaean eon (ca 3,800–2,500 mya)
First life-forms appear on Earth.

Proterozoic eon (2,500–542 mya)
In latter part of this eon, continental fragments join into one: Pannotia.

■ **PHANEROZOIC EON (542 MYA–PRESENT)**
Paleozoic era (542–251 mya)
Includes Cambrian, 500 mya: Multicellular animals leave abundant fossil evidence.

Includes Devonian, 400 mya: Freshwater fish migrate freely; plants colonize land.

Mesozoic era (251–65.5 mya)
Includes Triassic, 240 mya: Geologic catastrophes caused massive extinctions; surviving lizards evolved into dinosaurs.

Cenozoic era (65.5 mya–present)
Includes K-T extinction event, 65 mya: Half the plant and animal species become extinct.

Includes last great ice age, 18,000 ya: North and south are locked in ice; continents as we know them begin to form, further defined by retreating glaciers.

NORTH AMERICA

ALASKA
U.S.

Greenland
(Denmark)

C A N A D A

UNITED STATES

MEXICO

BELIZE

GUATEMALA HONDURAS

EL SALVADOR NICARAGUA

COSTA RICA

PANAMA

BAHAMAS

CUBA

HAITI

DOM.REP.

JAMAICA

ANTIGUA &
BARBUDA

ST. KITTS
& NEVIS DOMINICA

ST. LUCIA
BARBADOS
ST. VINCENT &
THE GRENADINES
GRENADA
TRINIDAD
& TOBAGO

HISTORY WRITTEN IN ICE
Scientists have been able to track the history of climate change though samples taken from Greenland's massive ice sheet. Core samples taken from the ice core show that an increase in melting coincided with the earliest human impacts, in the mid-19th century.

GREAT BEAR RAINFOREST
Along the coast of the Canadian province of British Columbia, the Great Bear Rainforest covers 15.8 million acres. This lush expanse is a temperate rainforest, filled with trees that are hundreds of years old and diverse wildlife. The rare cream-colored Kermode bear—also known as a spirit bear—lives only in these woods.

MISSISSIPPI RIVER WATERSHED
Draining a total of 1.2 million square miles—parts of 31 state, and two Canadian provinces—the Mississippi River watershed is one of the largest in the world. The river itself, more than 2,300 miles long, empties into the Gulf of Mexico.

MEXICO'S CAPITAL CITY
The streets of Mexico City are vibrant and colorful, with influences of Aztec, Spanish, French, and modern Mexican sensibilities. The city shines on September 15, the eve of Mexico's Independence Day, when a large crowd gathers outside the Palacio Nacional to celebrate the country's independence from Spain.

North Rim of Arizona's Grand Canyon

Continental FACTS

TOTAL NUMBER OF COUNTRIES
23

TOTAL AREA
9,449,000 square miles (24,474,000 sq km)

MOST POPULOUS COUNTRY
United States: 329,256,000

LEAST POPULOUS COUNTRY
Saint Kitts and Nevis: 53,000

LARGEST COUNTRY BY AREA
Canada: 3,855,101 square miles (9,984,670 sq km)

SMALLEST COUNTRY BY AREA
Saint Kitts and Nevis: 101 square miles (261 sq km)

HIGHEST ELEVATION
Denali (Mount McKinley),
United States: 20,310 feet (6,190 m)

LOWEST ELEVATION
Death Valley, United States: −282 feet (−86 m)

SOUTH AMERICA

BOGOTÁ, COLOMBIA
The capital city of Colombia is also the country's largest. It lies on a plateau of the Andes, and the nearby heights of Monserrate offer a bird's-eye view of Bogotá.

TRANS-AMAZONIAN HIGHWAY
Snaking through Brazil's Amazon—the world's largest and most diverse tropical rainforest—is a growing system of roads. Called the Trans-Amazonian highway, it is meant to ease transport for materials taken from the rainforest, such as timber, minerals, and farmed goods. But ongoing construction of this road poses even more risks to a vital ecosystem.

ATACAMA SALT FLATS
In the northeast region of Chile, surrounded by mountains, lies the Salar de Atacama, a massive salt flat that extends over nearly 1,200 square miles. In summer the rare Andean flamingos make their home in the flats, feeding off small organisms living in the salty pools spread throughout the landscape.

WILDLIFE OF PATAGONIA
At the southern end of the continent, Patagonia is a large region of steppe and desert climates poised at the meeting place of the Atlantic, Pacific, and Antarctic Oceans. Here you'll find most of the world's guanacos, a relative of the llama, and the black and white Commerson's dolphins swimming alongside boats.

VENEZUELA

GUYANA

COLOMBIA

SURINAME French Guiana
(France)

ECUADOR

P E R U

B R A Z I L

B O L I V I A

PARAGUAY

C H I L E

A R G E N T I N A

URUGUAY

Peru's Machu Picchu Inca ruins

Continental
FACTS

TOTAL NUMBER OF COUNTRIES
12

TOTAL AREA
6,880,000 square miles (17,819,000 sq km)

MOST POPULOUS COUNTRY
Brazil: 208,847,000

LEAST POPULOUS COUNTRY
Suriname: 598,000

LARGEST COUNTRY BY AREA
Brazil: 3,287,596 square miles (8,515,770 sq km)

SMALLEST COUNTRY BY AREA
Suriname: 63,251 square miles (163,820 sq km)

HIGHEST ELEVATION
Cerro Aconcagua, Argentina: 22,834 feet (6,960 m)

LOWEST ELEVATION
Laguna del Carbón, Argentina: −344 feet (−105 m)

THE SAMI PEOPLE
The Sami are an indigenous people native to the far northern regions of Europe. Today, some 80,000 Sami live in Norway, Sweden, Finland, and Russia. Many Sami still maintain the tradition as reindeer herders, following the massive animals through the tundra as they seek good grazing.

CITY OF CANALS
Founded nearly 750 years ago, Amsterdam is a city filled with history. Known for its many canals, rich artistic legacy, and iconic architecture, the Dutch capital is a tourist destination for many travelers.

ANDORRA
One of the smallest nations in Europe, Andorra is located between France and Spain in the Pyrenees mountains. The population is just under 77,000, and most of its people live in the capital city of Andorra la Vella.

EUROPE'S HIGHEST PEAK
At 18,510 feet, Mount El'brus, located in the Caucasus Mountains in Russia, is the tallest peak in Europe. El'brus is a volcano with two domes, with the second at the shorter height of 18,442 feet. The taller summit was first climbed in 1874 by a team led by the guide Akhia Sottaiev.

ICELAND

NORWAY

SWEDEN

FINLAND

RUSSIA

ESTONIA

LATVIA

LITHUANIA

RUSSIA

BELARUS

KAZAKHSTAN

(ÉIRE) IRELAND

UNITED KINGDOM

DENMARK

NETH.

BELG.

LUX.

GERMANY

POLAND

UKRAINE

CZECHIA
(CZECH REP.)

SLOVAKIA

MOLD.

FRANCE

LIECH.

SWITZ.

AUSTRIA

HUNGARY

ROMANIA

SLOV.

CROATIA

MONACO

SAN MARINO

BOSN. & HERZG.

SERBIA

ANDORRA

PORTUGAL

SPAIN

ITALY

VATICAN CITY

MONTEN.

KOS.

NORTH MACED.

BULGARIA

TURKEY

ALBANIA

GREECE

MALTA

Gondolas on the Grand Canal of Venice, Italy

Continental
FACTS

TOTAL NUMBER OF COUNTRIES
46

TOTAL AREA
3,841,000 square miles (9,947,000 sq km)

MOST POPULOUS COUNTRY
*Russia: 142,123,000

LEAST POPULOUS COUNTRY
Vatican City: 1,000

LARGEST COUNTRY BY AREA
*Russia: 6,601,665 square miles (17,098,242 sq km)

SMALLEST COUNTRY BY AREA
Vatican City: 0.17 square mile (0.44 sq km)

HIGHEST ELEVATION
El'brus, Russia: 18,510 feet (5,642 m)

LOWEST ELEVATION
Caspian Sea: −92 feet (−28 m)

* Area and population figures reflect
the total of Asian and European regions.

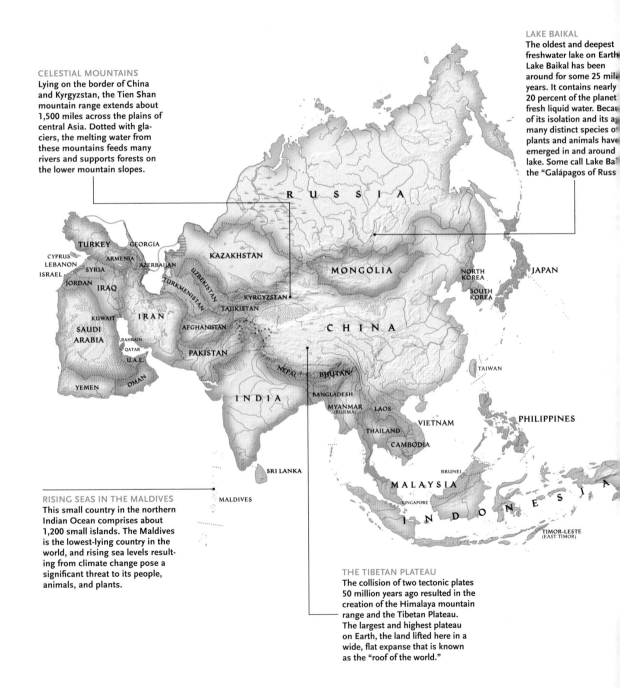

CELESTIAL MOUNTAINS
Lying on the border of China and Kyrgyzstan, the Tien Shan mountain range extends about 1,500 miles across the plains of central Asia. Dotted with glaciers, the melting water from these mountains feeds many rivers and supports forests on the lower mountain slopes.

LAKE BAIKAL
The oldest and deepest freshwater lake on Earth, Lake Baikal has been around for some 25 mill years. It contains nearly 20 percent of the planet fresh liquid water. Becau of its isolation and its a many distinct species o plants and animals have emerged in and around lake. Some call Lake Bai the "Galápagos of Russ

RISING SEAS IN THE MALDIVES
This small country in the northern Indian Ocean comprises about 1,200 small islands. The Maldives is the lowest-lying country in the world, and rising sea levels resulting from climate change pose a significant threat to its people, animals, and plants.

THE TIBETAN PLATEAU
The collision of two tectonic plates 50 million years ago resulted in the creation of the Himalaya mountain range and the Tibetan Plateau. The largest and highest plateau on Earth, the land lifted here in a wide, flat expanse that is known as the "roof of the world."

CYPRUS
LEBANON
ISRAEL
TURKEY
GEORGIA
ARMENIA
AZERBAIJAN
SYRIA
JORDAN
IRAQ
KUWAIT
SAUDI ARABIA
BAHRAIN
QATAR
U.A.E.
YEMEN
OMAN
IRAN
TURKMENISTAN
UZBEKISTAN
AFGHANISTAN
PAKISTAN
TAJIKISTAN
KYRGYZSTAN
KAZAKHSTAN
RUSSIA
MONGOLIA
NORTH KOREA
SOUTH KOREA
JAPAN
CHINA
TAIWAN
NEPAL
BHUTAN
BANGLADESH
MYANMAR (BURMA)
LAOS
VIETNAM
THAILAND
CAMBODIA
PHILIPPINES
BRUNEI
MALAYSIA
SINGAPORE
INDONESIA
TIMOR-LESTE (EAST TIMOR)
INDIA
SRI LANKA
MALDIVES

Hong Kong skyline at twilight

Continental
FACTS

TOTAL NUMBER OF COUNTRIES
46

TOTAL AREA
17,209,000 square miles (44,570,000 sq km)

MOST POPULOUS COUNTRY
China: 1,384,689,000

LEAST POPULOUS COUNTRY
Maldives: 392,000

LARGEST COUNTRY BY AREA
✷China: 3,705,405 square miles (9,596,960 sq km)

SMALLEST COUNTRY BY AREA
Maldives: 115 square miles (298 sq km)

HIGHEST ELEVATION
Mount Everest, China/Nepal: 29,035 feet (8,850 m)

LOWEST ELEVATION
Dead Sea, Israel/Jordan: –1,401 feet (–427 m)

✷ *Russia straddles both Asia and
Europe and exceeds China in area.*

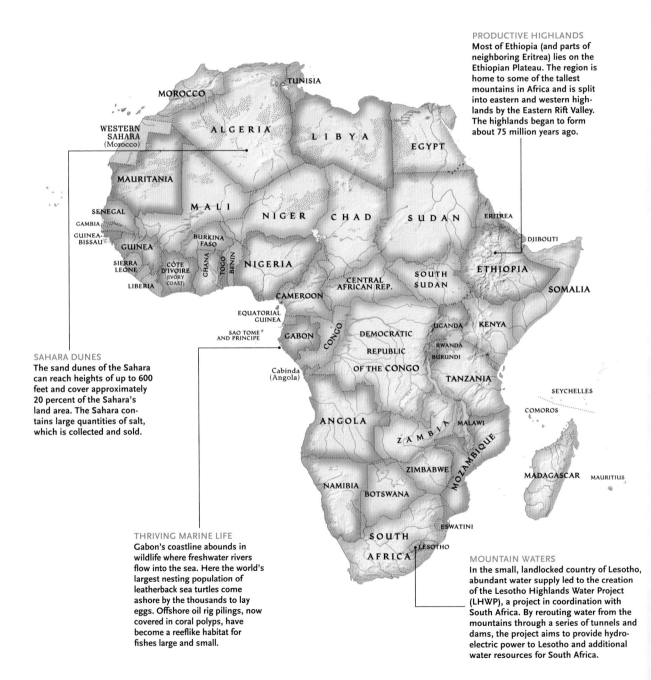

PRODUCTIVE HIGHLANDS
Most of Ethiopia (and parts of neighboring Eritrea) lies on the Ethiopian Plateau. The region is home to some of the tallest mountains in Africa and is split into eastern and western highlands by the Eastern Rift Valley. The highlands began to form about 75 million years ago.

SAHARA DUNES
The sand dunes of the Sahara can reach heights of up to 600 feet and cover approximately 20 percent of the Sahara's land area. The Sahara contains large quantities of salt, which is collected and sold.

THRIVING MARINE LIFE
Gabon's coastline abounds in wildlife where freshwater rivers flow into the sea. Here the world's largest nesting population of leatherback sea turtles come ashore by the thousands to lay eggs. Offshore oil rig pilings, now covered in coral polyps, have become a reeflike habitat for fishes large and small.

MOUNTAIN WATERS
In the small, landlocked country of Lesotho, abundant water supply led to the creation of the Lesotho Highlands Water Project (LHWP), a project in coordination with South Africa. By rerouting water from the mountains through a series of tunnels and dams, the project aims to provide hydroelectric power to Lesotho and additional water resources for South Africa.

Continental FACTS

TOTAL NUMBER OF COUNTRIES
54

TOTAL AREA
11,608,000 square miles (30,065,000 sq km)

MOST POPULOUS COUNTRY
Nigeria: 203,453,000

LEAST POPULOUS COUNTRY
Seychelles: 95,000

LARGEST COUNTRY BY AREA
Algeria: 919,590 square miles (2,381,741 sq km)

SMALLEST COUNTRY BY AREA
Seychelles: 176 square miles (455 sq km)

HIGHEST ELEVATION
Kilimanjaro, Tanzania: 19,340 feet (5,895 m)

LOWEST ELEVATION
Lake Assal, Djibouti: −509 feet (−155 m)

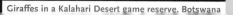
Giraffes in a Kalahari Desert game reserve, Botswana

AUSTRALIA & OCEANIA

HUNDREDS OF LANGUAGES
More than 8 million people live in Papua New Guinea, many of them belonging to the 700 or so tribes that call the nation home. Each of these tribes has its own language. The country lists 3 official languages but nearly 850 unofficial ones.

MARSHALL ISLANDS

PALAU

FEDERATED STATES OF MICRONESIA

K I R I B A T I

NAURU

SACRED ROCKS
In Australia's Northern Territory, a dome-shaped rock known as Uluru rises 2,831 feet from the sandy red plains. Uluru, along with a smaller rock formation known as Kata Tjuta, is sacred to the Anangu people indigenous to this area of the continent.

PAPUA NEW GUINEA

SOLOMON ISLANDS

TUVALU

SAM

VANUATU

FIJI

TONGA

AUSTRALIA

MONOTREMES
One of the most uncommon groups of animals in the world can be found only in Australia and New Guinea. Monotremes, including platypuses and echidnas, are mammals that lay eggs. Only five species of monotremes are known to exist in the world.

GLACIAL SYSTEMS
Both the North and South Islands contain glaciers, part of the diverse geological landscape of New Zealand. The Southern Alps, on the South Island, are a 300-mile-long mountain system that is home to hundreds of glaciers. Largest among them is Tasman Glacier, which measures 16.8 miles long and nearly 2 miles wide at some points.

NEW ZEALAND

Continental FACTS

TOTAL NUMBER OF COUNTRIES
14

TOTAL AREA
3,286,000 square miles (8,510,700 sq km)

MOST POPULOUS COUNTRY
Australia: 23,470,000

LEAST POPULOUS COUNTRY
Nauru: 10,000

LARGEST COUNTRY BY AREA
Australia: 2,988,901 square miles (7,741,220 sq km)

SMALLEST COUNTRY BY AREA
Nauru: 8 square miles (21 sq km)

HIGHEST ELEVATION
Mount Wilhelm, Papua New Guinea: 14,793 feet (4,509 m)

LOWEST ELEVATION
Lake Eyre, Australia: −52 feet (−16 m)

Australia's Sydney Opera House

ANTARCTICA

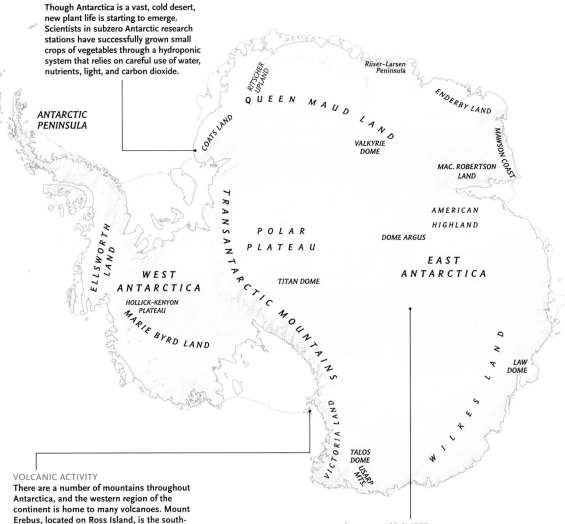

HYDROPONICS
Though Antarctica is a vast, cold desert, new plant life is starting to emerge. Scientists in subzero Antarctic research stations have successfully grown small crops of vegetables through a hydroponic system that relies on careful use of water, nutrients, light, and carbon dioxide.

ANTARCTIC PENINSULA

RITSCHER UPLAND

QUEEN MAUD LAND

Riiser-Larsen Peninsula

ENDERBY LAND

MAWSON COAST

COATS LAND

VALKYRIE DOME

MAC. ROBERTSON LAND

TRANSANTARCTIC MOUNTAINS

POLAR PLATEAU

AMERICAN HIGHLAND

DOME ARGUS

ELLSWORTH LAND

WEST ANTARCTICA

EAST ANTARCTICA

HOLLICK-KENYON PLATEAU

TITAN DOME

MARIE BYRD LAND

WILKES LAND

LAW DOME

VICTORIA LAND

TALOS DOME

USARP MTS.

VOLCANIC ACTIVITY
There are a number of mountains throughout Antarctica, and the western region of the continent is home to many volcanoes. Mount Erebus, located on Ross Island, is the southernmost active volcano on the planet, and its peak stands at 12,448 feet above sea level.

ICE SHEET
The continent of Antarctica is covered with ice—the largest single piece of ice on Earth. Measuring more than 5 million square miles, the area of the Antarctic Ice Sheet is equivalent to that of the Lower 48 United States and Mexico combined.

An iceberg arch off the Antarctic Peninsula

OCEANS
OF THE WORLD

A BLUE PLANET

Earth's predominant physical feature is the vast, continuous body of water that accounts for more than two-thirds of its surface, totaling some 139 million square miles. The global ocean is a dominant climate factor, with currents carrying heat from the Equator toward the poles, and a vital resource providing food to much of the world's population and serving as a key transportation route between continents.

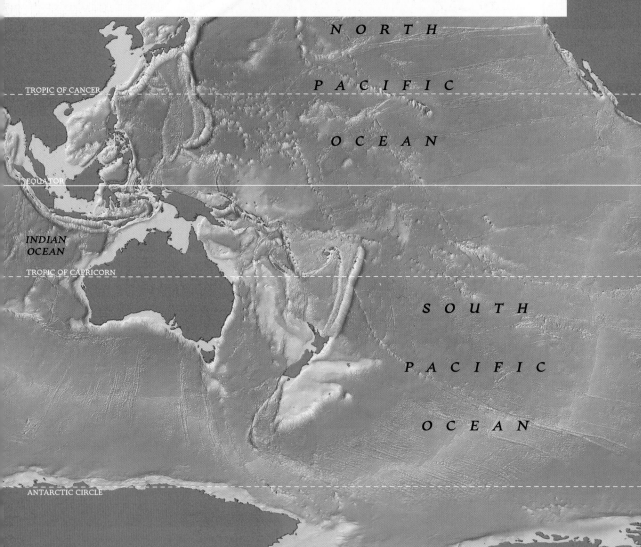

NORTH

PACIFIC

OCEAN

TROPIC OF CANCER

EQUATOR

INDIAN
OCEAN

TROPIC OF CAPRICORN

SOUTH

PACIFIC

OCEAN

ANTARCTIC CIRCLE

WHEREVER TWO CURRENTS MEET . . . THERE ARE ZONES OF GREAT TURBULENCE AND UNREST . . . AT SUCH PLACES THE RICHNESS AND ABUNDANCE OF MARINE LIFE REVEALS ITSELF MOST STRIKINGLY.

—RACHEL CARSON, IN *THE SEA AROUND US*

ARCTIC CIRCLE

NORTH

ATLANTIC

OCEAN

TROPIC OF CANCER

EQUATOR

SOUTH

ATLANTIC

OCEAN

INDIAN

OCEAN

TROPIC OF CAPRICORN

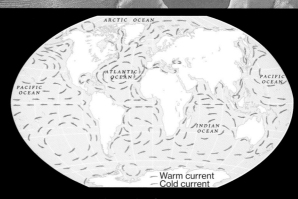

Warm current
Cold current

Rivers in the Ocean
Great surface currents circle the major
ocean basins, ferrying the heat of the tropical
sun north to warm and expand the temperate zones.

ANTARCTIC CIRCLE

ATLANTIC OCEAN

OCEAN TRENDS

Oceans are living things, with environments and processes that affect us all. They play huge roles in our lives as highways for travel and sources of food. Their vitality shapes the future of life on this planet. Here are a few indicators of ocean well-being today.

Marine Catch, 2014
■ Top 10 countries

Chlorophyll

Tiny phytoplankton are crucial to life inside and outside the oceans, and their blooming is tracked through the observation of chlorophyll concentrations. Nutrient-deficient areas are known as "deserts." Fluctuations and storms such as El Niño and Atlantic hurricanes can shift these patterns, causing some "deserts" to occasionally bloom.

Chlorophyll concentration (mg/m³), July 2002–Aug. 2013 average
>.01
1
20
■ No data

Fishing Activity

Roughly one billion people depend on fish as their main protein source. As demand for fish has risen, the global fishing industry has grown. Unfortunately, fishing is often practiced unsustainably, and current overfishing threatens ocean ecosystems. Crude fishing techniques can result in unintentional bycatch, which accounts for more than 40 percent of all marine catch globally.

Average annual marine catch metric tons per sq km/year
10
3
0.25

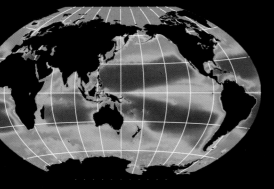

Sea Surface Temperatures

Sea surface temperature drives many of the oceans' most crucial systems. Destructive tropical storms are generated and sustained only in areas with high surface temperatures. So with ocean temperatures rising across the globe, the threat of more frequent and more destructive storms is increasing as well.

Sea surface temperature, July 2002–Aug. 2013 average
High
Low

KEY FACTS

About the
ATLANTIC

TOTAL AREA
35,400,000 square miles (91,700,000 sq km)

AVERAGE DEPTH
10,925 feet (3,300 m)

DEEPEST POINT
Puerto Rico Trench: –28,232 feet (–8,605 m)

LARGEST ISLAND
Greenland

THE DEEPEST POINT IN THE ATLANTIC OCEAN IS THE BOTTOM OF THE PUERTO RICO TRENCH, 28,232 FEET DOWN.

CONTINENTAL SHELF

GREENLAND

ICELAND
PLATEAU

ARCTIC CIRCLE

REYKJANES RIDGE

ROCKALL
PLATEAU

BATTLE OF THE ATLANTIC
Running from 1939 to 1945, the Battle of the Atlantic was the longest continuous military campaign of World War II. German U-boats clashed with Allied ships, and underwater wreckage from the years-long battle can still be found.

CELTIC
SHELF

*Flemish
Cap*

N O R T H

A T L A N T I C

O C E A N

MID-ATLANTIC RIDGE

TROPIC OF CANCER

PUERTO RICO
TRENCH

STRAIT OF GIBRALTAR
Measuring 36 miles long and eight miles wide at its most narrow point, the Strait of Gibraltar has played an important role in Atlantic trade for hundreds of years. This channel connects the Atlantic Ocean to the Mediterranean Sea, allowing ships to traverse the two important bodies of water.

VIKING CROSSINGS
Evidence of Viking settlements in Canada shows that Christopher Columbus wasn't the first European to set foot on North America. Indeed, Vikings were crossing the Atlantic Ocean nearly five centuries before the *Niña*, the *Pinta*, and the *Santa María* set sail.

M I D -

A T L A N T I C

S O U T H

A T L A N T I C

R I D G E

WALVIS RIDGE

TROPIC OF CAPRICORN

O C E A N

*RIO GRANDE
RISE*

*Agulhas
Bank*

S O U T H

P A C I F I C

O C E A N

UMVOTO RISE

PATAGONIAN SHELF

FALKLAND PLATEAU

NORTH SCOTIA RIDGE

SOUTH SANDWICH
TRENCH

ATLANTIC-INDIAN RIDGE

PACIFIC
OCEAN

CONTINENTAL S

ALEUTIAN BASIN

OKHOTSK
BASIN

A L E U T I A

KURIL-KAMCHATKA TRENCH

EMPEROR TROUGH

CHINOOK TROU

JAPAN BASIN

JAPAN TRENCH

N O R T H   P A

HAWAI

RYUKYU TRENCH

TROPIC OF CANCER

PHILIPPINE
BASIN

SOUTH CHINA BASIN

MARIANA TRENCH

PACIFIC GARBAGE PATCH
The largest collection of floating trash
on the planet lies in the Pacific Ocean
between California and Hawaii. Discovered in 1997, the garbage patch isn't
a solid island of plastic strong enough
to stand on, but a collection of broken-
down debris including fishing gear, plastic bags, bottles, and more.

PHILIPPINE TRENCH

Challenger Deep

CENTRAL PACIF

SUNDA SHELF

EQUATOR

M E L A N E S I A N

BASIN

I N D I A N

O C E A N

BASIN

VITYAZ TRENCH

ARAFURA SHELF

CORAL SEA
BASIN

FIJI
PLATEAU

Great Barrier Reef

TONG

TROPIC OF CAPRICORN

MACQUARIE RIDGE

TASMAN
BASIN

BOUNTY TROUGH

CAMPBELL
PLATEAU

KEY FACTS

About the
PACIFIC

TOTAL AREA
69,000,000 square miles (178,800,000 sq km)

AVERAGE DEPTH
14,040 feet (4,280 m)

DEEPEST POINT
Challenger Deep: −36,037 feet (−10,984 m)

LARGEST ISLAND
New Guinea

THE PACIFIC OCEAN IS THE WORLD'S LARGEST OCEAN BY FAR, COVERING ABOUT ONE-THIRD OF THE PLANET'S SURFACE—APPROXIMATELY 69 MILLION SQUARE MILES.

ALASKA PLAIN

TUFTS PLAIN

RENCH

NORTHEAST PACIFIC BASIN

PACIFIC OCEAN

CE

Kingman Reef

Christmas Ridge

NIHIKI ATEAU

TIKI BASIN

Society Ridge

Tuamotu Ridge

SOUTH PACIFIC OCEAN

SOUTHWEST PACIFIC BASIN

SVILLE GE

NORTH ATLANTIC OCEAN

Georges Bank

TROPIC OF CANCER

MIDDLE AMERICA TRENCH

GUATEMALA BASIN

COCOS RIDGE

PANAMA BASIN

EQUATOR

PERU BASIN

PERU-CHILE TRENCH

NASCA RIDGE

SALAS Y GÓMEZ RIDGE

TROPIC OF CAPRICORN

CHILE BASIN

CHILE TRENCH

HUMBOLDT PLAIN

GIANT KELP FORESTS
On the Pacific coast of North America, growths of giant kelp form a canopy that could compare to any rainforest. The kelp thrives in cool, shallow oceans where the water is rich in nutrients rising up from the deep sea. A diverse array of animals thrives in the kelp forests, from snails to sea otters.

SEAFARING HERITAGE
Starting in about 1500 BC, Indigenous cultures in the South Pacific were taking to the water. With their large, double-hulled outrigger vessels, these early seafarers traversed large swaths of the ocean, settling new islands and developing culture centered around the ocean that continues to this day.

INDIAN OCEAN

ARABIAN BASIN

CHAGOS-LACCADVE RIDGE

Chain Ridge

CARLSBERG RIDGE

MID-INDIAN BASIN

OFFSHORE DRILLING
Some of the world's largest reserves of oil can be found underneath the Persian Gulf. There are more than 150 offshore drilling rigs in the gulf, making it the world region with the third most rigs after the North Sea and the Gulf of Mexico.

EQUATOR

COCO-DE-MER SEAMOUNTS

SOMALI BASIN

Seychelles Bank

AMIRANTE TRENCH

MASCARENE PLATEAU

MID-INDIAN RIDGE

COMORO BASIN

MASCARENE BASIN

Madagascar

I N D I A N

MAURITIUS TRENCH

TROPIC OF CAPRICORN

MADAGASCAR BASIN

SOUTHWEST INDIAN RIDGE

SOUTHEA

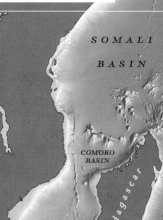

KEY FACTS

About the
INDIAN

TOTAL AREA
29,400,000 square miles (76,200,000 sq km)

AVERAGE DEPTH
12,990 feet (3,960 m)

DEEPEST POINT
Java Trench: –23,376 feet (–7,125 m)

LARGEST ISLAND
Madagascar

CROZET BASIN

CROZET PLATEAU

SEAMOUNTS AND BIODIVERSITY
Underwater mountains called seamounts, habitats for marine life, are being discovered in the Indian Ocean. Bustling ecosystems form around seamounts, built on large populations of microorganisms that support larger predators.

THE INDIAN OCEAN IS THE WARMEST OCEAN BASIN ON EARTH. THE WARMTH OF THE WATER INHIBITS THE GROWTH OF PHYTOPLANKTON AND SEVERELY LIMITS THE NUMBER OF MARINE ANIMALS IT CAN SUPPORT.

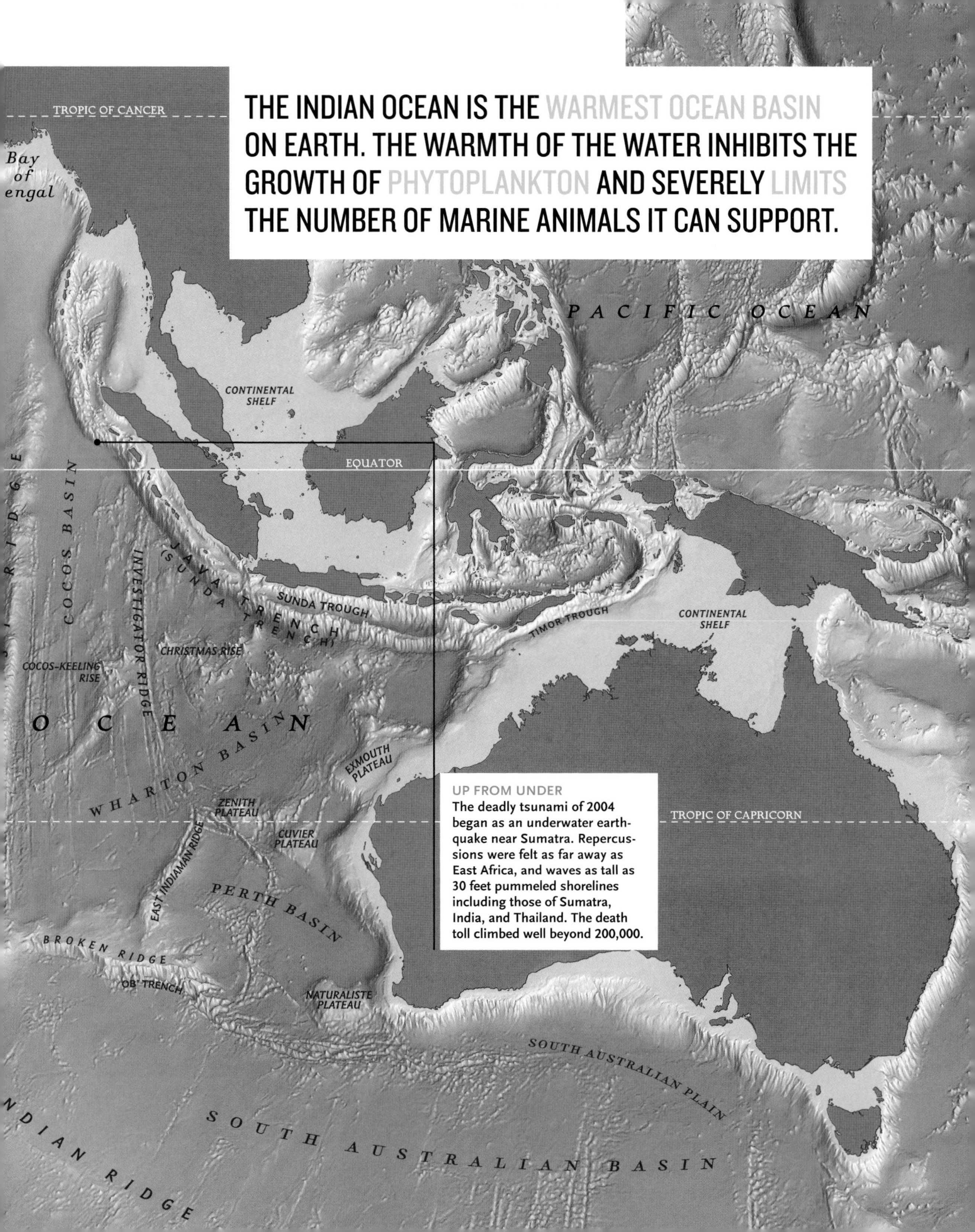

TROPIC OF CANCER

Bay of engal

PACIFIC OCEAN

CONTINENTAL SHELF

EQUATOR

COCOS BASIN

INVESTIGATOR RIDGE

JAVA (SUNDA) TRENCH

SUNDA TRENCH (JAVA)

SUNDA TROUGH

CHRISTMAS RISE

COCOS-KEELING RISE

TIMOR TROUGH

CONTINENTAL SHELF

O C E A N

WHARTON BASIN

EXMOUTH PLATEAU

ZENITH PLATEAU

TROPIC OF CAPRICORN

CUVIER PLATEAU

EAST INDIAMAN RIDGE

PERTH BASIN

BROKEN RIDGE

'OB' TRENCH

NATURALISTE PLATEAU

SOUTH AUSTRALIAN PLAIN

S O U T H   A U S T R A L I A N   B A S I N

NDIAN RIDGE

RIDGE

UP FROM UNDER
The deadly tsunami of 2004 began as an underwater earthquake near Sumatra. Repercussions were felt as far away as East Africa, and waves as tall as 30 feet pummeled shorelines including those of Sumatra, India, and Thailand. The death toll climbed well beyond 200,000.

ARCTIC
OCEAN

ARCTIC CIRCLE

POLAR VORTEX
Above the Arctic, a spinning mass of cold air called the polar vortex grows and shrinks with the changing seasons. Constantly spinning counterclockwise around the North Pole, it stays at a higher latitude in summer and a lower one in winter. Sometimes the intensely cold air at its bottom edge escapes the spin and heads south, causing extreme winter weather farther south.

NANSEN

GAKKEL

EURASDE

AMUNDSE

LOMONOSOV

CONTINENTAL SHELF

MAKAROV BASIN

MENDELEYEV RIDGE

SARGO PLATEAU

EURASIA

NAUTILUS BASIN

CHUKCHI PLATEAU

ALPHA RIDGE

AMERASIA BASIN

NORTHWIND RIDGE

STEFANSSON BASIN

CANADA BASIN

KEY FACTS

About the
ARCTIC

TOTAL AREA
5,600,000 square miles (14,700,000 sq km)

AVERAGE DEPTH
3,240 feet (987 m)

DEEPEST POINT
Molloy Deep: −18,599 feet (−5,669 m)

LARGEST ISLAND
Greenland

WARMING WATERS
As summer sea ice in the Arctic disappears, the diversity of life that relies on its presence will disappear as well. Since the 1980s, more than a million square miles of Arctic sea ice have been lost, and polar bears, walruses, seabirds, fish, even algae, and more have struggled to keep up with the changing environment.

THE ARCTIC OCEAN IS THE PLANET'S SMALLEST OCEAN, COVERING JUST 5.6 MILLION SQUARE MILES.

CENTRAL BASIN

SVYATAYA ANNA TROUGH

FRANTS-VIKTORIYA TROUGH

OLGA BASIN

BARENTS TROUGH

BASIN

YERMAK PLATEAU

Molloy Deep

KNIPOVICH RIDGE

MOHNS RIDGE

LOFOTEN BASIN

VORING PLATEAU

MERIDIAN OF GREENWICH (LONDON)

LENA TROUGH

BOREAS BASIN

TIC OCEAN

GREENLAND BASIN

CONTINENTAL SHELF

NORWEGIAN BASIN

AEGIR RIDGE

ICELAND-FAROE RISE

JAN MAYEN RIDGE

ICELAND PLATEAU

KOLBEINSEY RIDGE

GREENLAND

ARCTIC CIRCLE

ICELAND BASIN

ATLANTIC OCEAN

ELLESMERE ISLAND
Canada's Ellesmere Island is the northernmost piece of land in the Arctic archipelago. A polar desert, it receives very little rainfall and supports a small but unique collection of plants and animals.

REYKJANES RIDGE

IRMINGER BASIN

BAFFIN BASIN

OCEAN AROUND
ANTARCTICA

INDIA

KERGUELEN PLATEAU

PRINCESS ELIZ
TROUGH

B O U T H E

ANTARCTIC CONVERGENCE
There is no land boundary between the waters that comprise the Antarctic Ocean and the Pacific, Atlantic, and Indian Oceans. Instead, the boundary is an uneven line where the cold Antarctic waters flow north to meet the warmer waters of the world's other oceans.

ATLANTIC-INDIAN RIDGE

ATLANTIC-INDIANS BASIN

ATLANTIC

ATLANTIC OCEAN

MERIDIAN OF GREENWICH (LONDON)

AMERICA-ANTARCTICA RIDGE
(NORTH WEDDELL RIDGE)

ANTARCTIC CIRCLE

MID-ATLANTIC RIDGE

TROPIC OF CAPRICORN

SOUTH SANDWICH TRENCH

GEORGIA BASIN

FALKLAND RIDGE

CONTINENTAL SHELF

ICEBERGS
Most of the Earth's icebergs are found in Antarctica and the Arctic, where cold waters prevent large chunks that have broken off glaciers or ice sheets from melting. Scientists follow icebergs because they can offer insight into ocean currents, circulation, and the way that ice shelves break up over time.

South Shetland
Trough
DRAKE
PASSAGE

S O

NORTH SCOTIA RIDGE

FALKLAND TROUGH

FALKLAND PLATEAU

CHILE TRENCH

THE WATERS AROUND ANTARCTICA MAY PLUNGE DOWN MORE THAN 16,000 FEET AT THEIR DEEPEST POINT. AN EXPEDITION CURRENTLY UNDER WAY IS CONFIRMING THAT MEASUREMENT.

CEAN

SOUTH INDIAN OCEAN BASIN

ANTARCTIC CIRCLE

INDIAN-ANTARCTIC RIDGE

TASMAN BASIN

MACQUARIE RIDGE

HJORT TRENCH

EMERALD BASIN

CAMPBELL PLATEAU

BALLENY TROUGH

BALLENY BASIN

South Pole

ROSS SEA

PACIFIC-ANTARCTIC RIDGE

SOUTHWEST PACIFIC

HUMPBACK WHALES
In the chilly waters around Antarctica, humpback whales are a common sight. They feed on krill—small, shrimp-like creatures that are also prey for many seabirds and other marine mammals. Humpback whales have one of the longest animal migrations, traveling from their breeding grounds in warm tropical areas to feed in the colder waters near the poles.

THERN OCEAN

SOUTHEAST PACIFIC BASIN

EAST PACIFIC RISE

PACIFIC OCEAN

PACIFIC BASIN

TROPIC OF CAPRICORN

BEST OF @NATGEO

TOP PHOTOS OF OCEANSCAPES

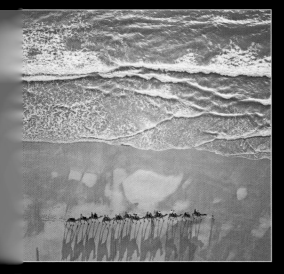

@geosteinmetz | GEORGE STEINMETZ
ourists riding camels cast shadows on the white sand of
Cable Beach, a popular travel destination in Broome,
Australia.

@jenniferhayesig | JENNIFER HAYES
Southern stingrays float in the North Sound of Grand Cayman, where sandbars and shallow waters are ideal habitat.

@paulnicklen | PAUL NICKLEN
A pod of narwhals surfaces in Arctic waters. The distinctive
vory tusk seen on males is actually a tooth growing through
ts lip.

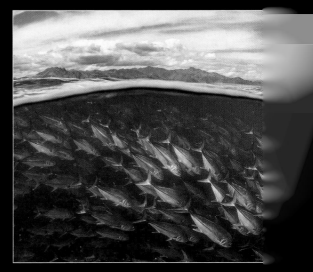

@thomaspeschak | THOMAS PESCHAK
A school of bigeye jacks moves through the Cabo Pulmo
Marine Reserve, a protected area of reefs off the Baja Cali-
fornia peninsula.

@jimmychin | JIMMY CHIN
The Ilulissat Icefjord is a gateway for icebergs calving from an active glacier to enter Disko Bay on Greenland's west coast.

@thomaspeschak | THOMAS PESCHAK
A double rainbow arcs from blue water between D'Arros Island and St. Joseph Atoll in the Seychelles.

@ladzinski | KEITH LADZINSKI
Sunset tints the sky above Keyhole Arch at Pfeiffer Beach, a secluded stretch of Big Sur coastline.

@daviddoubilet | DAVID DOUBILET
Brown boobies perch on coral in Tubbataha Reefs Natural Park, reachable only by boat in the Sulu Sea in the Philippines.

FLAGS OF THE WORLD

EACH OF TODAY'S 195 COUNTRIES FLIES AN HONORED AND SYMBOLIC FLAG

AFGHANISTAN
AREA 251,827 sq mi
(652,230 sq km)
POPULATION 34,941,000
CAPITAL Kabul

ALBANIA
AREA 11,100 sq mi
(28,748 sq km)
POPULATION 3,057,000
CAPITAL Tirana

ALGERIA
AREA 919,590 sq mi
(2,381,741 sq km)
POPULATION 41,657,000
CAPITAL Algiers

ANDORRA
AREA 181 sq mi
(468 sq km)
POPULATION 86,000
CAPITAL Andorra la Vella

ANGOLA
AREA 481,351 sq mi
(1,246,700 sq km)
POPULATION 30,356,000
CAPITAL Luanda

ANTIGUA AND BARBUDA
AREA 171 sq mi
(443 sq km)
POPULATION 96,000
CAPITAL St. John's

ARGENTINA
AREA 1,073,518 sq mi
(2,780,400 sq km)
POPULATION 44,694,000
CAPITAL Buenos Aires

ARMENIA
AREA 11,484 sq mi
(29,743 sq km)
POPULATION 3,038,000
CAPITAL Yerevan

AUSTRALIA
AAREA 2,988,901 sq mi
(7,741,220 sq km)
POPULATION 23,470,000
CAPITAL Canberra

AUSTRIA
AREA 32,383 sq mi
(83,871 sq km)
POPULATION 8,793,000
CAPITAL Vienna

AZERBAIJAN
AREA 33,436 sq mi
(86,600 sq km)
POPULATION 10,047,000
CAPITAL Baku

BAHAMAS, THE
AREA 5,359 sq mi
(13,880 sq km)
POPULATION 330,000
CAPITAL Nassau

BAHRAIN
AREA 293 sq mi
(760 sq km)
POPULATION 1,443,000
CAPITAL Manama

BANGLADESH
AREA 57,321 sq mi
(148,460 sq km)
POPULATION 159,453,000
CAPITAL Dhaka

BARBADOS
AREA 166 sq mi
(430 sq km)
POPULATION 293,000
CAPITAL Bridgetown

BELARUS
AREA 80,155 sq mi
(207,600 sq km)
POPULATION 9,528,000
CAPITAL Minsk

BELGIUM
AREA 11,787 sq mi
(30,528 sq km)
POPULATION 11,571,000
CAPITAL Brussels

BELIZE
AREA 8,867 sq mi
(22,966 sq km)
POPULATION 386,000
CAPITAL Belmopan

BENIN
AREA 43,484 sq mi
(112,622 sq km)
POPULATION 11,341,000
CAPITALS Porto-Novo (official capital),
Cotonou (administrative)

BHUTAN
AREA 14,824 sq mi
(38,394 sq km)
POPULATION 766,000
CAPITAL Thimphu

BOLIVIA
AREA 424,164 sq mi
(1,098,581 sq km)
POPULATION 11,138,000
CAPITALS La Paz (administrative),
Sucre (constitutional)

BOSNIA AND HERZEGOVINA
AREA 19,767 sq mi
(51,197 sq km)
POPULATION 3,850,000
CAPITAL Sarajevo

BOTSWANA
AREA 224,607 sq mi
(581,730 sq km)
POPULATION 2,215,000
CAPITAL Gaborone

BRAZIL
AREA 3,287,956 sq mi
(8,515,770 sq km)
POPULATION 208,847,000
CAPITAL Brasília

BRUNEI
AREA 2,226 sq mi
(5,765 sq km)
POPULATION 451,000
CAPITAL Bandar Seri Begawan

" PRIDE AND INDUSTRY."

—NATIONAL MOTTO OF BARBADOS

BULGARIA

AREA 42,811 sq mi
(110,879 sq km)
POPULATION 7,058,000
CAPITAL Sofia

BURKINA FASO

AREA 105,869 sq mi
(274,200 sq km)
POPULATION 19,743,000
CAPITAL Ouagadougou

BURUNDI

AREA 10,745 sq mi
(27,830 sq km)
POPULATION 11,845,000
CAPITAL Gitega

CABO VERDE

AREA 1,557 sq mi
(4,033 sq km)
POPULATION 568,000
CAPITAL Praia

CAMBODIA

AREA 69,898 sq mi
(181,035 sq km)
POPULATION 16,450,000
CAPITAL Phnom Penh

CAMEROON

AREA 183,568 sq mi
(475,440 sq km)
POPULATION 25,641,000
CAPITAL Yaoundé

CANADA

AREA 3,855,101 sq mi
(9,984,670 sq km)
POPULATION 35,882,000
CAPITAL Ottawa

CENTRAL AFRICAN REPUBLIC

AREA 240,535 sq mi
(622,984 sq km)
POPULATION 5,745,000
CAPITAL Bangui

CHAD

AREA 495,755 sq mi
(1,284,000 sq km)
POPULATION 15,833
CAPITAL N'Djamena

CHILE

AREA 291,932 sq mi
(756,102 sq km)
POPULATION 17,925,000
CAPITAL Santiago

CHINA

AREA 3,705,407 sq mi
(9,596,960 sq km)
POPULATION 1,384,689,000
CAPITAL Beijing

COLOMBIA

AREA 439,735 sq mi
(1,138,910 sq km)
POPULATION 48,169,000
CAPITAL Bogotá

COMOROS

AREA 863 sq mi
(2,235 sq km)
POPULATION 821,000
CAPITAL Moroni

CONGO

AREA 132,047 sq mi
(342,000 sq km)
POPULATION 5,062,000
CAPITAL Brazzaville

CONGO, DEMOCRATIC REPUBLIC OF THE

AREA 905,354 sq mi
(2,344,858 sq km)
POPULATION 85,281,000
CAPITAL Kinshasa

COSTA RICA

AREA 19,730 sq mi
(51,100 sq km)
POPULATION 4,987,000
CAPITAL San José

CÔTE D'IVOIRE

AREA 124,504 sq mi
(322,463 sq km)
POPULATION 26,261,000
CAPITALS Abidjan (administrative),
Yamoussoukro (legislative)

CROATIA

AREA 21,851 sq mi
(56,594 sq km)
POPULATION 4,270,000
CAPITAL Zagreb

CUBA

AREA 42,803 sq mi
(110,860 sq km)
POPULATION 11,116,000
CAPITAL Havana

CYPRUS

AREA 3,572 sq mi
(9,251 sq km)
POPULATION 1,237,000
CAPITAL Nicosia

CZECHIA (CZECH REPUBLIC)

AREA 30,451 sq mi
(78,867 sq km)
POPULATION 10,686,000
CAPITAL Prague

DENMARK

AREA 16,639 sq mi
(43,094 sq km)
POPULATION 5,810,000
CAPITAL Copenhagen

DJIBOUTI

AREA 8,958 sq mi
(23,200 sq km)
POPULATION 884,000
CAPITAL Djibouti

DOMINICA

AREA 290 sq mi
(751 sq km)
POPULATION 74,000
CAPITAL Roseau

DOMINICAN REPUBLIC

AREA 18,792 sq mi
(48,670 sq km)
POPULATION 10,299,000
CAPITAL Santo Domingo

ECUADOR

AREA 109,483 sq mi
(283,561 sq km)
POPULATION 16,499,000
CAPITAL Quito

EGYPT

AREA 386,662 sq mi
(1,001,450 sq km)
POPULATION 99,413,000
CAPITAL Cairo

EL SALVADOR

AREA 8,124 sq mi
(21,041 sq km)
POPULATION 6,187,000
CAPITAL San Salvador

EQUATORIAL GUINEA
AREA 10,831 sq mi
(28,051 sq km)
POPULATION 797,000
CAPITAL Malabo

ERITREA
AREA 45,406 sq mi
(117,600 sq km)
POPULATION 5,971,000
CAPITAL Asmara

ESTONIA
AREA 17,463 sq mi
(45,228 sq km)
POPULATION 1,244,000
CAPITAL Tallinn

ESWATINI
AREA 6,704 sq mi
(17,364 sq km)
POPULATION 1,087,000
CAPITALS Mbabane (administrative),
Lobamba (legislative and royal)

ETHIOPIA
AREA 426,372 sq mi
(1,104,300 sq km)
POPULATION 108,386,000
CAPITAL Addis Ababa

FIJI
AREA 7,056 sq mi
(18,274 sq km)
POPULATION 926,000
CAPITAL Suva

FINLAND
AREA 130,558 sq mi
(338,145 sq km)
POPULATION 5,537,000
CAPITAL Helsinki

FRANCE
AREA 248,573 sq mi
(643,801 sq km)
POPULATION 67,364,000
CAPITAL Paris

GABON
AREA 103,347 sq mi
(267,667 sq km)
POPULATION 2,119,000
CAPITAL Libreville

GAMBIA, THE
AREA 4,363 sq mi
(11,300 sq km)
POPULATION 2,093,000
CAPITAL Banjul

GEORGIA
AREA 26,911 sq mi
(69,700 sq km)
POPULATION 4,926,000
CAPITAL Tbilisi

GERMANY
AREA 137,847 sq mi
(357,022 sq km)
POPULATION 80,458,000
CAPITAL Berlin

GHANA
AREA 92,098 sq mi
(238,533 sq km)
POPULATION 28,102,000
CAPITAL Accra

GREECE
AREA 50,949 sq mi
(131,957 sq km)
POPULATION 10,762,000
CAPITAL Athens

GRENADA
AREA 133 sq mi
(344 sq km)
POPULATION 112,000
CAPITAL St. George's

GUATEMALA
AREA 42,042 sq mi
(108,889 sq km)
POPULATION 16,581,000
CAPITAL Guatemala City

GUINEA
AREA 94,926 sq mi
(245,857 sq km)
POPULATION 11,855,000
CAPITAL Conakry

GUINEA-BISSAU
AREA 13,948 sq mi
(36,125 sq km)
POPULATION 1,833,000
CAPITAL Bissau

GUYANA
AREA 83,000 sq mi
(214,969 sq km)
POPULATION 741,000
CAPITAL Georgetown

HAITI
AREA 10,714 sq mi
(27,750 sq km)
POPULATION 10,788,000
CAPITAL Port-au-Prince

HONDURAS
AREA 43,278 sq mi
(112,090 sq km)
POPULATION 9,183,000
CAPITAL Tegucigalpa

HUNGARY
AREA 35,918 sq mi
(93,028 sq km)
POPULATION 9,826,000
CAPITAL Budapest

ICELAND
AREA 39,769 sq mi
(103,000 sq km)
POPULATION 344,000
CAPITAL Reykjavík

INDIA
AREA 1,269,219 sq mi
(3,287,263 sq km)
POPULATION 1,296,834,000
CAPITAL New Delhi

INDONESIA
AREA 735,358 sq mi
(1,904,569 sq km)
POPULATION 262,787,000
CAPITAL Jakarta

IRAN
AREA 636,371 sq mi
(1,648,195 sq km)
POPULATION 83,025,000
CAPITAL Tehran

IRAQ
AREA 169,235 sq mi
(438,317 sq km)
POPULATION 40,194,000
CAPITAL Baghdad

IRELAND
AREA 27,133 sq mi
(70,273 sq km)
POPULATION 5,068,000
CAPITAL Dublin

ISRAEL
AREA 8,019 sq mi
(20,770 sq km)
POPULATION 8,425,000
CAPITAL Jerusalem

ITALY
AREA 116,348 sq mi
(301,340 sq km)
POPULATION 62,247,000
CAPITAL Rome

JAMAICA
AREA 4,244 sq mi
(10,991 sq km)
POPULATION 2,812,000
CAPITAL Kingston

JAPAN
AREA 145,914 sq mi
(377,915 sq km)
POPULATION 126,168,000
CAPITAL Tokyo

JORDAN
AREA 34,495 sq mi
(89,342 sq km)
POPULATION 10,458,000
CAPITAL Amman

KAZAKHSTAN
AREA 1,052,089 sq mi
(2,724,900 sq km)
POPULATION 18,745,000
CAPITAL Nur-Sultan (Astana)

KENYA

AREA 224,081 sq mi
(580,367 sq km)
POPULATION 48,398,000
CAPITAL Nairobi

KIRIBATI
AREA 313 sq mi
(811 sq km)
POPULATION 109,000
CAPITAL Tarawa

KOSOVO
AREA 4,203 sq mi
(10,887 sq km)
POPULATION 1,908,000
CAPITAL Prishtina

KUWAIT
AREA 6,880 sq mi
(17,818 sq km)
POPULATION 4,622,000
CAPITAL Kuwait City

KYRGYZSTAN
AREA 77,201 sq mi
(199,951 sq km)
POPULATION 5,849,000
CAPITAL Bishkek

LAOS
AREA 91,429 sq mi
(236,800 sq km)
POPULATION 7,234,000
CAPITAL Vientiane

LATVIA
AREA 24,938 sq mi
(64,589 sq km)
POPULATION 1,924,000
CAPITAL Riga

LEBANON
AREA 4,015 sq mi
(10,400 sq km)
POPULATION 6,100,000
CAPITAL Beirut

LESOTHO
AREA 11,720 sq mi
(30,355 sq km)
POPULATION 1,962,000
CAPITAL Maseru

LIBERIA
AREA 43,000 sq mi
(111,369 sq km)
POPULATION 4,810,000
CAPITAL Monrovia

LIBYA
AREA 679,362 sq mi
(1,759,540 sq km)
POPULATION 6,755,000
CAPITAL Tripoli

LIECHTENSTEIN
AREA 62 sq mi
(160 sq km)
POPULATION 39,000
CAPITAL Vaduz

LITHUANIA
AREA 25,212 sq mi
(65,300 sq km)
POPULATION 2,793,000
CAPITAL Vilnius

LUXEMBOURG
AREA 998 sq mi
(2,586 sq km)
POPULATION 606,000
CAPITAL Luxembourg

MADAGASCAR

AREA 226,658 sq mi
(587,041 sq km)
POPULATION 25,684,000
CAPITAL Antananarivo

MALAWI
AREA 45,747 sq mi
(118,484 sq km)
POPULATION 19,843,000
CAPITAL Lilongwe

MALAYSIA

AREA 127,355 sq mi
(329,847 sq km)
POPULATION 31,810,000
CAPITAL Kuala Lumpur

MALDIVES
AREA 115 sq mi
(298 sq km)
POPULATION 392,000
CAPITAL Male

MALI
AREA 478,841 sq mi
(1,240,192 sq km)
POPULATION 18,430,000
CAPITAL Bamako

MALTA

AREA 122 sq mi
(316 sq km)
POPULATION 449,000
CAPITAL Valletta

MARSHALL ISLANDS

AREA 70 sq mi
(181 sq km)
POPULATION 76,000
CAPITAL Majuro

MAURITANIA

AREA 397,955 sq mi
(1,030,700 sq km)
POPULATION 3,840,000
CAPITAL Nouakchott

MAURITIUS
AREA 788 sq mi
(2,040 sq km)
POPULATION 1,364,000
CAPITAL Port Louis

MEXICO

AREA 758,449 sq mi
(1,964,375 sq km)
POPULATION 125,959,000
CAPITAL Mexico City

MICRONESIA

AREA 271 sq mi
(702 sq km)
POPULATION 104,000
CAPITAL Palikir

MOLDOVA

AREA 13,070 sq mi
(33,851 sq km)
POPULATION 3,438,000
CAPITAL Chisinau

MONACO

AREA 1 sq mi
(2.0 sq km)
POPULATION 38,000
CAPITAL Monaco

MONGOLIA

AREA 603,908 sq mi
(1,564,116 sq km)
POPULATION 3,103,000
CAPITAL Ulaanbaatar

MONTENEGRO

AREA 5,333 sq mi
(13,812 sq km)
POPULATION 614,000
CAPITAL Podgorica

MOROCCO

AREA 172,414 sq mi
(446,550 sq km)
POPULATION 34,314,000
CAPITAL Rabat

MOZAMBIQUE

AREA 308,642 sq mi
(799,380 sq km)
POPULATION 27,234,000
CAPITAL Maputo

MYANMAR (BURMA)

AREA 261,228 sq mi
(676,578 sq km)
POPULATION 55,623,000
CAPITAL Nay Pyi Taw

NAMIBIA

AREA 318,261 sq mi
(824,292 sq km)
POPULATION 2,533,000
CAPITAL Windhoek

NAURU

AREA 8 sq mi
(21 sq km)
POPULATION 10,000
CAPITAL No official capital; government offices in Yaren District

NEPAL

AREA 56,827 sq mi
(147,181 sq km)
POPULATION 29,718,000
CAPITAL Kathmandu

NETHERLANDS
AREA 16,040 sq mi
(41,543 sq km)
POPULATION 17,151,000
CAPITAL Amsterdam

NEW ZEALAND
AREA 103,799 sq mi
(268,838 sq km)
POPULATION 4,546,000
CAPITAL Wellington

NICARAGUA
AREA 50,336 sq mi
(130,370 sq km)
POPULATION 6,085,000
CAPITAL Managua

NIGER
AREA 489,191 sq mi
(1,267,000 sq km)
POPULATION 19,866,000
CAPITAL Niamey

NIGERIA
AREA 356,669 sq mi
(923,768 sq km)
POPULATION 203,453,000
CAPITAL Abuja

NORTH KOREA
AREA 46,540 sq mi
(120,538 sq km)
POPULATION 25,381,000
CAPITAL Pyongyang

NORTH MACEDONIA
AREA 9,928 sq mi
(25,713 sq km)
POPULATION 2,119,000
CAPITAL Skopje

NORWAY
AREA 125,021 sq mi
(323,802 sq km)
POPULATION 5,372,000
CAPITAL Oslo

OMAN
AREA 119,499 sq mi
(309,500 sq km)
POPULATION 3,494,000
CAPITAL Muscat

PAKISTAN

AREA 307,374 sq mi
(796,095 sq km)
POPULATION 207,863,000
CAPITAL Islamabad

PALAU
AREA 177 sq mi
(459 sq km)
POPULATION 22,000
CAPITAL Melekeok (on Babelthuap)

PANAMA
AREA 29,120 sq mi
(75,420 sq km)
POPULATION 3,801,000
CAPITAL Panama City

PAPUA NEW GUINEA
AREA 178,703 sq mi
(462,840 sq km)
POPULATION 7,027,000
CAPITAL Port Moresby

PARAGUAY
AREA 157,048 sq mi
(406,752 sq km)
POPULATION 7,026,000
CAPITAL Asunción

PERU
AREA 496,224 sq mi
(1,285,216 sq km)
POPULATION 31,331,000
CAPITAL Lima

PHILIPPINES
AREA 115,831 sq mi
(300,000 sq km)
POPULATION 105,893,000
CAPITAL Manila

POLAND
AREA 120,728 sq mi
(312,685 sq km)
POPULATION 38,421,000
CAPITAL Warsaw

PORTUGAL
AREA 35,556 sq mi
(92,090 sq km)
POPULATION 10,355,000
CAPITAL Lisbon

QATAR
AREA 4,473 sq mi
(11,586 sq km)
POPULATION 2,364,000
CAPITAL Doha

ROMANIA

AREA 92,043 sq mi
(238,391 sq km)
POPULATION 21,457,000
CAPITAL Bucharest

RUSSIA

AREA 6,601,665 sq mi
(17,098,242 sq km)
POPULATION 142,123,000
CAPITAL Moscow

RWANDA

AREA 10,169 sq mi
(26,338 sq km)
POPULATION 12,187,000
CAPITAL Kigali

SAINT KITTS AND NEVIS

AREA 101 sq mi
(261 sq km)
POPULATION 53,000
CAPITAL Basseterre

SAINT LUCIA

AREA 238 sq mi
(616 sq km)
POPULATION 166,000
CAPITAL Castries

SAINT VINCENT AND GRENADINES

AREA 150 sq mi
(389 sq km)
POPULATION 102,000
CAPITAL Kingstown

SAMOA

AREA 1,093 sq mi
(2,831 sq km)
POPULATION 201,000
CAPITAL Apia

SAN MARINO

AREA 24 sq mi
(61 sq km)
POPULATION 34,000
CAPITAL San Marino

SÃO TOMÉ AND PRINCIPE

AREA 372 sq mi
(964 sq km)
POPULATION 204,000
CAPITAL São Tomé

SAUDI ARABIA

AREA 830,000 sq mi
(2,149,690 sq km)
POPULATION 33,091,000
CAPITAL Riyadh

SENEGAL

AREA 75,955 sq mi
(196,722 sq km)
POPULATION 15,021,000
CAPITAL Dakar

SERBIA

AREA 29,913 sq mi
(77,474 sq km)
POPULATION 7,078,000
CAPITAL Belgrade

SEYCHELLES

AREA 176 sq mi
(455 sq km)
POPULATION 95,000
CAPITAL Victoria

SIERRA LEONE

AREA 27,699 sq mi
(71,740 sq km)
POPULATION 6,312,000
CAPITAL Freetown

SINGAPORE
AREA 269 sq mi
(697 sq km)
POPULATION 5,996,000
CAPITAL Singapore

SLOVAKIA
AREA 18,933 sq mi
(49,035 sq km)
POPULATION 5,445,000
CAPITAL Bratislava

SLOVENIA
AREA 7,827 sq mi
(20,273 sq km)
POPULATION 2,102,000
CAPITAL Ljubljana

SOLOMON ISLANDS

AREA 11,157 sq mi
(28,896 sq km)
POPULATION 660,000
CAPITAL Honiara

SOMALIA
AREA 246,201 sq mi
(637,657 sq km)
POPULATION 11,259,000
CAPITAL Mogadishu

SOUTH AFRICA
AREA 470,693 sq mi
(1,219,090 sq km)
POPULATION 55,380,000
CAPITALS Pretoria (Tshwane) (administrative),
Cape Town (legislative), Bloemfontein
(judicial)

SOUTH KOREA
AREA 38,502 sq mi
(99,720 sq km)
POPULATION 51,418,000
CAPITAL Seoul

SOUTH SUDAN
AREA 248,777 sq mi
(644,329 sq km)
POPULATION 10,205,000
CAPITAL Juba

SPAIN

AREA 195,124 sq mi
(505,370 sq km)

POPULATION 49,331,000
CAPITAL Madrid

SRI LANKA

AREA 25,332 sq mi
(65,610 sq km)
POPULATION 22,577,000
CAPITALS Colombo (administrative),
Sri Jayewardenepura Kotte (legislative)

SUDAN

AREA 718,723 sq mi
(1,861,484 sq km)
POPULATION 43,121,000
CAPITAL Khartoum

SURINAME

AREA 63,251 sq mi
(163,820 sq km)
POPULATION 598,000
CAPITAL Paramaribo

SWEDEN
AREA 173,860 sq mi
(450,295 sq km)
POPULATION 10,041,000
CAPITAL Stockholm

SWITZERLAND

AREA 15,937 sq mi
(41,277 sq km)
POPULATION 8,293,000
CAPITAL Bern

SYRIA

AREA 71,498 sq mi
(185,180 sq km)
POPULATION 19,454,000
CAPITAL Damascus

TAJIKISTAN

AREA 55,637 sq mi
(144,100 sq km)
POPULATION 8,605,000
CAPITAL Dushanbe

TANZANIA

AREA 365,754 sq mi
(947,300 sq km)
POPULATION 55,451,000
CAPITAL Dar es Salaam (administrative);
Dodoma (official)

THAILAND
AREA 198,117 sq mi
(513,120 sq km)
POPULATION 68,616,000
CAPITAL Bangkok

TIMOR-LESTE (EAST TIMOR)

AREA 5,743 sq mi
(14,874 sq km)

POPULATION 1,322,000
CAPITAL Díli

TOGO

AREA 21,925 sq mi
(56,785 sq km)
POPULATION 8,176,000
CAPITAL Lomé

TONGA

AREA 288 sq mi
(747 sq km)
POPULATION 106,000
CAPITAL Nuku'alofa

TRINIDAD AND TOBAGO

AREA 1,980 sq mi
(5,128 sq km)
POPULATION 1,216,000
CAPITAL Port of Spain

TUNISIA

AREA 63,170 sq mi
(163,610 sq km)
POPULATION 11,516,000
CAPITAL Tunis

TURKEY

AREA 302,535 sq mi
(783,562 sq km)
POPULATION 81,257,000
CAPITAL Ankara

TURKMENISTAN

AREA 188,456 sq mi
(488,100 sq km)
POPULATION 5,411,000
CAPITAL Ashgabat

TUVALU

AREA 10 sq mi
(26 sq km)
POPULATION 11,000
CAPITAL Funafuti

UGANDA

AREA 93,065 sq mi
(241,038 sq km)
POPULATION 40,854,000
CAPITAL Kampala

UKRAINE
AREA 233,032 sq mi
(603,550 sq km)
POPULATION 43,952,000
CAPITAL Kiev

UNITED ARAB EMIRATES

AREA 32,278 sq mi
(83,600 sq km)
POPULATION 9,701,000
CAPITAL Abu Dhabi

UNITED KINGDOM

AREA 94,058 sq mi
(243,610 sq km)
POPULATION 65,105,000
CAPITAL London

UNITED STATES

AREA 3,796,741 sq mi
(9,833,517 sq km)
POPULATION 329,256,000
CAPITAL Washington, D.C.

URUGUAY

AREA 68,037 sq mi
(176,215 sq km)
POPULATION 3,369,000
CAPITAL Montevideo

UZBEKISTAN

AREA 172,742 sq mi
(447,400 sq km)
POPULATION 30,024,000
CAPITAL Tashkent

VANUATU

AREA 4,706 sq mi
(12,189 sq km)
POPULATION 288,000
CAPITAL Port-Vila

VATICAN CITY (HOLY SEE)

AREA 0.17 sq mi
(0.44 sq km)
POPULATION 1,000
CAPITAL Vatican City

VENEZUELA

AREA 352,144 sq mi
(912,050 sq km)
POPULATION 31,689,000
CAPITAL Caracas

VIETNAM

AREA 127,881 sq mi
(331,210 sq km)
POPULATION 97,040,000
CAPITAL Hanoi

YEMEN

AREA 203,850 sq mi
(527,968 sq km)
POPULATION 28,667,000
CAPITAL Sanaa

ZAMBIA

AREA 290,587 sq mi
(752,618 sq km)
POPULATION 16,445,000
CAPITAL Lusaka

ZIMBABWE

AREA 150,872 sq mi
(390,757 sq km)
POPULATION 14,030,000
CAPITAL Harare

UNITED NATIONS

IN SEARCH OF A PEACEFUL WORLD

The UN works to maintain international peace, develop friendly relations among nations, and achieve international cooperation in solving world problems.

In 1945, the 51 original Member States represented more than 80 percent of the world's population.

MORE OF THE
WORLD

BEYOND COUNTRY STATUS

There are 195 countries, 36 dependencies, and five other political units that make up the world today. Of those, 14 are U.S. territories, also considered dependencies, and are listed on page 323.

FIVE OTHER POLITICAL **ENTITIES** EXIST TODAY: **GAZA STRIP, NORTHERN CYPRUS, TAIWAN, WEST BANK, AND WESTERN SAHARA.**

Atoll islands surround Bora Bora, part of French Polynesia.

THE WORLD

Dependencies Listed by SOVEREIGNTY

AUSTRALIA
Christmas Island, Cocos (Keeling) Islands, Norfolk Island

DENMARK
Faroe Islands, Greenland (Kalaallit Nunaat)

FRANCE
French Polynesia, New Caledonia, Saint-Barthélemy, Saint Martin, Saint-Pierre and Miquelon, Wallis and Futuna

NETHERLANDS
Aruba, Curaçao, Sint Maarten

NEW ZEALAND
Cook Islands, Niue, Tokelau

UNITED KINGDOM
Anguilla, Bermuda, British Virgin Islands, Cayman Islands, Falkland Islands, Gibraltar, Guernsey, Isle of Man, Jersey, Montserrat, Pitcairn Islands, Saint Helena and Dependencies, Turks and Caicos Islands

FUTURE
OF THE PLANET

TAKING EARTH'S TEMPERATURE

Temperatures are increasing at different rates around the planet, and regions will feel the consequences of climate change differently. This map—created based on analysis of more than 40 social, economic, and environmental factors, including poverty, population growth, infrastructure, and areas of flooding and drought—represents patterns of vulnerability over the next 30 years.

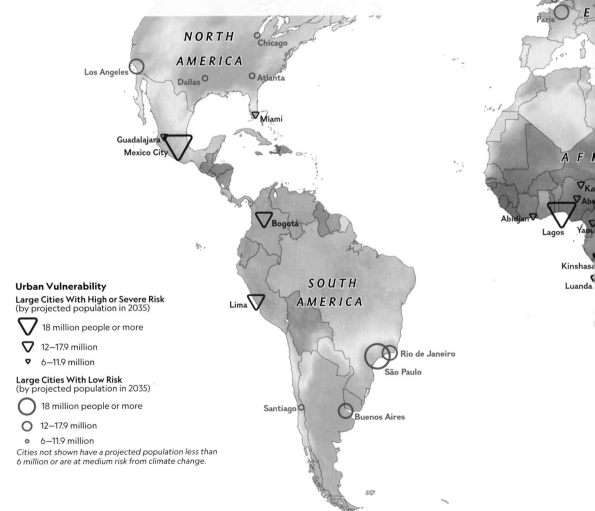

Urban Vulnerability

Large Cities With High or Severe Risk
(by projected population in 2035)

▽ 18 million people or more

▽ 12–17.9 million

▽ 6–11.9 million

Large Cities With Low Risk
(by projected population in 2035)

◯ 18 million people or more

◯ 12–17.9 million

◦ 6–11.9 million

Cities not shown have a projected population less than 6 million or are at medium risk from climate change.

SAO PAULO, BRAZIL, IS AMONG THE PLACES AT LOWEST RISK AS A RESULT OF CLIMATE CHANGE. THE CITY HAS BEEN IMPLEMENTING A MUNICIPAL CLIMATE LAW, INCLUDING LOWERING GREENHOUSE GAS EMISSIONS, SINCE 2009.

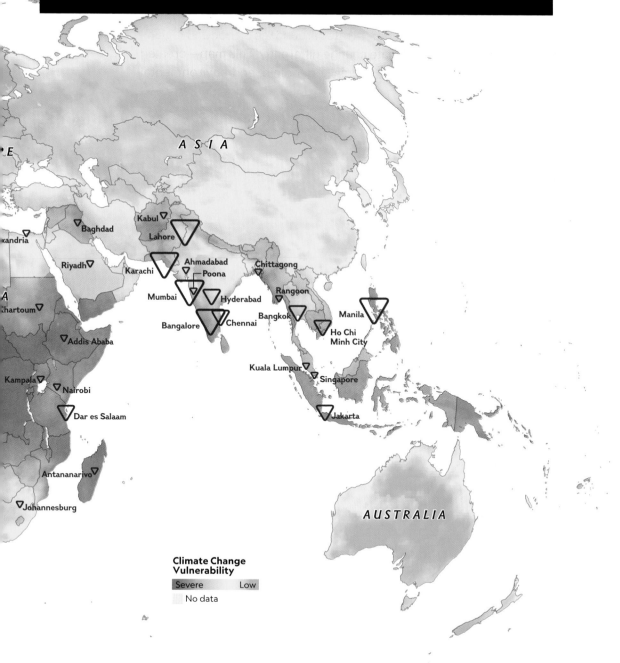

E

ASIA

Kabul

Baghdad

Lahore

xandria

Riyadh

Karachi

Ahmadabad

Poona

Chittagong

Mumbai

Hyderabad

Rangoon

Khartoum

Bangalore

Chennai

Bangkok

Manila

Addis Ababa

Ho Chi
Minh City

Kuala Lumpur

Kampala

Nairobi

Singapore

Dar es Salaam

Jakarta

Antananarivo

Johannesburg

AUSTRALIA

**Climate Change
Vulnerability**

Severe   Low

No data

FUTURE OF
THE WILD ON EARTH

WHERE NATURE STILL PREVAILS

Every continent on Earth contains landscapes that are still relatively untouched by the impact of human developments. Of the 14 biomes, or types of plant and animal community, those least affected by human development are deserts, tropical forests, and northern forests.

NORTH AMERICA

SOUTH AMERICA

Low Impact Areas by Biome

- Montane grasslands & shrublands
- Temperate grasslands, savannas, & shrublands
- Desert & xeric shrublands
- Mediterranean forests, woodlands, & scrub
- Tropical & subtropical grasslands, savannas, & shrublands
- Temperate coniferous forests
- Tropical & subtropical coniferous forests
- Tropical & subtropical dry broadleaf forests
- Temperate broadleaf & mixed forests
- Tropical & subtropical moist broadleaf forests
- Flooded grasslands & savannas
- Boreal forests/taiga
- Tundra
- Mangroves
- Ice and rock

  Human-impacted area

MORE THAN 70% **OF THE PLANET'S REMAINING WILDERNESS LIES WITHIN THE BORDERS OF** FIVE COUNTRIES: **AUSTRALIA, BRAZIL, CANADA, RUSSIA, AND THE UNITED STATES.**

FUTURE OF
HUMANS ON EARTH

ARE THINGS GETTING BETTER?

Health, wealth, education, nutrition, housing, safety, connections—
many factors contribute to quality of life. But improvements in lifestyle
are not felt equally throughout the world. This map provides a picture of
human development, or how well the average person is flourishing.
Where data is available, the map looks beyond the national level to
regional differences.

NORTH AMERICA

SOUTH AMERICA

Human Develpment, 2017

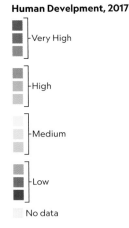

Very High

High

Medium

Low

No data

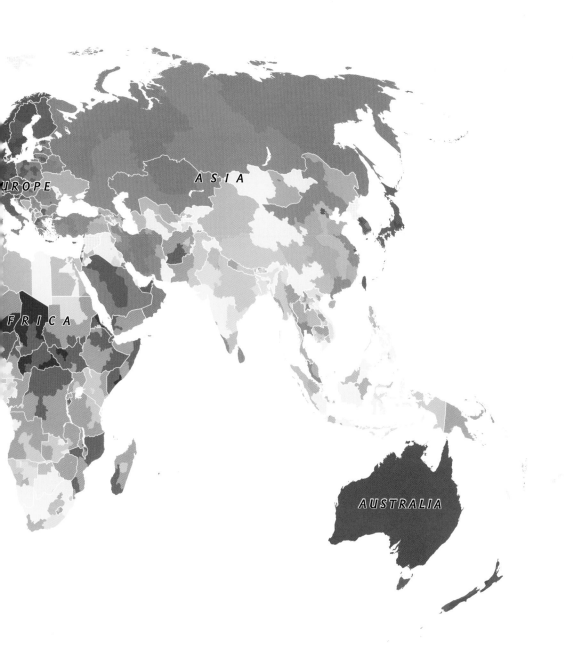

IN GHANA, TOGO, BENIN, AND NIGERIA, OIL DEVELOPMENT AND TRADE HAVE HELPED TO INCREASE WEALTH WHILE BRINGING NEW CHALLENGES, SUCH AS POLLUTION.

EUROPE

ASIA

AFRICA

AUSTRALIA

FURTHER

THE BEAT GOES ON

The Unisphere stood 140 feet tall at the heart of the 1964 New York World's Fair. Showing the Earth as one, with three rings representing the earliest orbiting space missions, the massive stainless-steel structure symbolized the fair's theme, "Peace Through Understanding." Thanks to persistent community effort and public investment, it still stands in Queens, New York, today. Its nearby fountain system took a beating from superstorm Sandy but, now renovated, the fountains offer refreshing cool to summer visitors.

A long-exposure shot turns visitors and fountains ghostly at the base of the Unisphere in New York City's Flushing Meadows–Corona Park.

"IT ISN'T ENOUGH TO TALK OF PEACE. ONE MUST BELIEVE IN IT. AND IT ISN'T ENOUGH TO BELIEVE IN IT. ONE MUST WORK AT IT."

—ELEANOR ROOSEVELT, POLITICAL ACTIVIST AND FIRST LADY OF THE UNITED STATES

CREDITS

Cover: (MAIN), Carsten Peter/National Geographic Image Collection; (CTR), Joel Sartore/National Geographic Photo Ark, photographed at Jurong Bird Park, Singapore; (LO LE), Warren Marr/Panoramic Images/National Geographic Image Collection; (LO RT), NASA/JPL-Caltech/STScI. Back cover: (UP LE), Frans Lanting/National Geographic Image Collection; (UP RT), George Steinmetz; (CTR), Joel Sartore/National Geographic Photo Ark, photographed at Audubon Insectarium, New Orleans; (LO), Markel Redondo.

2-3, Paul Zizka; 4, Frans Lanting/lanting.com; 4-5, Anand Varma/National Geographic Image Collection; 5 (LE), NASA, ESA, Hubble Heritage Team; 5 (RT), Tran Tuan Viet; 6, Ira Block; 6-7, Frans Lanting/lanting.com; 7, Joel Sartore/National Geographic Photo Ark, photographed at Audubon Insectarium, New Orleans; 8-9, Janne Kahila; 9, Greg Foot; 10-11, Markel Redondo; 12 (UP), NASA/JPL; 12 (LO), Robert Hurt/Caltech-JPL/Science Source; 13 (LE), Juan Carlos Alonso Lopez/Shutterstock; 13 (CTR), Bignai/Shutterstock; 13 (RT), oticki/Shutterstock; 14-15, Frans Lanting/lanting.com; 16 (UP), Abdul Raheem Mohamed/EyeEm/Getty Images; 16 (LO), Laura Kate Bradley/Getty Images; 17 (LE), Hakan Hjort/Getty Images; 17 (RT), ufokim/Getty Images; 18-19, Luca Locatelli/National Geographic Image Collection; 20 (UP), Brian Skerry; 20 (LO), anyaivanova/Getty Images; 21 (UP), Macduff Everton/National Geographic Image Collection; 21 (CTR), Brian Finke; 21 (LO), Robin Marchant/Getty Images; 22-3, Elen11/Getty Images; 24-5, NG Maps; 26-7, Mario Tama/Getty Images; 28 (UP), Eliza R. Scidmore; 28 (LO), ATWOOD Margaret – Date: 20091001/Photo © Basso Cannarsa/Opale/Bridgeman Images; 29 (UP), Yu Ruidong/China News Service/VCG via Getty Images; 29 (LO), Alex Wong/Getty Images; 30-31, NASA/JPL-Caltech/SwRI/MSSS; 32 (UP), Space Frontiers/Getty Images; 32 (LO), NASA/Desiree Stover; 33 (LE), © National Astronomical Observatory Japan; 33 (RT), Ella Marus Studio/Science Source; 33 (LO), Mickey Adair/Getty Images; 34-5, Whit Richardson/Getty Images; 36 (UP), Andy Bardon/National Geographic Image Collection; 36 (LO), Matteo Colombo/Getty Images; 37 (LE), Wangkun Jia/Shutterstock; 37 (RT), Patrick Poendl/Shutterstock; 37 (LO), Anthony Heflin/Shutterstock; 38 (UP LE), Herbert Kane/National Geographic Image Collection; 38 (UP CTR), ViewStock/Getty Images; 38 (UP RT), Sergey Melnikov/Shutterstock; 38 (LO LE), Prisma Bildagentur/UIG via Getty Images; 38 (LO CTR), Mark Graves/Shutterstock; 38 (LO RT), Spain: A caravan on the Silk Road as represented in the Catalan Atlas, 1375/Pictures from History/Bridgeman Images; 38-9, RTimages/Shutterstock; 39 (UP LE), Archiv/Photo Researchers/Science Source; 39 (UP CTR), Jose Ignacio Soto/Shutterstock; 39 (UP RT), AP Photo, File; 39 (LO LE), byvalet/Shutterstock; 39 (LO CTR LE), Songsak P/Shutterstock; 39 (LO CTR RT), New York Times Co./Getty Images; 39 (LO RT), NASA, ESA, HEIC, and The Hubble Heritage Team (STScI/AURA); 40-41, NG Maps; 42-3, Ocean Exploration Trust; 43, Emory Kristof/National Geographic Image Collection; 44 (UP), Great Wight Productions Pty Ltd and Earthship Productions, Inc.; 44 (LO), Norbert Wu/Minden Pictures/National Geographic Image Collection; 45, Emory Kristof/National Geographic Image Collection; 46, Frank Siteman/Getty Images; 47, JMichl/Getty Images; 48 (UP LE), Jimmy Chin/National Geographic Image Collection; 48 (UP RT), Renan Ozturk; 48 (LO LE), Carlton Ward, Jr./National Geographic Image Collection; 48 (LO RT), Pete McBride; 49 (UP LE), Jimmy Chin; 49 (UP RT), Stephen Alvarez/National Geographic Image Collection; 49 (LO LE), Renan Ozturk; 49 (LO RT), Paul Nicklen; 50, Noam Galai/WireImage/Getty Images; 50-51, Barry Bishop/National Geographic Image Collection; 52 (UP), Maria Stenzel/National Geographic Image Collection; 52 (LO), George Steinmetz/National Geographic Image Collection; 53 (UP), Onfokus/Getty Images; 53 (RT), Stephen Alvarez/National Geographic Image Collection; 54-5, Luis Javier Sandoval/Getty Images; 56-7, Jason Treat, NGM staff; Meg Roosevelt. Art: Sergio Ingravalle. Icons: Álvaro Valiño. Sources: Adrien Marck, National Institute of Sport, Expertise and Performance, France; IAAF; 58-9, Jenny Nichols; 59, Jenny Nichols; 60 (UP), Cameron Spencer/Getty Images; 60 (LO), Patrick Smith/Getty Images; 61 (LE), Oliver Hardt - International

Skating Union (ISU)/Getty Images; 61 (RT), Quinn Rooney/Getty Images; 62 (UP LE), Bill McKelvie/Shutterstock; 62 (UP CTR), Iara-sh/Shutterstock; 62 (UP RT), Valentyna Zhukova/Shutterstock; 62 (LO LE), Egyptian boat/Private Collection/De Agostini Picture Library/Bridgeman Images; 62 (LO CTR LE), A youth on horseback/Universal History Archive/UIG/Bridgeman Images; 62 (LO CTR RT), British Library/Science Source; 62 (LO RT), NASA; 62-3, Adisa/Shutterstock; 63 (UP LE), Dave King/Dorling Kindersley/Science Museum, London/Science Source; 63 (UP CTR LE), Car Culture/Getty Images; 63 (UP CTR RT), Sam Shere/Getty Images; 63 (UP RT), Olga Popova/Shutterstock.com; 63 (LO LE), SPL/Science Source; 63 (LO CTR), General Photographic Agency/Getty Images; 63 (LO RT), Noah Berger/AFP/Getty Images; 64-5, NG Maps; 66 (UP), Bernardo Galmarini/Alamy Stock Photo; 66 (LO), Starcevic/Getty Images; 67 (LE), Mike Hewitt/Getty Images; 67 (RT), Haitao Zhang/Getty Images; 68, America's Test Kitchen/Daniel J. van Ackere; 68-9, Xsandra/Getty Images; 70 (UP), Igor Plotnikov/Shutterstock; 70 (LO), s_jakkarin/Shutterstock; 71 (UP), Gunter Grafenhain/Huber Images/eStock Photo; 71 (CTR), Skip Brown/National Geographic Image Collection; 71 (LO), Tim Sloan/AFP/Getty Images; 72-3, NG Maps; 74-5, Miva Stock/DanitaDelimont/Alamy Stock Photo; 76 (UP LE), Jennifer Hayes; 76 (UP RT), Ira Block; 76 (LO LE), Simon Norfolk; 76 (LO RT), Stephen Wilkes; 77 (UP LE), Gabriele Galimberti & Paolo Woods; 77 (UP RT), Juan Arredondo; 77 (LO LE), David Guttenfelder/National Geographic Image Collection; 77 (LO RT), Renan Ozturk; 78, Courtesy Darryl Wee; 78-9, visualspace/Getty Images; 80 (UP), Courtesy Topas Travel; 80 (LO), Courtesy Geoffrey Weill Associates, Inc. 81, Courtesy Lapa Rios Ecolodge; 82-3, Grant Rooney Premium/Alamy Stock Photo; 84 (UP), darekm101/Getty Images; 84 (LO), helovi/Getty Images; 84-5, NG Maps; 85 (UP), coolbiere photograph/Getty Images; 85 (LO LE), Jody MacDonald/National Geographic Image Collection; 85 (LO RT), David Hannah/Getty Images; 86 (UP), Shaiith/Shutterstock; 86 (LO), Lauri Patterson/Getty Images; 87 (UP), Africa Studio/Shutterstock; 87 (CTR), pilipphoto/Shutterstock; 87 (LO), Michael Piazza; 88-9, Alexander Cimbal/Alamy Stock Photo; 90-91, Catherine Aeppel; 92-3, Frans Lanting/National Geographic Image Collection; 94 (LE), British Library, London, UK/© British Library Board. All Rights Reserved/Bridgeman Images; 94 (RT), Valeriy Poltorak/Shutterstock; 95 (UP LE), Sebastian Janicki/Shutterstock; 95 (UP RT), Trong Nguyen/Shutterstock; 95 (CT LE), NASA/JPL; 95 (CT RT), Elena11/Shutterstock; 95 (LO), NASA; 96 (UP LE), robert_s/Shutterstock; 96 (UP CTR LE), © Abderrazak EL ALBANI/Arnaud MAZURIER/CNRS Photothèque; 96 (UP CTR RT), National Science Foundation/Science Source; 96 (UP RT), Quang Ho/Shutterstock; 96 (CTR LE), CHIARI VFX/Shutterstock; 96 (CTR RT), Derek Siveter; 96 (LO LE), Sebastian Knight/Shutterstock; 96 (LO CTR), Stocktrek Images/National Geographic Image Collection; 96 (LO RT), Sebastien Plailly & Elisabeth Daynes/Science Source; 96-7, Yuriy Vahlenko/Shutterstock; 97 (UP LE), Warpaint/Shutterstock; 97 (UP CTR LE), New York Public Library/Science Source; 97 (UP CTR RT), Claus Lunau/Science Source; 97 (UP RT), Keystone/Hulton Archive/Getty Images; 97 (LO LE), Sheila Terry/Science Source; 97 (LO CTR), New York Public Library/Science Source; 97 (LO RT), USGS/NASA Landsat data/Orbital Horizon/Gallo Images/Getty Images; 98-9, NG Maps; 100 (UP), Chris Winsor/Getty Images; 100 (LO), Pablo Lopez Luz/Barcroft Media Ltd.; 101, Pete McBride/National Geographic Image Collection; 102, Jared Travnicek; 103, Beau Van Der Graaf/EyeEm/Getty Images; 104, Rebecca Hale, NG Staff; 104-105, Tom Zeller, Jr., NG Staff. Art by Bruce Morser. Sources: National Wildfire Coordinating Group; U.S. Forest Service; Colorado Firecamp; 106-107, Stocktrek Images/Getty Images; 108, Universal History Archive/UIG via Getty images; 108-109, Hernán Cañellas/National Geographic Image Collection; Alejandro Tumas, NG Staff; Shelley Sperry; 110-11, Carsten Peter/National Geographic Image Collection; 111, Robert Clark/National Geographic Image Collection; 112 (UP LE), Keith Ladzinski; 112 (UP RT), Randy Olson/National Geographic Image Collection; 112 (LO LE), Frans Lanting/lanting.com; 112 (LO RT), Charlie Hamilton James; 113 (UP LE), Michael Yamashita/National Geographic Image Collection; 113 (UP RT), Francisco J. Perez;

113 (LO LE), Keith Ladzinski/National Geographic Image Collection; 113 (LO RT), Carlton Ward, Jr.; 114 (1a), Scientifica/Getty Images; 114 (1b), Mark A. Schneider/Science Source; 114 (1c), Marli Miller/Visuals Unlimited, Inc.; 114 (1d), Charles D. Winters/Science Source; 114 (1e), DEA/Photo 1/Getty Images; 114 (2a), Gary Cook/Visuals Unlimited, Inc.; 114 (2b), Roberto de Gugliemo/Science Source; 114 (2c), Biophoto Associates/Science Source; 114 (2d), Manamana/Shutterstock; 114 (2e), Science Stock Photography/Science Source; 114 (3a), Joel Arem/Science Source; 114 (3b), National Museum of Natural History, Smithsonian Institution; 114 (3c), Scientifica/Getty Images; 114 (3d), Ted Kinsman/Science Source; 114 (3e), Science Stock Photography/Science Source; 114 (4a), National Museum of Natural History, Smithsonian Institution; 114 (4b), National Museum of Natural History, Smithsonian Institution; 114 (4c), Nadezda Boltaca/Shutterstock; 114 (4d), Scientifica/Getty Images; 114 (4e), National Museum of Natural History, Smithsonian Institution; 114 (5a), carlosdelacalle/Shutterstock; 114 (5b), National Museum of Natural History, Smithsonian Institution; 114 (5c), Vitaly Raduntsev/Shutterstock; 114 (5d), National Museum of Natural History, Smithsonian Institution; 114 (5e), Juraj Kovac/Shutterstock; 115, Orsolya Haarberg/National Geographic Image Collection; 116, Enric Sala; 117 (UP), NG Maps; 117 (LO), Rebecca Hale, NG Staff; 118-9, U.S. Geological Survey; 120-21, Wil Tirion; 121, Courtesy Andrew Fazekas; 122-3, Wil Tirion; 124, Brown Reference Group; 125, tdubphoto/Getty Images; 126 (UP LE), Davis Meltzer/National Geographic Image Collection; 126 (UP CTR LE), The Emperor Julius Caesar (oil on panel), Rubens, Peter Paul (1577–1640)/Private Collection/Photo © Christie's Images/Bridgeman Images; 126 (UP CTR RT), Atlas Photo Bank/Science Source; 126 (UP RT), NASA, ESA, J. Hester, A. Loll (ASU); 126 (CTR), NASA Images/Shutterstock; 126 (LO LE), © The British Library/The Image Works; 126 (LO RT), NASA/JPL-Caltech; 126-7, Brian Lula; 127 (UP LE), Larry Landolfi/Science Source; 127 (UP CTR LE), Library of Congress/Getty Images; 127 (UP CTR RT), Rolls Press/Popperfoto/Getty Images; 127 (UP RT), NASA/JPL/Cornell University/Maas Digital; 127 (LO LE), Royal Astronomical Society/Science Source; 127 (LO CTR LE), NASA/Johns Hopkins University Applied Physics Laboratory/Southwest Research Institute; 127 (LO CTR RT), National Air and Space Museum/Smithsonian Institution; 127 (LO RT), NASA/JHUAPL/SwRI; 128-9, NASA/JPL; 130, Universal History Archive/UIG via Getty Images; 131, John R. Foster/Science Source; 132-5, NG Maps; 136-7, Graphic: Matthew Twombly. Sources: NASA, European Sapce Agency, Indian Space Research Organisation; 138, ©Walt Disney Studios Motion Pictures/Lucasfilm Ltd./Courtesy Everett Collection; 138-9, NASA/JPL; 139, NASA/JPL/DLR; 140 (UP LE), Renan Ozturk; 140 (UP RT), George Steinmetz; 140 (LO LE), Stephen Alvarez/National Geographic Image Collection; 140 (LO RT), Jimmy Chin; 141 (UP LE), Pete McBride; 141 (UP RT), Luca Locatelli/National Geographic Image Collection; 141 (LO LE), Renan Ozturk; 141 (LO RT), John Stanmeyer; 142-3, Graphic by Jason Treat, NG Staff; 144, Tony Korody, Courtesy of Druyan-Sagan Associates; 145, Bryan Bedder/Getty Images for Breakthrough Prize Foundation; 146, John Zich; 146-7, Tom Abel and Ralf Kaehler, Stanford KIPAC; 148 (UP), Mark Garlick/Science Source; 148 (LO), Paul Nicklen/National Geographic Image Collection; 149 (UP), Brookhaven National Laboratory/Science Source; 149 (CTR), Claus Lunau/Science Source; 149 (LO), Roscosmos/GCTC; 150, Steve Schapiro/Corbis via Getty Images; 150-51, Pobytov/Getty Images; 151, PHL @ UPR Arecibo (phl.upr.edu) April, 2013; 152 (UP), NASA, ESA and the Hubble SM4 ERO Team; 152 (LO), Hubble Image: NASA, ESA, K. Kuntz (JHU), F. Bresolin (University of Hawaii), J. Trauger (Jet Propulsion Lab), J. Mould (NOAO), Y.-H. Chu (University of Illinois, Urbana) and STScI; CFHT Image: Canada-France-Hawaii Telescope/J.-C. Cuillandre/Coelum; NOAO Image: G. Jacoby, B. Bohannan, M. Hanna/NOAO/AURA/NSF; 153 (LE), CERN/Science Source; 153 (RT), Volker Springel/Max Planck Institute for Astrophysics/Science Source; 154-5, Keith Ladzinski/National Geographic Image Collection; 156-7, Marsel van Oosten, Squiver; 158 (UP LE), DEA/M. Seemuller/Getty Images; 158 (UP RT), Paulphin Photography/Shutterstock; 158 (CTR), nobeastsofierce/Shutterstock; 158 (LO LE), DeAgostini Picture Library/Getty Images; 158 (LO RT), Rainbow Black/Shutterstock; 159 (UP), Richard Ellis/Science Source/Getty Images; 159 (CTR LE), Sanoh Khamduang/Shutterstock; 159 (CTR), Bettmann/Getty Images; 159 (CTR RT), Svetlana Iakovets/Shutterstock; 159 (LO), Auscape/UIG/Getty Images; 160 (UP LE), Szasz-Fabian Jozsef/Shutterstock; 160 (UP CTR), Illustration of a page of text showing music making angels around two united reptiles around a circle from Historia Naturalis, by Pliny the Elder (vellum)/Biblioteca Nazionale Marciana, Venice, Italy/Roger-Viollet, Paris/Bridgeman Images; 160 (UP RT), The Picture Art Collection/Alamy Stock Photo; 160 (LO LE), Portrait bust of male, copy after a Greek fourth-th century b.c. original (marble), Roman (firstst century a.d.)/Museo Archeologico Nazionale, Naples, Campania, Italy/De Agostini Picture Library/A. Dagli Orti/Bridgeman Images; 160 (LO CTR LE), Wellcome Library, London; 160 (LO CTR RT), Granger.com – All rights reserved; 160 (LO RT), International Mammoth Committee, photo by Francis Latreille; 160-61, vitstudio/Shutterstock; 161 (UP LE), Stocktrek Images/Science Source; 161 (UP RT), Eric Isselee/Shutterstock; 161 (CTR LE), Joe Tucciarone/Science Source; 161 (CTR RT), Nata-Lia/Shutterstock; 161 (LO LE), 3D4Medical/Science Source; 161 (LO CTR LE), Daniel Prudek/Shutterstock; 161 (LO CTR RT), Michael Nichols/National Geographic Image Collection; 161 (LO RT), John Weinstein/Field Museum Library/Getty Images; 162 (UP LE), Dennis Kunkel Microscopy/Science Source; 162 (UP CTR), Dennis Kunkel Microscopy/Science Source; 162 (UP RT), Eye of Science/Science Source; 162 (LO LE), Kateryna Kon/Shutterstock; 162 (LO RT), Tatiana Shepeleva/Shutterstock; 163 (Fungi – UP LE), Denis Vesely/Shutterstock; 163 (Fungi – UP RT), Passakorn Umpornmaha/Shutterstock; 163 (Plants – UP LE), surajet.l/Shutterstock; 163 (Plants - UP RT), Mizuri/Shutterstock; 163 (Plants – LO LE), Alexandra Lande/Shutterstock; 163 (Plants – LO RT), Mike Ver Sprill/Shutterstock; 163 (Animals – UP LE), Ondrej Prosicky/Shutterstock; 163 (Animals – UP RT), frantisekhojdysz/Shutterstock; 163 (Animals – LO LE), Claudia Paulussen/Shutterstock; 163 (Animals – LO RT), Abeselom Zerit/Shutterstock; 164, Bret Hartman/TED; 164-5, © Martin Oeggerli/Micronaut 2018, supported by Pathology, Univ. Hospital Basel, C-CINA, Biozentrum, University Basel; 166-7, Art: Beau Daniels. Sources: Suzanne Simard and Camille Defrenne, University of British Columbia; Kevin Beiler, Eberswalde University for Sustainable Development; 168 (LE), ©MCA/Courtesy Everett Collection; 168 (RT), Jared Travnicek; 169, Michael Melford/National Geographic Image Collection; 170-71, Dinoraul/Alamy Stock Photo; 172 (UP LE), Ronan Donovan/National Geographic Image Collection; 172 (UP RT), Frans Lanting/lanting.com; 172 (LO LE), Kenneth Geiger; 172 (LO RT), Aaron Huey/National Geographic Image Collection; 173 (UP LE), Stefano Unterthiner; 173 (UP RT), Frans Lanting/lanting.com; 173 (LO LE), Ami Vitale/National Geographic Image Collection; 173 (LO RT), Florian Schulz/visionsofthewild.com; 174, Jared Travnicek; 175 (UP), Konrad Wothe/LOOK-foto/Getty Images; 175 (LO), Hugh Morton, courtesy North American Bear Center; 176 (UP), Ryan J. Lane/Getty Images; 176 (LO), Robert Clark/National Geographic Image Collection. Wolf and Maltese dog provided by Doug Seus's Wasatch Rocky Mountain Wildlife, Utah.; 177 (LE), Vincent J. Musi/National Geographic Image Collection; 177 (RT), Fuse/Getty Images; 178-9, CraigRJD/Getty Images; 180 (UP), Joel Sartore/National Geographic Photo Ark, photographed at Night Safari, Singapore; 180 (CTR), Joel Sartore/National Geographic Photo Ark, photographed at Lincoln Children's Zoo; 180 (LO), Joel Sartore/National Geographic Photo Ark, photographed at Indianapolis Zoo; 181 (UP LE), jeep2499/Shutterstock; 181 (UP RT), Joel Sartore/National Geographic Photo Ark, photographed at Gladys Porter Zoo; 181 (LO LE), Joel Sartore/National Geographic Photo Ark, photographed at Lowry Park Zoo; 181 (LO RT), Brendan Smialowski/Getty Images; 182-3, Bettmann/Getty Images; 183, Ron Cohn © The Gorilla Foundation/Koko.org; 184 (UP LE), Brian Skerry/National Geographic Image Collection; 184 (UP RT), Cristina Mittermeier/National Geographic Image Collection; 184 (LO LE), Brian Skerry/National Geographic Image Collection; 184 (LO RT), Carlton Ward, Jr.; 185 (UP LE), Mattias Klum; 185 (UP RT), Tim Laman; 185 (LO LE), Enric Sala/National Geographic Image Collection; 185 (LO RT), Justin Hofman; 186-7, David Doubilet/National Geographic Image Collection; 188 (UP), Flip Nicklin/Minden Pictures; 188 (LO), Kate Westaway/Getty Images; 189 (LE), Patricio Robles Gil/Sierra Madre/Minden Pictures; 189 (RT), Andy Mann/National Geographic Image Collection; 189 (LO), Mark Thiessen, NG Staff; 190, Jared Travnicek; 190 (3e – Marine Mussel), Carlyn Iverson/Science Source/Getty Images; 190 (4d – Red Abalone), Illustration © Emily S. Damstra; 191, Paul Nicklen/National Geographic Image Collection; 192-3, David Liittschwager/National Geographic Image Collection; 194 (UP LE), Frans Lanting/National Geographic Image Collection; 194 (UP RT), Tim Laman/National Geographic Image Collection; 194 (LO LE), Carlton Ward, Jr./National Geographic Image Collection; 194 (LO RT), Joel Sartore/National Geographic Photo Ark, photographed at

Jr., 1942–1998/Bridgeman Images; 285 (UP RT), "Signing the Declaration of Independence, July 4th, 1776" (oil on canvas), Trumbull, John (1756–1843)/Capitol Collection, Washington, USA/Bridgeman Images; 285 (CTR), Chiffanna/Shutterstock; 285 (LO), Smithsonian Institution/Science Source; 286 (UP LE), Joe McNally; 286 (UP CTR), Seal depicting a mythological animal and pictographic symbols, from Mohenjo-Daro, Indus Valley, Pakistan, 3000–1500 b.c. (stone), Harappan/National Museum of Karachi, Karachi, Pakistan/Bridgeman Images; 286 (UP RT), Aranami/Shutterstock; 286 (CTR LE), anyaivanova/Shutterstock; 286 (CTR RT), Greece: Marble bust of Alexander the Great at the British Museum, London/Pictures from History/Bridgeman Images; 286 (LO LE), Weeding, The Rice Culture in China (color woodblock print), Chinese School (19th century)/Private Collection/Archives Charmet/Bridgeman Images; 286 (LO CTR LE), DEA/G. Dagli Orti/De Agostini/Getty Images; 286 (LO CTR RT), Rodolfo Parulan, Jr./Getty Images; 286 (LO RT), Photos.com/Getty Images; 286-7, Leeuwtje/Getty Images; 287 (UP LE), Boris Vetshev/Shutterstock; 287 (UP CTR LE), Fine Art Images/Heritage Images/Getty Images; 287 (UP CTR RT), Ms FR 22495 f.265v Battle of Damietta in Egypt in 1218–19, during the fifth crusade (1217–1221) from Historia by Guillaume de Tyr, 1337 (vellum), French School (14th century)/Bibliotheque Nationale, Paris, France/Tallandier/Bridgeman Images; 287 (UP RT), KHM-Museumsverband, Weltmuseum Vienna; 287 (CTR), Luther as Professor, 1529 (oil on panel), Cranach, Lucas, the Elder (1472–1553)/Schlossmuseum, Weimar, Germany/Bridgeman Images; 287 (LO LE), clu/Getty Images; 287 (LO CTR), rimglow/Getty Images; 287 (LO RT), Pilgrim's "Blue and White" Gourd With Floral Decorations, ca1403–1424 (ceramic), Chinese School (15th century)/Musee Guimet, Paris, France/Bridgeman Images; 288-9, Jason Treat, NGM Staff. Art: Sam Falconer. Sources: Sara Graça da Silva, Institute for the Study of Literature and Tradition (IELT), New University of Lisbon, Portugal; Jamie Tehrani, Durham University; 290 (UP LE), Asante funerary mask, from Ghana (ceramic), African School/Private Collection/Photo © Boltin Picture Library/Bridgeman Images; 290 (UP RT), Universal History Archive/Getty Images; 290 (CTR LE), Powhatan, Father of Pocahontas, Engraving/Private Collection/J. T. Vintage/Bridgeman Images; 290 (CTR LE CTR), Portrait of Grand Duchess Catherine Alekseevna, future Empress Catherine II the Great, ca 1760 (oil on canvas), Antropov, Alexei Petrovich (1716–1795)/Radishchev State Art Museum, Saratov, Russia/Bridgeman Image; 290 (CTR RT CTR), Portrait of Simon Bolivar; Retrato de Simon Bolivar, ca 1925 (oil on canvas), Colombian School (19th century)/Private Collection/Photo © Christie's Images/Bridgeman Images; 290 (CTR RT), Photo Researchers/Getty Images; 290 (LO LE), Portrait of King Charles I (1600–1649) (oil on canvas), Dyck, Anthony van (1599–1641) (workshop of)/Private Collection/Photo © Philip Mould Ltd, London/Bridgeman Images; 290 (LO CTR), Cross-section of H.M.S. Endeavour, Captain Cook's ship from his first voyage (1768–1771) (color litho), Adams, Dennis (1914–2001)/Alecto Historical Editions, London, UK/Bridgeman Images; 290 (LO RT), Queen Victoria, 1877 (oil on panel), Angeli, Heinrich von (1840–1925)/Private Collection/Photo © Christie's Images/Bridgeman Images; 290-91, ArtisticPhoto/Shutterstock; 291 (UP), Keystone/Getty Images; 291 (CTR LE), Soviet poster featuring Lenin (color litho), Russian School (20th century)/Private Collection/Peter Newark Historical Pictures/Bridgeman Images; 291 (CTR), Hulton Archive/Getty Images; 291 (CTR RT), David Hume Kennerly/Getty Images; 291 (LO LE), Dinodia Photos/Getty Images; 291 (LO CTR LE), swim ink 2/Corbis via Getty Images; 291 (LO CTR RT), Catalina M/Shutterstock; 291 (LO RT), Chris Jackson/Getty Images; 292-3, Fine Art Images/Heritage Image Partnership Ltd/Alamy Stock Photo; 294 (UP), Pascal Deloche/Getty Images; 294 (LO), Departure of the Pilgrim Fathers for America (gouache on paper), Embleton, Ron (1930–1988)/Private Collection/© Look and Learn/Bridgeman Images; 295 (LE), Todd Gipstein/National Geographic Image Collection; 295 (RT), Franck Prevel/Getty Images; 296-7, Universal Images Group/Getty Images; 297, De Agostini Picture Library/Getty Images; 298 (UP LE), Michael Yamashita/National Geographic Image Collection; 298 (UP RT), Stephen Alvarez; 298 (LO LE), Simon Norfolk; 298 (LO RT), Stephen Alvarez; 299 (UP LE), David Guttenfelder; 299 (UP RT), Ira Block; 299 (LO LE), Aaron Huey/National Geographic Image Collection; 299 (LO RT), Simon Norfolk; 300-301, Tom Till/Getty Images; 302 and 303, Kenneth Garrett/National Geographic Image Collection; 304 (UP LE), Paul Paladin/Shutterstock; 304 (UP CTR LE), asharkyu/ Shutterstock; 304 (UP CTR RT), Seated Mastiff, ca 100 (earthenware), Chinese School, Eastern Han dynasty (25–220)/Indianapolis Museum of Art at Newfields, USA/Eleanor Evans Stout and Margaret Stout Gibbs Memorial Fund/in memory of Wilbur D. Peat/Bridgeman Images; 304 (UP RT), fotohunter/Shutterstock; 304 (CTR), Agnieszka Skalska/Shutterstock.com; 304 (LO LE), Pecold/Shutterstock; 304 (LO CTR), Marques/Shutterstock; 304 (LO RT), Jan Schneckenhaus/Shutterstock; 304-305, Luis Castaneda Inc./Getty Images; 305 (UP LE), De Agostini Picture Library/Getty Images; 305 (UP CTR LE), SSPL/Getty Images; 305 (UP CTR RT), ullstein bild/ullstein bild via Getty Images; 305 (UP RT), SSPL/Getty Images; 305 (LO LE), Portrait of Benjamin Franklin (Boston, 1706–Philadelphia, 1790), American scientist and politician/De Agostini Picture Library/M. Seemuller/Bridgeman Images; 305 (LO CTR), New York Public Library/Science Source; 305 (LO RT), Nerthuz/Shutterstock; 306, George Rolhmaller/U.S. Air Force/Getty Images; 307, Delil Souleiman/AFP/Getty Images; 308 (UP LE), The Arrival of the English in Virginia, from Admiranda Narratio, 1585–88 (colored engraving), Bry, Theodore de (1528–1598)/Service Historique de la Marine, Vincennes, France/Bridgeman Images; 308 (UP RT), Loyalist/Tory, King's American Regt. Officer, 2007 (w/c & gouache on paper), Troiani, Don (b.1949)/Private Collection/Bridgeman Images; 308 (CTR LE), Illustration for the Young Pilgrims, Hardy, Evelyn Stuart (1865–1935)/Private Collection/© Look and Learn/Bridgeman Images; 308 (LO CTR LE), Pontiac (1720–1769) 1763 (oil on canvas), Stanley, John Mix (1814–1872)/Private Collection/Peter Newark American Pictures/Bridgeman Images; 308 (LO CTR RT), Gilbert Stuart/National Gallery of Art, Washington, D.C./Getty Images; 308 (CTR RT), stoonn/Getty Images; 308 (LO), Visions of America/Purestock/Alamy Stock Photo; 308-309, Stock Montage/Getty Images; 309 (UP LE), Harriet Tubman (1820–1913), American Abolitionist, Portrait, Circa 1885/Private Collection/J. T. Vintage/Bridgeman Images; 309 (UP CTR LE), John Parrot/Stocktrek Images/Getty Images; 309 (UP CTR RT), U.S. National Archives; 309 (UP RT), AFP/Getty Images; 309 (LO LE), 39th North Carolina flag (textile), American School (19th century)/Private Collection/Photo © Civil War Archive/Bridgeman Images; 309 (LO CTR LE), GHI/Universal History Archive via Getty Images; 309 (LO CTR RT), NASA/The LIFE Premium Collection/Getty Images; 309 (LO RT), Scott Olson/Getty Images; 310-11, Matt Chwastyk, NGM; Scott Elder. Art: David Stevenson. Sources: Larry E. Tise, East Carolina Univ.; Bradley Dixon, Univ. of Texas at Austin; Trustees of the British Museum; Library of Congress; David B. Quinn, "Explorers and Colonies"; Carl Ortwin Sauer, "Sixteenth Century North America"; 312 (UP), Ricky Carioti/the Washington Post via Getty Images; 312 (LO), Women's Suffrage in the USA: Women Voting in the Wyoming Territory After Winning That Right in 1869 (color engraving), American School (19th century)/Private Collection/Peter Newark American Pictures/Bridgeman Images; 313, FPG/Getty Images; 314-15, Sean Pavone Photo/Getty Images; 324-5, Paolo Woods and Gabriele Galimberti. Artwork © 2019 Estate of Pablo Picasso/Artists Rights Society (ARS), New York; 326-7, va103/Getty Images; 328 (LE), NPeter/Shutterstock; 328 (RT), TommoT/Shutterstock; 328 (LO), Daniel J. Cox/Getty Images; 329 (UP), Dmitrijs Kaminskis/Shutterstock; 329 (CTR LE), Paul Nicklen/National Geographic Image Collection; 329 (CTR RT), Tetiana Yurchenko/Shutterstock; 329 (LO), Sergii Nagornyi/Shutterstock; 330-33, NG Maps; 334 (UP LE), Frans Lanting/lanting.com; 334 (UP RT), Renan Ozturk; 334 (LO LE), George Steinmetz; 334 (LO RT), Simon Norfolk; 335 (UP LE), Keith Ladzinski; 335 (UP RT), Pete McBride; 335 (LO LE), Ira Block; 335 (LO RT), Matthieu Paley; 336-7 and 338, NG Maps; 339, Michele Falzone/Getty Images; 340, NG Maps; 341, emicristea/Getty Images; 342, NG Maps; 343, Werner Bertsch/Huber Images/eStock Photo; 344, NG Maps; 345, travellinglight/Getty Images; 346, NG Maps; 347, Westend61/Getty Images; 348, NG Maps; 349, Richard Taylor/SIME/eStock Photo; 350, NG Maps; 351, Robin Galloway/Getty Images; 352-63, NG Maps; 364 (UP LE), George Steinmetz/National Geographic Image Collection; 364 (UP RT), Jennifer Hayes; 364 (LO LE), Paul Nicklen/National Geographic Image Collection; 364 (LO RT), Thomas Peschak/National Geographic Image Collection; 365 (UP LE), Jimmy Chin; 365 (UP RT), Thomas P. Peschak/National Geographic Image Collection; 365 (LO LE), Keith Ladzinski; 365 (LO RT), David Doubilet/National Geographic Image Collection; 372, Osugi/Shutterstock.com; 373, Mint Images/Frans Lanting/Getty Images; 372-79, NG Maps; 380-81, Matthew Pillsbury.

INDEX

Boldface indicates illustrations.

A

A Rocha 248
Aconcagua, Argentina 330, 341
Adad-nirari III, King (Babylon) 293
Adventure photos **48–49**
Adventure travel 46–47, **46–47,**
    84–85, **84–85**
Afghanistan **195, 238, 253,** 307, 366,
    366
Africa
    C-section rates 259
    human origins 230, 231
    map and facts 346–347
    tourism 333
African elephants **172**
African gray parrots 200, 201, **201**
Agriculture 18–20, **18–20,** 231,
    256–257
Akhenaten, Pharaoh 302, 303
Al-Shamahi, Ella 40
Alabama: state flag **318**
Alaska 73, 81, **318, 334**
Albania 366, **366**
Alberta, Canada **2–3**
Aldrin, Edwin "Buzz" 132
Alex (parrot) 183, 201, **201**
Algeria 98, 347, 366, **366**
Amazon region, South America 52,
    84, **211,** 240, **253**
American Samoa **322**
American Sign Language 182–183
Amsterdam, Netherlands 342
Anangu people 348
Andean flamingos 340
Andes, South America 98, **141,** 330
Andorra 342, 366, **366**
Anemones **185**
Angola 366, **366**
Animal kingdom 163, **163**
Animal tracks 174, **174**
Anker, Conrad **49,** 50, **50**
Antarctica
    climate change 154–155, **154–155**
    extremes 53
    icebergs **351,** 362

map and facts 350–351
oceans 362–363
travel **49,** 71, 89
wildlife **184**
Anthony, Marek 55
Antibiotic resistance 270–271,
    270–271
Antigua and Barbuda 366, **366**
Apollo missions 132, **216**
Apostle Islands National Lakeshore,
    Wisconsin 47, **47**
Archaea 162, **162**
Arctic Ocean **44,** 360–361
Argentina
    Cerro Aconcagua 330, 341
    disappearing languages 240
    flag and facts 366, **366**
    Nat Geo explorers 40
    @natgeo photos **141**
    Patagonia 340
    travel 66, **66**
Aristi, Greece 80
Aristotle 294
Arizona 73, **113, 318, 339**
Arkansas 89, **318**
Armenia 366, **366**
Armstrong, Neil 132
Asia
    human origins 231
    map and facts 344–345
Asteroid belt 131
Asteroids 147
Astronauts 149, **149**
Astronomy see Skywatching; Space
Asylum seekers, map of 236–237
Atacama Desert, Chile 53, **53**
Atacama salt flats, Chile 340
Athabasca Glacier, Canada **2–3**
Athens (city-state) 294, **294**
Atlantic, Battle of the (1939–1945) 355
Atlantic Forest, Brazil **211**
Atlantic Ocean 354–355
Atwood, Margaret 28, **28**
Aung, Ther Wint 40
Aurora borealis **140, 141, 148**
Austin, Texas 21
Australia
    climate change 99

dependencies 373
disappearing languages 241
drought 100
flag and facts 366, **366**
Great Barrier Reef 74–75, **74–75,**
    186, **186–187**
human origins 230
map and facts 348–349
Nat Geo explorers 41
Outback region 331
Sydney Opera House **349**
travel 65, 74–75, **74–75,** 80, 85,
    85, 364
wildlife 75, 178–179, **178–179, 209,**
    348
Australian king parrots **201**
Australian palm cockatoos 201
Austria 366, **366**
Azerbaijan 366, **366**

B

Babbage, Charles 297
Baboons 180, **180**
Bacteria 162, **162,** 270–271
Baha'i faith 251, **251**
Bahamas 366, **366**
Bahrain 366, **366**
Baikal, Lake, Russia 52, 344
Baker Island 323
Bali, Indonesia 89
Ballard, Robert **42,** 42–43
Bananas 21, **21**
Banff, British Columbia, Canada 89
Bangladesh 366, **366**
Banjar, Bali, Indonesia 89
Barbados 366, **366**
Barcelona, Spain 231
Barred owls **194**
Bats **209**
Bears **173,** 175, **175, 210,** 338
Bears Ears National Monument,
    Utah **334**
Bedouin **298**
Beef 256, 270
Bees **4–5,** 204–205, **204–205**
Belarus 366, **366**
Belgium 366, **366**

Belize 40, 366, **366**
Bellamy, Francis 317
Belyaev, Dmitry 177
Benin 366, **366**
BepiColombo spacecraft 128
Beppu, Japan 89
Berg, Pierre 66
Berger, Lee 227
Bering Strait **335**
Bhutan 41, 70, **70**, 366, **366**
Big bang theory 142, 143
Big Bend NP, Texas 73
Bigeye jacks (fish) **364**
Biking *see* Cycling
Bin Laden, Osama 307
Biodiversity 210–211, **210–211**, 358,
    360
Bioluminescence 44, **44**
Birds
    backyard 196–197, **196–197**
    hummingbirds 198–199, **198–199**
    killed by house cats 177
    @natgeo photos **194–195**, 365
    parrots 183, **194**, 200–201,
      200–201, 252
    sleep 255
Birds of paradise **194**
Biscayne NP, Florida **113**
Bishop, Barry **50–51**
Bishop, Jack 68, **68**
Black bears 175, **175**
Black holes 147
Black macaques **173**
Blacktip reef sharks 75
Blackwater National Wildlife Refuge,
    Maryland 47
Blue whales 188, **189**
Bobot (language) 241
Bodh Gaya, India 249
Bogotá, Colombia 244, 340
Boivin, Jean-Marc 51
Bolivia 24, 100, 313, 366, **366**
Bolshoi (Grand) Express (train) 65
Bolt, Usain 57
Boobies **365**
Books, travel 66–67
Bora Bora (island), Tahiti 64, **373**
Borges, Jorge Luis 66
Borneo, Indonesia **14–15**, 172
Bosnia and Herzegovina 366, **366**
Botswana 71, **173**, 347, 366, **366**

Bottlenose dolphins 183
Brain, human
    mindfulness 278–279, **278–279**
    psychobiome 274–275, **274–275**
    sleep and 254–255
Brand, Stewart 216
Brando, Marlon 81
Brazil
    Amazon rainforest 84
    Atlantic Forest **211**
    C-section rates 259
    flag and facts 341, 366, **366**
    greener cities 247
    Lençóis Maranhenses NP **334**
    Trans-Amazonian highway 340
    wildlife 180, **180**
British Columbia, Canada 84, **84**, 89
Brown boobies **365**
Brunei 366, **366**
Bubble Nebula **5**
Buchanan, James 315
Buddhism **5**, 76, 248–249, 251, **251**,
    299
Buenos Aires, Argentina 66, **66**,
    244
Bulgaria 367, **367**
Burgess Shale, Canada **169**
Burke, Bernard 139
Burkina Faso 367, **367**
Burma *see* Myanmar
Burundi 245, 367, **367**
Bush, George H. W. 315
Butterflies **202–203**
Byron, Annabelle 296
Byron, Lord 296

C
C-sections 258–259
Cabo Pulmo Marine Reserve, Mexico
    364
Cabo Verde 367, **367**
Cairngorms NP, Scotland **239**
Cairo, Egypt 245, 247
California
    best eats 86, **86**
    climate change 14
    extremes 53
    fires 14, **112**
    @natgeo photos **48**, **77**, **112**,
      365

    state flag **318**
    travel 47, **48**, 64, 73, **77**
Cambodia 367, **367**
Camels **364**
Cameron, James **44**
Cameroon 367, **367**
Canada
    disappearing languages 240
    Ellesmere Island 361
    flag and facts 339, 367, **367**
    fossils **169**, 170
    Great Bear Rainforest 338
    oldest rocks 330
    talking trees 166–167, **166–167**
    travel 70, 84, **84**, 89
    Viking settlements 355
Canary Islands 33
Cane toads 178
Cape Town, South Africa 100, 101
Capuchin monkeys **253**
Carbon pollution 17
Cassini spacecraft 129
Cassowaries 179
Cataracts 269, **269**
Caterpillars 202, **202**
Cats, domesticated 176, 177
Cauliflower coral 75
Caves 49, 53, **53**
Central African Republic 307, 367,
    367
Central American refugees 236
Central Park, New York City **246**
Ceres (dwarf planet) 131
Cesarean sections 258–259
Chaco Canyon, New Mexico 248
Chad 259, 367, **367**
Challenger Deep, Pacific Ocean **44**,
    52, 356
Chantek (orangutan) 183
Charote (language) 240
Cherrapunji, India 53
Cherry trees 314–315, **314–315**
Chesapeake Bay 191
Chicken 256, 270–271, **270–271**
Chile
    Atacama Desert 53, **53**
    Atacama salt flats 340
    copper mines 332
    disappearing languages 240
    Easter Island **298**
    flag and facts 367, **367**

Patagonia 340
travel 80, 89
Chiller, Tom 270
Chimpanzees 181, **181**
China
  climate change 99
  diplomatic gifts 315
  economic power 229
  female scientists 29
  flag and facts 345, 367, **367**
  Great Wall of China 65, **298**
  greener cities 247
  Hong Kong **345**
  Internet use 25
  lunar calendar 251
  Olympic athletes 60, 61, **61**
  populous cities 245
  pro-democracy protests 295
  space exploration 133, 136
  terra-cotta warriors 300–301,
    300–301
  Tien Shan mountains 344
  traditional medicine 262–263,
    262–263
  travel 65, 67, **67**
  Urumqi 53
  wildlife **156–157,** 173
Chisholm, Shirley 313
Chlorophyll, in oceans 354
Choche, Ethiopia **238**
Christianity 248–249, 251, **251**
Cincinnati, Ohio 86
Circuses **253**
Cities 244–247, **246–247,** 332
Cleisthenes 294
Climate change
  causes 17
  evidence 154–155, **154–155,** 338
  human migration and 231
  impact 14–15, 100–101, **100–101,**
    189, 344
  map 374–375
  predictions 98, 99
Climate zones map 98–99
Climbing 8–9, 48, 50–51, **50–51,** 334;
    see also Ice climbing; Trekking
Clinton, Hillary 313
Clouded leopards **208–209**
Clouds 102, **102,** 112
Clownfish 75, **185**
Cochrane, Chile 80

Cockatoos 201
Coding 296–297, **296–297**
Coffee **238**
Colombia 109, 236, 340, 367, **367**
Colonial era 294–295, 310–311,
    310–311
Colorado 47, 73, 89, 90, **90–91,** 318
Colorado River Delta, Mexico **101**
Comets 131, 147
Common ravens **197**
Communication
  animals 182–183, **182–183,** 188,
    201
  Internet access 22–25
  trees 164, 166–167, **166–167**
Comoros 367, **367**
Computer programmers 296–297,
    296–297
Confucianism 251, **251**
Congo, Democratic Republic of the
    237, 307, 367, **367**
Congo, Republic of 367, **367**
Connecticut: state flag **318**
Conservation
  biodiversity 210–211, **210–211**
  jellyfish 218–219, **218–219**
  marine biology 214–215, **214–215**
  Photo Ark 208–209, **208–209**
  plastics and 212–213, **212–213**
  time line 206–207, **206–207**
  see also Earth Day
Constellations 120–124, **120–124**
Constitution, U.S. 295, **295,** 312, 323
Continental drift 336
Continents 336–351, **336–351**
  Africa 346–347, **347**
  Antarctica 350–351, **351**
  Asia 344–345, **345**
  Australia & Oceania 348–349,
    349
  Europe 342–343, **343**
  North America 338–339, **339**
  Pangaea 336–337
  South America 340–341, **341**
Copernicus 139
Copper mines 332
Coral reefs 186–187, **186–187**
  Australia 74–75, **74–75**
  Gabon 346
  Philippines 215
  reef life 75, 210

Corvids 197, **197**
Cosmic radiation 148–149, **148–149,**
    153
Cosmos (television series) 145
Costa Rica 81, **81,** 367, **367**
Côte d'Ivoire 236, 367, **367**
Countries: flags and facts 366–373
Cousteau, Jacques 45
Cranes, sandhill **195**
Crater Lake NP, Oregon 73
Crawford Notch State Park, New
    Hampshire 47
Crimson-fronted parakeets **201**
Crispr (gene-editing technology)
    264–265, **264–265**
Croatia 367, **367**
Crocodiles 75, **173**
Crows 197
Cruises 71, **71**
Cuba 367, **367**
Culture 234–253
  female writers 28, **28**
  folk tales 288–289, **288–289**
  intangible 234–235, **234–235**
  landscape architecture 242–243,
    242–243
  languages 240–241
  map of refugees 236–237
  @natgeo photos **238–239,**
    252–253
  urbanization 244–247
  see also Religion
Curiosity (Martian rover) 128, 136
Cycling **34–35,** 60
Cyprus 307, 367, **367**
Czechia 367, **367**

D

Danakil Depression, Africa 53
Dante Alighieri 293
Danum Valley Conservation Area,
    Borneo **14–15**
Dark energy 142, 143, **143**
Dark matter 142, **142,** 152–153,
    152–153
Darwin, Charles 64
Death Valley NP, California-Nevada
    53
Deception Island, Antarctica 89
Declaration of Independence 295

Deepsea Challenger sub **44**
Delaware: state flag **318**
Delhi, India 245
Dementia 254
Democracy 294–295, **294–295**
Democratic Republic of the Congo 237, 307, 367, **367**
Deng Wei 60
Denmark 270, **299**, 367, **367**, 373
Deserts 98, 361
Dhendup, Tashi 41
Día de los Muertos 235, **235**
Dinosaurs 168, 170–171, **170–171**, 337
Diodorus Siculus 293
Diomede Islands, Bering Strait **335**
Diving 45, 49, 54–55, **54–55**, 187
Djibouti 53, 347, 367, **367**
DNA
    Crispr-Cas9 264–265, **264–265**
    Egyptians 302–303, **302–303**
    GMOs 21, **21**
    human migration 230–231
    Neanderthal 233
    track your own ancestry 231, 233
Dogs 176–177, **176–177**
Dolgan (language) 241
Dolphins 183, **184**, 255
Domestication 176–177, **176–177**
Dominica 367, **367**
Dominican Republic 367, **367**
Donadio, Emiliano 40
Doudna, Jennifer **264**, 264–265
Douglas fir trees 166–167, **166–167**
Dragon blood trees **334**
Drones 306, **306**
Drought 100–101, **100–101**, 112
Druyan, Ann 144–145, **144–145**
Dry Valleys, Antarctica 53
Dugongs 75
Dunton, Colorado 89
Dwarf planets 130–131, **130–131**

E

e-NABLE 273
Eagles 75
Earth 92–119
    clouds 102, **102**, 112
    cosmic radiation 149, **149**
    drought 100–101, **100–101**
    Earthrise photo **216**

extremes 52–53, **52–53**
future 374–375
hurricanes 106–107, **106–107**
land surface 331
map of climate zones 98–99
map of temperature trends 374–375
minerals 114–115, **114–115**
@natgeo photos **112–113**
population growth 280
storm chasers 110–111, **110–111**
time line 96–97, **96–97**
tornadoes 110–111, **110–111**
volcanic islands 118–119, **118–119**
volcanoes 108–109, **108–109**
wildfires 104, **104–105**
Earth Day 216–217, **217**
Earth Day every day
    diving coral reefs 187
    ethnobotany 235
    healthier planet 217
    honeybees 205
    insects as food 256–257, **256–257**
    light pollution 123
    plastic pollution 213
    religion 248
    travel 81
East Timor (Timor-Leste) 371, **371**
Easter Island, South Pacific Ocean **298**
Eclipses 125
Ecuador 17, 64, 367, **367**
Egypt
    adventure travel 85
    ancient DNA 302–303, **302–303**
    C-section rates 259
    flag and facts 367, **367**
    Giza Pyramids 64, **282–283**
    greener cities 247
    Nat Geo explorers 40
    night sky **140**
    primates 180, **180**
Eiffel Tower, Paris, France 67, **67**, 76
El Salvador 367, **367**
Elbrus, Mount, Russia 342
Elephants **172**
Ellesmere Island, Canada 361
Endangered and threatened species **156–157**, 210–211, **210–211**
Energy, solar **10–11**

Equatorial Guinea 367, **367**
Eris (dwarf planet) 130
Eritrea 25, 53, 368, **368**
ESA (European Space Agency) 128, 136
Estonia 368, **368**
Eta Aquarids meteor shower 125
Ethiopia 53, **112**, 226, **226**, 238, 259, 368, **368**
Ethiopian Plateau 346
Ethnobotany 235, 277
Eukarya 163, **163**
Eurasian magpies 197
Europa (Jupiter's moon) 139, **139**
Europe
    human origins 231
    map and facts 342–343
European Space Agency (ESA) 128, 136
Everest, Mount, China-Nepal 50–51, **50–51**, 53, 345
Evolution
    causes 211
    human 226–227, **226–227**
    key dates 163, 337
    time line 224–225, **224–225**
    of weapons 306
    whales 189
Exoplanets 147, 150–151, **150–151**
Exploration 34–55
    adventure 46–49, **46–49**, 90–91, **90–91**
    deep oceans 42–45, **42–45**
    extremes 50–57, **50–57**
    female explorers 28
    map 40–41
    oceans **42**, 42–43
    solar system 128–129, **128–129**
    South Pacific seafarers 357
    time line 38–39, **38–39**
Extinctions 210
Extremes 50–57, **50–57**
Extremophiles 43, 45, **45**
Eyes 268–269, **268–269**

F

Fairy tales 288–289, **288–289**
Falkland Islands 24
Fazekas, Andrew 121, **121**
Félicité, Seychelles 81

Festivals **231**, 235, **235**, 250–251, **250–251**
Fiji 368, **368**
Finland 17, **17**, 259, 368, **368**
Finley, Kristin **253**
Fir trees 166–167, **166–167**
Fires 14, 104, **104–105**, **112**
Fish 75, **76**, **364**
Fishing industry 20, **20**, 214–215, 354
Flags
  countries of the world **366–372**
  United States 316–317, **316–317**
  U.S. states **318–321**
  U.S. territories 322–323, **322–323**
Flamingos **195**, 340
Flint Hills, Kansas 47
Florida 47, **48**, 54–55, **113**, **184**, **280–281**, 318
Flying foxes (bats) **209**
Fo Guang Shan Buddha Museum, Kaohsiung, Taiwan **76**
Folk tales 288–289, **288–289**
Food
  America's best eats 86–87, **86–87**
  coffee **238**
  farming 2.0 18–19, **18–19**
  herbs & spices 276–277, **276–277**
  insects as 256–257, **256–257**
  Italy 68–69, **68–69**
  lab-grown meat 20, **20**
  meat consumption in U.S. 270
  sustainable seafood 20, **20**
  waste 21
Forests
  communication 164, 166–167, **166–167**
  rainforests 84, 211, **211**, 338
Fossils **168–169**, 168–171, 226–227, **226–227**
Foxes 177
France 67, **67**, **76**, 235, **235**, 295, 315, 368, **368**, 373
Frankfurt, Germany 247
Franklin, Kenneth 139
Freedman, Wendy 146, **146**
French Polynesia 64, 71, 81, **373**
Frogs 84
Fuji, Mount, Japan 65
Fungi 163, **163**

Future
  agriculture 18–19, **18–19**
  Earth 374–375
  humans on Earth 378–379
  life on Earth 376–377

G

Gabon 25, 346, 368, **368**
Gaffrey, Justin 55
Gagarin, Yuri 133
Gagnan, Émile 45
Galápagos Islands, South Pacific Ocean 64
Galápagos Rift, Pacific Ocean 43, 45, **45**
Galápagos sea lions **185**
Galileo 139
Galves, Jamal Allen 40
Gambia 368, **368**
Ganges River, India 52, 249
Gardens 66, **66**, 199
Geminids meteor shower 125
Gender issues 260–261, **260–261**
General relativity 33
Genetically modified organisms (GMOs) 21, **21**
Genetics see DNA
Genographic Project 233
Gentoo penguins **195**
Georgia (republic) 368, **368**
Georgia (state) 87, **87**, 318
Geothermal energy 89
Germany 25, 41, 236, 247, 368, **368**
Ghana 201, 368, **368**
"Ghost nets" 214–215
Giant kelp forests 357
Giant Magellan Telescope 146
Giant pandas **173**, 315
Giant tube worms **45**
Gibraltar, Strait of 355
Giraffes **347**
Giza, Egypt 64, **282–283**
Glaciers 348
Glaucoma 269, **269**
Global connectivity **22–23**, 22–25
Global warming 15, 17, 154–155, **154–155**; see also Climate change
GMOs (genetically modified organisms) 21, **21**
Gobi Desert, Mongolia 80, 85, **85**

Golden jellyfish 218–219, **218–219**
Golden lion tamarins 180, **180**
Golden snub-nosed monkeys **156–157**
Goldilocks zone 150
Gorillas 181, **181**, 182–183, **182–183**
Grand Canyon, Arizona **113**, 339
Grand Cayman (island) **364**
Grant, Ulysses S. 315
Gravitational waves 33, **33**
Gray parrots 183
Gray whales 189
Great Barrier Reef, Australia 74–75, **74–75**, 186, **186–187**
Great Bear Rainforest, Canada 338
Great Britain see United Kingdom
Great frigatebirds 255
Great Ocean Road, Australia 85, **85**
Great Pacific Garbage Patch 356
Great Wall of China 65, **298**
Greece 65, 80, 84, 119, **253**, 368, **368**
Green cities 246–247, **246–247**
Green sea turtles 75, **184**
Greenhouses 18, **18–19**
Greenland 338, **365**
Grenada 368, **368**
Griffith-Joyner, Florence 57
Grimm, Wilhelm and Jacob 288
Guam **322**
Guatemala **299**, 368, **368**
"Guernica" (Picasso) 324, **324–325**
Guinea 368, **368**
Guinea-Bissau 368, **368**
Gulf Stream 98
Gulf Wars 307
Guyana 368, **368**

H

Hahn, Dave 51
Haida (language) 240
Haiti 307, 368, **368**
Hamadryas baboon 180, **180**
Hammer throw **60**
Han (dolphin) 183
Hana Highway, Hawaii 64
Hang gliding **48**
Haumea (dwarf planet) 131
Hawaii **6–7**, 14, 33, 53, 64, 118–119, **118–119**, **184**, 318

Hayabusa2 spacecraft 128
Hayes, Rutherford B. 315
Health and medicine
    antibiotic resistance 270–271,
      270–271
    C-section births 258–259
    Crispr (gene-editing technology)
      264–265, **264–265**
    eyes 268–269, **268–269**
    gender 260–261, **260–261**
    herbs & spices 276–277,
      276–277
    mindfulness 278–279, **278–279**
    perpetuating the species 280–
      281, **280–281**
    prosthetics 272–273, **272–273**
    psychobiome 274–275, **274–275**
    sleep 254–255, **254–255**
    time line 266–267, **266–267**
    traditional Chinese medicine
      262–263, **262–263**
Hector (dolphin) 183
Herbs 276–277, **276–277**
Hercules (submersible) **42**, 43
Herodotus (historian) 293
Herring, Rachel 55
High Atlas Mountains, Morocco 80
Highlining 90, **90–91**
Hill, Elsie 312
Hillary, Edmund 51
Hinduism 234, **234**, 248–250, **250**
History
    America's lost colonies 310–311,
      310–311
    computer programming 296–297,
      296–297
    democracy 294–295, **294–295**
    diplomatic gifts 314–315, **314–315**
    DNA from ancient Egypt 302–
      303, **302–303**
    exploration time line 38–39, **38–39**
    innovations time line 304–305,
      304–305
    @natgeo photos **298–299**
    100-meter dash 56–57, **56–57**
    prehistory to 1600 time line
      286–287, **286–287**
    Sammu-ramat, Queen (Babylon)
      292–293, **292–293**
    1600 to recent past time line
      290–291, **290–291**

terra-cotta warriors 300–301,
    300–301
transportation time line 62–63,
    62–63
U.S. time line 308–309, **308–309**
war 306–307, **306–307**
woman suffrage 312–313,
    312–313
Hockey **48**
Holidays 250–251, **250–251**
Honduras 368, **368**
Honeybees **4–5**, 204–205, **204–205**
Hong Kong **345**
Honnold, Alex 48, **48**
Hoover Dam, Arizona-Nevada **100**
Hopkinson, Francis 316
Hornbein, Thomas 51
Hot springs 88–89, **88–89**
Hot Springs, Arkansas 89
Howland Island 323
Hubble Space Telescope 32
Huis, Arnold van 256
Human body, in space 149
Human origins
    human ancestors 226–227,
      226–227
    journalism 228–229, **228–229**
    migrations 230–231
    in movies 227
    Neanderthals 232–233, **232–233**
    time line 224–225, **224–225**
Humans
    gender issues 260–261, **260–261**
    map of development 378–379
    map of influence on nature
      376–377
    science of 220–281
    see also Culture; Food; Health
      and medicine
Hummingbirds 198–199, **198–199**
Humpback whales 75, **184**, **188**, 363
Hunga Tonga-Hunga Ha'ipi, Polyne-
    sia 118
Hungary 368, **368**
Hurricanes 106–107, **106–107**, 243
Hydroelectricity 346
Hydroponics 350
Hydrothermal vents 42–43, 45, **45**
Hyner View State Park, Pennsylva-
    nia 47

Ice climbing **2–3, 49, 141**
Ice hockey **48**
Ice sheets 338, 350
Ice skating 61, **61**
Icebergs **351**, 362, **365**
Iceland
    flag and facts 368, **368**
    history of democracy 294
    hot springs 88–89, **88–89**
    @natgeo photos **49, 140, 141, 335**
    urbanization 245
    volcanoes 109, 119
Idaho: state flag **318**
Igbo society 294
Illinois: state flag **319**
Immigration: refugees map 236–237
Inca **341**
India
    culture 234, **234, 238**
    extremes 52, 53
    flag and facts 368, **368**
    history of democracy 295
    holidays 251
    space exploration 136, 137, **137**
    travel 65
    UN peacekeeping mission 307
    urbanization 245
Indian Ocean 358–359
Indiana: state flag **319**
Indigenous peoples 17, **17**
Indonesia
    Borneo **14–15**, 172
    diplomatic gifts 315
    disappearing languages 241
    drought 100
    flag and facts 368, **368**
    hot springs 89
    urbanization 245
    volcanoes 109, 119
    wildlife **172, 181, 181, 185**
Innovations 56–57, **56–57**, 304–305,
    304–305
Insects 16, 256–257, **256–257**
Intelligence, animal 197, 201
Internet access 22–25
Iowa 86, 317, **319**
Iran 76, 368, **368**
Iraq 236, 307, 368, **368**
Ireland 368, **368**
Isfahan, Iran **76**

Islam 237, 248–249, 251, **251**
Israel 101, 368, **368**
Italy **68–69**, 68–70, 89, 109, **298**, **343**, 368, **368**
Ivory Coast *see* Côte d'Ivoire

J

Jakarta, Indonesia 100, 245
Jamaica 368, **368**
James Webb Space Telescope 32, **32**
Japan
 aging population 333
 diplomatic gifts 314–315, **314–315**
 flag and facts 368, **368**
 @natgeo photos **77, 113**
 Olympic athletes 61
 space exploration 128, 136
 travel 65, **77**, 78–79, **78–79**, 89
 urbanization 245
 washi paper 235
Jarvis Island 323
Jasper National Park, Canada 2–3
Java Trench, Indian Ocean 358
Jayewardene, Junius R. 315
Jedediah Smith Redwoods State
 Park, California 47
Jellyfish **44**, 218–219, **218–219**
Jerusalem 249
Jeter, Carmelita 57
John, King (England) 294
Johnson, Michael 60
Johnson, Robert 288, 289
Johnston Atoll 323
Jones, Holly 41
Jones, John Paul 317
Jordan 236, **298**, 368, **368**
Joshua Tree NP, California 73
Journalists 228–229, **228–229**
Juana Inés de la Cruz, Sor 28
Judaism 248–249, 250, **250**, 251
Juno spacecraft 30, 138, 139
Jupiter (planet) **30–31**, 125, **128–129**, 138–139, **138–139**

K

Kabul, Afghanistan **195**
Kalahari Desert, Botswana **347**
Kami Rita Sherpa 51

Kangaroos 179
Kansas 47, **319**
Kaohsiung, Taiwan **76**
Karen people 17
Katmai NP, Alaska 73
Katushemererwe, Fridah 41
Katydids **7**
Kayapó people **252**
Kazakh eagle hunters **239**
Kazakhstan 368, **368**
Kelly, Scott 149, **149**
Kelp forests 357
Kenai Peninsula, Alaska 81
Kentucky 53, **53**, **319**
Kenya 172, 234, **239**, 368, **368**
Kepler spacecraft 151
Kermode bears 338
Key, Francis Scott 316
Keystone species 210
Khonso Im-Heb 303
Kidd, Kenneth 231
Kilauea (volcano), Hawaii 118, **118–119**
Kilimanjaro, Mount, Tanzania 65, 347
King, William, Earl of Lovelace 297
Kingman Reef 323
King's Bay, Florida **184**
Kinshasa, Democratic Republic of
 the Congo 244, 245
Kiribati **191**, 369, **369**
Koalas 179
Kodaira, Nao 61
Koko (gorilla) **182–183**, **182–183**
Koldewey, Heather 214–215, **214–215**
Kookaburras 179
Kosovo 307, 369, **369**
Krakatau (Krakatoa), Indonesia 109, 119
Kuiper belt 131
Kulung culture **252**
Kuwait 245, 307, 369, **369**
Kyaiktiyo, Mount, Myanmar **299**
Kyrgyzstan **335**, 344, 369, **369**
Kyzylkum Desert, Uzbekistan **141**, 228

L

Lakes 52, **52**
Landscape architects 242–243, **242–243**
Landscapes, photos **334–335**

Languages 240–241, 348
Laos 369, **369**
Latvia 369, **369**
Laughing kookaburras 179
Leatherback sea turtles 346
Lebanon 236, 307, 369, **369**
Lemaître, Georges 143
Lençóis Maranhenses NP, Brazil **334**
Leopards **172**, **208–209**
Lesotho 346, 369, **369**
Liberia 369, **369**
Libya 369, **369**
Liechtenstein 245, 369, **369**
Life science 156–219
 domains of life 162–163, **162–163**
 map of future of wildlife 376–377
 @natgeo photos **172–173**, **184–185**, **194–195**
 time line 160–161, **160–161**
 see also Conservation; Health
  and medicine
Light pollution 123
Lightning 103, **103, 113**
Lincoln, Abraham 315
Lippincott, Donald 56
Lithuania 369, **369**
Livestock 20, 256, 257, 270–271, **270–271**
Living Breakwaters project 243
Los Angeles, California 244, 247
Louisiana 87, **319**
Lousios Gorge, Greece 84
Lovelace, Ada **296**, 296–297
Luxembourg 24, 369, **369**

M

Maasai Mara National Reserve,
 Kenya **172**
Macaques **173**
Macaws 200, **200, 252**
Macedonia 369, **369**
Machu Picchu, Peru **341**
Macron, Emmanuel 315
Macular degeneration 269, **269**
Madagascar **92–93**, 98, 369, **369**
Magna Carta 294
Magpies 197
Maine 87, **87, 319**
Majlis al Jinn, Oman **49**
Makemake (dwarf planet) 131, **131**

Malawi 369, **369**
Malaysia 369, **369**
Maldives 344, 345, 369, **369**
Mali 307, 369, **369**
Malraux, André 67
Malta 369, **369**
Mammoth Cave, Kentucky 53, **53**
Manatees **184**
Manta rays **116**
Maps
adventure travel 84–85
Africa 346
America's lost colonies 310–311
Antarctic oceans 362–363
Antarctica 350
Arctic Ocean 360–361
Asia 344
Atlantic Ocean 355
Australia & Oceania 348
C-section births 258–259
climate zones 98–99
disappearing languages 240–241
Europe 342
future of wild life 376–377
global connectivity 24–25
human development 378–379
human migration 230
iconic travel destinations 64–65
Indian Ocean 358–359
Nat Geo explorers 40–41
Neanderthal range 233
North America 338
ocean currents 353
ocean trends 354
oceans 352–353
Pacific Ocean 356–357
Pangaea 336–337
physical world 330–331
political world 332–333
Pristine Seas project 117
refugees 236–237
religions 248–249
South America 340
temperature trends 374–375
urbanization 244–245
U.S. national parks 72–73
Maracaibo, Lake, Venezuela 103
Marble 115, **115**
Maremma, Italy 89
Mariner missions 136, **136**
Marrakech, Morocco 66, **66**

Mars (planet) 125, 128, **128**, 134–137, **134–137**, 149
Marshall, Greg 189, **189**
Marshall Islands 369, **369**
Martinique 109
Maryland 47, 87, **319**
Massachusetts: state flag **319**
Matera, Italy **298**
Maui (island), Hawaii **6–7**
Mauna Kea, Hawaii 53
Mauritania 369, **369**
Mauritius 369, **369**
Mawsynram, India 53
Maxwell, Gavin 66
Maya 82–83, **82–83**, **299**
Mayer, Maria Goeppert 29
Mayflower Compact 294
McGowan, Kevin 197, **197**
Mead, Lake, Arizona-Nevada 100, **100**
Mealworms 257
Meat, lab-grown 20, **20**
Mecca, Saudi Arabia 249
Meditation 278
Meghalaya, India 53
Mercury (planet) 125, 128, **128**
Messner, Reinhold 51
Meteor showers 125, **125**
Mexico
culture 235, **235**, 239
diplomatic gifts 315
drought 100, **100**, 101
flag and facts 369, **369**
Mexico City 100, **100**, 244, 248, 338
@natgeo photos **49**, **239**, **364**
Riviera Maya 82–83, **82–83**
underwater art **54–55**
wildlife trade 200
Michigan: state flag **319**
Microbiome 274–275, **274–275**
Micronesia 369, **369**
Mid-Atlantic Ridge 43
Midway Islands 323
Migration, animal 71, **71**, **195**, 363
Migration, human 230–231, 236–237
Mijikenda people 234
Miles, Lyn 183
Milky Way **141**
Mindfulness 278–279, **278–279**
Minerals 114–115, **114–115**

Minnesota: state flag **319**
Misrach, Richard 243
Mississippi: state flag **319**
Mississippi River watershed 338
Missouri 317, **320**
Miura, Yuichiro 51
Moab, Utah **34–35**
Mohs' scale 114, 115
Moldova 369, **369**
Molina, Erina Pauline 41
Mollusks 191, **191**
Monaco 369, **369**
Monahans Sandhills State Park, Texas 47
Mongolia 80, 85, **85**, **239**, 369, **369**
Monkeys **156–157**, **173**, 180, **180**, **253**
Monotremes 348
Monsoons 53, **92–93**
Montana: state flag **320**
Montenegro 369, **369**
Monument Valley, Utah **48**
Moon 125, 132–133, **132–133**
Moore, Sir Patrick 122
Morocco 66, **66**, 70, 80, 169, 295, 369, **369**
Moths **202–203**
Mountain climbing *see* Climbing
Mountains 53, 330
Movies
dinosaurs 168, **168**
prehistoric fictions 227
space 138, **138**, 145
underwater worlds 54
volcanoes 108, **108**
Mozambique 85, **85**, 369, **369**
Multan, Pakistan **299**
Museums 54–55, **54–55**, **76**, 79
Music 46, 150
Myanmar 237, **299**, 369, **369**
Mývatn Nature Baths, Iceland **88–89**

N

Namibia 369, **369**
Narragansett Bay, Rhode Island 47
Narwhals **364**
NASA
Jupiter missions 138
Kepler spacecraft 151
Mars missions 128, 134–137, **136–137**

moon missions 132–133
solar system exploration 128–129, 130
Voyager missions 145
Nashville, Tennessee 64
National Geographic
    Adventurer of the Year 58–59, **58–59**
    Emerging Explorers 110–111, **110–111**
    explorers, map of 40–41
    Explorers-in-Residence 116–117, **117**
    Fellows 228–229, **228–229**
    female writers and photographers 28
    Genographic Project 230, 233
    Photo Ark 208–209, **208–209**
National parks, U.S. 72–73
Native Americans 77, 240
Nauru 349, 370, **370**
Navassa Island 323
Neanderthals 232–233, **232–233**
Nebraska **195, 320**
Nefertiti, Queen (Egypt) 302
Nelson, Christian Kent 86
Nelson, Gaylord 217
Nepal **252**, 370, **370**
Netherlands
    Amsterdam 342
    dependencies 373
    farming 18–19, **18–19**
    flag and facts 370, **370**
    microbead ban 215
    Olympic athletes 61
    travel 64
Neuroplasticity 278
Neutrinos 149, **149**
Nevada 53, **320**
New Hampshire 47, **320**
New Horizons probe 129, 130
New Jersey **313, 320**
New Mexico 80, **80, 320,** 321, **326–327**
New Orleans, Louisiana 87
New Year celebrations 251
New York 243, **320**
New York, New York 87, 244, **246, 335,** 380, **380–381**
New Zealand
    dependencies 373

female politicians 29
flag and facts 370, **370**
glaciers 348
Nat Geo explorers 41
travel 70, 89
voting rights 313
Newton, Isaac 152
Ngoteya, Hans Cosmas 41
Nicaragua 84, **84,** 370, **370**
Niger 259, 370, **370**
Nigeria 294, 347, 370, **370**
Nile River, Africa 52, **52**
Nixon, Richard 315
Nodosaur 170, **170–171**
Norgay, Tenzing 51
North America
    human origins 231
    map and facts 338–339
    urbanization 244
North Carolina: state flag **320**
North Dakota: state flag **320**
North Korea 370, **370**
North Pole 360
Northern lights **140, 141, 148**
Northern Mariana Islands **322**
Northern Territory, Australia 80
Norway **278–279,** 370, **370**

O

Oahu, Hawaii **184**
Ocasio-Cortez, Alexandria 29, **29**
Oceania: map and facts 348–349
Oceans 352–363
    Antarctica 362–363
    Arctic Ocean 360–361
    Atlantic Ocean 354–355
    chlorophyll 354
    deep-ocean exploration 42–45, **42–45**
    fishing industry 354
    Indian Ocean 358–359
    map of currents 353
    @natgeo photos **364–365**
    Pacific Ocean 356–357
    plastics in 214–215, **214–215**
    Pristine Seas project **116,** 116–117
    sea surface temperatures 354
    trends 354
    volcanic islands 118–119, **118–119**
    see also Sea life

O'Connor, Sandra Day 313
Octopuses 192–193, **192–193**
Offshore drilling 358
Ohio 86, 275, **320**
Oil industry 358
Okanogan-Wenatchee National Forest, Washington 47
Okavango Delta, Botswana 173
Oklahoma **112, 320**
Olympic Games 57, 60–61, **60–61,** 78
Oman **49,** 370, **370**
100-meter dash 56–57, **56–57**
Oort Cloud 131
Orangutans 181, **181,** 183
Oregon 73, **320**
Orff, Kate 242–243, **242–243**
Orlando, Florida **280–281**
Osa Peninsula, Costa Rica 81
Osaka, Japan 245
Outback region, Australia 331
Owens, Jesse 56
Owls **194**
Oysters 191, **243**

P

Pacific Coast Highway, California 64
Pacific Ocean
    Challenger Deep **44,** 52, 356
    Great Pacific Garbage Patch 356
    hurricanes **106–107**
    hydrothermal vents 45, **45**
    map and facts 356–357
Pakicetus 189
Pakistan **299,** 307, 370, **370**
Palau **116,** 218–219, **218–219,** 370, **370**
Paleontology see Dinosaurs; Fossils
Palmyra Atoll 323
Pamukkale, Turkey 89
Panama 370, **370**
Pandas, giant **173,** 315
Pangaea 336–337
Papua New Guinea **194, 238,** 245, 348, 349, 370, **370**
Paradise, California 14
Paraguay 24, 240, 370, **370**
Parakeets **201**
Paris, France 67, **67, 76,** 244
Parrots 183, **194,** 200–201, **200–201, 252**

Pasca Palmer, Cristiana 211
Patagonia, Argentina-Chile 340
Patterson, Francine **182,** 183
Paul, Alice 312
Pelosi, Nancy 313
Penguins **195**
Pennsylvania 47, **320**
Pepperberg, Irene 183, 201, **201**
Performance-enhancing drugs 57
Perfume 235, **235**
Perseids meteor shower 125, **125**
Persian Gulf 358
Persian Gulf Wars 307
Peru 234, **234,** 240, **252, 341,** 370,
    370
Petra, Jordan **298**
Petroglyphs **140**
Pets 176–177, **176–177**
Pfaff, Anna **49**
Philippines 41, **76,** 215, **365,** 370,
    370
Photo Ark 208–209, **208–209**
Photography
    adventure **48–49**
    birds **194–195**
    Earth **112–113**
    history **298–299**
    land life **172–173**
    landscape **334–335**
    ocean **364–365**
    people **252–253**
    sea life **184–185**
    skywatching **140–141**
    traditions **238–239**
    travel **76–77**
Photosynthesis 165
Picasso, Pablo 324, **324–325**
Pigs 256, 257, 270
Pink helmet jellyfish **44**
Pinwheel Galaxy 152
Planets 125, **128–129,** 130–131, **130–**
    131; see also specific planets
Plants
    fossils 168, **168**
    herbs & spices 276–277,
        276–277
    kingdom 163, **163**
    microscopic view 164–165,
        164–165
Plastics 16, **16,** 212–215, **212–215**
Platypuses 179

Pledge of Allegiance 317
Pluto (dwarf planet) 130, **130**
Poland 60, **60,** 370, **370**
Polar bears **173, 210**
Polar vortex 360
Politicians, female 26, 29, **29**
Pollination 204–205, **204–205**
Pollution 123, 213
Polynesia 64, 71, 81, 118, **191**
Population
    largest cities 244–245
    world 244, 280
Portugal 370, **370**
Poultry 270
Prehistory time line 286–287,
    286–287
Primate family tree 180–181, **180–181**
Pringle, Anne 40
Pristine Seas project **116,** 116–117
Prosthetics 272–273, **272–273**
Psychobiome 274–275, **274–275**
Púcon, Chile 89
Pueblo peoples 248
Puerto Rico **322**
Pulsars 148
Pyeongchang, South Korea 61
Pyramids 64, **282–283**

Q

Qatar 370, **370**
Qin Shi Huang Di, Emperor (China)
    300–301
Quebec, Canada 330
Quechua-speaking peoples 234,
    234
Quolls 178–179, **178–179**

R

Radiation, space 148–149, **148–149**
Railroads 70, **70**
Rainbows **365**
Rainforests 84, 211, **211,** 338
Rankin, Jeannette 313
Ravens **197**
Reagan, Ronald 315
Red bird-of-paradise **194**
Red kangaroos 179
Red-winged parrots **194**
Redwood trees **77**

Reefs see Coral reefs
Refugees 236–237, **253**
Reilly, Kevin 55
Reindeer 17, **17,** 342
Relativity theory 33
Religion
    holidays 239, **239,** 250–251,
        250–251
    India **234, 238**
    Mexico **235,** 239, **239**
    mythical birds 197
    @natgeo photos **238, 239, 299**
    world map 248–249
    see also specific religions
Resigaro (language) 240
Rey, H. A. 122
Rhode Island 47, **320**
Rio de Janeiro, Brazil 60, **60,** 244,
    247
Rivers 52, **52**
Riviera Maya, Mexico 82–83, **82–**
    83
Roanoke colony, Virginia 311
Robotics 273, **273**
Rock climbing see Climbing
Rock Island State Park, Tennessee
    47
Rocks, oldest 330
Rocky Mountain NP, Colorado 73
Rocky Mountains, North America 70,
    89, 98, 104, **104–105**
Rogers, Lynn 175, **175**
Rohingya Muslims 237
Romania 370, **370**
Romero, Jordan 51
Rosemary 164–165, **164–165**
Rossini, Gioacchino Antonio 293
Rotorua, New Zealand 89
Rowing races **252**
Rumph, Samuel Henry 87
Running 56–60, **56–60**
Russia
    disappearing languages 241
    expanse 331
    flag and facts 343, 370, **370**
    Lake Baikal 52, 344
    Mount Elbrus 342
    @natgeo photos **140**
    space exploration 129, 136
    travel 65, 70
Rwanda 29, 313, 370, **370**

S

Sa Pa, Vietnam 80, **80**
Safaris 71, **71**
Safina, Carl 173, 211, **211**
Sagan, Carl 33, **33**, 124, **144**, 145
Saguaro NP, Arizona 73
Sahara, Africa **6**, 346
Saint Kitts and Nevis 339, 370, **370**
Saint Laurent, Yves 66
Saint Lucia 370, **370**
Saint Vincent and Grenadines 370, **370**
Sala, Enric 116–117, **117**, 219
Salopek, Paul **141**, 228–229, **228–229**
Saltwater crocodiles 75
Samaras, Tim 110–111, **110–111**
Samburu people **239**
Sami people 17, **17**, 342
Sammu-ramat, Queen (Babylon) 292–293, **292–293**
Samoa 370, **370**
San Francisco, California 215
San Marino 370, **370**
Sand dunes **334**, 346
Sandhill cranes **195**
Santa Maria, Cara **9**
Santorini, Greece 119
São Paulo, Brazil 244, 375
São Tomé and Principe 370, **370**
Sápara people 17
Sarah, Aziz Abu 87
Sartore, Joel 208–209, **209**
Satellites 22
Saturn (planet) 125, 129, **129**
Saudi Arabia 313, 370, **370**
Scarlet macaws **200**
Schwabe, Samuel Heinrich 139
Scidmore, Eliza 28
Scotland **239**
Scuba diving see Diving
Sculpture, underwater 54–55, **54–55**
Sea eagles 75
Sea ice 360
Sea level rise 344
Sea life 184–193
  biodiversity 358, 360
  coral reefs 186–187, **186–187**
  mollusks 191, **191**
  @natgeo photos **184–185**
  octopuses 192–193, **192–193**

sea shells 190, **190**
seamounts and 358
whales 188–189, **188–189**
Sea lions **185**
Sea stars **185**
Sea surface temperatures 354
Sea turtles 75, **184**, 346
Seafood 20, **20**
Seahorses **185**
Seamounts 358
Seaver, Barton 87, **87**
Semiramis (mythical queen) 292–293, **292–293**
Senegal 370, **370**
Serbia 370, **370**
Serengeti NP, Tanzania 71, **71**
Seychelles 81, 347, **365**, 370, 370–371
Shamshi-Adad V, King (Babylon) 293
Shanghai, China 67, **67**, 245
Sharks 75, **76**
Shawki, Nora 40
Shells 190, **190**
Shenandoah NP, Virginia 73
Shenzhen, China 245, 247
Sheppard, Kate 29
Sherpas 51
Shinkansen Trans-Siberian Railway 70
Shooting stars see Meteor showers
Siam: diplomatic gifts 315
Sierra Leone 371, **371**
Sikhism 250, **250**
Silva, Sara Graça da 288
Silver foxes 177
Sima Qian (historian) 301
Simard, Suzanne 164, **164**, 166
Simenon, Georges 67
Sinai Peninsula, Egypt 85
Singapore 77, 371, **371**
Skywatching 120–125
  constellations 120–124, **120–124**
  events (2020) 125
  @natgeo photos **140–141**
  summer sky 122–123, **122–123**
  winter sky 120–121, **120–121**
Sleep 254–255, **254–255**
Slovakia 371, **371**
Slovenia 371, **371**
Smooth cauliflower coral 75
Snow 112, **113**

Socotra (island), Arabian Sea **334**
Solar eclipses 125
Solar energy **10–11**
Solar system 128–141
  dwarf planets 130–131, **130–131**
  exploration 128–129, **128–129**
  key features 131
  night sky photos **140–141**
  space science time line 126–127
  see also Moon; specific planets
Solomon Islands 371, **371**
Somalia 237, 371, **371**
Song Köl lake, Kyrgyzstan **335**
Soter, Steven 145
Sotomayor, Sonia 313
Sottaiev, Akhia 342
South Africa 60, **60**, 100, 101, 227, **227**, 295, 371, **371**
South America
  map and facts 340–341
  urbanization 244
  wildlife 340
South Carolina 47, **321**
South Dakota 73, **110**, 321
South Korea 61, **61**, 371, **371**
South Sudan 307, 371, **371**
Southern cassowaries 179
Southern stingrays **364**
Space
  cosmic radiation 148–149, **148–149**, 153
  human body in 149
  movies about 138, **138**
  time line 126–127, **126–127**
  trends 30–33, **30–33**
  see also Constellations; Moon; NASA; specific planets
Space shuttles 133
SpaceX 128
Spain **10–11**, 33, **141**, 231, 235, 324, **324–325**, 371, **371**
Spectral tarsiers 180, **180**
Speed skating 61, **61**
Spelman, Lucy 181, **181**
Sperm whales 188, **189**
Spices 276–277, **276–277**
Spinach 272, **272**
Spinner dolphins 184
Spirit bears 338
Sports 48, 56–61, **56–61**, 90–91, **90–91**

Sri Lanka 315, 371, **371**
St. Croix, U.S. Virgin Islands **184**
St. Lucia **71**
St. Peter's Basilica, Vatican City **77**
Star Wars movies 138, **138**
Starfish **185**
Stars 121, 146–147, **146–147**, 152; *see also* Constellations
Statue of Liberty, New York 315
Sternberg, Samuel H. 265
Steroids 57
Stingrays **364**
Storm chasers 110–111, **110–111**
Strickland, Donna 29, **29**
Stuart, Tristram 21, **21**
Sudan **52**, 307, 371, **371**
Suffrage 312–313, **312–313**
Sufism **299**
Sumatra (island), Indonesia 181
Summer Olympics 60, **60**, 78
Summer Triangle (asterism) 122
Supercell thunderstorms **103**
Superior, Lake, Canada-U.S. 47, **47**, 52, **52**
Supermoons 125
Supernovae 146–147, **146–147**
Supervolcanoes 108, **108**
Supreme Court, U.S. 313
Suriname 341, 371, **371**
Sustainable living
    cities 246–247, **246–247**
    creative solutions 16–17, **16–17**
    food 18–21
    travel 80–81, **80–81**
    see also Earth Day every day
Swaziland 371, **371**
Sweden 371, **371**
Switzerland 70, **70**, 371, **371**
Sydney, Australia 65, 247, **349**
Syria 234, 236, 307, **307**, 371, **371**

T

Tabei, Junko 51
Taft, Helen 314
Taft, William Howard 314, 317
Tahiti 64
Taiwan **76**
Taj Mahal, Agra, India 65
Tajikistan 371, **371**
Tamarins 180, **180**

Tambora, Mount, Indonesia 109
Tanzania 41, 65, 71, **71**, 227, **227**, 347, 371, **371**
Taoism 251, **251**
Tarsiers **172**, 180, **180**
Tasmanian devils 179
Tatum, Vince 55
Tehrani, Jamie 288
Telescopes 32, **32**, 33, **33**, **141**, 146
Tennessee 47, 64, **321**
Ter Mors, Jorien 61
Terra-cotta warriors 300–301, **300–301**
Tetiaroa, French Polynesia 81
Texas 47, 73, **321**
Thailand 17, 371, **371**
Thayore (language) 241
Thiessen, Mark 104, **104**
Thompson, Pete 90, **90–91**
3-D printing **272**, 273
Thunderstorms 103, **103, 112, 113**
Tibetan Plateau 344
Tickle, Evelyn 55
Tien Shan mountains, Asia 344
Tijuana, Mexico **239**
Tikal (site), Guatemala **299**
Timor-Leste 371, **371**
Titanic, R. M.S. **43**
Toads 178
Togo 371, **371**
Tokyo, Japan **77**, 78–79, **78–79**, 245
Tonga 371, **371**
Tornadoes 110–111, **110–111, 113**
Toucans **194**
Tourism 333
Tourtellot, Jonathan 71, **71**
Track and field 56–60, **56–60**
Trains 70, **70**
Trans-Amazonian highway, Brazil 340
Trans-Siberian Railroad 70
Transportation time line 62–63, **62–63**
Travel, adventure 46–47, **46–47**
Travel, classic 62–77
    best cities 66–67, **66–67**
    Great Barrier Reef, Australia 74–75, **74–75**
    greatest expeditions 70–71, **70–71**
    map of iconic destinations 64–65

map of U.S. national parks 72–73
@natgeo photos **76–77**
taste of Italy 68–69, **68–69**
transportation time line 62–63, **62–63**
Travel trends 78–89
    America's best eats 86–87, **86–87**
    Iceland's hot springs 88–89, **88–89**
    map of adventure travel 84–85
    Maya marvels 82–83, **82–83**
    sustainable travel 80–81, **80–81**
    Tokyo 78–79, **78–79**
Trees 17, **17**, **77**, 98, 164, 166–167, **166–167, 334**
Trekking 70, **70**; *see also* Climbing
Trelleborg, Denmark **299**
Trilobites 169, **169**
Trinidad and Tobago 371, **371**
Tristan da Cunha Islands 119
Trolltunga rock formation, Norway **278–279**
Trump, Donald 315
Truth or Consequences, New Mexico 80, **80**
Tsunamis 359
Tubbataha Reefs NP, Philippines **365**
Tube worms **45**
Tulips 64
Tulum (site), Mexico **82–83**, 83
Tunisia 295, **295**, 371, **371**
Turing, Alan 297
Turkey (country) 89, 236, 371, **371**
Turkey (food) 270
Turkmenistan 371, **371**
Turner, Ted 80
Turtles 75, **184**, 346
Tutankhamun, Pharaoh 302, **302**, 303
Tuvalu 371, **371**
Twins **220–221**

U

Uganda 21, **21**, 41, 257, 371, **371**
Ukraine 371, **371**
Ultralight trikes **48**
Ultramarathons 58–59, **58–59**
Uluru-Kata Tjuta NP, Australia 80, 348

Underwater art 54–55, **54–55**
Unisphere, Queens, New York 380, **380–381**
United Arab Emirates 372, **372**
United Kingdom 40, 60, 294, 315, 372, **372**, 373
United Nations 211, 236, 237, 307, 313, 372, **372**
United States
colonial era 294–295, 310–311, **310–311**
Constitution 295, **295**, 323
diplomatic gifts 314–315, **314–315**
flag and facts 316–317, **316–317**, 339, 372, **372**
greener cities 247
history 308–323
history of democracy 294–295
holidays 251
Internet surveillance 24
megacities 332
Nat Geo explorers 40
Olympic athletes 60
state flags **318–321**
territories, flags of 322–323, **322–323**
travel 64, 72–73, 86–87, **86–87**, 89
women in Congress 26, 29, **29**, 313
Universe 142–153
birth of 142–143, **142–143**
dark matter 142, **142**, 152–153, **152–153**
distances 147
Druyan, Ann 144–145, **144–145**
exoplanets 150–151, **150–151**
space radiation 148–149, **148–149**
star explosions 146–147, **146–147**
time line 126–127, **126–127**
Unsoeld, Willi 51
Urbanization 244–247, **246–247**
Uruguay 245, 372, **372**
Urumqi, China 53
U.S. Virgin Islands **184**, 322
Utah **34–35**, 48, 140, 321, 334
Uzbekistan **141**, 228, 372, **372**

V

Valerio, Mirna 58–59, **58–59**

Valle de la Luna, Chile **53**
Van Niekerk, Wayde 60, **60**
Vandebroek, Ina 277, **277**
Vanuatu 372, **372**
Vaquita 189
Vatican City **77**, 343, 372, **372**
Vatnajökull glacier, Iceland **49**
Venezuela 103, 372, **372**
Venice, Italy **343**
Vermont: state flag **321**
Vesuvius, Mount, Italy 109
Victoria, Queen (United Kingdom) 315
Victoria Falls, Zambia-Zimbabwe 71
Vietnam 80, **80**, 372, **372**
Viking landers 136, **136**
Vikings **299**, 355
Vilankulo, Mozambique 85, **85**
Vinther, Jakob 170
Virgin Islands, U.S. **184**, 322
Virginia 73, **321**
Vision 268–269, **268–269**
Volcanoes 108–109, **108–109**, 118–119, **118–119**, 140, 350
Voltaire 293
Vostok Station, Antarctica 53
Voting rights 312–313, **312–313**
Voyager spacecraft 30, 31, 32, **32**, 139, 145

W

Wake Island 323
Wald, Beth 28
Walkerton, Ohio 275
Wang Zhenyi 29
War 306–307, **306–307**
Washington (state) 47, 86, 321
Washington, D.C. **26**, 314–315, **314–315**, 323, **323**
Watanabe, Tamae 51
Water resources 346
Waterfalls **335**
Wax worms 16
Weather 53, 102–103, **102–103**, **112–113**, 360
Wee, Darryl Jingwen 78, **78**
Wendover, Peter 316
West Virginia: state flag **321**
Western Sahara 307
Whale sharks **76**

Whales 75, **184**, 188–189, **188–189**, 363
White-bellied sea eagles 75
White Desert, Egypt **140**
Wickey, Allison 55
Wiggins, Bradley 60
Wikelski, Martin C. 41
Wildebeests 71, **71**
Wildfires 14, 104, **104–105**
Wildlife trade 200, 201
Wind Cave NP, South Dakota 73
Winnie Palmer Hospital, Orlando, Florida **280–281**
Winter Olympics 61, **61**
Wisconsin 47, **47**, 86, **86**, 321
Włodarczyk, Anita 60, **60**
Wolong Nature Reserve, China **173**
Wolves **172**, 176, **176**, **210**
Women
pioneers 26–29, **26–29**, 313
suffrage 312–313, **312–313**
World War I 306, 315
World War II 306, 355
Wrangell–St. Elias NPP, Alaska **334**
Wu Dajing 61, **61**
Wyoming **112**, **113**, 312, **321**

X

X Games 90
Xi'an, China 300–301, **300–301**
Xinjiang, China 53

Y

Yellowstone NP, U.S. **4**, 108, **172**
Yemen 307, 372, **372**
Yoho NP, Canada 84, **84**
Yosemite NP, California **48**
Yucatán Peninsula, Mexico 82–83, **82–83**
Yurok people 77

Z

Zambezi River, Zambia-Zimbabwe 71
Zambia 71, 372, **372**
Zebras **71**
Zimbabwe 71, 372, **372**
Zwicky, Fritz 152

Since 1888, the National Geographic Society has funded more than 13,000 research, exploration, and preservation projects around the world. National Geographic Partners distributes a portion of the funds it receives from your purchase to National Geographic Society to support programs including the conservation of animals and their habitats.

National Geographic Partners
1145 17th Street NW
Washington, DC 20036-4688 USA

Get closer to National Geographic explorers and photographers, and connect with our global community. Join us today at nationalgeographic.com/join

For information about special discounts for bulk purchases, please contact National Geographic Books Special Sales: specialsales@natgeo.com

For rights or permissions inquiries, please contact National Geographic Books Subsidiary Rights: bookrights@natgeo.com

ISBN: 978-1-4262-2052-4
ISBN: 978-1-4262-2053-1 (U.K. edition)

Printed in the United States of America

19/WOR/1